Critical Essays on
RICHARD WRIGHT'S
Native Son

CRITICAL ESSAYS
ON
AMERICAN LITERATURE

James Nagel, General Editor
University of Georgia, Athens

◆

Critical Essays on
RICHARD WRIGHT'S
Native Son

◆

edited by
KENETH KINNAMON

Twayne Publishers
An Imprint of Simon & Schuster Macmillan
New York

Prentice Hall International
London   Mexico City   New Delhi   Singapore   Sydney   Toronto

G.K. Hall & Co.
An Imprint of Simon & Schuster Macmillan
1633 Broadway
New York, NY 10019

Library of Congress Cataloging-in-Publication Data

Critical Essays on Richard Wright's Native Son / edited by Keneth Kinnamon.
    p.   cm. — (Critical Essays on American literature)
    Includes bibliographical references and index.
    ISBN 0-7838-0013-4 (alk. paper)
    1. Wright, Richard, 1908–1960. Native Son.   2. African American men in literature.   I. Kinnamon, Keneth.   II. Series.
PS3545.R815N337   1997
813'.52—dc21   96-40463
                                                                   CIP

The paper used in this publication meets the minimum requirements of American National Standard for Information Sciences—Permanence of Paper for Printed Library Materials. ANSI Z39.48-1984.∞™

10 9 8 7 6 5 4 3 2

Printed in the United States of America

For
John, Louis, and Ted

Contents

General Editor's Note

◆

This series seeks to anthologize the most important criticism on a wide variety of topics and writers in American literature. Our readers will find in various volumes not only a generous selection of reprinted articles and reviews but original essays, bibliographies, manuscript selections, and other materials brought to public attention for the first time. This volume, *Critical Essays on Richard Wright's* Native Son, is the most comprehensive gathering of essays ever published on Richard Wright's famous novel, a landmark of African American literature and the last great work of American Naturalism. The collection contains both a sizable gathering of early reviews and a broad selection of more modern scholarship. Among the authors of reprinted articles and reviews are Ralph Ellison, Sterling A. Brown, Malcolm Cowley, Donald B. Gibson, James Nagel, and Andrew Delbanco. In addition to a substantial introduction by Keneth Kinnamon, there are also three original essays commissioned specifically for publication in this volume: Yoshinobu Hakutani's discussion of the racial discourse in *Pudd'nhead Wilson* and *Native Son;* Caren Irr's exploration of the presentation of "space" in the novel, which leads her to an assessment of Wright as a critic of communism; and Alessandro Portelli's linguistic analysis of the interplay of sound and meaning in Wright's fiction. We are confident that this book will make a permanent and significant contribution to the study of American literature.

JAMES NAGEL
University of Georgia, Athens

Publisher's Note

♦

Producing a volume that contains both newly commissioned and reprinted material presents the publisher with the challenge of balancing the desire to achieve stylistic consistency with the need to preserve the integrity of works first published elsewhere. In the Critical Essays series, essays commissioned especially for a particular volume are edited to be consistent with G. K. Hall's house style; reprinted essays appear in the style in which they were first published, with only typographical errors corrected. Consequently, shifts in style from one essay to another are the result of our efforts to be faithful to each text as it was originally published.

Introduction

KENETH KINNAMON

Richard Wright's *Native Son,* published on 1 March 1940, is now widely recognized as the culminating work of the socially conscious fiction of the Great Depression and as the most important watershed in the history of African American literature. Growing up poor and black in Mississippi in the early years of the century, Wright had gone north to Chicago in 1927, fleeing from racism and hoping to find there some measure of safety, dignity, and, even, the possibility of a literary career. While subsisting on a variety of menial jobs, he continued to read avidly and to write, publishing a story in *Abbott's Monthly Magazine* in 1931 and, after joining the Communist-sponsored John Reed Club, his first poem in 1933 in its organ *Left Front.* Becoming increasingly known in leftist and in black literary circles, Wright moved to New York in 1937 and published his first book, *Uncle Tom's Children: Four Novellas,* in 1938. A *succès d'estime,* it helped him to win a Guggenheim Fellowship, allowing him to devote himself full time to the completion of the novel that was to change American literature.

The fullest account we have of Wright's intentions in the novel is that extraordinary essay, first delivered as a lecture at the 135th Street Branch of the New York Public Library, *How "Bigger" Was Born.* In it he makes clear that he anticipated a variety of responses to his protagonist. By presenting Bigger Thomas as he was—"resentful toward whites, sullen, angry, ignorant, emotionally unstable, depressed and unaccountably elated at times, and unable even, because of his own lack of inner organization which American oppression has fostered in him, to unite with the members of his own race"—Wright knew that he risked confirming in white minds a racist stereotype, that his own comrades in the Communist party might reject his complex emotional and artistic honesty, and that the black bourgeoisie would be shamed by his frankness and would urge him to accentuate the positive in his racial portrayal. In a real sense, then, Wright was not so much appealing to his audiences as he was confronting them with a harsh and unpalatable truth, forcing them through his uncompromising fidelity to his terrible vision to undergo such emotional turmoil as to reexamine their attitudes and expand their awareness of the meaning, universally existential and politically revolutionary as well as racially revealing, of Bigger Thomas. He would assault his readers' sensibilities, not curry their favor or indulge their sentimentality. He would not repeat his mistake in *Uncle Tom's Children:* "When the reviews of that book began to appear, I realized that I had made an awfully naive mistake. I found that I had written a book which even bankers' daughters could read and weep over and feel good about. I swore to myself that if I ever wrote another book, no one would weep over it; that it would be so hard and deep that they would have to face it without the consolation of tears."[1]

If there is one common denominator to the 423 reviews, notices, essays, lectures, sermons, editorials, letters to the editor, and poems that appeared in the two years after the publication of the novel, it is their testimonial to the *power* of the work, the searing emotional force that gripped the reader with or against his will. "Shock our sensibilities," "tremendous wallop," "power and drama and truth," "throbs from the opening line, with a wallop propelled to the end," "tremendous power," "a terrible story, a horrible story," "its frank brutalities . . . will horrify many readers," "powerful story," "powerful novel," "engrossing, terrible story," "a super-shocker," "grim and frightening," "one of the most powerful novels of all time"—such phrases recurred many scores of times in the reviews of *Native Son.* So powerful was its impact that one reviewer could only describe it as "a book which takes you by the ears and gives you a good shaking, whirls you on your toes and slaps you dizzy against the wall." When the reader regained full consciousness, one supposes, he could then ponder the message Wright had conveyed with such overpowering force.[2]

When he did so, he was likely to note the thematic issues of race and politics and the literary qualities of narration and characterization. Whatever its universal dimensions, *Native Son* is first of all a novel about the American racial situation, and this aspect of its theme elicited comment from almost all of its reviewers. For most, regardless of race or region, Wright made a cogent as well as a moving case against white racism. As far north as Maine an anonymous reviewer noted that Bigger was a victim of environmental determinism: "a mean Negro who might have been a solid asset in another environment." As far south as Houston another claimed that "Wright makes a masterful, unrelenting appeal" for racial understanding, however much other Southerners may object to the novel's theme. In the Midwest a reviewer judged that "the picture of the Negro, against the white world as presented by Wright, is the most illuminating I have ever read," and in California students emphasized its importance as a revelation of social injustice and a demand for change. In the black press reviews, editorials, and letters to the editor praising Wright's racial theme appeared in the *New York Amsterdam News, Kansas City Call, Chicago Metropolitan Post,* the *Chicago Defender,* the *New York Age,* the *Baltimore Afro-American,* the *Philadelphia Tribune,* and other newspapers as well as in such important periodicals as *The Crisis, Phylon,* and the *Journal of Negro History.* There were, of course, dissenters from this consensus. Many feared that Bigger was so unrepresentatively brutish that he would shame blacks and alienate whites. A lively debate on this subject appeared in the *Baltimore Afro-American* and the *Philadelphia Tribune,* and it also figured prominently in Communist discussions of the novel. A similar opinion was expressed by only a few nonradical white reviewers. Joseph McSorley feared that the "bestial, treacherous, utterly unlovable" Bigger would only stimulate more white oppression, and William E. Gilroy made a similar point. Wilbur Needham gave the controversy an interesting turn when he argued that instead of confirming racist stereotypes, Bigger's characterization was weak because it represented "the sort of Negro who has absorbed all white vices and retained none of the Negro virtues." Many white Southern reviews were surprisingly sympathetic to Wright's racial thesis, for example, those in the *Alabama Baptist,* the *Augusta Chronicle,* the *Charleston News and Courier,* the *Dallas Morning News,* the *Louisville Courier-Journal,* and the *Memphis Commercial Appeal,* but others expressed reservations or hostility, such as the *Jacksonville Florida Times-Union, Fort Worth Star-Telegram,* the *Galveston News, Chattanooga Sunday Times,* and the *Times-Picayune New Orleans States.* In a national periodical David L. Cohn of Mississippi, a writer of sorts himself, called the novel "a blinding and corrosive study in hate" and advised black people to emulate the patience of Jews. Cohn was outdone by a white Northern reviewer, Burton Rascoe, who considered the social message both obtrusive and erroneous.[3]

Rascoe's political preferences were involved in his extreme hostility to Wright's book, as indicated by his later accusation that as a Communist, Wright was deliberately inciting racial hatred. Other reviewers also voiced objections to the "warped idealogy" which attempted "to make the Communist party seem the friend of the Negro." The Columbia, South Carolina, *State* ("strong odor of Communist and Negro propaganda"), the *Des Moines Sunday Register,* the *Newark Sunday Call,* and the *St. Louis Globe-Democrat* were especially blunt in their criticism of Wright's politics. Other anti-Communist reviewers capitalized on Wright's treatment of the Jan-Mary-Bigger relationship, called by *Time* magazine "one of the most devastating accounts yet printed of that tragicomic, Negrophilous bohemianism which passes among Communists as a solution of the Negro problem." In the other camp, Communists themselves debated the merits of the novel and its political implications, with influential spokesmen on both sides but the prevailing opinion favorable to Wright. One of the most thoughtful political analyses of the novel was by a Trotskyite who emphasized Bigger's self-realization through revolutionary struggle but warned Wright about the Stalinists. Finally, one might note the inevitable white liberals who congratulated themselves and the country on the book's publication and Wright's success. The rabbi of Temple Israel in New York cited this evidence of "the fact that here in our democracy we do not study a man's blood cells to evaluate genius but merely his creative ability," and *Newsweek,* admitting white responsibility for Bigger's plight, consoled itself that "in our system of government" such a book "can be openly printed, discussed, and answered."[4]

Concerning the strictly literary qualities of the novel, discussion centered around narration and characterization, with only a few perceptive observers noting Wright's symbolism. A clear consensus of praise for the work's literary artistry emerged, even from many who objected to its themes. Repeatedly, the driving narrative momentum with its strong dramatic quality was singled out for favorable comment: "for the first two-thirds of the book," an influential Midwestern reviewer wrote, "no tale of pursuit and capture has rivaled it." Likewise, Wright's characterization, especially of Bigger, was widely admired, many reviewers agreeing with Henry Seidel Canby's early comment that "only a Negro could have written" such a psychologically penetrating book. Canby and a few others, indeed, seemed to emphasize the psychological dimension of Wright's story as a way of evading the social message. But more often, reviewers considered characterization as well as narrative pace and structure as a means of realizing the author's theme. Many agreed with a reviewer in Albany, New York: "He has proven with this vigorous novel that for psychological imagination, for power of dramatic construction, for the convincingness and reality of his characters, he has few equals." Reviewers who noted Wright's symbolism, his crisp dialogue, his "prose . . . as firm as steel," and his satiric touches helped to amplify the artistic particulars of the craft that had produced such a powerful effect.[5]

In assessing this achievement, reviewers inevitably compared Wright to other writers, most frequently to Steinbeck, whose *The Grapes of Wrath* had appeared the year before; to Dostoevsky, author of another psychologically acute story of crime and punishment; and to Dreiser, author of another American tragedy. The socially conscious novelists Erskine Caldwell, Charles Dickens, James T. Farrell, Maxim Gorky, and Harriet Beecher Stowe were likened to Wright by several reviewers, and other writers, religious leaders, and a single filmmaker mentioned a time or two included Bontemps, Millen Brand, Joyce Cary, Humphrey Cobb, Pietro Di Donato, Thomas Dixon, Dos Passos, Dumas, Faulkner, Jessie Fauset, the Greek tragedians, D. W. Griffith, Hemingway, Victor Hugo, George Lee, Richard Llewellyn, Malraux, Albert Maltz, McKay, Margaret Mitchell, Conrad Richter, Shakespeare, Upton Sinclair, Stein, Tolstoy, Toomer, Turgenev, Waters E. Turpin, Van Vechten, Len Zinberg, Zola, Abraham Lincoln, the biblical Samson, and Jesus Christ. However singular Wright's novelistic vision may have been, it was immediately placed by reviewers in various literary traditions, most notably that of social protest.

Native Son very quickly became a popular as well as critical success. Advance sales, Book-of-the-Month Club distribution, and first-week sales totaled 215,000 copies, an extremely large printing for a first novel. In its issue of 16 March 1940, two weeks after publication, the *Publishers' Weekly* alerted the book trade to high rates of reorders from bookstores and to

Harper's heavy advertising campaign. An advertisement entitled "Public Stampedes for 'Native Son' " that appeared in various black newspapers was only mildly hyperbolical. On the national best seller charts, the novel first appeared in the second week of March, ranked very high though never in first place (a position held by Richard Llewellyn's *How Green Was My Valley*) through May, began to fade in June, wilted in July, and did not appear in August or thereafter. In particular cities in particular weeks—New York, Chicago, Philadelphia, San Francisco, St. Louis—*Native Son* did rise to the top of the best seller list. Moreover, library copies were circulated briskly, although at least one library in a major Southern city refused to purchase the book.[6]

Literary America was not yet ready to award a black writer a major prize in fiction, but the frequency with which Wright was nominated was another indication of the strong impact of *Native Son.* Only a few days after publication, F.[ranklin] P. A.[dams] penned the following versified "Book Review" in his widely read column: "All the prizes should be won / By Richard Wright's 'Native Son.' " Soon afterward black journalists expressed similar sentiments, Frank Marshall Davis predicting a Pulitzer Prize, and Arthur Huff Fauset an eventual Nobel Prize for Wright. By May, such diverse voices as Walter Winchell and an editorial writer for *New Masses* had joined the chorus, though ultimately to no avail. Still, *Native Son* was a serious contender for a Pulitzer Prize.[7]

Another measure of the novel's effect is the way it was used in discussions of the actual social conditions reflected so graphically in the fictional work. Several journalists and sociologists cited *Native Son* in discussions of poor housing in Chicago and elsewhere. Others drew parallels between Bigger Thomas and actual living individuals. A writer in the denominational organ of the Disciples of Christ suggested that *Native Son* "would be a good book for all judges, police officers, and prosecutors who have to do with the Negro to read."[8]

It is always difficult to gauge precisely the effect of a problem novel on the future of the problem it treats, but from the available evidence it seems safe to claim that Wright's intention to shock his readers into a new awareness of the terrible dimensions of American racism was to a large degree accomplished. Irving Howe once wrote that "the day *Native Son* appeared, American culture was changed forever."[9] The change was not basic or profound, but it was real. The several hundred thousand readers of the work could no longer see racial issues in quite the same way. *Native Son* did not start a war, as Lincoln claimed that *Uncle Tom's Cabin* did, or directly effect legislation, as *The Jungle* did, but it did alter the social as well as literary sensibilities of many of its readers.

In the years during and immediately after World War II, interest in *Native Son*—and in literature generally—subsided somewhat, but several critical essays deserve notice. The first of these is Harry Slochower's essay viewing

Bigger and his creator as "black Jews," that is, disinherited exiles in their own country. Unlike the submissive victims of European fascism, however, Bigger strikes back, his violence constituting a daring, creative response to his plight. Slochower also provides perceptive analysis of fire imagery in the novel. Another leftist critic, Edwin Berry Burgum, placing Wright in the progressive tradition of American literature, praises his realistic portrayal of social forces, especially as they bear down on the protagonist. But in "Book Three," Burgum argues, Wright fails to make convincing the measure of social hope that he seems to feel. A third white critic, Charles I. Glicksberg, wrote numerous articles in the forties and fifties on African American literature. The first of these (1944) differentiates *Native Son,* with its objectivity, realism, and detachment, from traditional attitudes based on romantic primitivism. His later articles emphasize Bigger's aggressive hatred of whites.[10]

In the forties, black critics were also heard on the greatest black novel. Hugh M. Gloster treated *Native Son* in terms of its critique of a prejudiced and capitalistic social order. Waters E. Turpin, a novelist himself, praised the "bitter honesty" of *Native Son,* but found its solution of racial problems inadequate. Admitting its bitter melodrama and propaganda, G. Lewis Chandler nevertheless considered *Native Son* a powerful and professional work marking the maturation of the black novelist in a novel that applies to victims of oppression everywhere. But the most important early critic of *Native Son* was assuredly Wright's erstwhile friend and protégé James Baldwin. The opening blast at *Native Son* was "Everybody's Protest Novel," in which both Wright's novel and *Uncle Tom's Cabin* are castigated as protest novels that reduce complex human beings to stereotypes. Two years later (1951) Baldwin treated *Native Son* more fully and less unfairly in "Many Thousands Gone," which considers the work's structure, artistry, and impact. He still objects to oversimplified characterization, but concedes that *Native Son* is "the most powerful and celebrated statement of what it means to be a Negro in America."[11]

Bigger's characterization was also an issue in the forties for two psychiatrists whose contributions appeared in specialized medical journals. Dr. Charles V. Charles surely misses the point in diagnosing Bigger as "basically a neurotic individual" whose race is "only incidental" to his problems. Much more helpful is the contribution of Dr. Frederic Wertham, who psychoanalyzed Wright, recovering submerged memories that appear in fictive guise in his novel. Wertham subsequently treated *Native Son* in his important psychological study of violence, *A Sign for Cain* (1966).[12]

One should also mention in passing that *Native Son* was widely noted abroad in the forties. Even before translations began to appear in 1941, Sven Møller Kristensen had considered the novel favorably in a Danish study of American literature *entre deux guerres.* Some important early foreign reviews are those by Loló de la Torriente in Spanish; George-Albert Astre, Albert Balthazar, Jean Blanzat, Raymond Dumay, Pierre Fauchery, Madeleine Gautier, René Lalou, Pierre Lesdain, Claude-Edmonde Magny, Maurice Nadeau,

Magdeleine Paz, Jean Rabaud, André Rousseaux, and Jean-Jacques Sorel in French; J. W. Crom in Dutch; and Emilio Cecchi and Achille Colombo in Italian.[13]

In the fifties and early sixties, a period of political conservatism in the country and the New Criticism in the academy, *Native Son* was of little interest to white critics. Charles Glicksberg's 1950 essay "The Alienation of Negro Literature" added nothing to what he had already said about the novel. More interesting is Morris Weitz's discussion in *Philosophy of the Arts* of depth-meaning and his analysis of the final paragraphs of the novel, but Robert A. Bone in his landmark work *The Negro Novel in America* (1958) provides a really good analysis. Like numerous other readers of *Native Son,* he finds Book Three the weakest because "Wright has failed to digest Communism artistically."[14]

On the other hand, African American scholars continued to ponder the implications of *Native Son* throughout the McCarthy and Eisenhower years. Most discussion of the novel had mentioned white stereotypes of blacks, but in 1950 Tilman C. Cothran employs sociological content analysis of *Native Son* to illustrate black stereotypes of whites. In the same year, the veteran critic and Howard University professor Alain Locke anticipated Robert Bone's later judgment by praising the first two books as universal art and deeming the third book propagandistic. Hugh M. Gloster and Thomas D. Jarrett both universalized Bigger's plight, the latter going so far as to say that "his experiences might well have been those of a white youth in the ghettoes." Nick Aaron Ford similarly deracializes *Native Son* by comparing it unfavorably to *The Outsider.* The distinguished critic Nathan A. Scott characterized Wright's movement from *Native Son* to *The Outsider* as a journey from the sociological to the metaphysical, noting that the author is still searching for a mode of rebellion that is not self-destructive. One of the better treatments of the novel during the fifties is William T. Fontaine's analysis of its symbolism and characterization, in which he finds Wright using materialism, Marxism, and "the psychoanalytic mechanisms of fear-shame-guilt-hate" to explore the behavior of both races. Better still is Esther Merle Jackson's existential reading of *Native Son* against *Light in August* and *Crime and Punishment.*[15]

Beginning in 1957, reprint editions made *Native Son* available to a new generation of readers. William A. Owens's introduction to the first of these makes familiar comments about naturalism and determinism, while Richard Sullivan is condescending in his afterword to another reprint four years later. Better are afterwords in 1964 and 1966 by Theodore Solotaroff and John Reilly. The former sensibly approaches the novel through *How "Bigger" Was Born,* noting that Wright attempted to find a general social meaning in black violence. Thus he raised issues that still confront the nation. Reilly, who was to become one of the major Wright scholars, emphasizes Wright's powerful realism, but adds the useful qualification that *Native Son* is an exposé of social injustice, not an objective report.[16]

As these editions were appearing, other voices were being raised, some quite influential. The most important of these was Irving Howe's in his celebrated (and reviled) essay "Black Boys and Native Sons" (1963). Morris Beja, concentrating on the theme of identity in both *Native Son* and *The Outsider*, is also laudatory, as is Walter Allen in his survey of the English and American novel since the twenties. Leslie Fiedler and Nathan A. Scott, on the other hand, both consider Bigger's characterization offensive and Wright's artistry deficient.[17]

Interest in *Native Son* increased in the late sixties. Warren French offered the novel view that Wright was victimized by his own talent with language. In a revaluation of the social novels of the thirties and forties, Gerald Green gives first place to *Native Son* in an article appropriately entitled "Back to Bigger." The 1967 inaugural issue of *Negro American Literature Forum*, eventually to become *African American Review*, carried complementary—indeed, contradictory—articles on Wright's novel, David Britt arguing its importance as racial protest and John F. Bayliss viewing it as a psychological study of a neurotic personality, only incidentally concerned with race. In a somewhat later article, Bruno Cartosio, like Britt, emphasized the protest element, too didactic, perhaps, but achieving a degree of universality.[18]

By the end of the decade, Wright criticism was becoming more analytical and less evaluative, a welcome development. Clifford Hand, for example, analyzes Wright's method of developing characters, noting a recurrent pattern of a struggle for rebirth from an environment of fear and hatred. In a work too little noticed, the philosopher William T. Fontaine shows that Bigger develops as a human being under the tutelage of his attorney, Boris Max. One of the very best of the early essays, Donald B. Gibson's "Wright's Invisible Native Son," emphasizes Bigger as an individual person rather than a social symbol, a person who cannot be wholly defined by Max's Marxist formulas. Another area for analysis is the imagery of *Native Son*, largely ignored by the disparagers of Wright's fictional craft. James A. Emanuel focuses on such images as the furnace, Bigger's propensity for standing in the middle of the floor, the cross, blindness, walls and curtains, the desire to "blot out" what is troublesome, and the white blur—all of which contribute to Bigger's characterization as a black "man of feeling." More narrowly focused but equally helpful is James Nagel's study of the imagery of vision, the development of which shapes both the plot and the point of view of the novel. Analyzing the genesis of the novel, Keneth Kinnamon emphasizes Wright's personal experiences in Mississippi and Chicago, his knowledge of urban ecology and the Nixon trial, and Communist ideology.[19]

Other essays linked *Native Son* with other works. Numerous reviewers in 1940 had connected Wright's novel to *Crime and Punishment*. Robert Stanton in 1969 notes close similarities in plot and theme before going on to explore Wright's use of Dostoevsky's "outrageous" idea that society can deprive a person of selfhood, which can then be recovered only through revolt. Darwin T.

Turner compares *Native Son* to Wright's next novel, *The Outsider,* showing how the author reworked the earlier book. If *The Outsider* is more intellectually persuasive, *Native Son* is more successful emotionally and artistically. Finally, Keneth Kinnamon in a brief note argues for the influence of *Othello* on Wright's novel.[20]

Broader approaches also continued in the late sixties. Nelson Manfred Blake, a historian, places the dramatis personae of *Native Son* against their social background. Robert Bone's pamphlet *Richard Wright* is trenchant, pointing out the picaresque pattern in *Native Son* and other works. Although it also deals with other works in addition to *Native Son,* George Kent's "Richard Wright: Blackness and the Adventure of Western Culture" is a seminal essay, especially in its identification of the "dramatic articulation of black and white culture" as an important source of Wright's power. Edward Margolies's chapter on *Native Son* in his *Native Sons* is also excellent, identifying in the novel three kinds of revolution: Communist, black nationalist, and metaphysical. For all its proletarian trappings, Margolies believes, the work is finally more psychological than sociological. Dan McCall also emphasized what he calls the "psychodrama" of the novel. Drawing on both naturalism and the gothic romance of Hawthorne and Poe, Wright's story concerns the "beast in the skull" of Bigger as a representative victim of racial oppression acting out the violence that is his birthright as a native son. From a more detached perspective, James W. Tuttleton raises the issue of propaganda vs. art, suggesting that Wright does not resolve their conflicting claims in *Native Son.* Raman K. Singh argues that Wright's Marxist ideology and even his Christian background allow him to transcend strictly racial issues in both *Native Son* and *The Outsider.* Linking *Native Son* to the racial situation of the late sixties, Addison Gayle Jr., the major spokesman of the Black Aesthetic movement, praises Wright's militance and asserts the continuing relevance of Bigger's situation and his struggle to transcend it through violence.[21]

The seventies began with the first collection of pieces on *Native Son,* Richard Abcarian's still useful though long out-of-print *Richard Wright's Native Son: A Critical Handbook.* Well conceived and executed, this volume contains 4 essays and a letter by Wright, 21 reviews, 11 essays on the novel, 6 essays on related topics, a chronology, a bibliography, and even a couple of poems on Wright. The other book appearing in 1970 was Russell C. Brignano's *Richard Wright: An Introduction to the Man and His Works.* The topical organization of this work results in three separate treatments of *Native Son,* the first emphasizing the racial theme, the second Marxist ideology, and the third the existential dimension. Interest in imagery and symbolism continued in 1970. Dan M. Donlan's catalog of white color symbolism and Ron Samples's examination of light, darkness, and fire seldom get beyond the obvious. Thomas LeClair's study of imagery of vision and blindness complements but does not surpass Nagel's essay of the year before. Lloyd W. Brown deals well with an important topic in "Stereotypes in Black and White: The Nature of

Perception in Richard Wright's *Native Son,*" showing how Bigger's sense of identity changes in the course of the novel. Kathleen Gaffney is also concerned with character change, but her essay on Bigger can be safely ignored. Like Robert Stanton the preceding year, Kenneth T. Reed comments, briefly, on Bigger and Dostoevsky's Raskolnikov. Several writers focused on *Native Son* as a paradigm relevant to the racial climate three decades after its publication. The South African expatriate Keorapetse Kgositsile agrees with Addison Gayle's support of black liberation through violence, which he believes *Native Son* to endorse, but he rejects the novel's theme of interracial brotherhood. Clifford Mason, celebrating the 30th anniversary of the novel, emphasizes its prophetic quality. Campbell Tatham uses *Native Son* to argue that black literature and white literature cannot be judged by the same criteria.[22]

Many reviewers and subsequent critics of *Native Son* have deemed "Book Three" the weakest section of the novel. In the best essay of 1971, Edward Kearns disputes this view, arguing that Book Three has a closer relation to what precedes it than previously assumed, for it pursues the theme of the conflict between abstraction and concreteness and carries out the motif of blindness. Also very good is Edward A. Watson's analysis of the characterization of Bessie Mears as an embodiment of the blues. Much lower in the scale are Donald R. Merkle's elementary observations on the symbolic import of the furnace and the water tower. Charles James's analysis of the novel as a black search for maturity belabors the obvious. Much more valuable are two short influence studies, one by Michel Fabre on Wright's use of methods derived from Poe, and the other by Morris Dickstein on the influence of *Native Son* (and *Black Boy*) on James Baldwin and Eldridge Cleaver. Also noteworthy is the commentary on *Native Son* in Daniel Aaron's "Richard Wright and the Communist Party." And although Michael Harper's moving "Poems for Richard Wright: *A Sequence*" are not conventional literary criticism, no one with an interest in *Native Son* should miss them.[23]

Two books on Wright came out in 1972, one of them a collection of essays on *Native Son.* The editor, Houston A. Baker Jr., includes "How 'Bigger' Was Born" as well as commentary by James Baldwin, Irving Howe, Robert Bone, Dan McCall, George Kent, Donald Gibson, Dorothy Canfield Fisher, Malcolm Cowley, and Nelson Algren. Baker's introduction, also appearing as "Racial Wisdom and Richard Wright's *Native Son*" in another collection this same year, stresses Wright's immersion in folk culture and his reflection of it in the novel. Bigger is both trickster and rebel, familiar figures in the folk tradition. Eugene E. Miller tries less successfully to establish links with folklore in "Voodoo Parallels in *Native Son.*" The other book in 1972 was Keneth Kinnamon's *The Emergence of Richard Wright: A Study in Literature and Society.* His chapter on *Native Son* incorporates his 1969 article on the novel's background; analyzes its structure, characterization, and symbolism; and examines its reception. Among the essays, R. B. V. Larsen's is one of the first to address the important issue of narrative voice—or voices, since Larsen identifies four. Raman Singh analyzes Bigger and other Wright protagonists as Christian heroes or antiheroes. In "The Content and Form of *Native Son*," James G. Kennedy takes a Marxist approach, finding rather predictably that the content is working class in character and that the form consists of a main plot denying the possibility of personal relationships across class and racial lines, and a subplot concerned with Bigger's radicalization. Louis Graham adds a new twist to the identity theme by arguing that the white characters, as well as Bigger, have difficulty in distinguishing between the appearance and the reality of what they are. In his book on the escape motif in American fiction, Sam Bluefarb strains to make Bigger fit, arguing that his "escape" is not spatial or geographical, but a movement into a larger self-understanding. And again this year there were two influence studies. Comparing Clyde Griffiths of *An American Tragedy* and Bigger, Friederike Hajek finds that unlike Dreiser's really bourgeois protagonist, Wright's achieves revolutionary class consciousness with the help of Boris Max. Linda J. Prior elaborates on Poe's influence on Wright by demonstrating elements of "The Murders in the Rue Morgue" in *Native Son*.[24]

The most important contribution to Wright studies in 1973 (or before or after) was Michel Fabre's biography *The Unfinished Quest of Richard Wright*. Here the reader will find the biographical matrix out of which *Native Son* emerged. The other book of this year was David Bakish's brief chronological account of Wright's life and works. The treatment of *Native Son* is a plot summary with running commentary. The debate continued this year over the meaning of Wright's protagonist. Richard E. Baldwin analyzes Bigger's perspective and personality, finding that despite the social obstacles placed in his way, he does manage to create a vision of self that is full of meaning. James O. Young, on the other hand, considers him a complete antihero: "Bigger is ignorant. He is mean. He is a coward. He is a murderer." Albert Murray, who never misses a chance to compare Wright unfavorably to Ralph Ellison, finds the novel not a tragedy but merely "a social science–oriented melodrama with an unhappy ending" and a protagonist who is not racially representative. Several scholars addressed the ideology of the novel, but not primarily in Marxist terms. Monika Plessner sees existentialism emerging from Marxism, and Richard Lehan discusses existentialism in *Native Son* and the fictional works that immediately followed it. Christian—or anti-Christian—themes concern John Killinger and Jerold J. Savory, the latter being especially concerned with Wright's use of the Book of Job. Louis D. Mitchell makes a tentative effort to describe the picaresque element in *Native Son* (and *Black Boy*), but Robert Bone's earlier comments are more penetrating. Saundra Towns's "The Black Woman as Whore: Genesis of the Myth" launches an early attack on Wright from a feminist position, the harbinger of more to come. Like Sarah in "Long Black Song," Bessie in *Native Son* is a "simple, sexual animal, incapable of any kind of transcendence." The Italian scholar Piero Boitani uses a more conventional approach in his substantial analysis of *Native Son* as a naturalistic novel.[25]

Less effective is the 1974 treatment of the novel in its social context by Loretta Valtz Mannucci, but some very strong essays did appear this year, including the first (and, to date, only) *PMLA* article, Paul N. Siegel's "The Conclusion of Richard Wright's *Native Son,*" which is devoted mainly to Boris Max, in Siegel's view more reformer than radical. In the following year *PMLA* published David Lank's response to this article and Siegel's rejoinder. Bigger's characterization, especially his inner conflict, is treated routinely by Lola Jones Amis, but much more interestingly by Sheldon Brivic. A sturdy defence of Bigger's characterization is mounted by Amritjit Singh, who refutes charges that Bigger is too melodramatically violent, that his characterization is more sociological than artistic, and that he is an example of "negative" rather than "positive" protest. An onomastic approach is taken by Frank McConnell, who asserts that the novel focuses on the positive (expansionist) and negative (racist) implications of the name *Bigger.* Phyllis R. Klotman makes good use of a critical concept of Wayne Booth, that of "moral distancing." Analyzing the rat scene at the beginning of the novel and the cell scene between Bigger and Max at the end, she demonstrates that Wright widens the distance between events and the reader when he wants to induce moral judgment and narrows it when he wants judgment suspended. Less helpful is Robert Felgar's brief study of animal imagery. Roger Rosenblatt's thesis that the heroes of black fiction are trapped in a cyclical nightmarish history and society from which all efforts to break free are doomed may be overgeneralized, but it does fit *Native Son* quite well. Also not to be missed among the 1974 offerings is June Jordan's trenchant contrast between *Native Son* and *Their Eyes Were Watching God*—black protest and black affirmation.[26]

Scholarship on *Native Son* in 1975 fell slightly below that of 1974 both qualitatively and quantitatively. The most substantial achievement is to be found in Fritz Gysin's *The Grotesque in American Negro Fiction,* containing a section on Wright running more than 70 pages, much of it dealing with *Native Son.* Focusing on grotesque *situations* rather than grotesque figures or objects, Gysin makes good points about the outsider motif, point of view, split personality, violence, and the like. Violence, viewed as a means of self-liberation for the racially oppressed, is endorsed by Ronald G. Billingsley and Addison Gayle. Another African American critic, Marilyn Nelson Waniek, pursues Baldwin's comment that violence replaces sex in *Native Son.* This year's comparative study, by Vivian I. Davis, examines *Native Son, The Plague,* and *The Stranger,* finding that both Wright and Camus "write of man's despair, estrangement, separateness, fear, suffering and hopelessness" in a godless world. Jerold J. Savory adds to his 1973 article on Job and *Native Son* the point that the Job of Job 3:31 is a defiant rebel achieving self-realization, thus providing a model for Bigger. The psychological emphasis was represented this year by H. Philip Bolton, who diagnoses Bigger as a paranoid.[27]

Jeffrey Sadler and Jerry Wasserman in 1976 both call on the existential psychology of R. D. Laing to explain *Native Son.* Other articles during this year take a variety of approaches. Dennis Baron was the first to apply linguistics to Wright, but his article on "the syntax of perception" adds little to what James Nagel and others had already established without Baron's jargon. Better were Jerry H. Bryant comparing *Native Son, Invisible Man,* and *Go Tell It on the Mountain,* and Patricia D'Itri's ingenious examination of "a pattern of frustrated black identity" in *Black Boy, Native Son,* and *Lawd Today* corresponding to childhood, adolescence, and adult life. Johnny Tolliver's pamphlet introduction to *Native Son* is elementary, and Dorothy Redden's notion that the novel reveals Wright's belief that the racial issue is more moral than sociopolitical is dubious, but Joel Roache's examination of the theme and structure of "How 'Bigger' Was Born" leads him to argue plausibly that Bigger is a revolutionary hero, and Wright's ideology is dialectical materialism. After surveying black and white response to *Native Son,* Barry Gross makes the point that Bigger can act but not express himself, while Wright can express himself but not act. His additional comparison of Bigger to Ahab, and the killing of Mary to the pursuit of the white whale is not, unfortunately, offered with tongue in cheek.[28]

Katherine Fishburn's book *Richard Wright's Hero: The Faces of a Rebel-Victim* appeared in 1977. It calls *Native Son* "a tragedy written in the ironic mode" with a protagonist who is "an existential hero, a metaphysical rebel." Clearly by now the interpretive pendulum is swinging away from naturalism toward existentialism. Morris Dickstein, always a critic worth reading, finds *Native Son* more hallucinatory and poetic than naturalistic, and Alessandro Portelli argues that the novel transcends the formulas of protest and proletarian fiction because Bigger is a "victim as aggressor." Even the Chicago setting, Vimala Rao maintains, is mythic and symbolic as well as factual. Barry Gross contributed another article this year, more plausible than the Melville reference, noting that Bigger's black self-awareness is more important than any help Boris Max can provide. The comparative articles this year were Mary Ann Witt's on Meursault and Bigger, and M. E. Grenander's on the theme of criminal responsibility (society's) in *Native Son* and Willard Motley's *Knock on Any Door.* The year's remaining essay was Willi Real's pedagogical piece containing a sensible discussion of role behavior and prejudice.[29]

Foreign scholars were especially active in 1978, with T. L. Morozova of the Soviet Union, Ileana Verzea of Romania, and Janasdan M. Waghmare of India providing rather conventional discussions of *Native Son* as a protest novel. Another Soviet scholar, Sergei Chakovsky, is more interesting in his contention that the work is less consistently Marxist than its bourgeois critics suppose. The comparative article this year was Kurt Otten's. In *Native Son,* he argues, Wright was moving away from a Dreiserian emphasis on victimization to a Dostoevskian explanation of metaphysics. A different kind of comparison is undertaken by Peter Brunette in his study of the film version of the novel, which itself utilizes some filmic techniques. Changes made by Wright and Pierre Chenal compromised and softened the novel's meaning. Two excellent essays appeared in 1978: Michael Cooke's analysis of the novel "as the consummate story of the possibilities of being in the annihilating adverse world of the twentieth century," and Charles Scruggs's careful study of the development of the theme of the human need for community through the conflicting visions of the city held by Bigger, Buckley, and Max. Both of the essays were revised and expanded in subsequent books by these two distinguished scholars.[30]

As the decade of the seventies ended, comparative studies flourished. The best was Yoshinobu Hakutani's careful contrast of *Native Son* and *An American Tragedy* on the issues of crime and guilt. Stephen Corey's well-focused article on *Native Son* and *Light in August* compares Buckley to Percy Grimm in Faulkner's novel. Both are malevolent individuals embodying the wishes of a vengeful racist society. In his book on Frantz Fanon, Chester Fontenot has a brief but suggestive discussion of *Native Son,* pointing out that Bigger's plight symbolizes that of the black person caught between the tension "to see the language and values of the dominant society as a means to liberation and enlightenment, and to see them as a way of manipulating white society." Thus the novel serves as a gloss on Fanon's ideas. Evelyn Gross Avery's disappointing *Rebels and Victims: The Fiction of Richard Wright and Bernard Malamud* falls well below the intellectual level of Hakutani, Corey, and Fontenot. In an article, Fontenot also discusses briefly but cogently Bigger's self-realization through rejecting the linear conception of history, and creating through violence his "own private dystopia." Two European scholars offer general views of Wright with substantial comments on his greatest novel. Willi Real is impressed by the intensity of *Native Son* while recognizing some aesthetic problems. Michel Terrier considers it basically Marxist and naturalistic, but also notes existentialist themes. Maria Diedrich published this year a massive study of Communism in the African American novel, with a chapter on Wright of over a hundred pages, essential reading for an understanding of Wright's ideology in his early career. The mixture of naturalism and existentialism in *Native Son,* noted by so many other scholars, presages for Diedrich the open break with Communism that Wright was to make. Taking a different view, Esther Terry thinks that Communism is overvalued in *Native Son* and African American culture undervalued. In a similar vein Nathan Scott states once again his by-now familiar complaint that Wright's strident protest has the effect of dehumanizing his protagonist. One should also note briefly Nelson Algren's piece quoting from a letter his friend Wright wrote to him commenting on the black response to *Native Son,* and Michelle Wallace's objection to the novel because it was "the starting point of the black writer's love affair with Black Macho."[31]

Books on Wright by Robert Felgar and Addison Gayle appeared in 1980. The former's volume in the Twayne series contains a chapter on *Native Son* exemplifying Felgar's overall theme that oppression dehumanizes both victim and victimizer. Addison Gayle's biography *Richard Wright: Ordeal of a*

Native Son makes good use of information released under the Freedom of Information Acts, but his discussion of *Native Son* adds little to what he had said earlier. A chapter on Wright in the British critic C. W. E. Bigsby's book *The Second Black Renaissance* examines Wright's use of "the Negro as metaphor" to address the problem of self and society. Another British critic, Ian Walker, makes a point similar to Morris Dickstein's in 1977 as he argues that Wright, in *Native Son* and elsewhere, is more a writer of psychological nightmare than naturalistic social and political emphasis. Priscilla Ramsey is also treading familiar ground in "Blind Eyes, Blind Quests in Richard Wright's *Native Son*," but her point that only when Bigger is alone with Bessie does he share clarity of vision with another person is novel and interesting. The strongest essay of the year is John P. McWilliams Jr.'s long "Innocent Criminal or Criminal Innocence: The Trial in American Literature," in which he discusses *Native Son* in the context of American legal history and in comparison to *The Pioneers, Billy Budd,* and *An American Tragedy.*[32]

The general level of the half-dozen items appearing in 1981 was higher than in 1980. Bonnie Barthold's wide-ranging book *Black Time* includes an analysis of the role of time in *Native Son,* finding Bigger in rebellion against white linear time in an effort to affirm his own inner temporal rhythms. But he is cut off from "the time of Western history and of the traditional African cycle." She goes on to make some comparisons to Chinua Achebe's *Things Fall Apart.* Another solid contribution is Jerry Bryant's analysis of violence in Wright's novel in relation to racial protest and historical trends, to existentialist ideas, and to the need for community. Apposite comparisons are made to works by West, Farrell, Sartre, and Camus. Comparison is the point of Horst-Jürgen Gerigk's excellent article on *The Brothers Karamozov, An American Tragedy,* and *Native Son,* all of which turn on a judicial error condemning the protagonist for a crime he did not commit. In Dostoevsky, human freedom and moral agency are affirmed through acceptance of guilt, but Bigger, a social victim, achieves freedom by rejecting the injustice of white racism and affirming his revolutionary identity. Marcus Klein's chapter "Black Boy and Native Son" in his *Foreigners* analyzes Wright's relation to leftist politics with comments on *Native Son,* but Diedrich's 1979 book is fuller and better. In *Images of the Preacher in Afro-American Literature,* Walter C. Daniels contrasts the protagonist of "Fire and Cloud" to Reverend Hammond in *Native Son.* Günter H. Lenz considers the northern urbanization of southern folk culture in Hurston and Wright. *Native Son* is discussed, as well as *Lawd Today, 12 Million Black Voices,* and *Black Boy.*[33]

Five relevant items were published in 1982, two by the Japanese Wright scholar Toru Kiuchi. One is an onomastic study of the protagonist of *Native Son,* the other a comparison of the novel to Alan Paton's *Cry, The Beloved Country,* which also focuses on an accidental murder, fear, and racial rebellion. Kathryn Hunter uses *Native Son,* among other works, to argue that unlike their white counterparts, "black novelists, whatever their style or story, have conveyed their values by other means than the character's identification with or quest for objects." Exceptions spring to mind on each side of the equation. *Native Son* is only one of Wright's works treated in Sherley Anne Williams's astringent but fair-minded essay "Papa Dick and Sister-Woman: Reflections on Women in the Fiction of Richard Wright." Even while honoring Wright's overall achievement, African American women readers must reject his "racist misogyny" and "male narcissism." And Craig Werner's book on the presence of Joyce in American fiction has a chapter on Faulkner and Wright. Although *Lawd Today* and *Uncle Tom's Children* are more obviously Joycean, Werner points out, *Native Son* develops Bigger's "expanding awareness of the symbolic significance of his naturalistic fate" in a way analogous to the psychological progression of Stephen Dedalus.[34]

Only three articles appeared in 1983, but two of them opened a new line of inquiry, Wright's relation to popular culture. Ross Pudaloff examines the influence of popular media on "Long Black Song," *Lawd Today,* and *Native Son.* In his view, image becomes more important than character, especially in the case of Bigger Thomas. Harold Hellenbrand is more concrete, treating the general influence of film and photography on Wright, and the specific influence of *King Kong* on *Native Son.* "Mythically and sociologically, the movie and the novel tell the same story. The movie, though, tells it largely from the white point of view and the novel largely from the black." As Hellenbrand admits, however, we do not know whether Wright actually saw the film. The third essay, Robert Lee's "Richard Wright's Inside Narratives," agrees with other critics that in *Native Son* and other works by the author, a mythic, hallucinatory dimension coexists with naturalistic protest.[35]

The long-awaited Wright volume in Maynard Mack's Twentieth Century Views series came out in 1984. Among the 14 reprinted essays editors Richard Macksey and Frank E. Moorer selected, those by Margaret Walker, George Kent, Keneth Kinnamon, Donald Gibson, Nathan Scott, Darwin Turner, Paul Siegel, Esther Merle Jackson, and Nick Aaron Ford deal with *Native Son* in whole or in part. Of the two new essays, Maria Mootry's feminist reprimand of Wright describes Bigger Thomas and Jake Jackson of *Lawd Today* in these terms: "Narcissistic, they value the company of men above all; they are childless; and they define themselves in opposition to women, either by using them, by perceiving themselves to be used by them, or in extreme situations, by transmuting the impulse to love to the impulse to violence and even death." Two important books this year treat *Native Son*, Michael Cooke's *Afro-American Literature in the Twentieth Century: The Achievement of Intimacy* and Trudier Harris's *Exorcising Blackness: Historical and Literary Lynching and Burning Rituals.* For Cooke, Wright's novel represents the stage of solitude in the evolution of black writers from self-veiling to intimacy. Harris argues that ritualized lynching shapes Wright's artistic vision, creating a pervading atmosphere of apprehension. This holds true for the legal lynching of Bigger in Chicago as well as for the traditional Southern lynching depicted in

"Between the World and Me," "Big Boy Leaves Home," and *The Long Dream.* Two of the other three items are comparative, Judith Brazinsky comparing Wright's novel to Paul Green's stage adaptation of it, and Robert Butler pointing out similarities between *Native Son* and Zola's *Thérèse Raquin* and *La Bête Humaine.* Butler does not explicitly claim that the Zola novels are sources for *Native Son,* but the parallels are striking. Finally, Kathleen Gallagher finds a new way to consider imagery in *Native Son,* focusing on Bigger's reaction to images rather than Wright's deployment of them. "At the end, he breaks through to a comprehension of the metaphor of his life," but it is too late. Qualitatively, 1984 was a very good year for *Native Son* studies.[36]

In contrast, 1985 was a lean year. Robert Fleming adduces persuasive internal evidence that Eugene O'Neill's *The Hairy Ape* was a source for elements of Wright's novel. Mary F. Sisney is less original in pointing out yet once more the presence of Poe in the work. Only two other items merit attention. George Goodin in his book *The Poetics of Protest* states that "a major achievement of *Native Son* consists of showing the confusion which oppression can foster in its victims, a confusion in which the various alternatives for remedy tend to cancel each other out." Didn't we already know this? Doyle W. Walls is more original in making his small point that whites in the novel fail to detect the Black English verb form in Bigger's ransom note ("*Do what this letter say.*").[37]

Whatever momentum was lost in 1985, the following year more than made up for it. Joyce Ann Joyce's *Richard Wright's Art of Tragedy* focuses on the artistry of *Native Son,* paying especially close attention to its structure and its imagery, which work together to achieve "the awe and power" characteristic of tragedy. Dispensing with the biographical, social, naturalistic, and existential approaches, Joyce offers instead a close reading that enhances our appreciation of Wright's literary skill. Also rewarding is James A. Miller's perceptive Bakhtinian approach to the issue of voice in the novel. Rejecting the notion that Max is authorial spokesman, Miller focuses on Bigger's "quest for voice and audience." In such a pursuit he must repudiate Max as well as white racists, ending in isolation as "a soloist listening to the sound of his own song." Louis Tremaine is also concerned with Bigger's voice, which is caught up in a "conflict between experience and expression." Tremaine analyzes character and plot as well as narrative voice to argue that they work expressionistically, not naturalistically, to convey Bigger's sensibility. More closely argued than Jerry Bryant's 1981 essay on violence, Robert Butler's article this year shows how carefully Wright used it to express Bigger's personality split between romantic aspiration and naturalistic entrapment. Killing Mary and Bessie, he is destroying these two aspects of himself. His effort to achieve wholeness in Book Three falls short, however. As usual, comparative studies appeared in 1986. Willfried Feuser's essay is refreshing in its concern with Wright's influence on another writer rather than another writer's influence on Wright. Discussing similarities in theme, structure, style, characterization, and worldview between *Native Son* and *Le Docker Noir,* Feuser convinces us that it had a profound effect on Ousmane Sembène's novel. Many reviewers of *Native Son* found that it called to mind *Crime and Punishment,* but Tony Magistrale goes beyond plot similarities and the theme of crime leading to spiritual growth to emphasize Wright's Dostoevskian use of "parallel characters, atmospheric effects, and a similar belief in the power of the human spirit to transform itself." There were two naysayers in 1986. In a widely read piece, the distinguished novelist David Bradley relates his four readings of the novel over a period of 15 years. Originally he thought "the plot . . . improbable, the narrative voice intrusive, the language often stilted, and the characters . . . stereotypical," especially the bestially repulsive Bigger. He finally comes round to viewing it as a sad reminder of the racism of its time. All of this is more interesting to the student of Bradley than to the student of Wright. Completeness requires the mention of Chester Hedgepeth Jr.'s talk of the "Samson syndrome" and "Sartrian nihilism" of *Native Son,* but this is not essential reading.[38]

Treatments of *Native Son* in 1987 were more numerous than in 1986, but they were not as good. Two important books on general topics have substantial discussions of the novel. Valerie Smith argues that Bigger, like his creator, learns to overcome his isolation and gain control of his life by telling his story. In the chapter entitled "Richard Wright and the Triumph of Naturalism" of his now standard history of *The Afro-American Novel and Its Tradition,* Bernard Bell faults Wright for rejecting in *Native Son* and elsewhere "both the concept of black nationalism and the values of Afro-American culture," but he recognizes the importance of Wright's "complex and controversial naturalistic vision of urban black characters and culture, his creation of the best-known character in black fiction . . . , and his projection of the Afro-American as the metaphor for America and modern man." Much more negative and much less thoughtful is Harold Bloom, who argues that the serious aesthetic shortcomings of *Native Son* derive from Wright's "bad authorial ear." The best refutation of this assertion is Alessandro Portelli's careful study appearing in the present volume. Bloom admits the social importance of *Native Son,* but finds it more interesting for its Oedipal theme. Not many readers will agree. James Robert Saunders, on the other hand, emphasizes the social import of the novel and adduces classroom experience to demonstrate its universal appeal, but his essay does little to enhance our understanding. Two essays on religion appeared in 1987, but neither was very helpful. Robert L. Douglas compares *Uncle Tom's Children* and *Native Son* with respect to "the treatment of the minister, the concept of religion . . . , and the use of religious music," concluding that Wright fluctuates between orthodoxy and skepticism. James H. Evans Jr. also tries hard to impute faith, maintaining that the key to Bigger's development is the use of religious language. But Evans is forced to admit that Bigger's faith is "restless" and "questioning," not firm or traditionally Christian. In his provocative book *The Sexual Mountain and Black Women*

Writers, Calvin Hernton comments on the depiction of women in *Native Son,* comparing it to Ann Petry's in *The Street.* John Orr also makes comparisons—to Faulkner—but the main point of his "psychocritical" approach to *Native Son* is an emphasis on "Southern identity . . . ostensibly suppressed, only to dominate the narrative through its haunting absences." The next step, one supposes, is to claim Northern identity for *Black Boy.* Language and voice are the concerns of the year's two most substantial contributions. Lynda Hungerford's linguistic approach goes farther than Doyle Walls's did two years earlier. She shows that Wright's use of Black English for Bigger, his family, and his friends makes for a realistic portrayal, but his representation of dialect orthographically for the speech of Reverend Hammond and the two black workers, Jack and Jim, in Book Two is deliberately stereotypical to emphasize their Tomish ways. Laura Tanner argues for a sharp distinction between Bigger and the narrative voice in the novel, identical with Max's voice in Book Three. Tanner considers the narrative voice unreliable, "white," at times almost racist. Perhaps the best article of the year is Barbara Foley's comparison of *An American Tragedy,* a novel of "the tragic consequences of false consciousness," to *Native Son,* a "grotesque rather than tragic . . . bitter social commentary." Her theoretical point is that proletarian fiction should be judged by a proletarian, not bourgeois, aesthetic.[39]

We can begin 1988 with two collections, *Richard Wright's Native Son* edited by Harold Bloom, and *Richard Wright: Myths and Realities* edited by C. James Trotman. Of the 11 essays in the Bloom collection, 9 are reprints on which this introduction has already commented. The new ones are Barbara Johnson's "The Re(a)d and the Black" and Joseph T. Skerrett Jr.'s "Composing Bigger: Wright and the Making of *Native Son,*" both worth close attention. Johnson analyzes Bigger's ransom note in relation to Wright's effort to combine Marxist vision with black experience. Just as Bessie reads the note inferring that Mary is dead, so Wright in *Black Boy* reads his story of the death of an Indian maiden to another black woman. For Wright, Johnson asserts, "the figure of the black woman as *reader* in his work is fundamental." Skerrett takes a psychological approach in arguing that *Native Son* "objectified, in symbolic terms," Wright's own "conflicts and passions." These center around his rebellious nature, his rejection of family, women, religion, society, and finally the Communist Party. Like Wright, Bigger must create his own values. The Trotman book collects papers from a 1985 symposium, one of which (Douglas) is discussed above. Of the three remaining, Joseph Bodziock's "Richard Wright and Afro-American Gothic" makes the point that *Native Son* uses the American gothic of Poe and Hawthorne to shock readers into confronting the reality of American racism; Alison Rieke examines in an interesting way the role of polemics in the narrative structure of *Native Son,* "The Man Who Lived Underground," and *The Outsider;* and Paul Newlin's "Why 'Bigger' Lives On: Student Reaction to *Native Son*" draws on long teaching experience to state that the novel elicits strong student response. This will not come as news to anyone who has even short experience teaching it. A teacher who is growing tired of emphasizing the social relevance may turn to Susanne Bullock-Kimball's interpretation "from the mytho-metaphoric perception," in which Bigger is the Minotaur, Mr. Dalton "a modern Minos," Mary a sacrifice to the beast, Bessie "the Ariadne-figure," and the police "the collective Theseus." Whereupon the teacher will be glad to get back to social relevance. Another weak effort is Jane Davis's "Self-Hatred in the Novels of Richard Wright," which belabors the obvious. The year's remaining three are better. Robert A. Coles sees Wright's early work (especially the poetry and *Native Son*) and career as an effort to synthesize literary forms, to unite art and social science, and to merge the black and white dispossessed in order to effect social change. Alan W. France's feminist, poststructuralist study of *Native Son* is not easy reading, but the main point is that the repressed absence, sexism, is a theme as important as the authorial theme of racism. More conventional, more accessible, and more useful is Yoshinobu Hakutani's well-informed "Richard Wright and American Naturalism." Positing the tension between the individual will and social determinism as characteristic of the best American versions of naturalism, Hakutani analyzes *Native Son* as successful and *Lawd Today* as unsuccessful.[40]

With only two items worth noting, 1989 marked a pause between two highly productive periods of *Native Son* criticism. Swimming against the current of feminist criticism, Kathleen Ochshorn defends the women characters in *Native Son,* asserting that "the black women in particular do represent a community," which Bigger, not Wright, underestimates. But one of the most productive scholars of twentieth-century fiction, Linda Wagner-Martin, takes issue with this view, finding in *Native Son* hostility to women. Other emphases in her general treatment of the book in a critical history of the American novel from 1914 to 1945 are its literary connections, its ambivalence, and its disbelief in American justice.[41]

As the 1990s began, an important collection appeared—*New Essays on Native Son* edited by Keneth Kinnamon. The editor's introduction, following Janice Thaddeus's example in her study of *Black Boy,* analyzes manuscripts, proofs, and unpublished letters to show how *Native Son* was shaped by external pressures as well as by the author's creative imagination, especially in the areas of sex and politics. Kinnamon also reviews the reception of the novel in the two years following its publication. Of the four other essays in this collection, two address the characterization of women. In "Native Sons and Foreign Daughters," Trudier Harris explores some of the social ironies involved in the novel's unfavorable presentation of female characters. As Bigger, responding to the American cultural values of individualism and freedom, aspires to soar, his mother, sister, and lover attempt to hold him down in the subservient place designated by society as appropriate for black people. Houston A. Baker Jr. focuses precisely on the concept of place in a new historicist treatment of black male and female roles in *Native Son* against the background of

Wright's own interpretation of African American history in *12 Million Black Voices*. The resulting indictment of Bigger and endorsement of Bessie complement the Harris essay while challenging much received opinion about Wright's protagonist. The other two essays are also rewarding. John M. Reilly demonstrates how narrative techniques are carefully used to subvert conventional American racial discourse and to establish the authority and authenticity of the protagonist's voice. And this voice reverberates beyond the covers of the book: "Bigger's achievement of voice stands as a symbol of the purpose of Afro-American literature." Craig Werner comes to a somewhat similar conclusion in his essay relating *Native Son* to modernism as a literary movement. Alienated and inarticulate, Bigger repeatedly struggles to tell as well as understand his story, becoming in the process a bluesy, modernist black hero in a racist wasteland. Harold Bloom brought out his third collection of Wright criticism this year, *Bigger Thomas,* with an introduction modifying his earlier "purely aesthetic reservations about Wright's tormented and now classic work" and placing it in the context of the racism displayed in the 1988 Presidential campaign. The collection presents nine "critical extracts" and a dozen critical essays, all reprinted. Another book on Wright also appeared in 1990, Eugene E. Miller's *Voice of a Native Son: The Poetics of Richard Wright.* Emphasizing the "intuitive, emotional, even visionary and semi-mystical Wright," Miller argues that Zaka, Erzulie, Ogun, Legba, Baron Samedi, and the color blue are keys to unlock the meaning of Wright's great novel of the South Side of Chicago, even though the author himself was not aware of this "mythic voodoo dimension." The originality of such an argument is more apparent than its plausibility. Two of the other four items this year compare Wright to other African American novelists. Maryemma Graham treats Frank London Brown and Ronald Fair as well as Wright as social realists writing in the protest vein about black Chicago. In a book chapter, Cushing Strout compares *Native Son* and *Invisible Man,* finding Ellison's novel superior in its use of folklore and its rejection of political radicalism. Michael F. Lynch's *Creative Revolt: A Study of Wright, Ellison, and Dostoevsky* includes a chapter analyzing the influence of *Crime and Punishment* on *Native Son* and *The Outsider.* In the former, Lynch believes, Wright is moving away from deterministic naturalism and Communism. Finally, there was another feminist analysis of—and attack on—the portrayal of women in *Native Son* and three other Wright books. According to Nagueyalti Warren, women are "cast as nonfeminine asexual beings and as sex objects of little value," reflecting not only attitudes of male characters but also "the ambivalence of [Wright's] psychosexual self."[42]

Much commentary in 1991 and 1992 centered on the Library of America edition of Wright, especially the new version of *Native Son,* which restored cuts of sexual and political material made to render the book acceptable to the Book-of-the-Month Club. Predictably, debate on the expurgated version of 1940 and the new version with coerced deletions restored focused on the sexual passages. Arnold Rampersad, who provided the excellent notes and chronology for the Library of America edition, speaks for many when he urges that "in making Bigger almost asexual and unresponsive where Mary Dalton is concerned, the Book-of-the-Month Club has made him less alive and almost incomprehensible." Chicago novelist Leon Forrest agrees that "with this edition, we get more of Bigger's humanity and psychological motivation." Other reviewers echoed these points. In an excellent essay Andrew Delbanco emphasizes Wright's daring presentation, for the first time in American literature, of "the full, urgent sexuality of a young black man" in a highly physical novel that insists on "the imperatives of the body." Jack Miles, Louis Menand, and several others show how restoration of deleted passages resolves inconsistencies, as Kinnamon had also demonstrated in 1990. Not all who endorsed the restorations agree that they enhanced the protagonist's humanity by affirming his sensuality. John A. Williams claims that the masturbation scene tends "to minimize whatever sympathy the reader feels for Bigger at this early point in the novel." Nevertheless, Williams adds, Wright is positive in showing the negative effects of racism. In one of the most thoughtful commentaries, Cyrus Colter praises the Library of America edition but notes that the 1940 version still displays "Wright's powerful chemistry" as a "resourceful and intrepid author."[43]

On the other hand, four writers clearly prefer the novel as originally published by Harper; the new edition, they believe, should present the deleted passages in the notes, not the text. Charles Johnson objects to Wright's "heavy-handed" treatment of sexual material: "Wright struggled mightily and only with partial success to make Bigger's brief moment of masturbation work as social metaphor. . . . It's [sic] omission is, perhaps, an example of how a good editor can save a great writer from belaboring his point." Eugene Miller is of like mind but less temperate expression in his "Open Letter to Jerry Ward, Keneth Kinnamon, Arnold Rampersad, and the Wright Circle," where he caricatures the views of Kinnamon and Rampersad as the black superstud stereotype: "If Wright meant to indicate such an equation, he could easily have written Bigger as a former day Wilt Chamberlain." James Campbell develops the most cogent argument in favor of the 1940 text. Believing that the Book-of-the-Month Club objected only to the masturbation scene, Campbell thinks that all other changes were entirely voluntary, and some of these had nothing to do with sex. Even the deleted masturbation scene may have met with Wright's voluntary rather than coerced approval. Thus the 1940 edition was indeed the final approved version, even though Wright believed that he had completed the novel weeks earlier with the bound page proof Harper submitted to the Book-of-the-Month Club. Furthermore, so far as we know, Wright did not object to the 1940 version of *Native Son* in the numerous reprints after original publication. So says James Campbell. James Tuttleton in *The Hudson Review* follows a similar line of reasoning. Both Campbell and Tuttleton would agree that the 1940 version had a 50-year life span not easily ended by a new version of dubious bibliographical authenticity because it was not in fact the final version approved by the author.[44]

In addition to this lively debate, 1991 was remarkable for Robert Butler's *Native Son: The Emergence of a New Black Hero,* the most extended and perhaps the best reading Wright's novel has received. After a chronology of Wright's life and chapters on the cultural background, importance, and critical reception of *Native Son,* Butler provides an intensive original interpretation of the novel in some 90 pages with chapters on setting, structure, characterization, point of view, tone, and theme. A selected, annotated bibliography is also included. Butler's reading argues that Bigger moves from victimization by a hostile racist environment through a psychological process of increasing self-understanding to the status of a black existential hero, master of his consciousness if not his circumstances. In *Native Son* Butler concludes that Wright "achieved the originality, depth, and resonance of a genuine masterwork." But there was even more in 1991. Gayl Jones's *Liberating Voices: Oral Tradition in African American Literature* contains, among other good things, a discussion of the intertextuality of Alice Walker's *The Third Life of Grange Copeland* with *Native Son.* The veteran scholar James Cox offers a comparison of Faulkner, mainly *Light in August,* and Wright, mainly *Native Son,* as Southern writers. In discussing the final scene, Cox notices a detail that had previously been overlooked: Bigger's reiterated phrase, "I'm all right." Cox's gloss is that Wright is implying that he is Bigger's father and that Bigger is all Wright.[45]

Apart from pieces stimulated by the Library of America edition and a minor pedagogical exercise, five noteworthy items appeared in 1992. Abdul R. JanMohamed sets out to correct Foucault's failure to racialize sexuality, using *Native Son* as an example of the need to do so. Bigger commits three "rapes": Mary, Bessie, and, the first, Gus. In Bigger's attempt to achieve power and freedom through rape, "*Native Son* turns out to be a profoundly specular novel; it holds up a mirror to the structure and economy of phallocratic society, but it is unable to escape or undermine them." Under the catchy title of "The Zen of Bigger Thomas," Gayle Pemberton discusses Wright's protagonist in the context of continuing black violence. She also compares *Native Son,* "a comic tragedy," to *Invisible Man,* "a tragic comedy." In "The Cultural Work of Time in *Native Son,*" Robert Felgar identifies four kinds of time: "synchronic, biblical, linear (or diachronic), and modernist." Bigger rejects the first two, associated with racism and religion respectively, and embraces the second two, suggesting clock-regulated activity and subjective experience respectively. Felgar has an interesting idea, but he fails to develop it adequately in this four-page note. Hillary Holladay returns an unfavorable verdict on Boris Max in "*Native Son*'s Guilty Man." Max is analyzed as an inept attorney guilty of "generalizations, self-doubts, long-winded tangents, and logical fallacies" in defense of Bigger. By failing to plead not guilty or insanity, Max forfeits any chance Bigger may have to escape execution. Holladay does not explain how Wright would have realized his tragic purpose if Max had managed to save Bigger from the electric chair. This year's comparative article was the Shakespearean scholar James R. Andreas's examination of the uses of *Othello* by Wright in *Native Son*, Ellison in *Invisible Man*, and Baraka in *Dutchman*. "Wright restages and reinterprets the problematic relationship of Othello and Desdemona; Ellison represents it comically; and Baraka reverses or inverts it." Andreas also compares Emilia of the play and Mrs. Dalton.[46]

In 1993 Henry Louis Gates Jr. and K. A. Appiah published *Richard Wright: Critical Perspectives Past and Present,* reprinting reviews of *Native Son* by Clifton Fadiman, Malcolm Cowley, and Alain Locke as well as essays by Ralph Ellison, Keneth Kinnamon, Laura Tanner, Barbara Johnson, Ross Pudaloff, Joyce Ann Joyce, Barbara Foley, and Houston A. Baker Jr. Foley's book on proletarian fiction also came out this year. In contrast to Hillary Holladay, from her sturdy Marxist point of view Foley defends Max's courtroom speech and believes that *Native Son* is an antibildungsroman because Bigger does not achieve revolutionary class consciousness. There were two articles in 1993. Eugene Miller expands his 1990 comments on the Library of America edition to claim that the restored sexual passages suggest an androgynous Bigger and place Wright "at least on the edges of the radical profeminist camp." Most feminists will be surprised. Kimberly W. Benston analyzes *Native Son* as a modernist version of "the slave narrator's drama of self-realization." Bigger is the author of his story, not Max or Jan Erlone. Benston concludes with a comparison of Wright's novel and *Narrative of the Life of Frederick Douglass.* Throughout, the approach is poststructuralist. A more accessible comparison is Robert Butler's contrast of Wright's description of the South Side and James T. Farrell's in the Studs Lonigan trilogy. Wright uses Gothic imagery and description to reflect Bigger's subjective reality of alienation. Farrell's more mimetic, fully realized environment reflects a sense of possibility available to Studs but denied to Bigger.[47]

With a perspective different from her 1986 book, the second chapter of Joyce A. Joyce's *Warriors, Conjurers and Priests,* published in 1994, analyzes *Native Son* as a romance in the symbolic tradition and *The Long Dream* as a realistic novel. In each case Wright's careful use of language enhances his social message. Dale E. Peterson contributes a solid article arguing the strong influence of Gorky and Dostoevsky on Wright, first comparing *Black Boy* to Gorky's *Childhood,* then *Native Son* and "The Man Who Lived Underground" to *Crime and Punishment.* With childhood experiences quite similar to Gorky's, Wright came to share his "faith in collectivist culture and social engineering," but Bigger's anguish, like Raskolnikov's, "is experienced as a human conundrum, not as a sociological formula." Seodial Deena interprets *Native Son* in familiar terms of environmental determinism. Bigger's racist and irrational world "twists him and makes him a killer." The ratio of plot summary to analysis in this article is far too high.[48]

Two collections of Wright criticism appeared in 1995, the last year covered—partially—in this survey: Arnold Rampersad's *Richard Wright: A Collection of Critical Essays* and Robert Butler's *The Critical Response to Richard Wright*. Four essays on *Native Son* appear in Rampersad, all reprinted. Butler represents the novel with five reviews and five reprinted essays, but also publishes a new piece by Keneth Kinnamon, "The Library of America Edition of *Native Son*." This discussion of textual issues considers the work of Kinnamon, Arnold Rampersad, and Mark Richardson before examining the debate over the restoration in the 1991 edition of sexual passages deleted from the proofs of the 1940 edition. Kinnamon expresses a preference for an edition restoring the sexual cuts but retaining other changes made before publication in 1940. To a book on urban themes in African American literature he coedited with Robert Butler, Yoshinobu Hakutani contributes an essay surveying Wright's theme of the city as a site of freedom and self-creation, focusing on *Native Son* and *The Outsider.* Both Bigger and Cross Damon seek freedom; Bigger achieves it psychologically. Violence in *Uncle Tom's Children* and *Native Son* is the concern of Laurel J. Gardner, who finds that its use is to confer dignity on the protagonists through self-assertion and to shock readers into an awareness of racism. In her book *American Anatomies: Theorizing Race and Gender,* Robyn Weigman analyzes *Native Son* as "our literature's most compelling story of the black man caught in the mythology of the rapist." Weigman shows how sexual metaphors allow a gendered reading of several scenes in the novel. Kimberly Drake is also concerned with rape in a comparative study of *Native Son* and Toni Morrison's *The Bluest Eye.* In both the rape of Bessie and the rape of Pecola, the author's focus on the male's perspective, necessary to secure the reader's identification with a character brutalized by racism, denies access to the rape victim's experience and feelings.[49]

The three original essays in the present collection both connect with previous scholarly approaches and point the way to future work on Wright's greatest novel. Past comparative studies have generally focused on works by Wright's American and French contemporaries or upon nineteenth-century European novelists. Yoshinobu Hakutani presents here an intertextual reading of *Native Son* and an important nineteenth-century American fictional discourse on race, *Pudd'nhead Wilson.* Careful not to assert direct influence of Twain on Wright, Hakutani nevertheless finds many similarities, including the governing deterministic worldview, the roles of Max and Wilson, and the murders of Mary and Judge Driscoll, while noting the richly characterized Bigger contrasting to Twain's puppet-like figures, as well as Wright's deadly seriousness contrasting to Twain's dark humor and satire. Both are major statements on the nation's perennial problem of racism. Can we now look toward comparative studies of Wright and Melville, Wright and Stowe,

Wright and Crane? Caren Irr's fascinating study of the political as well as psychological implications of Bigger's claustrophobia and agoraphobia combines close reading with an informed understanding of the scholarly reevaluation of the Left literature of the thirties that has been under way for over a decade now. Far from being a Stalinist dupe, Wright in *Native Son* is "an internal critic of Communism," reformulating the proletarian novel to meet the realities and the needs of urban black America. More good revisionary work on the ideology of Wright's fiction is needed. Although linguistic approaches to *Native Son* had been taken by Dennis Baron and Lynda Hungerford, Alessando Portelli sets a new standard in his challenging and exhaustive study of what he calls "the grammar of sounds" in *Native Son*. Adducing massive evidence from computer-generated data on the recurrence of various sound patterns, Portelli demonstrates how closely sound and sense are joined in the work's texture, not adventitiously but as a result of Wright's stylistic artistry. One hopes that Portelli will apply his method to other works by Wright and that other scholars adept in stylistics will also turn their attention to our author.

Much has been written on *Native Son* since 1940, but the richness of its themes and the artistry of its execution will bear continuing scrutiny for the foreseeable future.[50]

Notes

1. Richard Wright, *How "Bigger" Was Born* (New York: Harper, 1940), 21, 29–30.
2. "*Afro* Readers Write about 'Native Son,'" *Baltimore Afro-American,* 1 June 1940, 13. "Among Books Reviewed in March *Boston Evening Transcript* Especially Recommends," *Boston Evening Transcript,* 13 April 1940, part 5, 1. "Highlights in New Books," *Bakersfield Californian,* 26 March 1940, 18. "'Native Son' Delves Into Race Problems," *Bloomington (Ill.) Sunday Pantagraph,* 10 March 1940, 9 (This Associated Press review appeared in several other newspapers). "Negro's Answer," *Newsweek,* 4 March 1940, 40–41. "A Remarkable Book by Negro," *Hartford Courant,* 3 March 1940, magazine sec., 6. "Wright, Richard. Native Son," *Booklist,* 37 (1940): 307. "Wright, Richard. Native Son," *Pratt Institute Library Quarterly Booklist,* 6 (October 1940): 24. A. M. F., "A Powerful Novel of Negro's Struggle in a White World," *Milwaukee Journal,* 3 March 1940, part V, 3. Helen K. Fairall, "An Engrossing, Terrible Story Is This Novel About a Negro by a Negro," *Des Moines Register,* 3 March 1940, 9. Lewis Gannett, "Books and Things," *New York Herald Tribune,* 1 March 1940, 17. James Gray, "A Disturbing View of Our Unsolved Race Problem," *St. Paul Dispatch,* 8 March 1940, 10. W. L., "Another 'American Tragedy,'" *Raleigh News and Observer,* 24 March 1940, sec. M, 5. Bennett Davis, "Books of the Week in Review," *Buffalo Courier-Express,* 3 March 1940, sec. 6, 1.
3. "Books and Bookfolk," *Portland Press Herald,* 9 March 1940, 13. "Negro's Novel Is Overwhelming, Bitter, Profound," *Houston Press,* 22 March 1940, 27. "Powerful Plea for Negro Race," *Akron Beacon Journal,* 10 March 1940, 8-D. Barbara Ball, "The Vicarious World," *Berkeley Daily Californian,* 26 March 1940, 4. Dalton, "First Novel Wins Acclaim for Young Negro Writer," *Stanford Daily,* 10 April 1940, 4. For a survey of nearly all printed black reactions to the novel in 1940, see my forthcoming article "The Black Response to *Native Son*." Joseph McSorley, "Native Son. By Richard Wright," *Catholic World,* 151 (1940): 243. William E. Gilroy, "What

Will Be Its Effects?" *Advance,* 132 (1940): 242, 274. Wilbur Needham, "Negro Author Pens Story of Racial Relationships," *Los Angeles Times,* 10 March 1940, part III, 7. David L. Cohn, "The Negro Novel: Richard Wright," *Atlantic Monthly,* 165 (May 1940): 659. Burton Rascoe, "Negro Novel and White Reviewers," *American Mercury* 50 (May 1940): 113–16.

4.   John Selby, "The Literary Guidepost," *Ashland Daily Independent,* 3 March 1940, 4 (This syndicated review appeared in at least eighteen other newspapers). Murray du Q. Bonnoitt, "Under the Covers," *Columbia* (S.C.) *State,* 18 August 1940, 5-B. Helen R. Fairall, *op. cit.* "Exploring the Book World," *Newark Sunday Call,* 3 March 1940, part III, 5. James E. Dougherty, "Powerful Novel of Negro Life," *St. Louis Globe-Democrat,* 9 March 1940, 1B. " 'Bad Nigger,' " *Time,* 4 March 1940, 72. William T. Rosenblum, "Some Notable Comment on *Native Son,"* in *Native Son,* "Seventh Edition," by Richard Wright (New York: Harper, 1940), 368. "Negro's Answer," *Newsweek,* 4 March 1940, 41.

5.   Fanny Butcher, "Negro Writes Brilliant Novel, Remarkable Both as Thriller and as Psychological Record," *Chicago Daily Tribune,* 6 March 1940, 19. Henry Seidel Canby, *"Native Son* By Richard Wright," *Book-of-the-Month Club News,* February 1940, 2–3. R. J. Lewis Jr., "Between the Book Covers," *Albany Times-Union,* 3 March 1940, 10A. Lee Berry, "This World of Books," *Toledo Blade,* 9 March 1940, 5.

6.   "Book Marks for Today," *New York Herald Tribune,* 12 March 1940, 17. " 'Native Son' Sells Rapidly," *Publishers' Weekly,* 137 (1940): 1161. *New York Amsterdam News,* 9 March 1940, 2. *New York Age,* 16 March 1940, 2. *Pittsburgh Courier,* 23 March 1940, 4, and several subsequent issues through 11 May 1940. Angelo Herndon, "Books Read at Harlem Library Show People Seek a Way Out of Poverty," *Sunday Worker,* 7 April 1940, 5. "Dixie Library Bans 'Native Son': Alabama Library Won't Place 'Native Son' on Its Shelves," *Pittsburgh Courier,* 20 April 1940, 1, 4.

7.   F.[ranklin] P. A.[dams], "The Conning Tower," *New York Post,* 4 March 1940, 14. Frank Marshall Davis, " 'Native Son' Greatest Novel Yet by American Negro," *Nashville Defender,* 9 March 1940. Arthur Huff Fauset, "I Write as I See: A Negro Renaissance?" *Philadelphia Tribune,* 4 April 1940, 4. Walter Winchell, "On Broadway," *New York Sunday Mirror,* 5 May 1940, 10. "Pulitzer Awards," *New Masses,* 35 (14 May 1940): 26.

8.   C. W. Lemon, "Book Chat," *World Call* 22 (May 1940): 23, 46.

9.   Irving Howe, "Black Boys and Native Sons," *Dissent,* 10 (1963): 354.

10.   Harry Slochower, "In the Fascist Styx," *Negro Quarterly,* 1 (Fall 1942): 227–40. Edwin Berry Burgum, "The Promise of Democracy and the Fiction of Richard Wright," *Science and Society,* 7 (Fall 1943): 338–52. Charles I. Glicksberg, "The Negro Cult of the Primitive," *The Antioch Review,* 4 (Spring 1944): 47–55; "Negro Fiction in America," *South Atlantic Quarterly,* 45 (October 1946): 477–88; "For Negro Literature: The Catharsis of Laughter," *Forum* (May 1947): 450–56; "The Furies in Negro Fiction," *Western Review,* 13 (Winter 1949): 107–14; "The Alienation of Negro Literature," *Phylon,* 11 (First Quarter 1950): 49–58.

11.   Hugh M. Gloster, "Richard Wright: Interpreter of Racial and Economic Maladjustments," *Opportunity,* 19 (December 1941): 361–65, 383. Waters E. Turpin, "Evaluating the Work of the Contemporary Negro Novelist," *Negro History Bulletin,* 11 (December 1947): 59–60, 62–64. G. Lewis Chandler, "Coming of Age: A Note on American Negro Novelists," *Phylon,* 9 (first quarter 1948): 25–29. James Baldwin, "Everybody's Protest Novel," *Zero,* no. 1 (Spring 1949): 54–58; *Partisan Review,* 16 (June 1949): 578–85; "Many Thousands Gone," *Partisan Review,* 18 (November–December 1951): 665–80.

12.   Charles V. Charles, M.D., "Optimism and Frustration in the American Negro," *The Psychoanalytic Review,* 29 (July 1942): 270–99. Frederic Wertham, M.D., "An Unconscious Determinant in *Native Son," Journal of Clinical Psychopathology and Psychotherapy,* 6 (July 1944): 111–15; *A Sign for Cain: An Exploration of Human Violence* (New York: Macmillan, 1966), 332–33.

13.   Sven Møller Kristensen, *Amerikansk Literatur 1920–1940* (Copenhagen: Athenaeum, 1942), 174–77. Loló de La Torriente, *"Sangre Negra,* por Richard Wright," *Afroamerica,* 1 (January and July 1945): 102–4. Georges-Albert Astre, "Un Grand Romancier

noir: Richard Wright," *Fraternité* (Paris), 10 October 1946, 3. Albert Balthazar, "L'Evolution de l'àme nègre: Un grand romancier noir: Richard Wright," *L'Occident* (Brussels), c. 10–11 August 1946. Jean Blanzat, "*Un Enfant du pays* de Richard Wright," *Le Figaro* (Paris), 5 July 1947. Raymond Dumay, "Wright (Richard): *Un Enfant du pays*," *La Gazette des Lettres*, 3 (23 August 1947): 10. Pierre Fauchery, "Comment peut-on être nègre?" *Action* (Paris), 25 July 1947, 11. Madeleine Gautier, "Un Romancier de la race noire: Richard Wright," *Présence Africaine*, no. 1 (October–November 1947): 163–65. René Lalou, "Le Livre de la semaine: *Un Enfant du Pays*, par Richard Wright," *Les Nouvelles Littéraires*, 17 July 1947, 3. Pierre Lesdain, "Richard Wright: *Un Enfant du Pays*," *Volonté*, 17 April 1948. Claude-Edmonde Magny, "Richard Wright ou l'univers n'est pas noir," *Une Semaine dans le monde*, 30 August 1947, 8. Maurice Nadeau, "Un Enfant d'Amerique," *Combat* (Paris), 11 July 1947, 2. Magdeleine Paz, "*Un Enfant du pays* par Richard Wright," *Paru*, no. 34 (September 1947): 44–47. Jean Rabaud, "Un Grand Ecrivain noir: Richard Wright," *Le Populaire de Paris*, 16 July 1947, 2. André Rousseaux, "Les Livres," *France Illustration*, nos. 104–6 (11 October 1947): 321. Jean-Jacques Sorel, "Richard Wright *Un Enfant du pays*," *La Nef*, no. 33 (August 1947): 148–49. J. W. Crom, "Een praatje over 'Zoon van Amerika' in de Wereldkronick," *Schakeling*. Emilio Cecchi, "L'angnoscia di avere le pelle diversa," *L'Europeo*, 7 March 1948, 10. Achille Colombo, "Wright Richard: *Paura*," *Letture*, 3 (January 1948): 6.

14. Charles I. Glicksberg, "The Alienation of Negro Literature," *Phylon*, 11 (First Quarter 1950): 49–58. Morris Weitz, *Philosophy of the Arts* (Cambridge, Mass.: Harvard University Press, 1950), 137–41. Robert A. Bone, *The Negro Novel in America* (New Haven, Conn.: Yale University Press, 1958), 140–52.

15. Tilman C. Cothran, "White Stereotypes in Fiction by Negroes," *Phylon*, 11 (Third Quarter 1950): 252–56. Alain Locke, "Self-Criticism: The Third Dimension in Culture," *Phylon*, 11 (Fourth Quarter 1950): 391–94. Hugh M. Gloster, "Race and the Negro Writer," *Phylon*, 11 (Fourth Quarter 1950): 369–71. Thomas D. Jarrett, "Toward Unfettered Creativity: A Note on the Negro Novelist's Coming of Age," *Phylon*, 11 (Fourth Quarter 1950): 313–17. Nick Aaron Ford, "The Ordeal of Richard Wright," *College English*, 15 (November 1953): 87–94. Nathan A. Scott, "Search for Beliefs: Fiction of Richard Wright," *University of Kansas City Review*, 23 (Autumn 1956): 131–38. William T. Fontaine, "Toward a Philosophy of the American Negro Literature," *Présence Africaine*, nos. 24–25 (February–May 1959): 165–76. Esther Merle Jackson, "The American Negro and the Image of the Absurd," *Phylon*, 23 (Fourth Quarter 1962): 359–71.

16. William A. Owens, "Introduction," in *Native Son* (New York: Harper, 1951), vii–xii. Richard Sullivan, "Afterword," in *Native Son* (New York: The New American Library, 1961), 394–99. Theodore Solotaroff, "Afterword," in *Native Son* (New York: The New American Library, 1964), 393–400. John M. Reilly, "Afterword," in *Native Son* (New York: Harper & Row, 1966), 393–98.

17. Morris Beja, "It Must Be Important: Negroes in Contemporary American Fiction," *Antioch Review*, 24 (Fall 1964): 323–36. Leslie A. Fiedler, *Waiting for the End* (New York: Stein and Day, 1964), 106–7. Nathan A. Scott Jr., "The Dark and Haunted Tower of Richard Wright," *Graduate Comment*, 7 (July 1964): 93–99.

18. Warren French, *The Social Novel at the End of an Era* (Carbondale: Southern Illinois University Press, 1966), 171–80. Gerald Green, "Back to Bigger," *Kenyon Review*, 28 (September 1966): 521–39. David Britt, "*Native Son:* Watershed of Negro Protest Literature," *Negro American Literature Forum*, 1 (Fall 1967): 4–5. John F. Bayliss, "*Native Son:* Protest or Psychological Study?" *Negro American Literature Forum*, 1 (Fall 1967): 5–6. Bruno Cartosio, "Due scrittori afroamericani: Richard Wright e Ralph Ellison," *Studi americani*, 15 (1969): 395–431.

19. Clifford Hand, "The Struggle to Create Life in the Fiction of Richard Wright," in *The Thirties: Fiction, Poetry, Drama*, ed. Warren French (Deland, Fla.: Everett/Edwards, 1967), 81–87. William T. Fontaine, *Reflections on Segregation, Desegregation, Power and Morals* (Springfield, Ill.: Charles C. Thomas, 1967), 22–30. Donald B. Gibson, "Wright's Invisible Native

Son," *American Quarterly,* 21 (Winter 1969): 728–38. James A. Emanuel, "Fever and Feeling: Notes on the Imagery in *Native Son,*" *Negro Digest,* 18 (December 1968): 16–24. James Nagel, "Images of 'Vision' in *Native Son,*" *University Review,* 36 (December 1969): 109–15. Keneth Kinnamon, "*Native Son:* The Personal, Social, and Political Background," *Phylon,* 30 (Spring 1969): 66–72.

20. Robert Stanton, "Outrageous Fiction: *Crime and Punishment, The Assistant,* and *Native Son,*" *Pacific Coast Philology,* 4 (1969): 52–58. Darwin T. Turner, "*The Outsider:* Revision of an Idea," *CLA Journal,* 12 (June 1969): 310–21. Keneth Kinnamon, "Richard Wright's Use of *Othello* in *Native Son,*" *CLA Journal,* 12 (June 1969): 358–59.

21. Nelson Manfred Blake, *Novelists' America: Fiction as History, 1910–1940* (Syracuse, N.Y.: Syracuse University Press, 1969), 226–53. Robert Bone, *Richard Wright* (Minneapolis: University of Minnesota Press, 1969). George Kent, "Richard Wright: Blackness and the Adventure of Western Culture," *CLA Journal,* 12 (June 1969): 322–43. Edward Margolies, *Native Sons: A Critical Study of Twentieth Century Negro American Authors* (Philadelphia: Lippincott, 1968), 65–86. Dan McCall, *The Example of Richard Wright* (New York: Harcourt, Brace, & World, 1969), 64–102. James W. Tuttleton, "The Negro Writer as Spokesman," in *The Black American Writer* (DeLand, Fla.: Everett/Edwards, 1969), vol. 1, 245–59. Raman K. Singh, "Some Basic Ideas and Ideals in Richard Wright's Fiction," *CLA Journal,* 13 (September 1969): 78–84. Addison Gayle Jr., "Richard Wright: Beyond Nihilism," *Negro Digest,* 18 (December 1968): 4–10.

22. Richard Abcarian, ed., *Richard Wright's Native Son: A Critical Handbook* (Belmont, Cal.: Wadsworth, 1970). Russell C. Brignano, *Richard Wright: An Introduction to the Man and His Works* (Pittsburgh: University of Pittsburgh Press, 1970). Dan M. Donlan, "The White Trap: A Motif," *English Journal,* 59 (October 1970): 943–44. Ron Samples, "Bigger Thomas and His Descendants," *Roots,* 1 (1970): 86–93. Thomas LeClair, "The Blind Leading the Blind: Wright's *Native Son* and a Brief Reference to Ellison's *Invisible Man,*" *CLA Journal,* 13 (March 1970): 315–20. Lloyd W. Brown, "Stereotypes in Black and White: The Nature of Perception in Richard Wright's *Native Son,*" *Black Academy Review,* 1 (Fall 1970): 35–44. Kathleen Gaffney, "Bigger Thomas in Richard Wright's *Native Son,*" *Roots,* 1 (1970): 81–85. Kenneth T. Reed, "*Native Son:* An American *Crime and Punishment,*" *Studies in Black Literature,* 1 (Summer 1970): 33–34. Keorapetse Kgositsile, "The Relevance of Bigger Thomas to Our Time," *Roots,* 1 (1970): 79–80. Clifford Mason, "Native Son Strikes Home," *Life,* 68 (8 May 1970): 18.

23. Edward Kearns, "The 'Fate' Section of *Native Son,*" *Contemporary Literature,* 12 (Spring 1971): 146–55. Edward A. Watson, "Bessie's Blues," *New Letters,* 38 (Winter 1971): 64–70. Donald R. Merkle, "The Furnace and the Tower: A New Look at the Symbols of *Native Son,*" *English Journal,* 60 (September 1971): 735–39. Charles James, "Bigger Thomas in the Seventies: A Twentieth-Century Search for Significance," *The English Record,* 22 (Fall 1971): 6–14. Michel Fabre, "Black Cat and White Cat: Richard Wright's Debt to Edgar Allan Poe," *Poe Studies,* 4 (June 1971): 17–19. Morris Dickstein, "Wright, Baldwin, Cleaver," *New Letters,* 38 (Winter 1971): 117–24. Daniel Aaron, "Richard Wright and the Communist Party," *New Letters,* 38 (Winter 1971): 170–81. Michael Harper, "Poems for Richard Wright: *A Sequence,*" *New Letters,* 38 (Winter 1971): 83–87.

24. Houston A. Baker Jr., ed., *Twentieth Century Interpretations of Native Son: A Collection of Critical Essays* (Englewood Cliffs, N.J.: Prentice-Hall, 1972). Eugene E. Miller, "Voodoo Parallels in *Native Son,*" *CLA Journal,* 16 (September 1972): 81–95. Keneth Kinnamon, *The Emergence of Richard Wright: A Study in Literature and Society* (Urbana: University of Illinois Press, 1972), 118–52. R. B. V. Larsen, "The Four Voices of Richard Wright's *Native Son,*" *Negro American Literature Forum,* 6 (Winter 1972): 105–9. Raman K. Singh, "Christian Heroes and Anti-Heroes in Richard Wright's Fiction," *Negro American Literature Forum,* 6 (Winter 1972): 99–104, 131. James G. Kennedy, "The Content and Form of *Native Son,*" *College English,* 34 (November 1972): 269–83. Louis Graham, "The White Self-Image Conflict in *Native Son,*" *Studies in Black Literature,* 3 (Summer 1972): 19–21. Sam Bluefarb, *The Escape Motif in the*

American Novel: Mark Twain to Richard Wright (Columbus: Ohio State University Press, 1972), 135–53. Friederike Hajek, *"American Tragedy*—zwei Aspekte. Dargestellt in Richard Wright's *Native Son* und in Theodore Dreiser's *An American Tragedy," Zeitschrift für Anglistik und Amerikanistik,* 20 (July 1972): 262–79. Linda J. Prior, "A Further Word on Richard Wright's Use of Poe in *Native Son," Poe Studies,* 5 (December 1972): 52–53.

25. Michel Fabre, *The Unfinished Quest of Richard Wright* (New York: William Morrow, 1973). David Bakish, *Richard Wright* (New York: Ungar, 1973), 30–40. Richard Baldwin, "The Creative Vision of *Native Son," The Massachusetts Review,* 14 (Spring 1973): 378–90. James O. Young, *Black Writers of the Thirties* (Baton Rouge: Louisiana State University Press, 1973), 232–35, 241–42. Albert Murray, *The Hero and the Blues* (Columbia: University of Missouri Press, 1973), 93–97. Monika Plessner, *Onkel Tom verbrennt seine Hütte: Die literarische Revolution der schwarzen Amerikaner* (Frankfurt am Main: Insel Verlag, 1973), 151–75. Richard Lehan, *A Dangerous Crossing: French Literary Existentialism and the Modern American Novel* (Carbondale: Southern Illinois University Press, 1973), 95–106. John Killinger, *The Fragile Presence: Transcendence in Modern Literature* (Philadelphia: Fortress Press, 1973), 129–34, 135, 139, 146, 153. Jerold J. Savory, "Descent and Baptism in *Native Son, Invisible Man,* and *Dutchman," Christian Scholar's Review,* 3 (Winter 1973): 33–37. Louis D. Mitchell, "The Picaresque Element in Richard Wright's Two Major Novels," *Journal of Afro-American Issues,* 1 (Summer/Fall 1973): 384–94. Saundra Towns, "The Black Woman as Whore: Genesis of the Myth," *The Black Position,* no. 3 (1973): 39–59. Piero Boitani, *Prosatori negri americani del novecento* (Rome: Edizioni di Storia e Letteratura), 123–64.

26. Loretta Valtz Mannucci, *I negri americani della depressione al dopoguerra* (Milan: Feltrinelli, 1974), 98–107. Paul N. Siegel, "The Conclusion of Richard Wright's *Native Son," PMLA,* 89 (May 1974): 517–23. Lola Jones Amis, "Richard Wright's *Native Son:* Notes," *Negro American Literature Forum,* 8 (Fall 1974): 240–43. Sheldon Brivic, "Conflict of Values: Richard Wright's *Native Son," Novel: A Forum on Fiction,* 7 (Spring 1974): 231–45. Amritjit Singh, "Misdirected Responses to Bigger Thomas," *Studies in Black Literature,* 5 (Summer 1974): 5–8. Frank McConnell, "Black Words and Black Becoming," *The Yale Review,* 63 (Winter 1974): 193–210. Phyllis R. Klotman, "Moral Distancing as a Rhetorical Technique in *Native Son:* A Note on 'Fate,' " *CLA Journal,* 18 (December 1974): 284–91. Robert Felgar, " 'The Kingdom of the Beast': The Landscape of *Native Son," CLA Journal,* 17 (March 1974): 333–37. Roger Rosenblatt, *Black Fiction* (Cambridge, Mass.: Harvard University Press, 1974). June Jordan, "On Richard Wright and Zora Neale Hurston: Notes Toward a Balancing of Love and Hatred," *Black World,* 23 (August 1974): 4–8.

27. Fritz Gysin, *The Grotesque in American Negro Fiction: Jean Toomer, Richard Wright, and Ralph Ellison* (Bern: Francke Verlag, 1975), 91–164. Ronald G. Billingsley, "The Burden of the Hero in Modern Afro-American Fiction," *Black World,* 25 (December 1975): 38–45, 66–73. Addison Gayle, *The Way of the New World: The Black Novel in America* (Garden City, N.Y.: Anchor Press/Doubleday, 1975), 200–220. Marilyn N. Waniek, "The Space Where Sex Should Be: Toward a Definition of the Black American Literary Tradition," *Studies in Black Literature,* 6 (Fall 1975): 7–13. Vivian I. Davis, "The Genius of Fantastic Feebleness (With Apologies to Richard Wright)," *Proceedings of the Comparative Literature Symposium,* 8 (1975): 99–116. Jerold J. Savory, "Bigger Thomas and the Book of Job: The Epigraph to *Native Son," Negro American Literature Forum,* 9 (Summer 1975): 55–56. H. Philip Bolton, "The Role of Paranoia in Richard Wright's *Native Son," Kansas Quarterly,* 7 (Summer 1975): 111–24.

28. Jeffrey Sadler, "Split Consciousness in Richard Wright's *Native Son," South Carolina Review,* 8 (April 1976): 11–24. Jerry Wasserman, "Embracing the Negative: *Native Son* and *Invisible Man," Studies in American Fiction,* 4 (Spring 1976): 93–104. Dennis E. Baron, "The Syntax of Perception in Richard Wright's *Native Son," Language and Style,* 9 (Winter 1976): 17–28. Jerry H. Bryant, "Wright, Ellison, Baldwin—Exorcising the Demon," *Phylon,* 37 (June 1976): 174–88. Patricia D'Itri, "Richard Wright in Chicago: Three Novels That Represent a Black Spokesman's Quest for Self Identity," *Midwestern Miscellany,* 4 (1976): 26–33. Johnny E.

Tolliver, *An Introduction to Richard Wright's Native Son* (Jackson: Mississippi Library Commission, 1976). Dorothy S. Redden, "Richard Wright and *Native Son:* Not Guilty," *Black American Literature Forum,* 10 (Winter 1976): 111–16. Joel Roache, "What Had Made Him and What He 'Meant': The Politics of Wholeness in 'How "Bigger" Was Born,' " *Sub-Stance,* no. 15 (1976): 133–45. Barry Gross, "Art and Act: The Example of Richard Wright," *Obsidian: Black Literature in Review,* 2 (Summer 1976): 5–19.

29.   Katherine Fishburn, *Richard Wright's Hero: The Faces of a Rebel-Victim* (Metuchen, N.J.: Scarecrow, 1977), 59–100. Morris Dickstein, *Gates of Eden: American Culture in the Sixties* (New York: Basic Books, 1977): 59–81. Alessandro Portelli, *Bianchi e neri nella letteratura americana* (Bari: De Donato, 1977), 85–89. Vimala Rao, "The Regionalism of Richard Wright's *Native Son," Indian Journal of American Studies,* 7 (1977): 94–102. Barry Gross, " 'Intellectual Overlordship': Blacks, Jews, and *Native Son," The Journal of Ethnic Studies,* 5 (Fall 1977): 51–59. Mary Ann Witt, "Race and Racism in 'The Stranger' and 'Native Son,' " *The Comparatist: Journal of the Southern Comparative Literature Association,* 1 (May 1977): 35–47. M. E. Grenander, "Criminal Responsibility in *Native Son* and *Knock on Any Door," American Literature,* 49 (May 1977): 221–33. Willi Real, "Richard Wright, *Native Son* (1940)," in *Der Roman im Englischunterrich der Sekundarstuffe II* (Paderborn: Schöningh, 1977), 169–84.

30.   T. L. Morozova, "Tipologija Geroja," in *Literatura SŠA XX Veka: Opyt tipologičeskogo issledovanija (Avtorskaja pozicija, konflikt, geroj)* (Moscow: Nauka), 1978, 485–88. Ileana Verzea, "Tradiţie şie modernitate in romanul American de culoare," *Revista de istorie şi teori literară,* 27, no. 2 (1978): 239–45. Janasdan Waghmare, *American Negro: Sahitya Anni Sanskruti* (Bombay: Lokvangamaya, 1978), 77–115. Sergei Chakovsky, "Rasovyj Konflikt Literatura SŠA XX Veka (Negritjanskaya literatura v 20-30-60-e gody)," in *Literatura SŠA XX Veka: Opyt tipologičeskogo issledovanija (Avtorskaya pozicija, konflikt, geroj)* (Moscow: Nauka, 1978), 302–6. Kurt Otten, "Der Protestroman Richard Wrights," in *Black Literature: zur afrikanischen und afroamerikanischen Literatur* (Munich: Fink, 1978), 317–44. Peter Brunette, "Two Wrights, One Wrong," in *The Modern American Novel and the Movies* (New York: Ungar, 1978), 131–42. Michael Cooke, "Naming, Being, and Black Experience," *The Yale Review,* 67 (Winter 1978): 167–86. Charles Scruggs, "The Importance of the City in *Native Son," Ariel,* 9 (July 1978): 37–47.

31.   Yoshinobu Hakutani, "*Native Son* and *An American Tragedy:* Two Different Interpretations of Crime and Guilt," *The Centennial Review,* 23 (Spring 1979): 208–26. Stephen Corey, "The Avengers in *Light in August* and *Native Son," CLA Journal,* 23 (December 1979): 200–212. Chester Fontenot, *Frantz Fanon: Language as the God Gone Astray in the Flesh* (Lincoln: The University of Nebraska, 1979), 24, 27–28. Evelyn Gross Avery, *Rebels and Victims: The Fiction of Richard Wright and Bernard Malamud* (Port Washington, N.Y.: Kennikat, 1979). Chester Fontenot, "Black Fiction: Apollo or Dionysus?" *Twentieth Century Literature,* 25 (Spring 1979): 73–84. Willi Real, "Richard Wright (1908–1960)," in *Der moderne Roman des Amerikanischen Negers: Richard Wright, Ralph Ellison, James Baldwin* (Darmstadt: Wissenschaftliche Buchgesellschaft, 1979), 11–47. Michel Terrier, *Le Roman américain 1914–1945* (Paris: Presses Universitaires de France, 1979), 119–24. Maria Diedrich, *Kommunismus im afroamerikanischen Roman* (Stuttgart: J. B. Metzlersche Verbuchshandlung, 1979), 173–291. Esther Terry, "Wright's *Native Son:* The Burden It Bears," *Five College Contributions in Black Studies,* no. 2 (1979): 3–26. Nathan Scott, "Black Literature," in *Harvard Guide to Contemporary American Writing* (Cambridge, Mass.: Harvard University Press, 1979), 289–91. Nelson Algren, "Motley: He Was an Invisible Man Among Black Writers," *Chicago Tribune,* 25 February 1979, sec. 7, 1. Michelle Wallace, *Black Macho and the Myth of the Superwoman* (New York: Dial, 1979), 55–57.

32.   Robert Felgar, *Richard Wright* (Boston: Twayne, 1980), 78–108. Addison Gayle, *Richard Wright: Ordeal of a Native Son* (Garden City, N.Y.: Anchor/Doubleday, 1980), 115–18. C. W. E. Bigsby, *The Second Black Renaissance* (Westport, Conn.: Greenwood, 1980), 54–84. Ian Walker, "Black Nightmare: The Fiction of Richard Wright," in *Black Fiction: New Studies of the Afro-American Novel Since 1945* (London: Vision Press, 1980), 11–28. Priscilla Ramsey, "Blind

Eyes, Blind Quests in Richard Wright's *Native Son*," *CLA Journal,* 24 (September 1980): 48–60. John P. McWilliams Jr., "Innocent Criminal or Criminal Innocence: The Trial in American Literature," in *Law and American Literature* (Chicago: Commission on Undergraduate Education in Law and the Humanities of the American Bar Association, 1980), 1–109.

33.   Bonnie J. Barthold, *Black Time: Fiction of Africa, the Caribbean, and the United States* (New Haven, Conn.: Yale University Press, 1981), 62–69. Jerry H. Bryant, "The Violence of *Native Son,*" *Southern Review,* 17 (April 1981): 303–19. Horst-Jürgen Gerigk, "Culpabilité et liberté: Dostoevskij, Dreiser et Richard Wright," *Revue de Littérature Comparée,* 55 (July–December 1981): 358–76. Marcus Klein, *Foreigners: The Making of American Literature 1900–1940* (Chicago: University of Chicago Press, 1981), 270–87. Walter C. Daniels, *Images of the Preacher in Afro-American Literature* (Washington: University Press of America, 1981), 147–79). Günter H. Lenz, "Southern Exposure: The Urban Experience and the Re-Construction of Black Folk Culture and Community in the Works of Richard Wright and Zora Neale Hurston," *New York Folklore,* 7 (Summer 1981): 3–39.

34.   Toru Kiuchi, "Richard Wright's Naming of Bigger Thomas," in *Suzuki Yukio Sensei Koki Kinen Ronbunshu: Phoenix o Motomete* (Tokyo, Nanundo, 1982), 371–83. Toru Kiuchi, "Richard Wright's *Native Son* and Alan Paton's *Cry, the Beloved Country,*" *Waseda Daigaku Eibungaku,* 56 (25 January 1982): 71–79. Kathryn Hunter, "Possessions and Dispossessions: Objects in Afro-American Novels," *The CEA Critic,* 44 (March 1982): 32–40. Sherley Anne Williams, "Papa Dick and Sister-Woman: Reflections on Women in the Fiction of Richard Wright," in *American Novelists Revisited: Essays in Feminist Criticism* (Boston: G. K. Hall, 1982), 394–415. Craig Werner, *Paradoxical Resolutions: American Fiction Since James Joyce* (Urbana: University of Illinois Press, 1982), 9–32.

35.   Ross Pudaloff, "Celebrity as Identity: Richard Wright, *Native Son,* and Mass Culture," *Studies in American Fiction,* 11 (Spring 1983): 3–18. Harold Hellenbrand, "Bigger Thomas Reconsidered: 'Native Son,' Film and 'King Kong,' " *Journal of American Culture,* 6 (1983): 84–95. A. Robert Lee, "Richard Wright's Inside Narratives," in *American Fictions: New Readings* (London: Vision, 1983), 200–221.

36.   Richard Macksey and Frank E. Moorer, eds., *Richard Wright: A Collection of Critical Essays* (Englewood Cliffs, N.J.: Prentice-Hall, 1984). Maria K. Mootry, "Bitches, Whores, and Woman Haters: Archetypes and Typologies in the Art of Richard Wright," in *Richard Wright: A Collection of Critical Essays,* 117–27. Michael G. Cooke, *Afro-American Literature in the Twentieth Century: The Achievement of Intimacy* (New Haven, Conn.: Yale University Press, 1984), 86–97. Trudier Harris, *Exorcising Blackness: Historical and Literary Lynching and Burning Rituals* (Bloomington: Indiana University Press, 1984), 95–128. Judith Giblin Brazinsky, "The Demands of Conscience and the Imperatives of Form: The Dramatization of *Native Son,*" *Black American Literature Forum,* 18 (Fall 1984): 106–9. Robert J. Butler, "Wright's *Native Son* and Two Novels by Zola: A Comparative Study," *Black American Literature Forum,* 18 (Fall 1984): 100–105. Kathleen Gallagher, "Bigger's Great Leap to the Figurative," *CLA Journal,* 27 (March 1984): 293–314.

37.   Robert Fleming, "O'Neill's *The Hairy Ape* as a Source for *Native Son,*" *CLA Journal,* 28 (June 1985): 434–43. Mary F. Sisney, "The Power and Horror of Whiteness: Wright and Ellison Respond to Poe," *CLA Journal,* 29 (September 1985): 82–90. George Goodin, *The Poetics of Protest: Literary Form and Political Implication in the Victim-of-Society Novel* (Carbondale: Southern Illinois University Press, 1985), 105–11. Doyle W. Walls, "The Clue Undetected in Richard Wright's *Native Son,*" *American Literature,* 57 (March 1985): 125–28.

38.   Joyce A. Joyce, *Richard Wright's Art of Tragedy* (Iowa City: University of Iowa Press, 1986). James A. Miller, "Bigger Thomas's Quest for Voice and Audience in Richard Wright's *Native Son,*" *Callaloo,* 9 (Summer 1986): 501–6. Louis Tremaine, "The Dissociated Sensibility of Bigger Thomas in Wright's *Native Son,*" *Studies in American Fiction,* 14 (Spring 1986): 63–76. Robert J. Butler, "The Function of Violence in Richard Wright's *Native Son,*" *Black American Literature Forum,* 20 (Spring/Summer 1986): 9–25. Willfried Feuser, "Richard Wright's *Native Son* and Ousmane Sembène's [sic] *Le Docker Noir,*" *Komparatische Hefte,* 14 (1986): 103–16.

Tony Magistrale, "From St. Petersburg to Chicago: Wright's *Crime and Punishment*," *Comparative Literature Studies*, 23 (Spring 1986): 59–70. David Bradley, "On Rereading 'Native Son,' " *The New York Times Magazine*, 7 December 1986, 68, 70, 74, 78–79. Chester Hedgepeth Jr., *Theories of Social Action in Black Literature* (New York: Peter Lang, 1986), 15–21, 38–43, 144–45.

39.   Valerie Smith, *Self-Discovery and Authority in Afro-American Narrative* (Cambridge, Mass.: Harvard University Press, 1987), 65–87. Bernard Bell, *The Afro-American Novel and Its Tradition* (Amherst: The University of Massachusetts Press, 1987), 153–68. Harold Bloom, "Introduction," in his *Richard Wright* (New York: Chelsea House, 1987), 1–6. James Robert Saunders, "The Social Significance of Wright's Bigger Thomas," *College Literature*, 14 (Winter 1987): 32–37. Robert L. Douglas, "Religious Orthodoxy and Skepticism in Richard Wright's *Uncle Tom's Children* and *Native Son*," *Griot*, 6 (Fall 1987): 44–51. James H. Evans Jr., *Spiritual Empowerment in Afro-American Literature* (Lewiston, N.Y.: Edwin Mellen, 1987), 95–130. Calvin Hernton, *The Sexual Mountain and Black Women Writers* (New York: Anchor/Doubleday, 1987), 61–65. John Orr, *The Making of the Twentieth Century Novel: Lawrence, Joyce, Faulkner and Beyond* (New York: St. Martin's, 1987), 169–73. Lynda Hungerford, "Dialect Representation in *Native Son*," *Language and Style*, 20 (Winter 1987): 3–15. Laura E. Tanner, "Uncovering the Magical Disguise of Language: The Narrative Presence in Richard Wright's *Native Son*," *Texas Studies in Literature and Language*, 29 (Winter 1987): 412–31.

40.   Harold Bloom, ed., *Richard Wright's Native Son* (New York: Chelsea House, 1988). C. James Trotman, ed., *Richard Wright: Myths and Realities* (New York: Garland, 1988). Susanne Bullock-Kimball, "The Modern Minotaur: A Study of Richard Wright's *Native Son*," *Notes on Mississippi Writers*, 20, no. 2 (1988): 41–48. Jane Davis, "Self-Hatred in the Novels of Richard Wright," *Literary Griot*, 1 (Fall 1988): 75–97. Robert A. Coles, "Richard Wright's Synthesis," *CLA Journal*, 31 (June 1988): 375–93. Alan W. France, "Misogyny and Appropriation in Wright's *Native Son*," *Modern Fiction Studies*, 34 (Autumn 1988): 413–23. Yoshinobu Hakutani, "Richard Wright and American Naturalism," *Zeitschrift für Anglistik und Amerikanistik*, 36 (1988): 217–26.

41.   Kathleen Ochshorn, "The Community of *Native Son*," *Mississippi Quarterly*, 42 (Fall 1989): 387–92. Linda Wagner-Martin, *The Modern American Novel, 1914–1945: A Critical History* (Boston: Twayne, 1989), 117–21, 132–34.

42.   Keneth Kinnamon, ed., *New Essays on Native Son* (Cambridge: Cambridge University Press, 1990). A shorter version of Kinnamon's introduction appears as "How 'Native Son' Was Born" in *Writing the American Classics* (Chapel Hill: University of North Carolina Press, 1990), 209–34. Harold Bloom, ed., *Bigger Thomas* (New York: Chelsea House, 1990). Eugene E. Miller, *Voice of a Native Son: The Poetics of Richard Wright* (Jackson: University Press of Mississippi, 1990), 44–60. Maryemma Graham, "Bearing Witness in Black Chicago: A View of Selected Fiction by Richard Wright, Frank London Brown, and Ronald Fair," *CLA Journal*, 33 (March 1990): 280–97. Cushing Strout, *Making American Tradition: Visions and Revisions from Ben Franklin to Alice Walker* (New Brunswick, N.J.: Rutgers University Press, 1990). 164–76. Michael F. Lynch, *Creative Revolt: A Study of Wright, Ellison, and Dostoevksy* (New York: Peter Lang, 1990), 77–131. Nagueyalti Warren, "Black Girls and Native Sons: Female Images in Selected Works by Richard Wright," *Literary Griot*, 2 (Spring 1990): 52–67.

43.   Richard Wright, *Early Works: Lawd Today!, Uncle Tom's Children, Native Son* (New York: The Library of America, 1991), 443–850. Eleanor Blau, "The Works of Richard Wright as Written," *The New York Times*, 28 August 1991, sec. C, 11. John Blades, "The Uncut Vision of Richard Wright," *Chicago Tribune*, 7 October 1991, Tempo sec., 1, 7. Andrew Delbanco, "An American Hunger," *New Republic*, 206 (30 March 1992): 28–30, 32–33. Jack Miles, "The Lost (and Found) Turning Point of 'Native Son,' " *Los Angeles Times*, 3 November 1991, 19. Louis Menand, "The Hammer and the Nail," *The New Yorker*, 68 (20 July 1992): 79–84. John A. Williams, "Richard Wright: The Legacy of a Native Son," *Washington Post Book World*, 22 September 1992, 1, 10. Cyrus Colter, "His Thundering Texts Restored to Full Glory," *Chicago Sun Times Book Week*, 22 September 1991.

44. Charles Johnson, "Black Fiction's Father Figure," *Chicago Tribune,* 17 November 1991, sec. 14, 1, 4. Eugene Miller, "Open Letter to Jerry Ward, Keneth Kinnamon, Arnold Rampersad, and the Wright Circle," *The Richard Wright Newsletter,* 2 (Fall 1992): 7. James Campbell, "The Wright Version," *Times Literary Supplement* (London), 13 December 1991, 14. James Tuttleton, "The Problematic Texts of Richard Wright," *Hudson Review,* 45 (Summer 1992): 261–71.

45. Robert Butler, *Native Son: The Emergence of a New Black Hero* (Boston: Twayne, 1991). Gayl Jones, *Liberating Voices: Oral Tradition in African American Literature* (Cambridge, Mass.: Harvard University Press, 1991), 151–60. James Cox, "Beneath My Father's Name," *Sewanee Review,* 79 (Summer 1991): 412–33.

46. Abdul JanMohamed, "Sexuality on/of the Racial Border: Foucault, Wright, and the Articulation of 'Racialized Sexuality,' " in *Discourses of Sexuality: From Aristotle to AIDS* (Ann Arbor: The University of Michigan Press, 1992), 94–116. Gayle Pemberton, *The Hottest Water in Chicago: On Family, Race, Time, and American Culture* (Boston: Faber and Faber, 1992), 162–75. Robert Felgar, "The Cultural Work of Time in *Native Son,*" *Notes on Mississippi Writers,* 24 (July 1992): 99–103. Hillary Holladay, "*Native Son*'s Guilty Man," *The CEA Critic,* 54 (Winter 1992): 30–36. James R. Andreas, "Othello's African American Progeny," *South Atlantic Review,* 57 (November 1992): 39–58.

47. Henry Louis Gates Jr. and K. A. Appiah, eds., *Richard Wright: Critical Perspectives Past and Present* (New York: Amistad, 1993), 6–25, 110–225. Barbara Foley, *Radical Representations: Politics and Form in U.S. Proletarian Fiction, 1929–1941* (Durham, N.C.: Duke University Press, 1993), 206–12. Eugene E. Miller, "Authority, Gender, and Fiction," *African American Review,* 27 (Winter 1993): 687–91. Kimberly W. Benston, "The Veil of Black: (Un)masking the Subject of African-American Modernism's 'Native Son,' " *Human Studies,* 16 (April 1993): 69–99. Robert Butler, "Farrell's Ethnic Neighborhood and Wright's Urban Ghetto: Two Visions of Chicago's South Side," *MELUS,* 18 (Spring 1993): 103–11.

48. Joyce Ann Joyce, *Warriors, Conjurers and Priests: Defining African-Centered Literary Criticism* (Chicago: Third World Press, 1994), 49–72. Dale E. Peterson, "Richard Wright's Long Journey from Gorky to Dostoevsky," *African American Review,* 28 (Fall 1994): 375–87. Seodial Deena, "The Irrationality of Bigger Thomas's World: A Frightening View for the Twenty-First Century Urban Population," *CLA Journal,* 38 (September 1994): 20–30.

49. Arnold Rampersad, ed., *Richard Wright: A Collection of Critical Essays* (Englewood Cliffs, N.J.: Prentice Hall, 1995), 12–62. Robert Butler, ed., *The Critical Response to Richard Wright* (Westport, Conn.: Greenwood, 1995), 15–59, 173–76, 181–84. Yoshinobu Hakutani, "The City and Richard Wright's Quest for Freedom," in *The City in African-American Literature* (Madison/Teaneck, N.J.: Fairleigh Dickinson University Press, 1995), 50–63. Laurel J. Gardner, "The Progression of Meaning in the Images of Violence in Richard Wright's *Uncle Tom's Children* and *Native Son,*" *CLA Journal,* 38 (June 1995): 420–40. Robyn Weigman, *American Anatomies: Theorizing Race and Gender* (Durham, N.C.: Duke University Press, 1995), 100–104. Kimberly Drake, "Rape and Resignation: Silencing the Victim in the Novels of Morrison and Wright," *LIT: Literature Interpretation Theory,* 6 (Winter/Spring 1995), 63–72.

50. Some of the material in this introduction is derived from previous writings by the author. For comprehensive coverage of commentary on *Native Son* and everything else pertaining to Wright, see *A Richard Wright Bibliography: Fifty Years of Criticism and Commentary, 1933–1982* (Westport, Conn.: Greenwood, 1988) by Keneth Kinnamon with the help of Joseph Benson, Michel Fabre, and Craig Werner. Kinnamon is gradually updating this annotated bibliography in the *Richard Wright Newsletter,* published at Northeastern University.

REVIEWS

◆

The Case of Bigger Thomas

Malcolm Cowley

"Native Son" is the most impressive American novel I have read since "The Grapes of Wrath." In some ways the two books resemble each other: both deal with the dispossessed and both grew out of the radical movement of the 1930's. There is, however, a distinction to be drawn between the motives of the two authors. Steinbeck, more privileged than the characters in his novel, wrote out of deep pity for them, and the fault he had to avoid was sentimentality. Richard Wright, a Negro, was moved by wrongs he had suffered in his own person, and what he had to fear was a blind anger that might destroy the pity in him, making him hate any character whose skin was whiter than his own. His first book, "Uncle Tom's Children," had not completely avoided that fault. It was a collection of stories all but one of which had the same pattern: a Negro was goaded into killing one or more white men and was killed in turn, without feeling regret for himself or his victims. Some of the stories I found physically painful to read, even though I admired them. So deep was the author's sense of the indignities heaped on his race that one felt he was revenging himself by a whole series of symbolic murders. In "Native Son" the pattern is the same, but the author's sympathies have broadened and his resentment, though just as deep, is less painful and personal.

The hero, Bigger Thomas, is a Negro boy of twenty, a poolroom loafer, a bully, a liar and a petty thief. "Bigger, sometimes I wonder why I birthed you," his pious mother tells him. "Honest, you the most no-countest man I ever seen in all my life." A Chicago philanthropist tries to help the family by hiring him as chauffeur. That same night Bigger kills the philanthropist's daughter—out of fear of being discovered in her room—and stuffs her body into the furnace. This half-accidental crime leads to others. Bigger tries to cast the blame for the girl's disappearance on her lover, a Communist; he tries to collect a ransom from her parents; after the body is found he murders his Negro mistress to keep her from betraying him to the police. The next day he is captured on the snow-covered roof of a South Side tenement, while a mob howls in the street below.

Reprinted from *The New Republic*, 102 (18 March 1940): 382–83, with the permission of the journal.

In the last part of the book, which is also the best, we learn that the case of Bigger Thomas is not the author's deepest concern. Behind it is another, more complicated story he is trying hard to explain, though the words come painfully at first, and later come in a flood that almost sweeps him away. "Listen, you white folks," he seems to be saying over and over. "I want to tell you about all the Negroes in America. I want to tell you how they live and how they feel. I want you to change your minds about them before it is too late to prevent a worse disaster than any we have known. I speak for my own people, but I speak for America too." And because he does speak for and to the nation, without ceasing to be a Negro, his book has more force than any other American novel by a member of his race.

Bigger, he explains, had been trained from the beginning to be a bad citizen. He had been taught American ideals of life, in the schools, in the magazines, in the cheap movie houses, but had been denied any means of achieving them. Everything he wanted to have or do was reserved for the whites. "I just can't get used to it," he tells one of his poolroom buddies. "I swear to God I can't. . . . Every time I think about it I feel like somebody's poking a red-hot iron down my throat."

At the trial, his white-haired Jewish lawyer makes a final plea to the judge for mercy. "What Bigger Thomas did early that Sunday morning in the Dalton home and what he did that Sunday night in the empty building was but a tiny aspect of what he had been doing all his life long. He was *living,* only as he knew how, and as we have forced him to live. . . . The hate and fear which we have inspired in him, woven by our civilization into the very structure of his consciousness, into his blood and bones, into the hourly functioning of his personality, have become the justification of his existence. . . . Every thought he thinks is potential murder."

This long courtroom speech, which sums up the argument of the novel, is at once its strongest and its weakest point. It is strongest when Mr. Max is making a plea for the American Negroes in general. "They are not simply twelve million people; in reality they constitute a separate nation, stunted, stripped and held captive *within* this nation." Many of them—and many white people too—are full of "balked longing for some kind of fulfillment and exultation"; and their existence is "what makes our future seem a looming image of violence." In this context, Mr. Max's talk of another civil war seems not so much a threat as an agonized warning. But his speech is weakest as a plea for the individual life of Bigger Thomas. It did not convince the judge, and I doubt that it will convince many readers.

It is not that I think Bigger "deserved" the death sentence for his two murders. Most certainly his guilt was shared by the society that condemned him. But when he killed Mary Dalton he was performing the first free action in his whole fear-tortured life; he was accepting his first moral responsibility. That is what he tried so hard to explain to his lawyer. "I ain't worried none about them women I killed. . . . I killed 'em 'cause I was scared and mad. But I been scared and mad all my life and after I killed that first woman, I wasn't scared no more for a little while." And when his lawyer asks him if he ever thought he would face the electric chair, "Now I come to think of it," he answers, "it seems like something like this just had to be." If Mr. Max had managed to win a life sentence for Bigger Thomas, he would have robbed him of his only claim to human courage and dignity. But that Richard Wright makes us feel this, while setting out to prove something else—that he makes Bigger Thomas a human rather than a racial symbol—shows that he wrote an even better novel than he had planned.

Change the World: Dick Wright Gives America a Significant Picture in "Native Son"

MIKE GOLD

Only the day before yesterday, it seems, I met Dick Wright at the John Reed Club in Chicago. He was a shy and very young proletarian poet, earnest enough about the cause to be one of those actives who put away the chairs after the meeting and help to sweep the hall.

And only yesterday, modest Dick Wright was Harlem reporter for the Daily Worker, taking his newspaper work as seriously as his poetry, because it was part of the same cause.

But today, Dick Wright has himself become major news in the American literary world. His first novel, "Native Son," has sold over 200,000 copies in less than a month. It is no exaggeration to say that at one stroke he has become a national figure. Neither is it an exaggeration to claim that after ten years of fumbling, and experiment, of great visions and uneven fulfillments, our American social realism, our American proletarian literature or whatever critics wish to name it, has finally culminated in two sure classics—Steinbeck's "Grapes of Wrath" and Richard Wright's "Native Son."

The story of "Native Son" is one that will burn itself on the imagination of this country, I believe, as has no other novel about Negroes since Uncle Tom's Cabin.

It was surely his Communist training that gave Richard Wright the moral courage to reveal without fear every ugly secret of a democracy that is based on the blood and suffering of an oppressed nation within the nation.

His poor boy, Bigger, living with his mother, brother and sister in a single rat-infested room in one of those horribly decayed South Side tenements, commits two horribly revolting and senseless murders for which he dies at the hands of the State.

Richard Wright demonstrates that this poor boy was never a murderer by nature. He was only what white capitalism had made him—an unskilled, jobless, nervous, fear-ridden youth without a human future.

Reprinted from *Sunday Worker* (31 March 1940): Sec. 2, p. 7.

Bigger's first murder is an accident. He has been hired as chauffeur by a white philanthropist who is a "friend of Negroes," but whose wealth comes from the horrible Negro slum tenements he owns.

This man has himself created the Biggers he would "reform," but the Poor Boy feels however dimly that a few splashes of smug philanthropy cannot whitewash the great crime that was done him at birth.

This real estate philanthropist's collegey daughter, however, has developed some twinges of social conscience.

She even has Communist friends, and might be termed a parlor Bolshevik. Charming, well-meaning, she is essentially a dilletante [sic] having her brief flirtation with dangerous fealities before sinking back comfortably into the inevitable suburban swamp.

In a silly drunken spree, she drags Bigger into a situation that makes him ripe fodder for a lynching.

Henry Siedel [sic] Canby, a philosopher of the bourgeois literary suburbs, has seized upon the fact that this girl associated with Communists, and that Bigger resented her patronage, as evidence that these "Communist Negrophiles" (his elegant term) are somehow to blame.

Mr. Canby would torture such a conclusion, of course, out of even a nonpartisan turnip. Prejudice makes for stupidity, and Mr. Canby misses entirely the subtle and masterly psychology with which Richard Wright depicts the reactions of a poor Negro boy who has learned to hate and distrust all whites and then he meets white Communists.

Wright has pictured two Communists, though not typical, and shown how their courage and their self-sacrificing efforts to save Bigger finally penetrate through the mists, and help him, even though it be for a last few hours, to discover his own manhood and to rise to tragic heights. How could even a Mr. Canby miss this? It is one of the main points in the story.

It is a rare and special thing that Wright has done, as no American writer before him. He has written a story on the racial theme without sentimentalizing it.

And he has done it in the form of a melodrama that is simply a superb achievement in technique. Wright can teach anyone in Hollywood how to concoct a thriller. He will affect writers as much as Hemingway did.

I must admit that I fail to understand the process by which the shy, unformed Chicago poet of only a few years ago has become such a master. It is one of the literary miracles, and, though I don't understand, I say it is a good miracle, and I am proud it happened via the Daily Worker!

Maybe it is the miracle of complete honesty, of Communist honesty, that fierce morality which burns out all the bunk in a writer. Maybe the way to be a great writer is to love your poor, oppressed folk with the passionate loyalty of Dick Wright.

For it is his complete honesty and loyalty that enable him to take the worst that is charged against his folk, and to throw it back as a challenge in the face of the oppressor.

Do not miss this book. Dick Wright has put an uneradicable mark on the thought of America. Only a few books in one's time convey an immediate feeling that they express a whole nation. And the book of Richard Wright does just that.

Book Reviews: *Native Son,* by Richard Wright

RALPH ELLISON

Like Negro "swing" musicians, Negro bad-men constitute one of the most sensitive groups in American life; they both reflect and are products of its violence. It is an indictment of our society that their sensitivity and creativeness are not allowed to flow into socially more productive channels. In "Native Son," Richard Wright gives the bad-man a chance to be productive; the hero, Bigger Thomas, is a young bully, a coward, and petty thief. His story is told in three books titled "Fear," "Flight" and "Fate."

In the first, Bigger is taken from the Chicago Relief rolls and given a job as chauffeur in the home of Mr. Dalton, a wealthy white philanthropist who owns the tenement where he, his mother and a young sister and brother live in a single room. The first night on the job Bigger accidentally kills the philanthropist's daughter, Mary. Disposing of her body in a furnace, he attempts to cast suspicion on Jan, Mary's Communist lover.

Book two, "Flight," treats his escape upon detection, his murder of his girl Bessie to keep her from talking, and his capture after an exciting chase over the roofs of the South Side Slums. The third book, "Fate," deals with the trial and Bigger's defense by Max, a Communist lawyer, who explains Bigger's relation to the whole of American society and the part that American race prejudice played in forming Bigger's personality. Brutalized and conditioned to the deepest levels of his consciousness by fear and violence, Bigger did not know how to accept the friendly gestures of Mary and Jan, and when caught in a tabooed situation with Mary, out of fear, he killed her. Seeing in Mary a part of the white world that oppressed him, Bigger took the moral responsibility for her death. In killing he achieved the first realization of his personality; and it was in the vague comprehension of this, while awaiting the electric chair, that he achieved his first sense of dignity—murder had become creation, the seeds of violence had brought forth violent fruit.

This is a stern dialectic, and its message reaches beyond the narrow confines of Negro life to affect the whole of society. Max explains that there are many in our country, white and black, who are hungry for the same bread of

Reprinted from *TAC,* 2 (April 1940): 8, with the permission of Fannie Ellison and the William Morris Agency, Inc.

self-realization for which Bigger groped and who daily are handed the stones of violence, the grapes of wrath. Max warns that they will not continue to strive for the old ideals as more and more they find them empty. Like Bigger they might find release through violence. In Germany, Hitler's rise was possible because of the despair of the people. Disillusioned in their attempts to achieve a harmonious existence through the old political forms, they turned to Hitler because he promised a way out. Hitler is said by some writers to be a neurotic. Perhaps this is true, but no one can say that the German people are all neurotics, nor would an asylum for Hitler solve their problem. Hitler is an exaggerated product of the circumstance that conditioned them all.

Some reviewers are calling Bigger Thomas a neurotic, but it is a mistake to dismiss him as such. He is not crazy, he is the product of the restrictions placed upon 15,000,000 American citizens, in the narrow sense, and upon one-third of the nation in the broader sense. He could not accept the way out of Negro Christianity, nor could he create music of his violence; his reaction was direct, positive and physical. Deprived of education and forced by the reality of Jim-crow to reject the common American assumptions that all men are created equal and endowed with the right of health and the pursuit of happiness, Bigger reacted as life had taught him: violently.

"Native Son" jars our common assumptions concerning the Negro and concerning American society; one is a clue to the other. If America's promise is not to be fulfilled in violence, we must all, like Jan, realize the necessity of taking stock of both.

The Negro Novel: Richard Wright

David L. Cohn

Richard Wright, a Mississippi-born Negro, has written a blinding and corrosive study in hate. It is a novel entitled *Native Son.* The race hatred of his hero, Bigger Thomas, is directed with equal malevolence and demoniac intensity toward *all* whites, whether they are Mary Dalton, the moony Negrophile whom he murdered, or the vague white men who seemed to bar his youthful ambition to become an aviator or join the navy. This book has far-reaching qualities of significance above and beyond its considerable virtues as a novel, because Mr. Wright elects to portray his hero not as an individual merely but as a symbol of twelve million American Negroes.

Bigger is very young. His exact age is not stated, but we are told he is too young to vote, and he is therefore under twenty-one. Although his life has hardly begun, his career and hopes for the future have been blasted by the Negro-hating whites of Chicago. On page 14 of *Native Son,* Bigger and his friend Gus are watching an airplane above the city. "I *could* fly a plane if I had a chance," Bigger says. "If you wasn't black and if you had some money and if they'd let you go to that aviation school, you *could* fly a plane," Gus answers. And time after time, throughout the length of this book, Bigger bitterly complains that he is denied access to the broad, glittering world which the whites monopolize for themselves to the exclusion of Negroes. Toward the end of the novel (p. 302), Bigger, in jail for murdering a white girl and his Negro mistress, says: "I ain't asking nobody to be sorry for me . . . I'm black. *They don't give black people a chance*" (my italics). Bigger's crimes and his fate in the electric chair, the author makes clear to us, are consequently to be laid at the door of white society.

In the speech of Bigger's lawyer at his trial, one finds the fullest summation of Mr. Wright's point of view toward the Negro question in America, and the most explicit statement of his use of Bigger as a symbol of the oppressed Negro. "This boy," says lawyer Max, "represents but a tiny aspect of the problem whose reality sprawls over a third of a nation. . . . Multiply Bigger Thomas twelve million times, allowing for environmental and temperamental variations . . . and you have the psychology of the Negro people. . . . Taken collectively, they are not simply twelve million; in reality they constitute a separate nation, stunted, stripped, and held captive *within* this nation, devoid of political, social, economic and property rights."

Mr. Wright might have made a more manly and certainly more convincing case for his people if he had stuck to fact. In all of the non-Southern states, Negroes have complete political rights, including the suffrage, and even in the South Negro suffrage is constantly being extended. So powerful, indeed, is the Negro vote, and so solidly is it cast en bloc in Negro-populous Eastern and Midwestern states, that in closely contested Presidential elections the Negro vote may decide who shall become President of the United States. Hence the scramble of both parties for the Negro vote. Nowhere in America save in the most benighted sections of the South, or in times of passion arising from the committing of atrocious crime, is the Negro denied the equal protection of the laws. If he is sometimes put in jail for no reason at all in Memphis, so too are whites put in jail for no reason at all in Pittsburgh. This is the unjust fate, not of the Negro alone, but of the poor, the obscure, and the inarticulate everywhere, regardless of pigmentation. The ownership, also, of more than a billion dollars' worth of property by Negroes in the South alone, and the presence of prosperous Negro business concerns throughout the country, are some refutation of the sweeping statement that Negroes are denied property rights in this country.

Through the mouth of Bigger's lawyer we are told in unmistakable terms that the damming up of the Negro's aspirations, and the denial to him of unrestricted entry into the whole environment of the society in which he is cast, may lead Negroes, in conjunction with others, toward a new civil war in America. Mr. Wright seems to have completely forgotten the unparalleled phenomenon—unique in the world's history—of the *first* American Civil War, in which millions of white men fought and killed one another over the issue of the black slave. If it be granted that the original enslavement of Negroes was a crime against justice, then it must also be granted that its bloody expiation was filled with enough death and destruction to satisfy even the most hate-consumed Negro. But it doesn't seem to satisfy Mr. Wright. A second civil war must begin where the first one left off in order to bring about the eventual freeing of the Negro minority, even if it means the destruction of the society of the majority. Justice and understanding are to come through the persuasive snouts of machine guns.

Bigger's lawyer is a Jew. As a member of a race which has known something of oppression,—not for three centuries, the length of the Negro's residence in America, but for more than twenty centuries in nearly every country of the world,—he pleads extenuation for his client both on broad grounds of justice and on the ground that white society drove Biggers to crime by repressing him. If repression of the members of a minority drives them to slay members of the majority, it would follow that the principal occupation of

Jews in Tsarist Russia, Poland, Rumania, and other bitterly anti-Semitic countries would have been to use their oppressors as clay pigeons. Jewish revolutionists there have been, indeed, but over the whole sweep of two thousand years of dark Jewish history the mass of these people, enduring greater oppression than Negroes knew here even in slavery, created within the walls of their ghettos an intense family and communal life and constructed inexhaustible wells of spiritual resource. They used their talents and energies as best they could, serene in the belief either that a Messiah would ultimately come and deliver them out of bondage into the Promised Land or that justice would ultimately triumph. Mr. Wright uses a Jewish lawyer as his mouthpiece, but he has learned nothing from Jewish history, nor gleaned anything of the spirit of that group whom Tacitus called "a stubborn people."

It is beyond doubt that Negroes labor under grave difficulties in America; that economic and social discrimination is practised against them; that opportunities open to whites are closed to blacks. It is also beyond doubt that the position, if not the status, of the Negro is constantly improving in the United States. The evidence on this point is overwhelming. But there is one hard and inescapable fact which must be courageously faced. The social structure of America, despite many racial admixtures, is Anglo-Saxon. And nowhere on earth—save in isolated instances—do whites and Negroes in Anglo-Saxon communities intermingle socially or intermarry. And so long as this is a fact, neither the Negro—and this is what completely escapes Mr. Wright—*nor the white man* will function as a full-fledged personality. It could easily be demonstrated that Southern whites living in the presence of masses of Negroes, and maintaining at least tolerable racial relations through the exercise of exquisite, intuitive tact on both sides, suffer aberrations and distortions of the spirit only slightly less severe than those suffered by Negroes.

It is no fault of the Negro or of the present generation of whites that the Negro is here. But the preaching of Negro hatred of whites by Mr. Wright is on a par with the preaching of white hatred of Negroes by the Ku Klux Klan. The position, moreover, of a minority struggling toward the sun must be gauged at any given time by its relative rather than its absolute state, and in accordance with this postulate it is clear that the Negro's lot in America is constantly being ameliorated.

It is highly significant of the whole hate-headlong point of view of Mr. Wright that he has chosen to make his hero so hopelessly despairing of making a good life for himself because of white repressions, that he drives him to crime and execution when his adult life has hardly begun. Contrast this with the experience of the Jews in England, who were first granted full civil rights only after five centuries of living in the country.

Mr. Wright obviously does not have the long view of history. He wants not only complete political rights for his people, but also social equality, and he wants them now. Justice demands that every right granted to others shall be granted to Negroes, but men are not gods. A hard-headed people will be conscious of the Pauline law of expediency: "All things are lawful unto me, but all things are not expedient."

Justice or no justice, the whites of America simply will not grant to Negroes at this time those things that Mr. Wright demands. The Negro problem in America is actually insoluble; all profound, complex social problems are insoluble, and only a politically naïve people will believe otherwise. In the meanwhile, recognition by both sides that the question is insoluble, followed by tempered, sincere efforts to make the best of the situation within its frame of reference, will produce the most equitable results for both. Hatred, and the preaching of hatred, and incitement to violence can only make a tolerable relationship intolerable.

Even Abraham Lincoln did not envisage a time when the Negro question would be solved upon Mr. Wright's terms. In 1862 he said to a Negro delegation who called on him: "You and we are different races. . . . But even when you cease to be slaves you are yet far from being placed on an equality with the white race. . . . The aspiration of men is to enjoy equality with the best when free, but on this continent not a single man of your race is made the equal of a single man of ours. . . . Go where you are treated best, and the ban is still upon you."

And Mr. Wright's hero kills and dies in Mr. Lincoln's state of Illinois.

Native Son and Revolution

J. R. JOHNSON [C. L. R. JAMES]

Black Bigger Thomas, native son, stifled by and inwardly rebellious against white America's treatment of him, by accident murders a white girl. For him this murder is the beginning of a new life. In striking such a blow against his hated enemies, in the struggle to outwit them and evade capture, his stunted personality finds scope to expand. Before he is sentenced to death, the sincere efforts of two white Communists to save him teach him that all whites are not his enemies, that he is not alone, that there is a solidarity of all the oppressed.

Such, finely audacious and magnificently simple, is the theme, sprung from such a wealth of emotional vitality and presented with such power of literary realization that it forces discussion and unwilling reconsideration of the world's No. 1 minority problem, the Negro question in America. The book therefore is not only a literary but also a political event. Here we are concerned with a revolutionary interpretation of Bigger Thomas, an aspect, not unnaturally, neglected or misunderstood by all reviewers, "Marxist" or otherwise. The career of Bigger Thomas is a symbol and prototype of the Negro masses in the proletarian revolution.

Bigger hates white people with a consuming hatred. So do the great masses of Negroes. Quite often the hate is hidden, sometimes it is buried deep out of sight, sometimes it is twisted into its opposite, a passionate religiousity. But it is there, and speakers, particularly Negro speakers, can always elicit it from any Negro gathering. It represents ten generations' experience of injustice, of humiliation, of suppressed resentment and bitterness. But if Negroes hate whites, they also fear them, their knowledge, their power, their ruthlessness—also the accumulated experience of the generations.

THE SLEEPING VOLCANO

This hate will be one of the most powerful forces in the Negro revolution. In the South an iron system holds the Negroes down. But Southern whites

Reprinted from *The New International*, 6 (May 1940): 92–93, with the permission of the Estate of C. L. R. James.

know quite well what fires smoulder behind the deference and the humility. "If you let a nigger forget himself, you have to kill him" is one of their commonest expressions. As long as society in the South maintains its integrity, the Negroes will continue to be docile. But if the solid South does not remain solid, if that society ever goes to pieces, then, wherever the Negroes outnumber the whites, we shall see some of the bloodiest massacres that this continent has known. Whoever doubts this should study the slave revolt of Spartacus, and the black revolt in San Domingo: the end of the San Domingo revolt was the complete annihilation of the white population.

America differs from San Domingo in one important respect: the Negroes are a minority and in a proletarian revolution the white proletariat of the North will be dominant. Its aim will be to tear the poor whites of the South from the leadership of the Southern landlords and capitalists, by precept and example to make them aware of their solidarity with the Negroes. The strength and organization of the Northern proletarians; the extent of the social disintegration in the South driving blacks and poor whites closer together, will shape the course of the struggle.

In a profound sense Bigger Thomas is a "typical" Negro. His hatred of whites, his sense of his wrongs and his forcibly limited life, his passionate desire to strike at his enemies, all this is racial. He is different from other Negroes only in the fact that his nature is such that he cannot contain himself.

Bigger, having killed by accident, now has to save himself. He must match his wits against this whole powerful white world, which has hitherto held him chained, and in this conflict he finds himself. The murder of Mary is an accident, rooted though it is in the social order. But his acceptance of full responsibility for it is a revolutionary act. To scheme, to plan, to fight—this is to be free. In this bold stroke, the central theme of his book, Wright has distilled the very essence of what is the Negro's future. The great masses of Negroes carry in their hearts the heavy heritage of slavery, and their present degradation. Such has been their past, it is their present, and, as far as they can see, it is their future. It is the revolution which will lift these millions from their knees. Nobody can do it for them. Men, personalities, will be freed from the centuries of chains and shame, as Bigger's personality was freed, by violent action against their tyrants. It is on the evening after the battle, with smoking rifle and dripping bayonet, that the Negro will be able to look all white men in the face, will be able to respect himself and be respected. Wright notes that Bigger had no confidence in other Negroes; they were too afraid and too conscious of fear to trust one another. That confidence in himself which Bigger earned by the unwitting murder of Mary, millions of Negroes will gain only by the revolution. There is no other way for them.

BIGGER'S FIGHT

The finest passages in the book describe Bigger's fight against capture, and it is curious how blind all have been to the overwhelming significance of this. What hero in what literature ever fought his fight with such courage and such determination? As he reads in the paper that the crime has been pinned on him, "his right hand twitched. He wanted a gun in that hand. He got his gun from his pocket and held it. He read again." Thenceforward he fights. The murder of Bessie, his girl friend, is subordinate to his great purpose: to fight against these tyrants and torturers. He couldn't leave Bessie behind, and he couldn't take her. Therefore he had to destroy her. In the abstract it is a revolting crime. But whoever has entered into the spirit of the new Bigger must see it as he saw it. Eight thousand white men with guns and gas were out looking for him. Without bravado, without self-pity, he fought.

> A small black object fell near his head in the snow, hissing, shooting forth a white vapor, like a blowing plume, which was carried away from him by the wind. Tear gas! With a movement of his hand he knocked it off the tank. Another came and he knocked it off. Two more came and he shoved them off. The wind blew strong, from the lake. It carried the gas away from his eyes and nose. He heard a man yell,
> "Stop it! The wind's blowing it away! He's throwing 'em back!"
> The bedlam in the street rose higher; more men climbed through trapdoors to the roof. He wanted to shoot, but remembered that he had but three bullets left. He would shoot when they were closer and he would save one bullet for himself. They would not take him alive.
> "Come on down, boy!"
> He did not move; he lay with gun in hand, waiting. Then, directly under his eyes, four white fingers caught hold of the icy edge of the water tank. He gritted his teeth and struck the white fingers with the butt of the gun. They vanished and he heard a thud as a body landed on the snow-covered roof. He lay waiting for more attempts to climb up, but none came.
> "It's no use fighting, boy! You're caught! Come on down!"
> He knew that they were afraid, and yet he knew that it would soon be over, one way or another; they would either capture or kill him. He was surprised that he was not afraid. Under it all some part of his mind was beginning to stand aside; he was going behind his curtain, his wall, looking out with sullen stares of contempt. He was outside of himself now, looking out, he lay under a winter sky lit with tall gleams of whirling light, hearing thirsty screams and hungry shouts. He clutched his gun, defiant, unafraid.

More than the mere desire to live was at stake. It was the bursting pride of a spirit long cramped and oppressed that found itself free at last. All students of revolutionary history know it: the legions of Spartacus, Cromwell's Ironsides, the Paris enragés, the Russian workers defending Petrograd against

Udenitch, the Spanish workers defending Madrid, the march of the Chinese Communists across China in 1936. That was the spirit of defiance and determination in which Bigger fought.

In prison, fighting for a clear realization of what has happened to him, Bigger attains the highest stage of his development: he learns that the two white Communists are his friends. They prove it in action. Here again Bigger's experience typifies another important revolutionary truth. Masses learn by experience, not by propaganda, and the Negro masses in particular will have to be shown solidarity in action and not in logic. There will be many Negroes in the revolutionary party, but the vast majority will in all probability learn the lesson of class solidarity as Bigger learned it.

WRIGHT AS A REVOLUTIONARY NOVELIST

Did Wright consciously epitomize Negro revolutionary struggle in the career of Bigger Thomas? The question is irrelevant. The artist, by methods compounded of conscious logic and his own intuition, observes society and experiences life. He comes to his conclusions and embodies them in character, scene, and dramatic situation. According to the depth of his penetration and the sweep of his net, his capacity to integrate and reproduce, he writes his novel, paints his picture, or composes his symphony. Psychologist, historian, politician, or revolutionary, drawing on his own experience, sees symbols, parallelism, depth and perspective unsuspected by the creator. The artist can see the truth and nothing but the truth, but no one can expect him to see the whole truth.

In our age literature, especially literature of this kind, cannot be divorced from politics. Wright is a Stalinist. In this novel a scrupulous artistic integrity enables him to draw white Communists, if not with the same success as Negroes, yet without bias or subservience to the Stalinist conception of the party and the party "line." But he treads a dangerous road. Stalinism has destroyed the literary and artistic life of Russia, it has ruined Malraux, one of the most gifted of contemporary writers. In that evil garden nothing creative flourishes. The artist in uniform soon ceases to be an artist. The Stalinists are past masters in the art of enveloping, suborning, corrupting. It will be a pity if they succeed in perverting and blighting this splendid talent.

Insight, Courage, and Craftsmanship

STERLING A. BROWN

A Book-of-the-Month Club selection, its first edition sold out within three hours, a quarter million copies called for within six weeks, Richard Wright's *Native Son* is a literary phenomenon. Magazines have run articles about it after the first reviews. It is discussed by literary critics, scholars, social workers, journalists, writers to the editor, preachers, students, and the man in the street. It seems important to the reviewer that debates on *Native Son* may be heard in grills and "juke-joints" as well as at "literary" parties, in the deep South as well as in Chicago, among people who have not bothered much to read novels since *Ivanhoe* was assigned in high school English.

One commentator writes that the book "has torn the surface veneer from a condition which is awakening the conscience of the entire nation." Only the future can decide whether the revelations in *Native Son* awaken the conscience of the nation; according to history that conscience is not easily aroused. But, if such a great and difficult task could be achieved by a single book, *Native Son* is that book.

Richard Wright is, of course, not the first Negro to compound bitterness and wisdom eloquently, nor the first to see the terrible effects of frustration. He is the first, however, to give a psychological probing of the consciousness of the outcast, the disinherited, the generation lost in the slum jungles of American civilization. Mr. Wright has urged that novelists should have perspective and an integrated vision of their material. In *Native Son* he gives such a philosophical novel. With a narrative skill all of his own, with what he has elsewhere called "the potential cunning to steal into the inmost recesses of the human heart," with a surprising mastery of the techniques of fiction, tested in the past as well as the present, Mr. Wright has struck with tremendous impact. Earlier writers have likewise struck out; sometimes their blows were powerful; sometimes they were scattered, or glanced off, or missed altogether.

In one of Mr. Wright's short stories, Big Boy left "home"—a community in the deep South where white violence erupted spasmodically and where

Reprinted from *Opportunity,* 18 (June 1940): 185–86.

Negroes lived in a slow paralysis of fear. In Chicago Bigger meets with forces as destructive, but unlike Big Boy, he cannot leave this home. Daily, as with so many of his fellows on the Southside, or in Harlem, or in Philadelphia, Washington, Atlanta, Birmingham—wherever you choose—by insult, indignity, and injury, now petty, now gross, always constant—the iron is driven into Bigger's soul. The first scene, where Bigger and Buddy corner a rat and smash it with a skillet, sets the tone for the grim sequence. *Native Son* would be distinguished if for no other reason than the social realism with which Chicago's Southside is presented. Here are the rickety "kitchenette" flats, which produce such exorbitant returns for the realtors' little investment that the human wastage does not count. Here are the dives, the poolrooms, the ineffectual boys' clubs where crimes are planned. The crushed products of this environment—although slightly sketched, for Bigger gets the lion's share—are quite convincing: Bigger's gang of Jack, G. H., and Gus; Buddy the brother (the last two are brilliantly characterized); the tragic kid Vera, sensitive to the quick, gentle-hearted and doomed; Mrs. Thomas who seeks escape through religion but cannot find it there; and Bigger's sweetheart Bessie: *"She worked long hours, hard and hot hours seven days a week, with only Sunday afternoons off; and when she did get off she wanted fun, hard and fast fun, something to make her feel that she was making up for the starved life she led."*

The narrative *drive* of this novel from the killing of the rat, through the two murders, the flight, to the capture on the tenement roof is amazing. In contrast, the last section slows down. This is to be expected, but there is likewise some repetitiousness. *Native Son* is naturally compared to Dreiser's *An American Tragedy,* but there are great differences, and one of these involves technique. A naturalist, Dreiser piles detail upon detail to gain verisimilitude; but Wright, seeking truth to a reality beyond naturalism, makes use of the devices of the symbolic novel, as do such writers as Steinbeck, Faulkner, Caldwell and Dos Passos. He compresses a great deal in small space and time: for instance, a philanthropist interested in Negro education, a politician riding to power on Negro baiting, representatives of a sensational press, the overzealous young communist Jan, and Mary, the victim of the accidental murder; the older, more understanding Communist lawyer, Max, a Negro preacher, these and other symbolic personages cross Bigger's tragic path. With so much compression, verisimilitude is sometimes sacrificed. The hiding of the girl's body, the delay in discovering the crime, the ease with which the kidnapping note is delivered are details not completely convincing. From melodrama (even though of such a high order) some losses are as inevitable as the sure gains.

But Mr. Wright's greatest achievement is not his description of a setting—as revelatory as that is, nor his conduct of narrative—as thrilling as that is, but his characterization of Bigger Thomas. It took courage to select as hero, a wastrel, a sneak thief, a double-killer. Most writers of minority groups select as heroes those who disprove stereotypes. Here is the "bad nigger" set down without squeamishness, doing all that the "bad nigger" is supposed to do. But that is merely the start. Mr. Wright sees all around this "bad nigger" and through him, and we get the interpretative realism that shows how inevitable it was that he should get that way. Here in brief compass we see a youngster who could have been, should have been so much more, stunted and twisted into a psychopathic hater, feeling free and important only after a murder, exercising his new power in concocting a kidnapping plot absurdly fashioned after the movies which, with the poolrooms, were his chief educators. Mr. Wright uses more than once the symbol of the rat, now cornered, now dashing into a hole, and Bigger's concept of the meeting ground between whites and Negroes as a No Man's Land. "What can I do? They got me," he asked. He knew that they had had him for a long time.

The lawyer, Max, in a profound speech (less a courtroom plea for life imprisonment than a philosophical statement of the tragic race problem) says: "*Multiply Bigger Thomas twelve million times, allowing for environmental and temperamental variations, and for those Negroes who are completely under the influence of the church, and you have the psychology of the Negro people.*" Max's statement is considered to be Richard Wright's. If this point is debated one should give full weight to the words: "*allowing for environmental and temperamental variations.*" David Cohn in the current *Atlantic Monthly* considers *Native Son* "a blinding and corrosive study in hate," and lectures the author, reminding him of the Civil War "in which millions of white men fought and killed one another over the issue of the black slave." This seems to miss the point of the novel, especially the fine closing. Other critics disagree with Mr. Cohn; Henry Seidel Canby in the "Book-of-the-Month Club News," for instance, says that "this is not a vindictive book." Among so much else, Mr. Wright has established authentically and powerfully that hatred exists among the kicked around, the dispossessed. It is a further indication of the Negro's position in America that this inevitable fact, known so well by Negroes, recorded often by social scientists but never before so forcefully by our creative writers, has caused such perturbation. *Native Son* should silence many of the self-appointed white "interpreters" of the Negro, who, writing from a vantage (?) point above and outside of the race, reveal the Negro as one peculiarly endowed to bear the burdens and suffer the shame without rancor, without bitterness, and without essential humanity.

Negro Novel and White Reviewers

Burton Rascoe

Concerning no novel in recent times, with the possible exception of *The Grapes of Wrath,* have the reviewers in general displayed a more utterly juvenile confusion of values than they have shown in their ecstatic appraisal of Richard Wright's *Native Son.* The only way I can account for the cataclysmic impact this novel made upon their brains is by deducing that they have kept themselves virginally aloof from the sort of reading which daily gives millions of us the stimulation and catharsis of pity and terror in the tabloids and in the magazine fiction professionally described as the "pulps." To this may be added the further deduction that, so hysterical have the strains of the times made many of us, these good people, the reviewers, go easily haywire about anything which looks to them like a social document exposing "conditions."

Sanely considered, it is impossible for me to conceive of a novel's being worse, in the most important respects, than *Native Son.* It has many technical excellences. They are such as any Street & Smith editor would applaud, or as Walter B. Pitkin, in his writing classes at Columbia, would grade as A-1. But the editors for Street & Smith, and Mr. Pitkin, would probably say very sensibly that there are faults in this novel which even a tyro in fiction should not be guilty of. Let me enumerate some of them:

(1) If there is a moral message to be emphasized, that message should be made implicit in the consistent action and dialogue of the novel. It should not be in the form of a running commentary by the author, particularly not when the author is very confused about what he wants to prove.

(2) If a character is conceived as being inarticulate and dumb about the economic and social forces which have (in your mind) been responsible for his social and moral delinquency, it is an artistic error to portray that character, at times, as being fully conscious of the "conditions" which have mentally and emotionally crippled him. It is an elementary principle not only of art but of moral law, of legal principle, and of common sense, that, if you are aware of yourself and of the factors under which you live, you are, *yourself,* responsible

Reprinted from *The American Mercury,* 50 (August 1940): 495–98, with the permission of Legion for Survival of Freedom, Inc., Elisabeth Carto, Treasurer.

for what you do and you must accept that responsibility. Mr. Wright has Bigger Thomas, the hero of his story, commit two murders on the appalling theory that he is justified in so doing because, as ecstatic reviewers assure us, "he knows religion as something meant to lull people into submission" and because Bigger feels "powerless and afraid of the white world, which exploits, condescends to, and in turn fears the race it has segregated." (The quotes are, respectively, from Milton Rugoff in the New York *Herald Tribune* and Margaret Marshall in the *Nation*.)

(3) It is a violation of a fundamental esthetic principle—sanctioned from Aristotle on down—to portray a character in speech, thought or action in a way not consistent with what you, the writer, might conceivably do in similar circumstances and in similar conditions.

Recently I witnessed a *reductio ad absurdum* of Mr. Wright's fundamental thesis in *Native Son*. Mr. Wright was a luncheon guest, in New York, of a club whose membership comprises men who have achieved a degree of importance in the creative arts—writers, musicians, painters, illustrators, engineers, editors, etc. Mr. Wright was introduced eulogistically by Mr. William Chenery, editor of *Collier's*, who dwelt upon the young novelist's accomplishment as a writer who had achieved bestsellerdom. There was no reference, condescending or otherwise, to the guest's color.

Mr. Wright had been told that, as the club's guest, he need not make any speech unless he felt like doing so. He is a handsome young man; his face is fine, kind and intelligent. It was a spontaneous tribute to him and to the success he had attained that the club gave him an ovation such as it has rarely given to anyone but artists like Pablo Casals and Jascha Heifetz. Mr. Wright was, on this occasion (though he may not have realized it), an embodied refutation of his theme in *Native Son*. He was the only black man there, surrounded by white people. Yet they were all rejoicing in his success, eager to do him honor—even if there were many, of course, who had not read his book.

They were not, even unconsciously, trying to make things so difficult for Mr. Wright that he would have artistic or any other justification if he should choose to murder the first two debutantes he met after leaving the luncheon. Mr. Wright must have had some intimations of this anomaly—this contrast between himself and his fictional hero—when he arose to speak. In response to the spontaneous acclaim, he got up to say a few words. He was doubtless confused and embarrassed. Good writers, and Mr. Wright in his best vein is decidedly good, are rarely good speakers. He faltered, as most of us do who have not been trained to speak in public, and in his confusion he said, with the nicest air of camaraderie—as if to say "Come up and see me some time": "I hope you will all have a chance to meet Bigger Thomas."

I don't know what others who had read *Native Son* felt about the author's hope, but I for one shuddered. Bigger Thomas, in the novel, is a murderer because (so his creator tells us) he resents the white race. Bigger murders a rich white girl who is sentimentally interested in "the Negro problem" and whose family has contributed millions to alleviate conditions among the poor in the Negro quarters of Chicago. Bigger also murders his Negro mistress. He indulges in this slaughter not because of anything these poor, misguided women, white and black, have done to him, since they haven't harmed him at all, but because (Mr. Wright argues) all of us who happen to have white skins instead of black have made Bigger what he is.

II

In the midst of the hurrahing I rise to assert that I think the moral in *Native Son* is utterly loathsome and utterly insupportable as a "message." When I carefully examine all the evidence Mr. Wright offers to prove that Bigger Thomas should have become a murderer and that the guilt lies on our own heads, I remain emphatically unconvinced. I can't see that Bigger Thomas had anything more to contend with, in childhood and youth, than I had or than dozens of my friends had. Their lives and mine have not been velvety but we do not want to kill people because of this. And I have known fine priests, fine rabbis, fine Protestant ministers (black and white) whose "conditional environment" was even worse than this "conditional environment" which Mr. Wright would have us believe makes murderers out of Negro men.

Mr. Wright is as much an American as you are or I am. We Americans are constitutionally for the underdog, so long as it does not seriously interfere with the business at hand of getting along. It is quite the thing now, among our intellectuals, to contend that whites have given the Negroes a dirty deal, forgetting that whites have given themselves a dirty deal also. These intellectuals deplore Hitler, Stalin and Mussolini on psychopathic grounds, but they are unable to see that by their own logic Bigger Thomas is just a small-scale Negro Hitler. Or a Negro Stalin or Mussolini. The partiality of these dictators for bloodletting also can be traced to conditional environment. If I am supposed to start grieving over what I have done to Hitler and Stalin in their hard early life, I won't take any.

And the same applies to Bigger. This is also to serve notice that despite all the eloquence Bigger's lawyer and Wright's reviewers bring to Bigger's defense, if I were on the jury I would vote to hang Bigger. Bigger, I have been amply convinced, wouldn't hesitate two minutes to shoot me or his lawyer or his author, even if we were going about business and paying him no mind. I don't like the idea of being shot, even fictionally, just because my color is not like Bigger's. I wouldn't like it even if I knew that all the Bigger Thomases think I am somehow responsible because life hasn't been cushy for them. I'm just unreasonable in these matters of murder, where I'm the murderee.

Mr. Wright, one may note, is doing very well. A lot of white writers with talent doubtless are wishing they were making as much money as he is making. But they are not envious of him, nor do they begrudge his success in the least. They hope he prospers. For myself, I hope that now he has got *Native Son* out of his system, he will use his talents to more sensible ends. He is one of the two writers, white or black, who have ever had the ear to catch and transliterate Negro speech correctly. The other writer is Louis Paul, who is white.

REPRINTED CRITICISM

◆

The Promise of Democracy and the Fiction of Richard Wright

EDWIN BERRY BURGUM

Richard Wright is one of the latest and most intransigent representatives of a literary movement among our submerged nationalities that has been developing since the turn of the century as the literary analogy to the extension of our democratic ideals within the sphere of practical life.

The disappearance of the frontier around 1890 is usually accepted as the opening of a new period in our history when we became aware of the presence of minority races and underprivileged workers. From this time until the First World War a movement of "muckraking" and reformism gathered impetus in the area of politics and business. It was very largely negative in nature, an attack upon graft and corruption, and only incidentally sympathetic to the common man who was their victim. The movement in fiction reflected these characteristics in the work of Frank Norris and Upton Sinclair; except that the nature of fiction demanded and secured a greater emphasis on the human suffering. But it is noteworthy that the literary movement as it gathered momentum in the new century shifted to a positive emphasis. In the work of novelists like Willa Cather, Theodore Dreiser, and Sherwood Anderson, and poets like Vachel Lindsay and Carl Sandburg, we no longer see Anglo-Saxon writers bemoaning the misfortunes of the poor and the foreigners, but writers still Anglo-Saxon by birth or thoroughly assimilated to Anglo-Saxon attitudes of temperament beginning to find in the foreign stock qualities superior to their own. Whether these foreigners are workers or farmers, such writers admire their self-reliance, their endurance, their zest for living, in implicit contrast to the lack of these qualities in the dominant Puritan bourgeois stock. Even after the First World War, writers like Ernest Hemingway and Dos Passos carried over this interest in the social and cultural values of common people of other stocks than their own, but infused a new note of conscious envy or sense of inferiority on their own part. The man of foreign birth who had first been commiserated for his unfortunate economic position was

Reprinted from *The Novel and the World's Dilemma* by Edwin Berry Burgum (New York: Oxford University Press, 1947): pp. 223–40. The essay originally appeared in *Science and Society,* 7 (Fall 1943): 338–52.

now admired for his preservation of the more vital values of personality which the more prosperous native stock had sacrificed. I am here not concerned with the validity of these judgments, but only with their significance as denoting the rise in prestige of the foreign born in the eyes of certain native writers. It would be idle to claim that these writers represented the major tendency in our literature. But they were there to encourage the minorities themselves.

The 'thirties marked the coming of age of these submerged nationalities in the historical development of an independent American culture. When Van Wyck Brooks as a literary critic wrote *America's Coming of Age* in 1917, he was thinking only of Anglo-Saxon America. But no sooner, it would seem, had our Anglo-Saxon writers succeeded in throwing off their deference to English precedents (gaining the strength to do so through their new kinship to non-Anglo-Saxon America), than these other racial elements in American society demanded their share in the new culture. They began to point out their contribution to the national pattern. At first, through autobiography or sociological writing, in the work of Jacob Riis, Mary Antin, and Randolph Bourne, but later on, by the mid-twenties, in literature also, Americans of foreign birth began to make themselves felt, not as converts to the dominant Anglo-Saxon attitudes, but as modifiers of them. These new writers were now insisting upon their contribution to the newly forming pattern of national culture.

Within its limits, which they gladly accepted, they began to express in literary form the idioms they were introducing into the national language and to present with affectionate detail those idiosyncrasies of personality by which some of our Anglo-Saxon writers were already intrigued. Building upon this real but partial acceptance into the literary community, validated as it now was by the holding of political office and the possession of some economic power, these minority peoples could now, for the first time, express their awareness of the meaning of democracy and of the dignity of their share in it. But at the same time they could not fail to be acutely conscious of the partial character of their attainment. What had been achieved only made them the more cognizant of the long road ahead to anything like a real equality of opportunity and prestige. Their confidence in their potentialities as part of the amalgamation of a truly inclusive culture was contaminated by the knowledge that they had been forced to fight every inch of the way and a suspicion that the tolerance of the dominant Anglo-Saxon would lessen the more he found he had to tolerate.

The particular social relationship of the particular people to the Anglo-Saxon control determined the precise blend of suspicion and confidence in the literary expression.

The Negro, who has been treated worst of all despite a Civil War that ended in his specific emancipation, could not fall prey to any delusion of democracy, however personally prosperous. He could not share the optimism of other minorities in our society that their partial acceptance was either a temporary blot upon the escutcheon of our ideals or only part of the neglect of the working class in general. If self-assertion seemed to be winning acceptance for other minority groups, he could only conclude that his traditional policy of trust and co-operation was wrong. He developed a hatred of his old submissive self and a greater hatred for the whites who pretended to love and admire him in proportion as he remained without dignity. The Negro, once given a taste of dignity, drew the lesson that he had only himself to depend upon, and developed an inner core of tenacious resentment as he became aware that he was victim of the most glaring hypocrisy of all.

The new Negro, taught at length by our liberal tradition to trust himself and to expect equality, is alert for any manifestation of its spuriousness and is ready to die in shame or violence rather than submit any longer to the indignities of the past. His intransigence, it must be confessed, can hardly be palatable even to philanthropic whites. We must guard against a retreat into fear when we make the startling discovery that the roles have been reversed. It is no longer we whites who are in the position of granting equality if we please, but the Negroes who are wresting it from us whether we please or not. Such is the first shock that we get from Wright's novels. We are shaken once and for all from our complacency. If we are foolish and reactionary, we shall react by terror. If we are wise, we shall recognize that we have brought this impasse upon ourselves. But, above all, we shall become convinced that the impasse exists, and cannot be conjured away. This is the way the modern Negro feels. He is on the point of rebellion when he is mistreated. He is watchful for hypocrisy, scornful of the insufficiency of the good intention, determined not to sell his birthright for the small change of petty concessions. The Negro today feels that the gulf is absolute between the white skin and the black, save for two exceptions. They will trust those whites who stand shoulder to shoulder with them in a common fight to escape poverty and ignorance. They will trust those whites who risk a similar poverty and suffering to aid them in their own escape.

And so the new Negro literature, at its best when it is least influenced by white modes of feeling, is more bitter than that of any other minority group. This bitterness, turned inward and warped into melancholy during the period of the blues, becomes more and more direct in expression until it reaches an explosive violence, scarcely to be restrained, in Wright's fiction. Though neglected by white readers until the 'thirties, the new movement was actually earlier under way than the expression of other groups. Beginning about the year 1900 (as the *Negro Caravan* suggests), with the stories of Charles W. Chesnutt (whose work was at first taken for that of a white writer), it became a vigorous school early in the 'twenties, when the magazine *Opportunity* was founded and Claude McKay and Langston Hughes were beginning to attract attention. This later work, especially the poetry, carried into esthetic expression the idioms and cadences of Negro speech, and reflected Negro sentiments in such genuine detail that its Negro origin could never have been mistaken. But though often written in a tone of aggressive resentment, its themes are usually a grim exposure of suffering to which the Negro helplessly submits rather than a narration of his revolt.

Richard Wright, therefore, had the advantage of an already developing tradition of Negro literature of protest. His greatness is to be found in the honesty and the power with which he transfers into fiction these convictions of the new Negro where they presented themselves in their most direct and least sophisticated form, unmodified by bourgeois standards, either Negro or white. In most of Wright's short stories, for instance, the Negro is an uneducated poor farmer or share-cropper of the deep South, living in rigid ostracism apart from the white world. A few stories in which the Negroes have found a common basis of feeling and action with poor whites who know something about Communism are an exception. In most of them, the possibility of equality with whites, or even of any sort of co-operation with them, is beyond the limit of experience. But these men have nevertheless caught the contagious spirit of democracy as it has been sweeping through the masses of the nation generally. All of his Negroes are psychologically convinced that they are men with rights. When his young Negro is caught by a white swimming in a forbidden pond, he talks back, defying the segregation. When the white starts to shoot him, he grabs the pistol and kills. Even though he has to flee north, he carries with him a determined spirit without regret. The Negro who has spent years trying to enlarge his small farm and become prosperous like a white farmer, when he finds his ambition frustrated, discovers his mistake in accepting bourgeois ideals and destroys everything. When such men are put upon, their spontaneous reaction is no longer to cringe, but to fight back; and when the fight proves futile, they prefer to die rather than submit. They are simple persons in the terms of formal education, but circumstances have forced upon them an intensity of emotional conflict which is more like the stuff of classical tragedy than any other quarter of American life can present.

Native Son translates into a metropolitan environment such a temperament where the conflicts become more complex and cause the breakdown of the personality. It is an environment, also, paradoxically, where constructive contact with whites becomes a possibility. The novel treats of the difficulties of such a contact for both parties. For we must remember that, if the short stories were written to reveal the new Negro to whites, *Native Son* endeavors to disclose both to each other.

The first reaction of the white reader is probably an awareness of his own inadequacy in such a situation. It dawns upon him that he is probably only a variant of the Daltons in his good intentions towards the Negroes. If he has taken pride in his practice of equality, in his magnanimous freedom from prejudices, he begins to see how, from the Negro's point of view, he must have appeared as sentimentally patronizing as the informality of Jan and Mary. He begins to recognize that barriers of suspicion and prejudice do not drop on both sides when he wills it. There are two persons concerned in a relationship of equality; for equality, where individuals are involved, is a form of friendship, and friendship is a reciprocal activity.

Normally, the establishment of friendships is facilitated by the existence of a larger framework of common class or group beliefs and interests. When, in place of this preliminary awareness of common attitudes, the opposite exists, an awareness of hostile ones, the winning of friendship becomes a gradual process. Each side must assure the other that he is an exception to the group to which he would normally belong. It therefore becomes an instance of obtuseness and arrogance, of indifference to the individuality of the other person, when we assume in him an automatic response of delighted receptivity to our advances. Despite Mary's sophistication and Jan's radical beliefs, they have not realized that to Bigger Thomas they are no more individuals than Bigger is to them. When they make advances to him, it is not to him as individual, but to him as Negro, indeed, to him as a Negro of the old school, grateful for whatever charity a white may offer. If they do not see that they are treating him as a type, they cannot be expected to see how inevitably he at the same time is treating them as a different type. Bigger knows nothing of their radical theories. All he knows is that Mary is the sort of girl who is likely to get him into trouble with both whites and blacks, and ultimately with Jan himself, since she is his lover. When they insist upon his eating with them in a Negro café habituated by his friends, they seem to think he ought to appreciate this evidence of their democracy. They do not realize either that to his friends in the café his presence will seem a disloyalty to his race, evidence of his having sold out to the whites, or that his own wishes in the matter have been completely ignored. Their equality therefore becomes an act of racial superiority through the very compulsions they mistakenly think are causing its breakdown. The meaning of social equality has never been as adequately defined in a novel.

Our delusion, however, regarding the nature of equality is but one example of the larger problem of the actual limitation of our horizons. Direct experience is the intensest authentication of abstract statement. There is no financial depression in the effective sense of the phrase, as a determinant of man's immediate relationships with others, if his income and normal associations afford him a way of life bereft of emotional participation in deprivation, lacking any approximation of equality with the deprived, in pain or renunciation or spiritual suffocation. The prosperous, therefore, in all sincerity conclude that the underprivileged who complain are exaggerating, since their own circumstances do not set up a similar compulsion to rebel. Whatever lies beyond the horizon of close personal contacts becomes an abstraction. The poor man who is habitually seen from the window of a limousine is an allegorical man who is defined not in terms that he would himself understand, but those selected by the specific relationship between the two classes, which is to the profit of the person making the judgment. Similarly, the millionaire in his limousine is an abstraction to the man who never meets one in the subway. No amount of education or personal cleverness can overcome these limitations which testify to the authority of direct relationships within the group. Whatever is without the group is distorted, unknown and therefore frightening, or not worth knowing and complacently ignored. Only thus can history explain the psychology of fascists, who are certainly neither stupid nor illiterate.

When one's abstract views are contrary to the movement of history, this distortion is of what is essential in the unexperienced. But where it is precisely the essential or typical which is rightly known, the ignorance of the nonessential tends rather to guarantee the escape from a waste of effort upon the irrelevant. The essential, under such circumstances, is not distorted, but embodied instead in the large simple pattern of allegory. If, in other words, what falls without our immediate experience is always allegory, this allegory may be either a distortion of reality or only a simplified, larger-than-life presentation of it. In the latter case, one will not be in error in the long run, but he will make regrettable mistakes in specific actions. But it remains true, all the same, that even when a theory of society which history is proving to be valid is accepted by the group, whatever passes beyond the horizon of the group will be known only in an abstract way, symbolically, and will remain unknown or distorted in detail. The union worker, we may assume, knows the capitalist more accurately as a type than the employer his worker, because his first hand experience and superior understanding of social conditions affords him a valid insight into his general character. Each, nevertheless, will inflate the specific image of the other to an extent that will make it seem improbable to the other person. The sociological value of fiction is that it provides a partial solution of this dilemma. If it is constructed on the proper abstract basis, it pushes our horizon beyond the limits of our effective experiences, and provides a more authentic understanding of the individual. It is the particular value of *Native Son* that this service, which in most novels is only a by-product of the nature of fiction, becomes the conscious purpose that determines its method.

The conflicts that form the plot of *Native Son* take their particular form from the characters' ignorance of these limitations, just as Wright's firm hand in their delineation is a consequence of his awareness of them. Bigger Thomas, the Negro boy, weighed down by his illiteracy, is no more ignorant of the individuality of the rich philanthropists, the Daltons, than they are of his. They recognize him as a type, the underprivileged adolescent who has been in trouble with the police, and are prepared to treat him according to a formula which seems enlightened to them, rehabilitation through a job as their chauffeur in an atmosphere of kindly intentions. They fail to recognize that their theory is the approach of private charity which the Negro people are no longer willing to accept; and that, despite Bigger's apparent humility, circumstances have fashioned him into its incorrigible opponent. They know Bigger more specifically than he them, but their specific knowledge is worse than useless since it is used to justify an untenable premise. Bigger, on the other hand, who cannot be said to know the Daltons with any specificity, is right in his general view of them. For him they are allegorical figures from another world, millionaires who live sumptuously on rents torn from the poor Negroes of a segregated district. In this fundamental matter his underprivileged station has afforded him a superior insight. He senses their inconsistency and unfairness in attempting to conceal from themselves and the Negro population by the small benefactions of charity the monstrous oppression from which they draw an income, huge by comparison. Despite his illiteracy, then, Bigger's awareness of his relationship to the Daltons is more sound than theirs of him.

But Wright takes the errors of the Daltons for granted. He is concerned, rather, with the fact that Bigger, though his insights are basically more sound than the Daltons', cannot use them constructively. Sensing shame and futility in his mother's consolation from a religion that demands submission to misery and the renunciation of any hope for a better life, what might have been a healthy inner need to act is perverted by the sort of action his environment provides. At the outset, Wright keys his novel to this interpretation. Bigger kills the rat that has been frightening the women folks, and then frightens them the more by flaunting its dead body in their faces. His courage is that overcompensation for fear called bravado. It passes beyond the needs of the situation and defeats its own end here as in later crises in the novel. Its source is his acceptance of the ideals of the white race as they have penetrated his ghetto. Flying an airplane symbolizes the freedom and mastery of the white race he would like to share. Knowing that he cannot, his helplessness creates an inner state of fear which (as it has transformed his healthy impulse of courage into bravado) sets up the direct motivation of hatred, and transforms what might have been a healthy social activity into petty thievery. But, to this uneducated boy, hatred for the whites is too remote and turns inward. It vents itself upon his family with their misguided notion that decency is rewarded, upon his black neighbors from whom his gang steals, upon the gang for the pettiness of its objectives, and upon himself for his inability to attain more grandiose ends. When he accepts the job with the Daltons, it is to escape these pressures which he hates. But they have all the same been furnishing him with the uneasy stability of belonging to some grouping. In his new environment he is alone in a white world, which becomes the more formidable since he cannot treat it with the unalloyed hatred it seems to him to deserve. The apparent kindliness of the Daltons obscures the simplicity of their allegorical meaning and intensifies his inner conflicts by introducing an element of intellectual doubt to add to his fear.

Behind Wright's narrative is the unspoken assumption that Negroes must have some organization for common protest that shall enable them to bring the abstract objective into productive relationship to the specific situation, that will afford understanding and guidance in the specific situations as they arise. In its absence, as riots in the Negro sections of our large cities have shown, an inevitable demand will spend itself in anarchistic violence to the defeat of its profound and laudable intention. For Negroes, *Native Son* is a warning that there is no alternative to right organization except the futility of individual violence into which Bigger is led.

Alone with these whites, whom Bigger fears but is no longer so sure he should hate, his fear and hatred rise into a crescendo as the situation feeds his incompetence with more serious temptations. When it becomes part of his duty to put the drunken daughter of the Daltons to bed, the strain between abstract knowledge and ignorance of the immediate situation reaches the breaking point. His fear that he may be thought by her parents to be planning her rape would have been unjustified had he known the Daltons as individuals. But it is valid both as a generalization of the white world and as a temptation her previous freedom with her lover seemed to be proffering him. In his state of excitement his handling of this difficult situation defeats his intention. He smothers to death the girl he does not wish to be charged with raping. His motives here and elsewhere are quite different from those of Dostoevsky's Roskolnikov, to whom he has been wrongly compared.

His trial of constructive action has been a failure. What follows up to his arrest is the tale of one savage, misguided act after another. But Bigger has become blind to their savagery. His uncertain groping for some valid avenue of self-fulfilment before the murder now gives way to the authority of his excitement. He enters a world of paranoiac fantasy, in which his acts of frenzy seem to him not so much the clever concealment of his initial mistake as the unfolding of a grandiose plan of conquest. He has lost his sense of belonging with anybody, black or white, and his need to belong with anybody. His act of murder seems to him to have released immense potentialities that had lain imprisoned within his personality. While he is actually running away from pursuit in desperation, he conceives himself to be a Tamberlaine capable of reducing the whole world to the prostrate state it had imposed upon him and he has now escaped. He seems now to be flying the forbidden airplane above a remote and impotent world.

But this picture of his immediate reaction to his crime cannot be isolated from his subsequent attitudes. After his arrest he reverts to an apathy of complete worthlessness. His arrest and the white crowds howling for his lynching puncture his fantasy and restore him to the only contact with reality he has ever known. As long as he lacks a fraternal mechanism for its transformation, it is the only contact with reality the underprivileged Negro of our day can ever know: the certainty that there is nobody in our society who is worse treated. Now Bigger no longer possesses the illusion of power in individual hatred. He has reverted to the animal docility of slavehood. His self-respect reawakens when he finds a single man who understands him, and by understanding him enables him at last to bridge the gulf between the abstract and the particular. In the long final section of the novel his Jewish Communist lawyer repeats for him the therapeutic service David performed for the distraught Saul of Browning's poem.

Bigger, it is true, understands very little of the content of these discussions. But the lawyer's patience and kindliness of intention in conducting them are enough to convince him of their central meaning. It is enough that they are taking place in such a milieu. Through this elementary fact Bigger comes to feel that there is one man in the world who understands him better than he understands himself, and can bring to the surface of his consciousness that longing to be of some value to himself and to society which the distortions of his hatred had concealed. So starved and twisted has been his former emotional life, that this simple experience of a single friendship takes on the proportions of a sufficient achievement for a lifetime. He cannot conceive of a further goal to live for. The lawyer embodies that principle of equality which Bigger has been unable to articulate, though he reacted against Mary Dalton's mistaken bohemian notion of it that Jan had shared. Max's willingness to endure criticism for defending him and a social ostracism similar to his own has put them on a common basis of understanding. And from this common basis Bigger is able to see for the first time that he is not alone in his struggle and his torment.

Bigger Thomas is of course not a typical Negro. Some of his actions, like the slaying of the rat, are symbolic presentations of his personal traits. But though Bigger himself is an individual and not a symbolic figure, the reader accepts him as representative of other men unlike him in various respects. As often happens in contemporary fiction, the extreme disorders of personality which he exhibits are only an exaggeration of the latent characteristics of apparently more normal persons. In a world where there is scarcely a man so illiterate as not to be aware of our publicized ideals of democracy and apply them directly to his own circumstances, Bigger's hatred is shared in varying degrees by every Negro and every worker, and indeed by every individual who feels deprived of a chance to fulfill his potentialities. The only differences are in the depth to which the hatred is buried, the adequateness with which it is controlled, or in the extent to which it is diluted by compensations. Other characters besides Bigger turn out to be examples of this common hatred with the variety of qualifications I have just mentioned.

For a time, it is true, we do not get this impression. We follow Bigger's activities so closely that we share his collapse after his arrest. But in place of the apathy into which he falls, we recoil with loathing from a sudden recognition that we have been identifying ourselves too closely with his fantasies. His murders now stand forth in all their gruesome tabloid clarity. At this point, Wright introduces the insincere rhetoric of the district attorney and the white mob's demand for lynching. They reawaken our sympathy for Bigger, and bring home to us the relation between his depravity and the dominant social pressures which constantly verbalize the principles of justice and democracy but deny any adequate application of them. As though to prove that such hypocrisy does not merely produce Biggers in the black race but corrupts our whole social fabric, we become aware that this white mob is only concealing its affinity with what is vicious in Bigger by seeking from his lynching a similar paranoid satisfaction of its own frustration. Our loathing of the mob cancels out our reaction against Bigger, and our disgust turns toward the deplorable social system which is responsible for both of them. Bigger's hatred of the whites is itself a variant of the common insecurity of the common man in our culture.

Fortunately, there are forces at work to avert catastrophe in our national life. The demand for Negro labor in time of war, the growing acceptance of Negroes by the trade unions, the appearance of Negroes in the top ranks of virtually every cultural and intellectual profession, the committees on fair employment practices are but a few of the justifications for optimism. Wright might have chosen as his theme the conflict between these two groups of forces, and resolved it in an atmosphere of confidence that history cannot reverse itself and progress is inevitable. But if treated generally, with the stress on the social forces, a distortion of the good intention into sentimentality would be likely. If, on the other hand, the stress were on individual relationships, a powerful and beautiful novel might be written. But it would fail to give the right impression of the general state of affairs. Or it would become a novel not of the Negro people but of proletarian life, whites and blacks working together towards a common end, to the neglect, emotionally, of the racial element altogether.

Wright, on the contrary, has preferred to accept the general situation as it is today. He makes his reader intellectually aware of the economic and political forces at work. But he focuses our attention upon their effect on the individual personality. Desirous above all of banishing our complacency, he is not interested in the rosy promise of the future. He knows that this promise will not be valid unless whites are stimulated to action by a sense of guilt and blacks are guided by some better plan than anarchistic individualism. And so he translates the underlying social forces into their specific exhibition in the relationships of individuals. But he does not neglect the case for hope. Just as he depicts the crisis as the immediate consequence of wrong personal relationships, he seeks to show that the promise of the future depends immediately and specifically upon the capacity for making the right ones. Doubtless this capacity itself is contingent upon a plausible philosophical view of the general situation. But the important point Wright is making is that this general view needs to be written into the very structure of the personality as a capacity for friendship. The relation between Bigger and his lawyer, Max, to which the end of the book is devoted, is intended to serve as prototype of the proper constructive relationship between men generally.

Wright's accomplishment, unfortunately, is not as good as his intention. Though he conveys some impression of what he means, he is confused and repetitious in presenting the case for hope. This is in part the result of a change in method. Up to this point in the narrative, he has been following the general plan of Dreiser's *American Tragedy*. Using an objective method to reveal the subjective state of their hero's personality, on the theory of the influence of environment, both authors have tended to pile up an unnecessary quantity of substantiating detail. But Dreiser's trial scene is monotonous rather than confused. He continues to use the same technique. Wright, on the contrary, departs at this point from Dreiser's method and no longer follows the external probabilities of the situation. The character of Max's plea to the court can hardly be justified. His public speeches would never convince a jury, since they are only projections of his private conversations with Bigger in his cell. Even though during the entire novel we have been interested in Bigger's inner life, we have seen it largely through the frank interpretations of the author, without distortion of the probabilities of everyday life either in the action or the dialogue. Both are now distorted. What the lawyer says becomes ambiguous, and where he says it unlikely. The objective method is superseded by a symbolic one. Wright is no longer the detached commentator but allows his personality to merge with that of the lawyer. This change of technique was doubtless dictated by Wright's desire to involve his audience in a direct emotional appeal. He is addressing them symbolically when Max addresses the court symbolically, as though he were still clarifying Bigger's mind. His intention, if successful, would have brought the book to a crescendo of hope for the future, as Max and Bigger, the author, the court, and the readers merge in a common understanding of friendship and equality. But since Wright is unable to put his message in the clear detail of the earlier sections of the book, the effect is not that of the concluding speech in *Waiting for Lefty*, but of a sudden plunge into Dostoievsky. Wright begins to share the confusions and even something of the hysteria, the negative aspects of which he has been elucidating.

The tone of the book changes. What had given *Native Son* its refreshing atmosphere of sanity was the awareness its objective method assured, that the author had been untouched by the maladies he described. The characters, the situations, our whole social fabric, we had realized with consternation, are parallel to the decadence of Russia before the Revolution, which Dostoevsky exposed so thoroughly, and so obviously shared. Wright, like Dreiser, had stood aloof from the terrible deeds of his characters. But when he turns to the case for hope, the ambiguity of its statement is no more convincing than the frank mysticism of Dostoevsky. That social orientation towards the common man, which alone permits a genuine approach to groups beyond our immediate experience, has been clarified. But the clarification is a deduction the reader skims from the restless surface of its vague restatement. One feels that Wright has not understood Max much better than Bigger has done; and Bigger has surely not got the essence of what he was trying to say at all. From Max's fervid proffer of friendship he has drawn no further aid than the recovery of his self-esteem, and no further meaning than the dogged return to his original delusion (though it is now held in a spirit of tranquillity, as though his life had achieved a constructive aim) that his act of murder was an escape from oppression. It was easier, apparently, for Dostoevsky to accept the mystic belief of Christianity, that part of man is innately good and at war with his innately evil impulses, than for Wright to hunt with the aid of psychology for the ray of hope veiled in the depths of social decay. The anxious verbosity of Max's pleas evokes the suspicion that Wright, against his intention, shares that counterpart of the social neurosis he describes, which is the unconscious fear that hope itself is a fantasy.

Perhaps in a world where grounds for hatred are so valid, even so talented an author may be forgiven if he cannot present with equal skill the case for love and understanding. We may expect that among all our national minorities the Negro will be the last to do so, and that he will do so first in those areas of the working class where genuine friendships can be taken for granted. But as the Negro sees the white world yielding before the pressure of his merit as well as his demands, his psychology will change. He will then know that he has won a place of dignity in the American society, and the newest Negro literature is likely to be the story of his positive achievement.

Wright's Invisible Native Son

Donald B. Gibson

The difficulty most critics have who write about Richard Wright's *Native Son* is that they do not see Bigger Thomas.[1] They see him with their outer eyes, but not with the inner eyes, "those eyes with which they look through their physical eyes upon reality."[2] Of course there is a certain sense in which everyone is invisible, a certain sense in which the observer creates the observed, attributing to him qualities whose nature depends upon the viewer's own character. When we see a man in muddy work clothes, we are likely to see him only as a laborer and to have aroused in us whatever ideas we have toward laborers. We rarely look at a man so dressed (assuming that he is unknown to us) and see a father, a churchgoer, taxpayer or fisherman, though the man underneath the clothing may theoretically be all these things. If we think about him, we automatically assume certain things about his life style—about his values, his economic and social position, and even his occupation. To the extent that the clothes determine what we see, the person beneath them is invisible to us.

The difficulty comes about when we assume that the outer covering is the essential person. Most critics of Wright's novel see only the outer covering of Bigger Thomas, the blackness of his skin and his resulting social role. Few have seen him as a discrete entity, a particular person who struggles with the burden of his humanity. Wright has gone to great lengths in the novel to create Bigger as a person, to invest the social character with particularizing traits, to delineate the features of a face. The final meaning of the book, as a matter of fact, depends upon the awareness on the part of the reader of Bigger's individuality. The lack of such awareness has led most critics to misread the novel, for almost all of them interpret it as though the social person, Bigger Thomas, were the *real* and *essential* person. The following bit of dialogue, however, suggests a different perspective.

> MAX: "Well, this thing's bigger than you, son. . . ."
> BIGGER: "They going to kill me anyhow."[3]

Reprinted from *American Quarterly*, 21 (Winter 1969): 728–38, with the permission of The John Hopkins University Press.

This exchange between Max and Bigger reveals that each is looking at the problem at hand in an essentially different way. Max is thinking of the social implications of the situation; Bigger's attention is focused on his own impending doom. Which view is the truer, the more significant in the context of the novel? Wright's critics have generally opted for the view of Max, but if Max's view is true, then most of the whole final section does not make sense. For a careful reading of that third section, "Fate," indicates that the focus of the novel is not on the trial nor on Max, but on Bigger and on his finally successful attempt to come to terms with his imminent death. It need be noted that the trial does not take up the entire third section of the novel as has been often said. In the edition cited above, the third section comprises 126 pages; the trial itself consumes 37 pages and Max's address to the jury, 17 pages. The length of Max's speech and its bearing on what has preceded in the novel to that point have led experienced readers to neglect what else happens in that final section. It has led to many conclusions about the novel which are not borne out by the 89 pages of the last section describing what happens before and after the trial. The degree to which the reader focuses upon Max and Max's speech determines the degree to which Bigger is invisible to him.

In order to assess properly the meaning of the final section, it is necessary to understand what happens in the concluding pages of the novel. First of all it is too simple to say as Baldwin does that "he [Bigger] *wants* to die because he glories in his hatred and prefers, like Lucifer, rather to rule in hell than serve in heaven."[4] The point is that Bigger, through introspection, finally arrives at a definition of self which is his own and different from that assigned to him by everyone else in the novel. The many instances in the last of the three sections of the novel which show him exploring his deepest thoughts, feelings and emotions reveal Baldwin's statement to be patently false. Shortly after Bigger's capture and imprisonment he lies thinking in his cell.

> And, under and above it all, there was the fear of death before which he was naked and without defense; he had to go forward and meet his end like any other living thing upon the earth. . . . There would have to hover above him, like the stars in a full sky, a vast configuration of images and symbols whose magic and power could lift him up and make him live so intensely that the dread of being black and unequal would be forgotten; that even death would not matter, that it would be a victory. This would have to happen before he could look them in the face again: a new pride and a new humility would have to be born in him, a humility springing from a new identification with some part of the world in which he lived, and this identification forming the basis for a new hope that would function in him as pride and dignity. (pp. 234–35)

This quotation not only refutes Baldwin's statement about Bigger's motivations, but it as well indicates the focus of the novel at this point is on Bigger Thomas the private person. The emphasis is upon a problem that he faces as an isolated, solitary human whose problem is compounded by race though absolutely not defined by racial considerations. There follows from the point in the novel during which the above quotation occurs a pattern of advance and retrogression as Bigger gropes his way, privately and alone, toward that "new identification," that "pride and dignity" referred to in the passage. From this point on Bigger feels by turns guilt, hate, shame, remorse, fear, anger, and through the knowledge of himself engendered through acquaintance with his basic thoughts and feelings moves toward a sense of identity. There is a good deal of emphasis placed upon the solitary nature of his problem. At least twice he advances to the point at which he recognizes that salvation for him can come only from himself, from his own effort and knowledge.

> He was balanced on a hair-line now, but there was no one to push him forward or backward, no one to make him feel that he had any value or worth—no one but himself. (p. 305)
> He believed that Max knew how he felt, and once more before he died he wanted to talk with him and feel with as much keenness as possible what his living and dying meant. That was all the hope he had now. If there were any sure and firm knowledge for him, it would have to come from himself. (p. 350)

If we see the quotation above (from pp. 234–35) as defining Bigger's essential problem, then it is evident that the passage must have relevance to the concluding pages of the novel. When Bigger has achieved the "new humility," the "pride and dignity" referred to there, if he has achieved it, it should be evidenced somewhere later in the novel. And so it is. During the final two pages of the novel it is clear that Bigger no longer suffers, is no longer in terror about his impending death. "Aw, I reckon I believe in myself. . . . I ain't got nothing else. . . . I got to die" (p. 358 Wright's ellipses). He accepts himself as never before, and in realizing his identity is able to evaluate his past actions objectively. "I didn't want to kill! . . . But what I killed for, I *am*! It must have been pretty deep in me to make me kill! I must have felt it awful hard to murder. . . ."

Because he has come to terms with himself, because he no longer hates and despises himself as he has during most of his life, it is no longer necessary for him to feel hatred. For this reason he is able to pass along through Max a reassuring word to his mother: "Just go and tell Ma I was all right and not to worry none, see? Tell her I was all right and wasn't crying none . . ." (p. 358). Had he "died in hatred," as Bone says,[5] he would hardly have called out his final words to Max, "Tell Jan hello . . ." (p. 359). These words indicate that Bigger's contradictory feelings about himself and his situation have been resolved, for they could only be spoken by virtue of Bigger's having accepted the consequences of his actions and hence himself. He has no choice—if he is to achieve the degree of reconciliation to his fate necessary for him to face death and therefore assert his humanity—but to recognize that he *is* what he has *done*.

The two perspectives of Bigger Thomas contained in the novel exist in tension until in the final pages the focus shifts away entirely from the social emphasis. No matter what the social implications of Bigger's situation, the fact is that he, the private, isolated human must face the consequences. It is no wonder that Bigger is almost totally unable to understand Max's speech during the trial. He grasps something of the tone, but the meanings of the words escape him, for Max is not really thinking about Bigger the existential person, the discrete human entity. When Bigger and Max converse privately, they understand each other reasonably well. But during the trial Max is talking about a symbol, a representative figure. Hence the significant problem becomes not whether Max will save Bigger—the answer to that question is a foregone conclusion—but whether Bigger will save himself in the only possible way, by coming to terms with himself. This we see him doing as we observe him during long, solitary hours of minute introspection and self-analysis.

Probably the critic most responsible for the perception of Bigger Thomas as a social entity and that alone is James Baldwin, who conceived some rather convincing arguments about the limitations of the protest novel and especially of *Native Son*.

> All of Bigger's life is controlled, defined by his hatred and his fear. And later, his fear drives him to murder and his hatred to rape: he dies, having come, through this violence, we are told, for the first time, to a kind of life, having for the first time redeemed his manhood.[6]

Baldwin, for all the persuasiveness of his language, has failed to see Bigger the person. For it is clear enough that Bigger's feeling of elation, of having done a creative thing simply in murdering is not the final outcome. It is rather early in the novel when he feels release, free from the forces which have all his life constrained him. But after his capture he finds he is indeed not free; he still has himself to cope with. His final feeling is not—as the concluding pages of the novel explicitly show—exaltation for having "redeemed his manhood." Very soon after the first murder, to be sure, he does feel that it has had some redeeming effect.

> The thought of what he had done, the awful horror of it, the daring associated with such actions, formed for him for the first time in his fear-ridden life a barrier of protection between him and a world he feared. He had murdered and had created a new life for himself. It was something that was all his own, and it was the first time in his life he had had anything that others could not take from him. (p. 90)

But this response occurs after all about one-fourth of the way through the novel. These are not the feelings Bigger has at the end. One need only imagine this passage as among Bigger's thoughts as we last see him in order to see how inappropriate it would be as a concluding statement. He is not in the mood of prideful self-assertion which he feels so often from the time he disposes of Mary's body until his crime is discovered. Instead, the conclusion finds him feeling a calm assurance and acceptance of self. There is neither irony nor condescension in his final "Tell Jan hello," nor does the last scene in the denotative meanings of it words and the tone project "hatred and fear" on Bigger's part.

Baldwin's eloquent statement at the end of "Everybody's Protest Novel" describing how the protest novel fails does not describe the content of Wright's novel.

> The failure of the protest novel lies in its rejection of life, the human being, the denial of his beauty, dread, power, in its insistence that it is his categorization alone which is real and which cannot be transcended.[7]

The statement itself is not to be questioned; its applicability to *Native Son* is. There is too much in Wright's novel which suggests that Bigger's response to his situation does not stem from his categorization, his Negroness, but from his humanness. What has the following response, occurring after Bigger has returned from hearing his sentence, to do with his "categorization"?

> In self-defense he shut out the night and day from his mind, for if he had thought of the sun's rising and setting, of the moon or the stars, of clouds or rain, he would have died a thousand deaths before they took him to the chair. To accustom his mind to death as much as possible, he made all the world beyond his cell a vast grey land where neither night nor day was, peopled by strange men and women whom he could not understand, but with those lives he longed to mingle once before he went. (p. 349)

These are not the thoughts and feelings of a Negro, as such, but of a man who is about to die and who struggles to cope with the fact. Race, social condition, whatever category a reader might have placed him in, have no relevance here. There are many such passages in the third section of the book showing Bigger's individual response to his situation. For example, the following:

> He had lived and acted on the assumption that he was alone, and now he saw that he had not been. What he had done made others suffer. No matter how much he would long for them to forget him, they would not be able to. His family was a part of him, not only in blood, but in spirit. (p. 254)
>
> He would not mind dying now if he could only find out what this meant, what he was in relation to all the others that lived, and the earth upon which he stood. Was there some battle everybody was fighting, and he had missed it? (p. 307)
>
> His face rested against the bars and he felt tears roll down his cheeks. His wet lips tasted salt. He sank to his knees and sobbed: "I don't want to die. . . . I don't want to die. . . ." (p. 308)

His interpretation of the opening scene of the novel is likewise a measure of the degree to which Baldwin does not see Bigger.

> Rats live there too in the Thomas apartment . . . and we first encounter Bigger
> in the act of killing one. One may consider that the entire book, from that harsh
> "Brring!" to Bigger's weak "Good-by" as the lawyer, Max, leaves him in the
> death cell is an extension, with the roles inverted, of this chilling metaphor.[8]

This interpretation would be true if Bigger were *only* the social figure which critics have seen. But the figure on the final pages of the novel, no matter what he is,
is not a rat. He does not die as a rat dies, he is neither fearful nor desperate.

An alternative reading is offered by Edwin Burgum in his essay on
Native Son in which he says of Bigger's killing of the rat and flaunting it in the
faces of his mother and sister, "His courage is that overcompensation for fear
called bravado. It passes beyond the needs of the situation and defeats its own
end here as in later crises in the novel."[9] This interpretation gets beyond the
problem of comparing Bigger with a rat. Certainly Wright's sympathies are
with Bigger to a greater degree than his being likened to a rat implies.

It must be admitted that Bigger Thomas, the social figure whom Baldwin and others have seen, has a prominent place in the novel and is by no
means a figment. He is a representative figure to Buckley, to the policemen
investigating the murder of Mary, and to the public at large. Wright makes it
amply evident that the desire on the part of these people to do away with
Bigger reflects a primitive desire to perform ritual murder and, thereby, to do
away with the potential threat posed by all other Negroes through sacrificing
the representative black figure. But readers need to avoid the error of the
characters in the novel by distinguishing between Bigger's qualities as a representative figure and his qualities as a particular person (difficult though this
may be in our time and in our society) who, exclusive of race, faces death.

> If he were nothing, if this were all, then why could not he die without hesi-
> tancy? Who and what was he to feel the agony of a wonder so intensely that it
> amounted to fear? Why was this strange impulse always throbbing in him
> when there was nothing outside of him to meet it and explain it? Who or what
> had traced this restless design in him? Why was this eternal reaching for some-
> thing that was not there? Why this black gulf between him and the world:
> warm red blood here and cold blue sky there, and never a wholeness, a oneness,
> a meeting of the two. (pp. 350–51)

Feeling such things as these and about to die in the electric chair, Bigger
ceases to be representative of the Negro and becomes every man whose death
is imminent—that is, every man.

The view of Bigger as representative (and hence invisible) comes about
in part because Wright's novel has been too frequently seen as a "Negro"
novel or a protest novel, and all the limitations of these categories have been
ascribed to it. It has been extremely difficult for even the most sophisticated
readers to see Bigger's humanity because the idea of an ignorant, uneducated,
criminal Negro coming to terms with the human condition, as Bigger finally

does, is an alien idea. The novel should be compared not only to *Crime and Punishment,* the work with which it is most frequently compared, but with *The Stranger* as well. Wright's and Camus' novels were published two years apart (1940 and 1942 respectively) and there are many striking parallels between them. The most fruitful result of such a comparison may be to lift Wright's novel out of the context of the racial problem in America and to place it in larger perspective, or at least to reveal the extent to which *Native Son* is not so limited as it has appeared to be.

The limited view has also been responsible for the interpretation of the novel as a propaganda piece for the Communist Party.[10] On the contrary the novel points up the limitations of a system of ideas which by its very nature is incapable of dealing with certain basic human problems. Bigger is saved in the end, but not through the efforts of the Party, which constantly asserts that the individual cannot achieve meaningful salvation. This further implies that the thought processes leading to Wright's break with the Party were already in motion as early as 1939, and that his formal public announcement of the break in 1944[11] was a resolution of much earlier distress.

The interpretation of the novel as a propaganda piece for the Communist Party stems from the notion that Max is Wright's spokesman. As a result, a good deal of weight is placed upon Max's address to the jury. Though there is enough evidence to suggest that Max's personal view of Bigger allows for his existence as a discrete individual, the strategy he chooses to defend Bigger requires that he deal with him largely on an abstract level with the intention of convincing his hearers that the abstraction is embodied within the particular individual before them. Thus he says:

> "This boy represents but a tiny aspect of a problem whose reality sprawls over a third of this nation." (p. 330)
> "Multiply Bigger Thomas twelve million times, allowing for environmental and temperamental variations, and for those Negroes who are completely under the influence of the church, and you have the psychology of the Negro people." (p. 333)

The effect of his words on many is simply to enhance Bigger's invisibility.

Rather than being Wright's spokesman, in truth, Max presents one side of a dialogue whose totality is expressed through the dual perspective contained in the novel.[12] Max is indeed a sympathetic character, but for all his good intentions, he has limitations. He never, for example, entirely understands what Bigger is getting at during their conversations. Only in the end, during their final meeting, does he come to have some notion of the fact that he is not superior to Bigger, that he knows no more than Bigger about the kinds of questions the condemned man is asking and consequently is not in a position to explain anything. When Bigger tells Max that he *is* what he has *done* ("What I killed for, I *am!*"), Max's response is to recoil in horror, for even he ultimately is unable to accept any definition of man outside his own preconceived idea. Max cannot accept the implications of Bigger's conclusions nor, indeed, can he fully understand the position that Bigger has finally arrived at. Wright makes this point doubly clear with the line, "Max groped for his hat like a blind man." Now given the nearly explicit meanings which sight and blindness have had in the novel prior to this, it can hardly be a fortuitous simile. Not even Max is completely capable of recognizing and accepting the truth of Bigger's humanity.

Though Max's motivations are good, founded as they are upon his basic good character and good feeling, he is unable finally to save Bigger, for Bigger's salvation comes about through his own efforts, through his eventual ability to find freedom from the constraints of his past. All the characters in Wright's major works after *Native Son* achieve the same kind of freedom, or at least the promise of such freedom, in one way or another. This is true of the central character of *Black Boy* (which is more fictional in technique and intention than commonly recognized), *The Long Dream, The Outsider* and of "The Man Who Lived Underground." *Native Son* resolves the tension between the two alternatives, the one seeing the salvation of individuals through social change, the other seeing the salvation of individuals through their own efforts. After *Native Son* Wright was never again to suggest the possibility of any individual's achieving meaningful social salvation. The inescapable conclusion is that Wright lost faith entirely in social solutions to human problems and came to believe that ultimately the individual alone can save himself. During that final meeting between Max and Bigger it is made abundantly clear that Bigger has through the course of the third section of the novel come to terms with his most pressing problem, his impending doom. In so doing he achieves the only meaningful salvation possible. (Max speaks first.)

> "But on both sides men want to live; men are fighting for life. Who will win? Well, the side . . . with the most humanity and the most men. That's why . . . y-you've got to b-believe in yourself. Bigger. . . ."
> Max's head jerked up in surprise when Bigger laughed.
> "Aw, I reckon I believe in myself. . . . I ain't got nothing else. . . . I got to die." (p. 358)

Now if the conclusions I have come to here are valid, then two highly significant corollaries follow: 1) Wright did not *simply* emerge from the naturalistic school of Dreiser, Dos Passos and Farrell; he did not simply adapt the techniques and thoughts of the naturalists to the situation of the black man.[13] 2) The existentialist thinking of this later work did not derive from the influence on him of Camus, Sartre and other French existentialists, but grew out of his own experience in America.[14]

I do not want to argue that Wright was not strongly influenced by American literary naturalism; certainly he was. But he was not as confined by the tradition as has been generally believed. If my thesis about *Native Son* is correct, then Wright is not an author whose major novel reflects the final phases of a dying tradition, but he is instead one who out of the thought, techniques and general orientation of the naturalistic writers developed beyond their scope. *Native Son,* as I have described it in this essay, looks forward rather than backward. It is a prototype of the modern existentialist novel and a link between the fiction of the 1930s and a good deal of more modern fiction.

A kind of condescension and a preconception about the potential of a self-educated black man from the very depths of the South have combined to obscure the sources of Wright's proclivity toward existentialism. The following comments made by two writers and critics who were friends of Wright make the point.

REDDING   Dick was a small-town boy—a small-town Mississippi boy—all of his days. The hog maw and the collard greens. He was fascinated by the existentialist group for a while, but he didn't really understand them.

BONTEMPS: Essentially, of course, Wright was and remained not only an American but a Southerner. Negroes have a special fondness for that old saw, "You can take the boy out of the country, but you can't take the country out of the boy."[15]

In order to understand the sources of the existentialist concern in Wright's work and thought, one need only note the quality and character of the life described by Wright in *Black Boy* and realize as well that "existentialism" may be described as a mood arising out of the exigencies of certain life situations rather than as a fully developed and articulated systematic philosophy which one chooses to hold or rejects. Though we cannot say that existentialism resulted directly from the experience of Europeans under Nazi occupation, we can certainly say that the occupation, the war itself, created circumstances conducive to the nurturing and development of the existential response. Europeans during the war, especially those engaged in underground activities, daily faced the imminent possibility of death, and the constant awareness of impending death was largely responsible for the emergence of a way of interpreting the meaning of life consonant with that awareness. *Black Boy* of course does not describe a wartime situation, but one cannot help but feel the constant pressure on the person described there, a pressure from a world which threatens unceasingly to destroy him. The earliest of Wright's memories is of an episode which results in his being beaten unconscious, and this at a very young age. Thereafter we see described in the book the progress of an inward, alienated individual, distrustful of all external authority, who learns that his survival depends upon the repudiation of the values of others and a strong reliance upon his own private and personal sense of values. The existential precept, "existence precedes essence," stems as a mood from Wright's experience as described in *Black Boy*, but as a condition of his life and not as a consciously held philosophical principle. Herein lie the sources of Bigger Thomas' response to the condition brought about by his crime, capture and condemnation.

A comment made by Wright in response to an unfriendly review of *Native Son* is relevant as a final observation.

> If there had been one person in the Dalton household who viewed Bigger Thomas as a human being, the crime would have been solved in half an hour. Did not Bigger himself know that it was the denial of his personality that enabled him to escape detection so long? The one piece of incriminating evidence which would have solved the "murder mystery" was Bigger's humanity under their very eyes.[16]

We need only make the proper substitutions to see the relevance of Wright's comment to the views of most critics of his novel. "The denial of his personality," and the failure on their part to see "Bigger's humanity under their very eyes" have caused him to be invisible, to be Wright's own invisible native son.

Notes

1. Limitations of space preclude naming all the critics I have in mind. A few of them are the following: James Baldwin, "Everybody's Protest Novel" and "Many Thousands Gone," *Notes of a Native Son* (Boston, 1955), pp. 13–23, 24–25; Robert Bone, *The Negro Novel in America* (New Haven, 1958), pp. 140–52; Hugh M. Gloster, *Negro Voices in American Fiction* (Chapel Hill, N.C., 1948), pp. 222–34; John Reilly, "Afterword," *Native Son* (New York, 1966). Critics most nearly exceptions are Edwin Berry Burgum, *The Novel and the World's Dilemma* (New York, 1963), pp. 223–40; Esther Merle Jackson, "The American Negro and the Image of the Absurd," *Phylon*, XXIII (1962), 359–71; Nathan A. Scott, "Search for Beliefs: The Fiction of Richard Wright," *University of Kansas City Review*, XXIII (1956), 19–24.

2. Ralph Ellison, *Invisible Man* (New York, 1952), p. 3.

3. *Native Son* (New York, 1940), p. 312. Subsequent quotations from the novel are from this edition.

4. *Notes of a Native Son*, p. 44.

5. *The Negro Novel*, p. 150.

6. *Notes of a Native Son*, p. 22.

7. P. 23. Edward Margolies explores the opposite view of Wright's novel in *Native Sons: A Critical Study of Twentieth Century Negro American Authors* (New York, 1968), pp. 85–86.

8. P. 34.

9. P. 232.

10. Richard Sullivan, "Afterword" to *Native Son*, Signet, 1961.

11. "I Tried to Be a Communist," *Atlantic Monthly*, CLXV (Aug. 1944), 61–70; (Sept. 1944), 56.

12. Margolies believes that the duality of perspective referred to here is unresolved. Pp. 79–80.

13.   Wright's relation to the naturalistic tradition was first articulated by Alfred Kazin, *On Native Grounds* (New York, 1942), p. 372, and later by Bone in *The Negro Novel,* pp. 142–43.

14.   Margolies concurs with this conclusion. P. 68.

15.   Saunders Redding and Arna Bontemps in "Reflections on Richard Wright: A Symposium," *Anger and Beyond,* ed. Herbert Hill (New York, 1966), p. 207. Further comments on Wright and existentialism occur on pages 203, 205, 208, 209.

16.   "I Bite the Hand that Feeds Me," *Atlantic Monthly,* CLXV (June 1940), 826.

Images of "Vision" in *Native Son*

JAMES NAGEL

Perhaps it is understandable that a "race" novel as provocative as Richard Wright's *Native Son*[1] has evoked a critical response largely in terms of sociological analysis. Indeed, as a social document the work is a penetrating and controversial statement which has shocked the conscience of American complacency. But regardless of the accuracy of Wright's picture of the racial condition in this country, his book is not only a social study but a "novel," a work of art which transcends the limitations of sociological prose. In this work, as in all good fiction, the "art" of the novel supports the theme, and no reading of the book is complete until it has given careful attention to the relationship between "method" and "meaning."

One of the most prevalent aspects of the artistry of *Native Son* is the persistence of the images of "vision" which pervade almost every significant moment. The very frequency of these images would suggest that this book is not merely about racial violence, not only a vehicle of "chase adventure," nor a courtroom drama, nor a study of urban mechanization. It is, rather, an analysis of "perception" which documents the effect prejudice, alienation, oppression, and isolation have on one's ability to "see" and "be seen" clearly. In fact, the narrative device of this book is to relate nearly all events as they are "seen" by the protagonist, Bigger Thomas. And, further, the plot is described and developed in images of blindness, impaired vision, and "seeing" for the first time.

As several critics have already pointed out,[2] the central image in its various forms is that of blindness. Literally, blindness relates only to Mrs. Dalton who is in fact without sight, and whose disability permits and provokes the murder of her daughter. She is also blind, however, in a figurative sense (as are all the rest of the characters) in that she has virtually no insight into the realities of Negro life in Chicago. Like her husband, she sees Bigger only as a type, a generalized object of her cathartic altruism that is expected to respond

James Nagel's article, "Images of 'Vision' in *Native Son*" originally appeared in The *University Review* (36:2), Winter 1969. It is reprinted here with the permission of *New Letters/The University Review* and the Curators of the University of Missouri-Kansas City and with the permission of the author.

to generosity with gratitude and humility, but not with any overt expressions of individualism. Thus she is blind on two counts, a condition symbolic of the depth of the "blindness of the white liberal philanthropic community,"[3] as Edward Margolies has pointed out.

But Mrs. Dalton is not the only character whose vision and understanding have been impaired. Britten, for example, sees only "communists" and "niggers." To Dalton he says: "Well, you see 'em one way and I see 'em another. To me, a nigger's a nigger" (p. 154). It should be also noted that his attitude has been carefully foreshadowed by the frequent references to the peculiarities of his eyes (see pp. 146–53), beginning with Bigger's first exposure to him:

> The white man at Mr. Dalton's side [Britten] was squinting at him; he felt that tight, hot, choking fear returning. The white man clicked on the light. He had a cold, impersonal manner that told Bigger to be on his guard. In the very look of the man's eyes Bigger saw his own personality reflected in narrow, restricted terms. (p. 146)

And Bigger's first view of Britten is no better. He sees Mr. Dalton and the investigator only in "red darkness" and as "white discs of danger" (p. 146). To Bigger he is an enemy and easily recognizable: "Britten was familiar to him; he had met a thousand Brittens in his life" (p. 154). Thus both of them are reduced to a "type" in the eyes of the other.[4]

In fact, until the first murder Bigger is as blind as anyone: he does not understand himself and plays no clear role in either his family, gang, or society. Those around him are equally sightless: Bessie, for example, is twice mentioned as being blind (pp. 132, 165) as is Reverend Hammond, who casts his gaze on a more promising vision of the promised land.

At one point he asks Bigger to "Fergit yuh's black" (p. 263). Indeed, in Bigger's mind, at least, nearly everyone is blind: "His feet were cold and he stamped them in the snow, surrounded by people waiting, too, for a car. He did not look at them; they were simply blind people, blind like his mother, his brother, his sister, Peggy, Britten, Jan, Mr. Dalton, and the sightless Mrs. Dalton and the quiet empty houses with their black gaping windows"[5] (pp. 163–64).

Perhaps Bigger's inability to see and understand the world about him precludes the possibility of his realizing that anyone is more insightful than he.[6] In some respects he is right: the newspapers reduce him to a dehumanized "ape" and the police underestimate him to the extent of suspecting an accomplice on the grounds that "the plan of the murder and kidnapping was too elaborate to be the work of a Negro mind" (p. 229). Apparently they have not "seen" him at all, a fact he senses in counting on their blindness for his escape.

Thus blindness is operative throughout the novel as a metaphor of a lack of understanding and of a tendency to generalize individuals on the basis of race. It is both a rationalization for those who are looking and a disguise for those who are being looked at. This concept is expressed in other terms as well: Wright continually refers to a "curtain" or "barrier" which prevents his characters from fully seeing and communicating with others, particularly those of another race. Because of it, Bigger is alienated from even his friends and isolated behind his symbolic "curtain." Threatened by the shame of acknowledging the living conditions of his family, he erects a protective barrier: "he lived with them, but behind a wall, a curtain" (p. 14); and, again: "All that morning he had lurked behind his curtain of indifference and looked at things, snapping and glaring at whatever had tried to make him come out into the open" (p. 31).

Sometimes the "wall" seems the result of a deterministic force which prevents him from establishing rapport with anyone. Jan, for example, tries to reach Bigger on the street after being questioned at the Daltons', but despite his intentions, circumstances prevent full communication: "In the pale yellow sheen of the street lamp they faced each other; huge wet flakes of snow floated down slowly, forming a delicate screen between them" (pp. 161–62).

Throughout *Native Son* this metaphor is reminiscent of the "veil" concept explored in *The Souls of Black Folk*,[7] by W. E. Burghardt DuBois. DuBois, of course, was writing much earlier (1903), but the meaning of the device is, tragically, much the same. The veil, he points out, not only prevents whites and blacks from seeing each other, but also deters a Negro from truly seeing himself: "After the Egyptian and Indian, the Greek and Roman, the Negro is a sort of seventh son, born with a veil, and gifted with a second-sight in this American world—a world which yields him no true self-consciousness, but only lets him see himself through the revelation of the other world" (DuBois, p. 16).

The result is an imposed self-destruction of identity, with the white-ideal constantly at odds with the reality of blackness. This dichotomy, DuBois suggests, promotes a unique duality, perpetually schizophrenic, in one's view of himself: "It is a peculiar sensation, this double-consciousness, this sense of always looking at one's self through the eyes of others, of measuring one's soul by the tape of a world that looks on in amused contempt and pity. One ever feels his two-ness—an American, a Negro; two souls, two thoughts, two unreconciled strivings; two warring ideals in one dark body, whose dogged strength alone keeps it from being torn asunder" (DuBois, pp. 16–17).

Thus the veil, like blindness, creates a sense of isolation within impregnable walls and transfers a pathological dualism from society to the oppressed individual.

What DuBois is talking about seems very close to the situation Bigger finds himself in:

> But what was he after? What did he want? What did he love and what did he hate? He did not know. There was something he *knew* and something he *felt;* something the *world* gave him and something he *himself* had; something spread out in *front* of him and something spread out in *back:* and never in all his life, with this black skin of his, had the two worlds, thought and feeling, will and mind, aspiration and satisfaction, been together; never had he felt a sense of wholeness (p. 225)

In addition to the images of the "veil" and "blindness," there are other metaphors of vision which relate to the central theme. For example, Bigger's view of the white world is, essentially, a simplistic re-creation of the images in the popular media. Perhaps this process is best illustrated in the "movie scene" in which Jack and Bigger attend a local double feature. Wright has selected the two pictures very carefully: *The Gay Woman* depicts the sophisticated white cocktail set whirling through social crises against a background of swimming pools and golf courses and night clubs. Bigger takes this to be an accurate reproduction of upper-class society and this misconception informs both his goals and his disappointment upon meeting the Daltons, who do not fit the pattern.

The second movie presents another hyperbole in ironic contrast to the first: *Trader Horn* shows "black men and black women dancing against a wild background of barbaric jungle" (p. 32). For all its exaggeration, this scene is, unfortunately, much closer to the primitive conditions of his own life, yet it does not replace the first. It is, rather, at least in part, the lingering portrait of *The Gay Woman* which prompts him to work for the Daltons: "He looked at *Trader Horn* unfold and saw pictures of naked black men and women whirling in wild dances and heard drums beating and then gradually the African scene changed and was replaced by images in his own mind of white men and women dressed in black and white clothes, laughing, talking, drinking and dancing. Those were smart people; they knew how to get hold of money, millions of it. Maybe if he were working for them something would happen and he would get some of it. He would see just how they did it (pp. 35–36).

Thus his response to the movies underscores Bigger's refusal to identify himself with black society and reveals his quest for the amorphous splendor of the white world.

This fantasy of the white world, however, has a devastating effect on his thoughts and actions. "Whiteness," as an oppressive symbol, is omnipresent: there is the white world of Cottage Grove Avenue, the white cat which leaps upon his shoulder, the white snow which retards his escape, the white water which assists his capture, the white faces which glare at him in the court-room, and the "white mountain" which demands his execution. Whiteness becomes both the coveted goal and the oppressive enemy: he goes to work for the Daltons seeking the wealth of the white world; he finds not richness, but a "white blur," symbolizing hostility, manifested in the blind Mrs. Dalton. She is an abstraction to him, a white nebulous threat, and as such she frightens him into killing her daughter:

> He turned and a hysterical terror seized him, as though he were falling from a great height in a dream. A white blur was standing by the door, silent, ghost-like. It filled his eyes and gripped his body . . . Frenzy dominated him. He held his hand over her mouth . . . (p 84)

Significantly, it is a white image which motivates each of the murders: with Mary it was the "white blur"; with Bessie it is a whiteness in nearly the same form. As he prepares to kill her he watches her "white breath" in the cold air, resentment and hostility swelling within him.

When he is about to strike, the motivating image leaves him, and he pauses for it to return, suggesting that without the whiteness there would be no killing: "he had to stand here until that picture came back, that motive, that driving desire to escape the law. Yes. It *must* be this way. A sense of the white blur hovering near, of Mary burning, of Britten, of the law tracking him down, came back. Again, he was ready" (p. 222).

Thus violence being a weapon of the weak, both murders are born of fear and are a symbolic thrust against an enormous oppressor, a futile act of self-defense.

There are also a number of consistent images involving "visions" and "dreams." Perhaps the most important of these is Bigger's haunting memory of Mary's head severed from her body.[8] The picture recurs again and again as an immediate and constant reminder of the reality of his action. He had struck out against a white blur, but it was an individual he had killed, a girl whose memory provokes a feeling as close to guilt as he is capable of.

He becomes so preoccupied with the image that in a dream he substitutes his own head for Mary's: "he stood on a street corner in a red glare of light like that which came from the furnace and he had a big package in his arms so wet and slippery and heavy that he could scarcely hold onto it and he wanted to know what was in the package and he stopped near an alley corner and unwrapped it and the paper fell away and he saw—it was his *own* head—his own head lying with black face and half-closed eyes and lips parted with white teeth showing and hair wet with blood and the red glare grew brighter like light shining down from a red moon and red stars on a hot summer night . . ." (p. 156).

It is a vivid image, recalling the red glow of the furnace that had frightened him during the investigation, the heat in the furnace room; and it suggests, symbolically, that in killing Mary he has killed himself as well.

Perhaps it is suitably ironic that both the triumph and the tragedy of Bigger's life are realized in the same act: the murder is at once the culmination of his isolation and blindness and the inception of his ability to "see." The death scene is the pivotal point for not only the structure and theme, but for the imagery as well: it is a moment of "recognition" in the classical sense. From this moment on, the prevailing image for Bigger is one of "seeing."

He sees his home life as it really is (p. 100), and he seems to have gained a remarkable insight into character: he realizes that he has not been alone in his blindness, that ". . . Jan was blind. Mary had been blind. Mr. Dalton was blind. And Mrs. Dalton was blind; yes, blind in more ways than one . . . Bigger felt that a lot of people were like Mrs. Dalton, blind . . . Buddy, too, was blind . . . Looking at Buddy and thinking of Jan and Mr. Dalton, he saw in Buddy a certain stillness, an isolation, meaninglessness" (pp. 102–3).

Not all of his new insights are negative, however. In a splendid image, Bigger sees, for a moment, the amelioration of the racial "problem:"

> Another impulse rose in him, born of desperate need, and his mind clothed it in an image of a strong blinding sun sending hot rays down and he was standing in the midst of a vast crowd of men, white men and black men and all men, and the sun's rays melted away the many differences, the colors, the clothes, and drew what was common and good upward toward the sun . . . (p. 335)

Clearly, something has happened to Bigger. The act of killing, as Max later explains, was not only destructive but "creative" in the sense of giving Bigger a life he was denied before.[9] For the first time he has a sense of his own identity: he now understands the motivation of the Daltons (p. 122); he glimpses the incredulousness of his actions and is forced to laugh at himself (p. 175); and, ultimately, through a combination of his new perception and the compassion of his lawyer, he strikes through the "whiteness" to see individual people: "For the first time in his life he had gained a pinnacle of feeling upon which he could stand and see vague relations that he had never dreamed of. If that white looming mountain of hate were not a mountain at all, but people, people like himself, and like Jan—then he was faced with a high hope the like of which he had never thought could be, and a despair the full depths of which he knew he could not stand to feel" (p. 334).

Strangely, after the murder, Bessie too sees as she never could before: she realizes that Bigger has murdered Mary (p. 168), that she is irretrievably involved with Bigger (p. 173), and that the police will charge him with rape as well as murder (p. 213). She now understands the damaging effect of her entire relationship with him (p. 215) and her former blindness (p. 216).

The change is also manifested in Jan; he and Bigger find it possible to remove the veil: "He looked at Jan and saw a white face, but an honest face . . . Suddenly, this white man had come up to him, flung aside the curtain, and walked into the room of his life . . . He saw Jan as though someone had performed an operation upon his eyes, or as though someone had snatched a deforming mask from Jan's face" (p. 268).

Of all the characters, of course, Max sees most brilliantly. In appropriate visual imagery, he explains Bigger's situation to the court: "The central fact to be understood here is not who wronged this boy, but what kind of a vision of the world did he have before his eyes, and where did he get such a vision as to make him, without premeditation, snatch the life of another person so quickly and instinctively that even though there was an element of accident in it, he was willing after the crime to say: 'Yes; I did it. I had to' " (p. 364).

In the same terms he pleads for mercy for Bigger: "But our decision as to whether this black boy is to live or die can be made in accordance with what actually exists. It will at least indicate that we *see* and *know!* And our seeing and knowing will comprise a consciousness of how inescapably this one man's life will confront us ten million fold in the days to come" (p. 369).

Unfortunately, however, Max has not seen *all*. Despite his perceptive analysis of the racial situation in general, he too has failed to see the individual in the mass. He sees Bigger as one black man among twelve million, not as a boy suddenly aware of his own identity. He understands the cause of the crime, but not what it means to Bigger; thus he cannot acknowledge the murder as a "good" act in any sense. Even though the boy says, "But what I killed for, I *am*" (pp. 391–92), and "it must have been good! When a man kills, it's for something" (p. 392), Max does not understand and gropes for his hat like a "blind" man (p. 392).

And so the novel ends, deep in the themes and images with which it began. Bigger, on the basis of his new individuality, realizes that his real tragedy is not death; it is rather the fact of never having been clearly seen by anyone. Throughout the novel the images of vision have suggested this conclusion: blindness prompting isolation, impaired vision, alienation. Thus the imagery contributes to the central theme that the denial of personal identity is the worst form of oppression. Therefore, through the techniques of his fiction Richard Wright emphasizes the role of *perception* in the racial issue and develops the depth and greatness of the "art" of *Native Son*.

Notes

1. Richard Wright, *Native Son* (A Perennial Classic: New York, 1966).

2. See, for example, Robert A. Bone, *The Negro Novel in America* (New Haven, 1968), pp. 140–52, and Edward Margolies, "Richard Wright: *Native Son* and Three Kinds of Revolution,"

Native Sons: A Critical Study of Twentieth–Century Negro American Authors (New York, 1969), pp. 65–86.

3.   Margolies, p. 84.

4.   In addition, although the reader grows to know Bigger intimately, Britten remains stereotypic, the effect of which is to artistically restrict the vision of the reader. Thus he too becomes, very subtly, a participant in the blindness.

5.   On another occasion he sees the windows of the empty building as the "eye-sockets of empty skulls" (p. 216).

6.   Bigger's fear of and resistance to the white world is frequently symbolized by his gesture of throwing his hands up in front of his face. Generally this action occurs when he is attempting to blot out some detail which does not conform to his understanding of reality. For examples, see pp. 49–50, 95, 109, 133, 236, and 307.

7.   W. E. Burghardt DuBois, *The Souls of Black Folk* (A Fawcett Premier Book: Greenwich, Conn., 1967).

8.   See pp. 108, 110, 113, 123, 126, 183, 195, 204, and 220 for examples.

9.   See Margolies, p. 86.

The Conclusion of Richard Wright's *Native Son*

Paul N. Siegel

The conclusion of *Native Son* has perhaps caused more critics, distinguished and obscure, to go astray, reading into it their own preconceptions instead of perceiving the author's purpose, than any other significant portion of a major work of modern American literature. Both Max's lengthy speech in the courtroom and his final scene with Bigger have been grievously misunderstood.

Let us turn to Irving Howe as our prime example:

> The long speech by Bigger's radical lawyer Max . . . is ill-related to the book itself: Wright had not achieved Dreiser's capacity for absorbing everything, even the most recalcitrant philosophical passages, into a unified vision of things. . . . Yet it should be said that the endlessly repeated criticism that Wright caps his melodrama with a party-line oration tends to oversimplify the novel, for Wright is too honest simply to allow the propagandistic message to constitute the last word. Indeed, the last word is given not to Max but to Bigger. For at the end Bigger remains at the mercy of his hatred and fear, the lawyer retreats helplessly, the projected union between political consciousness and raw revolt has not been achieved—as if Wright were persuaded that, all ideology apart, there is for each Negro an ultimate trial that he can bear only by himself.[1]

Howe, therefore, finds that the "endlessly repeated criticism" that Max's speech is a "party-line oration"[2] "tends to oversimplify the novel" not because this criticism is incorrect but because it does not go beyond the speech to perceive that the union of Bigger's "raw revolt" and Max's "political consciousness" has not been effected. So, too, Alfred Kazin declares that Wright's method is "to astonish the reader by torrential scenes of cruelty, hunger, rape, murder and flight, and then enlighten him by crude Stalinist homilies."[3] By "crude Stalinist homilies" Kazin undoubtedly means Max's speech and his conversations with Bigger.

Howe, Kazin, Bone, McCall, Margolies, and Brignano and the numerous other critics referred to by Howe and McCall have responded to the

Reprinted by permission of the Modern Language Association of America from *PMLA*, 89 (May 1974): 517–23.

courtroom speech with a conditioned reflex: Richard Wright was a Communist; Boris Max is called a Communist (only, to be sure, by the red-baiting prosecuting attorney and newspapers, but that is overlooked); therefore, the speech must be a "party-line oration," a "crude Stalinist" homily. Before we examine the speech, let us see what Ben Davis Jr., a leading black official of the Communist party at the time, had to say about it in reviewing the book in the *Sunday Worker,* the official organ of the party.

Although Davis concedes that "certain passages in Max's speech show an understanding of the responsibility of capitalism for Bigger's plight," he checks off the following points against Max: "he accepts the idea that Negroes have a criminal psychology"; "he does not challenge the false charge of rape against Bigger"; "he does not deal with the heinous murder of Bessie, tending to accept the bourbon policy that crimes of Negroes against each other don't matter"; "he argues that Bigger, and by implication the whole Negro mass, should be held in jail to protect 'white daughters' "; he "should have argued for Bigger's acquittal in the case, and should have helped stir the political pressure of the Negro and white masses to get that acquittal." "His speech," Davis concludes, ". . . expresses the point of view held . . . by . . . reformist betrayers. . . . The first business of the Communist Party or of the I.L.D. would have been to chuck him out of the case."[4]

Whatever the distortions in the pronouncement of this party bureaucrat turned literary critic,[5] he is, it must be acknowledged, a more authoritative interpreter of the party line of the time than either Howe or Kazin. Davis obviously wants the simplified propaganda that *Native Son* does not give: a hero who is a completely innocent victim and a lawyer who thunders his client's innocence, who brilliantly exposes a frame-up rooted in a corrupt society, and who calls for giant demonstrations against this frame-up. The fact that Max is not a party-line expounder is one of the points that made the party leaders uneasy about *Native Son,* an uneasiness indicated by the review itself and by the fact that Davis' review appeared a month after the novel's publication.

The novel itself indicates that Max is not a Communist party member. Jan tells Mary (p. 66) that Max is "one of the best lawyers we've got." He does not refer to him as a "comrade," a member of the Communist party, but as one of the lawyers employed by the International Labor Defense, the legal defense organization controlled by the party. Although Max is obviously sympathetic to the causes espoused by the Communists, the fact that he is employed by the International Labor Defense does not indicate that he is a Communist any more than the employment of the noted criminal lawyer, Samuel S. Leibowitz, in the Scottsboro case meant that Leibowitz was a Communist. When he tells Bigger that others besides blacks are hated, he says (p. 295), "They hate trade unions. They hate folks who try to organize. They hate Jan." "They hate Jan"—not "Communists like me and Jan." Later he says, "I'm a Jew and they hate me" (p. 304)—not "I'm a Communist and a Jew and they hate me."

If, then, Max is not the novel's Communist spokesman who delivers a "party-line oration," what are his politics and what does he say in his speech? An old, wise, weary Jew, deeply aware of the radical defects of the society of which he is a member, Max, as we shall see in his courtroom speech, envisions a cataclysmic end to this society and seeks desperately to avert it by striving to have wrongs redressed. He is neither a revolutionist nor a Stalinist.[6]

His speech is not an address to a jury, as Edwin Berry Burgum, James Baldwin, Dan McCall, and Edward Margolies affirm.[7] Max clearly states that, not daring to put Bigger's fate in the hands of a white jury whose minds have been inflamed by the press, he has entered a plea of guilty, which by the laws of Illinois permits him to reject a trial by jury and to have the sentence rendered by the presiding judge. "Dare I," he asks the judge, ". . . put his fate in the hands of a jury . . . whose minds are already conditioned by the press of the nation. . . ? No! I could not! So today I come to face this Court, rejecting a trial by jury, willingly entering a plea of guilty, asking in the light of the laws of this state that this boy's life be spared."[8]

It is to this judge that Max is speaking. Beyond the judge he is speaking to "men of wealth and property," who, if they misread "the consciousness of the submerged millions today" (p. 338), will bring about a civil war in the future. It is amazing that James Baldwin can say that Max's speech "is addressed to those among us of good will and it seems to say that, though there are whites and blacks among us who hate each other, we will not; there are those who are betrayed by greed, by guilt, by blood, by blood lust, but not we; we will set our faces against them and join hands and walk together into that dazzling future when there will be no white or black" (p. 47). Baldwin is here carried away by his own rhetoric. There is not a sentence in the speech stating or implying a dazzling future to which black and white will walk hand in hand!

Nor is the speech a savage attack on capitalism or a statement of a "guilt-of-the-nation thesis,"[9] a plea for sympathy for one whose guilt we must all share. "Allow me, Your Honor," says Max (pp. 327–28), ". . . to state emphatically that I do *not* claim that this boy is a victim of injustice, nor do I ask that this Court be sympathetic with him. . . . If I should say that he is a victim of injustice, then I would be asking by implication for sympathy; and if one insists upon looking at this boy in the light of sympathy, he will be swamped by a feeling of guilt so strong as to be indistinguishable from hate."

The mob of would-be lynchers, he says, knowing in its heart of the oppression of Negroes, is as possessed of guilt, fear, and hate as Bigger is. In order to understand the full significance of Bigger's case, he urges the judge, one must rise above such emotion. To do so, he summons him to look upon it from a historical height. The "first wrong," the enslavement of the Negroes, was "understandable and inevitable" (p. 327), for in subduing this "harsh and wild country" (p. 328) men had to use other men as tools and weapons. "Men do what they must do" (p. 329). From that first wrong came a sense of guilt, in the attempted stifling of which came hate and fear, a hate and fear that matched that of the Negroes. Injustice practiced on this scale and over that length of time "is injustice no longer; it is an accomplished fact of life" (p. 330). This fact of life is a system of oppression squeezing down upon millions of people. These millions can be stunted, but they cannot be stamped out. And as oppression grows tighter, guilt, fear, and hatred grow stronger on both sides. Killing Bigger will only "swell the tide of pent-up lava that will some day break loose, not in a single, blundering, accidental, individual crime, but in a wild cataract of emotion that will brook no control" (p. 330). Sentencing him to life imprisonment, on the other hand, will give him an opportunity to "build a meaning for his life" (p. 338).

Max's speech is, in short, an agonized plea to the judge to understand the significance of Bigger and, understanding, to break through the pattern of hatred and repression that "makes our future seem a looming image of violence" (p. 337). It has been frequently pointed out that in Book III, which is entitled "Fate," we see realized the doom of Bigger that has been foreshadowed from the beginning. This is entirely true, of course, but "Fate" also refers to the doom of the United States, toward which Max sees us, "like sleepwalkers" (p. 324), proceeding. "If we can understand how subtly and yet strongly his life and fate are linked to ours,—if we can do this, perhaps we shall find the key to our future" (p. 324). Bigger killed "accidentally"—that is, he was not aware of killing as he killed, but this does not matter. What matters is that "every thought he thinks is potential murder" (p. 335). "Who knows when another 'accident' involving millions of men will happen, an 'accident' that will be the dreadful day of our doom?" (pp. 337–38).

Max's speech, far from being, as Howe says, "ill-related to the book," not a part of "a unified vision of things," grows out of the rest of the novel. It has, to be sure, a number of weaknesses. It and the prosecuting attorney's speech are not seen and heard from Bigger's point of view, which is otherwise rigidly adhered to in the novel, the vivid presentation of Bigger's visceral reactions, as events are registered on his consciousness, contributing to the novel's force and drive. Max's speech, which takes sixteen pages, is not, however, summarized and presented through Bigger's consciousness, and at its end we are told that Bigger "had not understood the speech, but he had felt the meaning of some of it from the tone of Max's voice" (p. 370). Moreover, the speech, far from being superimposed on what had gone on before and at variance with it, repeats too obviously what has already been said. Wright's awareness of this repetition and his desire to achieve a heightened effect in the final summing up may explain a rhetoric that is occasionally too highly wrought and too highly pitched.

That the speech, however, is not an obtrusion is indicated by the number of recurring themes and images in the novel that the speech brings together. The first theme that we might consider is that of blindness. Bigger, eating his breakfast the morning after he has killed Mary and looking upon his family and the world with new eyes, realizes that his mother, sister, and brother exclude from their vision of the world that which they do not wish to see. He also realizes that Mrs. Dalton is blind figuratively as well as literally, that Mr. Dalton and Jan are blind, and that Mary had been blind in not recognizing that which was in him, the propensity to kill. When he joins Bessie, he feels the same about her being blind as he does about his family. She knows nothing but hard work in white folks' kitchens and the liquor she drinks to make up for her starved life. In flight, despite the danger of death, Bigger feels a "queer sense of power" at having set the chase in motion, at being engaged in purposeful activity for the first time in his life, and thinks, "He was living, truly and deeply, no matter what others might think, looking at him with their blind eyes" (p. 203). When Jan visits him in prison, he tells Bigger, "I was kind of blind. . . . I didn't know we were so far apart until that night" (p. 244). Bigger, understanding that Jan is expressing his belief in him, for the first time looks upon a white man as a human being. "He saw Jan as though someone had performed an operation upon his eyes" (p. 246).

Max, in his image of the American people proceeding to their doom like sleepwalkers, catches up these images of darkness present on all sides. It is this blindness that he emphasizes throughout his speech. If the judge reacts only to what he has to say about the sufferings of Negroes, he states, he will be "blinded" by a feeling that will prevent him from perceiving reality and acting accordingly. "Rather, I plead with you to see . . . an existence of men growing out of the soil prepared by the collective but blind will of a hundred million people" (p. 328). "Your Honor," he exclaims, "in our blindness we have so contrived and ordered the lives of men" (p. 336) that their every human aspiration constitutes a threat to the state.

Max, then, sees the American people as going unseeingly to their doom because they—except, presumably, for a possibly saving remnant of them such as Max himself and his co-workers—either actively support or passively and unthinkingly accept the institutions of a repressive society. Bigger for his part sees whites as constituting an overwhelming natural force, a part of the structure of the universe. "To Bigger and his kind," says Wright early in the novel, "white people were not really people; they were a sort of great natural force, like a stormy sky looming overhead, or like a deep swirling river stretching suddenly at one's feet in the dark" (p. 97). The snowstorm that covers Chicago after Bigger's murder is symbolic of the hostile white world. When Bigger slips in running, "the white world tilted at a sharp angle and the icy wind shot past his face" (p. 205). The snow separates Jan and Bigger from each other, as Jan accosts Bigger in the street after Mary's disappearance and tries to speak to him, only to be driven away by Bigger's gun: "In the pale yellow sheen of the street lamp they faced each other; huge wet flakes of snow floated down slowly, forming a delicate screen between them" (p. 146). When Jan gets through to Bigger in prison, an image of the white world as a great natural force is used again, this time a force subject to erosion: "Jan had spoken a declaration of friendship that would make other white men hate him: a particle of white rock had detached itself from that looming mountain of white hate and had rolled down the slope, stopping still at his feet" (p. 246; see also p. 253).

With his fine sensitivity, Max understands Bigger's feeling about whites, which Bigger had conveyed to him in the prison interview, and tries to make the judge understand it, using the same image of the white world as a natural force, not made up of human beings: "When situations like this arise, instead of men feeling that they are facing other men, they feel that they are facing mountains, floods, seas" (p. 327). But the judge blindly does not understand.

Another recurring image is that of the wall or curtain or veil behind which Bigger withdraws and hides rather than face reality. "He knew that the moment he allowed himself to feel to its fullness how [his family] lived, the shame and misery of their lives, he would be swept out of himself with fear and despair. So he held toward them an attitude of iron reserve; he lived with them, but behind a wall, a curtain. And toward himself he was even more exacting. He knew that the moment he allowed what his life meant to enter fully into his consciousness, he would either kill himself or someone else."[10] So, Max says, the killing of Mary was "a sudden and violent rent in the veil behind which he lived" (pp. 330–31), tearing aside his alienated feelinglessness and enabling him for the first time really to live.

The theme that Bigger's killing has given him a freedom he never before had is sounded frequently. "He had murdered and created a new life for himself. It was something that was all his own, and it was the first time in his life he had had anything that others could not take from him" (p. 90). And again: "He felt that he had his destiny in his grasp. He was more alive than he could ever remember having been; his mind and attention were pointed, focussed toward a goal" (p. 127). And still again: "There remained to him a queer sense of power. *He* had done this. *He* had brought all this about. In all of his life these two murders were the most meaningful things that had ever happened to him" (p. 203).

This is what Max tells the judge. In order to seek to reach him, he dares to speak of the killing as "an act of *creation*" (p. 325). He is not only concerned with conveying to the judge the bondage in which Bigger had lived so that it took this killing to give him "the possibility of choice, of action, the opportunity to act and to feel that his actions carried weight" (p. 333). He is concerned with conveying to him the sense of an impending awful catastrophe in which millions of others learn to be free through killing: "How soon will someone speak the word that resentful millions will understand: the word to be, to act, to live?"[11]

The sense of freedom that Bigger received was only transitory. Caught and imprisoned, Bigger wonders concerning the meaning of his life. Were the intimations of freedom, of "a possible order and meaning in his relations with the people about him" real (p. 234)? Or would freedom and meaning elude him and would he "have to go to his end just as he was, dumb, driven, with the shadow of emptiness in his eyes" (p. 235)? "Maybe they were right when they said that a black skin was bad. . . . Maybe he was just unlucky, a man born for dark doom, an obscene joke."

The big question of Book III is whether Bigger will find himself. It is not answered until the very end of the novel, the farewell scene with Max. "At the end," says Howe, "Bigger remains at the mercy of his hatred and fear." It is hard to make men hear who will not listen. Seven times in the last page and a half of the novel Bigger cries out to Max, "I'm all right," the last time adding, "For real, I am" (p. 359). The repeated assurance "I'm all right" obviously means that Bigger is not at the mercy of fear, that he is sure that he will not, as he had dreaded, have to be dragged to the electric chair, kicking and screaming, filled with animal terror because he had not been able to find human dignity. He has found what he had sought, an understanding of himself that "could lift him up and make him live so intensely that the dread of being black and unequal would be forgotten; that even death would not matter, that it would be a victory" (p. 234). The meaning for his life, which Max had thought to gain him the opportunity to build during life imprisonment, he had grasped from his recent experience under the duress of death.

What was the understanding of himself that he had acquired? Bone believes that Bigger casts out fear by giving himself completely to hatred, thereby in reality suffering a defeat: "What terrifies Max is that Bigger, repossessed by hate, ends by accepting what life has made him: a killer. Bigger's real tragedy is not that he dies, but that he dies in hatred. A tragic figure, he struggles for love and trust against a hostile environment which defeats him in the end" (*The Negro Novel*, p. 150). Since the conclusion has been so misunderstood, it will be necessary to quote at some length from it in order to examine it closely.

Max does not wish to talk to Bigger about the significance of his life, but he is forced to do so by Bigger's insistence. He tells Bigger: "It's too late now for you to . . . work with . . . others who are t-trying to . . . believe [in life, which is thwarted by capitalism] and make the world live again. . . . But it's not too late to believe what you felt, to understand what you felt. . . . The job in getting people to fight and have faith is in making them believe in what life has made them feel, making them feel that their feelings are as good as those of others. . . . That's why . . . y-you've got to b-believe in yourself, Bigger" (pp. 357–58).

These words work upon Bigger. They give him what he wants. Ironically, however, they cause him to go further than Max intended. "Bigger, you killed," says Max. "That was wrong. That was not the way to do it." Bigger, however, accepts himself completely, including his overwhelming impulse to kill: "Sounds funny, Mr. Max, but when I think about what you say I kind of feel what I wanted. It makes me feel I was kind of right. . . . They wouldn't let me live and I killed. Maybe it ain't fair to kill, and I reckon I really didn't want to kill. But when I think of why all the killing was, I began to feel what I wanted, what I am. . . . I didn't want to kill! . . . But what I killed for, I *am!* It must've been pretty deep in me to make me kill! . . . What I killed for must've been good! . . . When a man kills, it's for something."[12]

Max's shock on hearing these words seems excessive for one who had shown such an understanding of Bigger and had said, "We are dealing here with an impulse stemming from deep down" (p. 333). Perhaps this is a flaw in the scene. However, we must remember that this is the third great blow he has received. The first was when the judge, the representative of the establishment, had disregarded his desperate plea. The second was when the governor had refused to exercise clemency. These blows make it all the more difficult for him to sustain the blow inflicted by Bigger, the representative of black millions. The catastrophe he foresees seems to him more than ever inescapable.

Is Bigger's acceptance of his feelings of hate a victory or a defeat? If Bone is, like Max, shocked by Bigger's words, and in his shock can only see that Bigger is defeated by his hostile environment, he should consider how Bigger's killing was presented as a means of liberation and so described by Max himself. Wright, of course, is not advocating murder. Murder gave Bigger a sense of freedom, but it also gave him a sense of guilt, and, not giving him a sense of relatedness to others, it finally left him empty. But hatred of the oppressor is a natural, human emotion; it is only unhealthy when it is kept stifled. Used as the motor power of an idea driving toward a goal, it can transform both the individual and society.

So Max in his courtroom speech said of the American Revolutionary War (p. 366): "Your Honor, remember that men can starve from a lack of self-realization as much as they can from a lack of bread! And they can *murder* for it, too! Did we not build a nation, did we not wage war and conquer in the name of a dream to realize our personalities and to make those realized personalities secure!" So, too, Sartre, in summarizing Fanon, echoes the statement that killing can be a creative act (the French existentialists, we may recall, acclaimed Wright and accepted him as one of their own):

In the period of their helplessness, their mad impulse to murder is the expression of the [colonial] natives' collective unconscious. If this suppressed fury fails to find an outlet, it turns in a vacuum and devastates the oppressed creatures themselves. In order to free themselves they even massacre each other. . . . This irrepressible violence [in a war of national liberation] is . . . man re-creating himself. . . . The native cures himself of colonial neurosis by thrusting out the settler through force of arms. When his rage boils over, he rediscovers his lost innocence and he comes to know himself in that he creates himself.[13]

Bone, moreover, overlooks completely—as does Howe—Bigger's last words before his final "good-bye": "Tell. . . . Tell Mister. . . . Tell Jan hello. . . ." (p. 359; Wright's ellipses). Bigger does not go to death hating all white men. He accepts the comradeship of Jan, for the first time in his life dropping the "mister" in front of a white man's name. But this comradeship he will extend only to those who have earned it in action, not to superficial sympathizers, patronizing philanthropists or bureaucratically arrogant radical sectarians. His pride in himself would not permit it otherwise.

Bigger realized in his death cell that "if there were any sure and firm knowledge for him, it would have to come from himself" (p. 350). And so it was. And just so, Wright indicates, the inner liberation of the blacks will have to come from within themselves. "There were rare moments," we were told early in the novel (pp. 97–98), "when a feeling and longing for solidarity with other black people would take hold of [Bigger]. . . . He felt that some day there would be a black man who would whip the black people into a tight band and together they would act and end fear and shame." Bigger in prison and in the face of death acquires the belief in himself and in his people that could propel the ghetto millions toward a goal that would catch "the mind and body in certainty and faith" (p. 98). Only between such blacks and such whites as Jan, the conclusion of *Native Son* implies, can there be genuine unity in a common struggle for a different and better form of society. This struggle for the third American revolution promises, in view of the adamant position of the ruling class that had rejected Max's plea and caused him to despair, to become, like the Revolutionary War and the Civil War, a bloody conflict before it is victorious.

Notes

1.   "Black Boys and Native Sons," *A World More Attractive* (New York: Horizon, 1963), p. 104.

2.   So, too, Dan McCall sums up "the usual objection voiced against the third part of Wright's novel": "The Party had interrupted Wright's project and falsified the message of 'the bad nigger' " (*The Example of Richard Wright,* New York: Harcourt, 1969, p. 90). McCall, who has written the best criticism on *Native Son,* himself speaks of Max (pp. 90, 101) as "the ideological spokesman" who "can only filter Bigger through the Party's vision." Robert A. Bone, who likewise has written well on *Native Son,* says similarly: "In Book III Wright has allowed his statement as a Communist to overwhelm his statement as an artist. . . . Bigger's lawyer . . . is at once a mouthpiece for the author and a spokesman for the party line" (*Richard Wright,* Min-

neapolis: Univ. of Minnesota Press, 1969, p. 23). For similar views, see Edward Margolies, *The Art of Richard Wright* (Carbondale: Southern Illinois Univ. Press. 1969), pp. 114–15, and Russell Carl Brignano, *Richard Wright: An Introduction to the Man and His Works* (Pittsburgh: Univ. of Pittsburgh Press, 1969), p. 81.

3. *On Native Grounds* (New York: Harcourt, 1942), p. 387.

4. *Sunday Worker,* New York, 14 April 1940, Sec. 2, p. 4, col. 6.

5. Max's statement that Bigger's existence is "a crime against the state" (Richard Wright, *Native Son,* New York: Harper, 1940, p. 367) is, insofar as it is an indictment at all, far more of an indictment of the state than it is of Bigger. Max does deal with the murder of Bessie (pp. 336–37), making the point that Bigger knew that the white world would be concerned with the murder only of Mary, not of Bessie. He nowhere argues that Bigger, let alone "the whole Negro mass," should be held in jail to protect white daughters.

6. James G. Kennedy, in an article ("The Content and Form of *Native Son,*" *College English,* 34, 1972, 269–86) published after I submitted this article to *PMLA,* assumed that Max is to be taken as a Communist party member but asserted (282) that Max reveals himself to be really "an idealist and no Marxist" because "he supposes there can be understanding above classes."

7. Edwin Berry Burgum, *The Novel and the World's Dilemma* (1947; rpt. New York: Russell, 1963), p. 238; James Baldwin, "Many Thousands Gone," *Notes of a Native Son* (New York: Dial Press, 1963), p. 42; McCall, p. 93; Margolies, p. 112.

8. P. 325. See also pp. 304 and 317. Clarence Darrow similarly pleaded guilty and rejected a trial by jury in the Loeb-Leopold case, to which the novel refers.

9. Robert Bone, *The Negro Novel in America* (New Haven: Yale Univ. Press, 1966), p. 151.

10. P. 19. See also pp. 24, 91, 203, 226, 240.

11. P. 337. The theme of blindness was mentioned in Bone, *The Negro Novel,* p. 147, James A. Emanuel, "Fever and Feeling: Notes on the Imagery in *Native Son,*" *Negro Digest,* 18 Dec. 1968, 20–21, and Brignano, p. 117; the theme of the white world as a great natural force in Bone, p. 147 and Brignano, p. 117; the image of the wall or curtain behind which Bigger withdraws in Emanuel, pp. 22–24; the theme of Bigger's killing as a means of liberation in Bone, p. 146, McCall, pp. 87, 100, Margolies, pp. 116–17, Brignano, p. 147. None of these takes note, however, of how these themes and images are gathered up in Max's speech.

12. P. 358. This was what Jan had told Bigger when he visited him in prison: "You believed enough to kill. You thought you were settling something, or you wouldn't have killed" (p. 246). Apparently, "all the killing" refers to all the times Bigger felt like killing.

13. Introd. to Frantz Fanon, *The Wretched of the Earth* (New York: Grove, 1966), pp. 16–18. With Sartre's point that the suppressed fury of the natives causes them to turn against each other, compare Bigger's violence in Doc's poolroom, when his fear of the hated white man forces him to attack Gus rather than to rob Blum's delicatessen.

Composing Bigger:
Wright and the Making of *Native Son*

Joseph T. Skerrett Jr.

More is going on in *Native Son* than a merely intellectual synthesis of literary naturalism and Marxist political economy. In an early review Malcolm Cowley sensed a widening of Wright's sympathies since the stories of *Uncle Tom's Children,* "a collection of stories all but one of which had the same pattern: a Negro was goaded into killing one or more white men and was killed in turn, without feeling regret for himself or his victims." Admiring the stories, Cowley thought them "painful to read," for he felt that in them Wright's indignation was expressing itself in the revenge of "a whole series of symbolic murders." "In *Native Son* the pattern is the same, but the author's sympathies have broadened and his resentment, though quite as deep, is less painful and personal." This suggestion that the intellectualization of the violent relationships portrayed in the short stories was doing something *for* Wright as well as for the reader is bolstered by Saunders Redding's insistence that Wright himself was behind Bigger Thomas's inarticulateness. Redding broadly asserted that "in a way that is more direct than is true of most important modern authors of fiction, Wright's heroes were in naked honesty himself, and not imaginary creations that served to express his complicated personality." Stanley Edgar Hyman accounted for the great power of *Native Son* by concluding that in the novel

> the tensions and guilts connected with sexuality, openly and deliberately manipulated in the fiction, fled into the color imagery, and gave it a sexual resonance and ambiguity not consciously contrived, which powerfully reflected the social undercurrents of American life.

Despite these strong indications of alternative directions of inquiry, critics have been reluctant to release the by now comfortable grasp they have on the "protest fiction" aspect of *Native Son*. It has, I think, blinded them to the meaning of *Native Son* as the culmination of Wright's first phase as a writer.

Reprinted from *Richard Wright's Native Son,* ed. Harold Bloom (New York: Chelsea House, 1987): pp. 125–42, with the permission of the author. © 1975, 1987 by Joseph T. Skerrett Jr.

Native Son is not only Wright's most ambitious and most achieved work of art, but it is also the work in which he most completely—whether or not "openly and deliberately" as Hyman says—related the materials of his personal biography to his intellectual and aesthetic activities. In the working out of *Native Son* Wright objectified, in symbolic terms, the conflicts and passions arising out of his life up to that time. *Native Son* is rooted in the fertile soil of his personal psychosocial and psychosexual "situation," to use Kenneth Burke's term.

II

Wright began to work on the story before leaving Chicago for New York in the spring of 1939; one of his Chicago acquaintances at that time later told Michel Fabre that he could remember having seen a draft of early parts of the story shortly before Wright left for New York. In Chicago Wright had been living with his family—his ailing mother, his brother, and grandmother Wilson, who had joined them during the summer of 1934. If the emotional record of *Black Boy* is to be trusted, as I think it may, Wright must have felt the continual pressure of aggression and guilt and responsibility. Age had not tempered his grandmother's religious zeal and narrow-mindedness, and Wright's mother, though supportive, "was still partially paralyzed after a recent attack of encephalitis." Neither can have approved of whatever hint they got of Richard's involvement with the Communists. Wright respected his mother, Fabre says, "Because of her indisputable moral authority, [but] her devoutness irritated him more and more, along with her resigned attitude toward social injustice and hatred of communism." His dependent and seemingly indolent brother Leon did not contribute to the support of the family; "Wright spent increasingly less time at home in order to avoid friction between them." The intrafamiliar tensions so vividly described in *Black Boy* continued to exert pressure on Wright's life, even as, through his contact with the Communists, he was discovering a community which valued his rebellious attitudes. Wright's imaginative response to this complex "situation" was an equally complex one, for at the same time, at various stages of development, in 1934, 1935, and 1936 he was at work on the "objective" description of Jake Jackson's day in *Lawd Today,* the "ameliorative" and integrationist stories of *Uncle Tom's Children;* and the "revolutionary" attitudes of Bigger Thomas.

In "How 'Bigger' Was Born" Wright indicates that he sat down to his typewriter sometime in 1934 with the meaning and characterization of Bigger all "thought out." Whether this is true or not, the cathartic event in the process of committing Bigger to paper was Wright's new job at the South Side Youth Club. Here he was able to observe the rebellious urbanized and alienated black youths of whom Bigger is a composite and symbolic projection. But more importantly, at the Youth Club Wright began to identify with the passions of the delinquents and, as Fabre remarks, "for once, to give free reign to his own antisocial feelings." He felt that the job had thrust him into "a kind of dressed-up police work" and he hated the work of distracting these potential rebels with "ping-pong, checkers, swimming, marbles and baseball in order that [they] might not roam the streets and harm the valuable white property which adjoined the Black Belt." Privately Wright identified with the damage and disturbance the boys caused when they left his clubhouse in the afternoons, for it was a meaningful demonstration that "life is stronger than ping-pong." This identification with the criminal rebellion of his youthful charges enabled him to tolerate the work: "that was the only way I could contain myself for doing a job I hated; for a moment I'd allow myself, vicariously, to feel as Bigger felt—not much, just a little, just a *little*—but still, there it was" ("How 'Bigger' Was Born").

In giving rein to even this littlest amount of fellow-feeling with the boys and with his own imaginative re-creation of them, Wright brought himself face to face with his own inner tension about literary expression. He thought of literature as an essentially criminal activity, which had to be carried out under the shadow of what he calls in "How 'Bigger' Was Born" a "mental censor—product of the fears which a Negro feels from living in America." The fear of disapproval from white audiences and black leaders, though he considers them in separate categories, are really one and the same: fear of reprisal for the act of aggression he knew the book to be. The writing of the novel became entangled with Wright's deepest aggressive drives. His dissatisfaction with the response to *Uncle Tom's Children* supports this contention, for he found that it inspired more pity than terror.

> I found that I had written a book which even bankers' daughters could read and weep over and feel good about. I swore to myself that if I ever wrote another book, no one would weep over it; that it would be so hard and deep that they would have to face it without the consolation of tears. ("How 'Bigger' Was Born")

This feeling that the stories had failed was not a reflection of disapproval from Wright's Communist friends: their approval had been unstinting. The disapproval arose from within: the stories did not do for Wright what he wanted from them. So it was shortly after the completion of *Uncle Tom's Children* that Bigger Thomas, spawned in Wright's memories of "bad" black boys in his Mississippi home and developed in his observation of other boys in the Chicago slums, made contact with Wright's deepest personal fears and obsessions and took possession of his imagination: the writing of the novel became a struggle of exorcism from the forces, both black and white, that attempted to censor Wright's feeling of it.

The more I thought of it the more I became convinced that if I did not write of Bigger as I saw and felt him, if I did not try to make him a living personality and at the same time a symbol of all the larger things I felt and saw in him, I'd be reacting as Bigger himself reacted: that is, I'd be acting out of *fear* if I let what I thought whites would say constrict and paralyze me.

As I contemplated Bigger and what he meant, I said to myself: "I must write this novel, not only for others to read, but to free *myself* of his sense of shame and fear." In fact the novel, as time passed, grew upon me to the extent that it became a necessity to write it; the writing of it turned into a way of living for me. ("How 'Bigger' Was Born")

III

Bigger Thomas's situation in the novel is an imaginative replication of Wright's own "situation." Trapped by the economics of the Depression and the resultant intensification of racial prejudice and discrimination, Bigger feels resentment against the demands of his family—his religious mother, his sister Vera, and his younger brother, Buddy—whose needs require that he submit to the near-slavery of the employment offered by the welfare relief program. Bigger struggles against the family strategies to control his actions without access to the violence that is characteristic of his behavior later in the story. His central counter-strategy is to numb himself to the family feeling within:

He shut their voices out of his mind. He hated his family because he knew that they were suffering and that he was powerless to help them. He knew that the moment he allowed himself to feel to its fullness how they lived, the shame and misery of their lives, he would be swept out of himself with fear and despair. So he held toward them an attitude of iron reserve; he lived with them, but behind a wall, a curtain. (*Native Son*)

This denial is, of course, not without its cost. Bigger must repress his own impulses even more stringently. "He knew that the moment he allowed what his life meant to enter fully into his consciousness, he would either kill himself or someone else. So he denied himself and acted tough."

Like Jake in *Lawd Today,* Bigger hesitates to follow out his occasional thoughts of rebellion. Each time he asks himself the question What can I do? "his mind hit[s] a blank wall and he [stops] thinking." Jake takes out his frustration and anger on his wife Lil, whom he blames for his troubles; Bigger is in many ways psychologically more sensitive. He has displaced his sensitivity and potential tenderness within the family circle in order to protect his ego from pain. Curiously, unlike Jake, Bigger has no symbolic outlet for his aggressive feeling, as Jake does in the elaborate verbal play of "the dozens" in which he engages his street buddy. Bigger's passion is too close to the surface, perhaps, to be assuaged by such verbal objectification. The engagement that excites him is the engagement with the whites, who have so suffocatingly circumscribed his life. Having revived the plan to rob Blum's Delicatessen, Bigger feels released from the numbed and half-dead existence that is normality to him.

> All that morning he had lurked behind his curtain of indifference and looked at things, snapping and glaring at whatever had tried to make him come out into the open. But now he was out; the thought of the job at Blum's and the tilt he had had with Gus had snarled him into things and his self-trust was gone. Confidence could only come again now through action so violent that it would make him forget.

The fear of the whites threatens Bigger's sense of manly self-control. Amongst the gang it is that fear which creates a brutal community. Bigger humiliates Gus, forcing him to lick the tip of Bigger's knife, in order to prevent the gang from carrying out the planned armed robbery of Blum's. He knew that "the fear of robbing a white man had had hold of him when he started the fight with Gus." But, as this is a knowledge too costly to be admitted, Bigger's psyche represses it. "He knew it in a way that kept it from coming to his mind in the form of a hard and sharp idea. . . . But he kept this knowledge of his thrust firmly down in him: his courage to live depended upon how successfully his fear was hidden from his consciousness."

This attitude on Bigger's part, this holding his own consciousness at arm's length, is perhaps Wright's most original achievement in his characterization of Bigger. Unlike his creator, Bigger has, as his story opens, almost no access to his own symbolic imagination, his own creative consciousness. His almost formalized imaginative act is the role-playing game he engages Gus in—"playing white." The roles—general, banker, President—are satiric (and thus aggressive) but they are quickly abandoned when their nasty double edge is felt: the absurd pomposity and venality of the powerful whites control the boys' imaginations even in parody. Bigger has never experienced the fulfillment Wright got from the act of writing, that Jamesian sense of an invigorating self-integration and self-satisfaction that is the hallmark of a stable identity. In Francis Fergusson's terminology, the central "action" of the novel, dictated by Bigger's "purpose" in this story, is "to discover an identity." The search for the murderer that occupies the Daltons, the police, and the reporters, the search for motives and evidence by the attorneys, the search for a mode of acquittal by Max are all counterpointed with Bigger's increasingly conscious search for an integrated and satisfying consciousness of who he is.

This important aspect of Wright's exclusive use of Bigger's point of view has been at the center of the critical contention surrounding the novel's achievement. Some, like John Bayliss, see Bigger as merely pathetic in his struggles with consciousness, slow-witted and environmentally unsuited for urban society. More astute critics characteristically lose track of the fact that it is Bigger's point of view we are dealing with, and begin to attribute what Fergusson would call "the movement of the spirit" in the novel entirely to the author's, and not the character's, psyche. Thus Robert Bone notes that Wright succeeds in balancing the "stark horror" of the story with the "spiritual anguish" promised in the novel's epigraph from the Book of Job—"Even today is my complaint rebellious; my stroke is heavier than my groaning"— but he finally sees this anguish in terms of Wright rather than Bigger:

> This note of anguish, which emphasizes Bigger's suffering, is so intense as to be almost physical in character. It is sustained by a style which can only be called visceral. The author writes from his guts, describing the emotional state of his characters in graphic psychosomatic terms. It is a characteristic device which has its source in Wright's aching memory of the deep south. (*The Negro Novel in America*)

The observation, as this essay attempts to demonstrate, is essentially true. But it is no less true that the critic here—and later in his essay as well— refuses to deal with the nature of Bigger's individuality as it comes to grips with itself. He winds up summing the novel's themes thus: "Bigger is a human being whose environment has made him incapable of relating meaningfully to other human beings except through murder." Surely this does not give much room to that "movement of the spirit" which Wright's epigraph from Scripture suggests we should seek. Donald Gibson has addressed himself to this curious obtuseness of critics who fail to deal with the totality of the character, charging them with sociocultural blindness: "most critics of Wright's novel see only the outer covering of Bigger Thomas, the blackness of his skin and his resulting social role. Few have seen him as a discrete entity, a particular person, who struggles with the burden of his humanity."

Considered as more than a representative figure or pawn in a sociological murder-melodrama, Bigger's story extends from the brilliantly epitomic opening domestic scene to his dismissal of Max on the last page of the narrative, and not, as many of Gibson's "blind" readers would have it, from Mary Dalton's murder to Boris Max's defense. Bigger's purpose, the action which this novel imitates, is the search for identity, an identity denied him by both his social milieu and his family situation. Bigger seeks a world in which he is not an alienated being, a world in which he can be "at home." Bigger's severe alienation from his human environments is matched by a sensual awareness (expressed in what Bone calls Wright's "visceral" prose style) which develops a nearly philosophical intensity. Thus, Wright manages to replicate, through the experience of Bigger, his own experience in coming to terms with his imagination as the "at home" identity that would save him from the familial and social threat that surrounded him. In Bigger's case it is not a mediated and formalized form of aggression that is the instrument of liberation, but rather the unmediated, literal, and violent murders of Mary Dalton and Bessie Mears.

Given the conflict that characterized Wright's relationship with his family womenfolk, it is, of course, highly significant that both of Bigger's victims are women. It is perhaps a more significant fact that one is white, the other black. In Wright's short stories the black men were victims and the women either bystanders and supporters or burdens and betrayers. The image of black woman as heroine and Communist in "Bright and Morning Star" was an afterthought, an anomaly. In *Native Son,* with its central image of the black man in rebellion against the victimizing strictures and constraints that retard his development, the targets of the attack are women.

Now Wright's difficulties with women were not, of course, limited to childhood traumas and adolescent misunderstandings of motive. He gave the name "Mary Dalton" to Bigger's first victim at least in part because it was the "nom de guerre" of a Communist Party member in Chicago whom Wright disliked intensely. More importantly, at the time he was writing *Native Son,* Wright's sexual relationships with women had begun to reflect and fulfill the patterns that had been established in his new home life.

After moving to New York in 1937, Wright lived for a time with the Sawyers, a modest black family, on 143rd Street in Harlem. Wright became sexually involved with the daughter of the household, Marian Sawyer, and their engagement was announced in the spring of 1938. Early in May, Wright rushed into the apartment of his friends, the Newtons, "announcing that according to the prenuptial physical examination Marian had an advanced case of syphilis." Feeling "outraged that he had been deceived and relieved that he had escaped from such a grave danger," Wright immediately broke with the Sawyers and moved into the Newtons' new apartment in Brooklyn (Michel Fabre, *The Unfinished Quest of Richard Wright*).

Jane Newton quickly became a significant literary confidante; Wright read to her from his manuscript and respected her suggestions for changes. Before completing the novel (in early June of 1939), he had seriously courted two more women, both white. When Ellen Poplar hesitated to commit herself to a marriage within a month or so, Wright married Dhima Rose Meadman "at the beginning of August 1939, in the sacristy of the Episcopal Church on Covenant Avenue, with Ralph Ellison as best man" (Fabre).

In the Marian Sawyer affair Wright can only have felt betrayed and nearly trapped by the sexual connection. Her illness, "advanced" or not, could only serve—as his mother's illness, so recently escaped—to limit or divert him. The whole business revived in him the sense of threat posed by women, a sense of threat deeply ingrained in him at home. A marriage, contracted in large part, it seems (judging by the precipitous and absolute rupture between the couple), on Wright's conventional sense of guilt and responsibility for the illicit sexual contact, is avoided when the woman is proven a "betrayer," threatening Wright with disease, disgrace, and/or the misery and limitation of continued guilt-ridden nursing duties. In the marriage, Wright seems to have been reacting rather than acting. The evidence suggests that while Dhima Rose Meadman was attractive to Wright, his strongest reason for marrying her was the apparent rejection of his proposal by Ellen Poplar. After an unhappy season in Mexico, Wright and Dhima separated and divorced. Fabre indicates that Wright "had never stopped blaming himself for his impatience and injustice" toward Ellen, and when they met at the Newtons' late in 1940 their union was quickly sealed. Benefit of clergy was bestowed in March 1941, after which the Wrights moved out of the Newtons' apartment and set up housekeeping on their own. Ellen Poplar's hesitation was a challenge to Wright's ego; the marriage to Dhima was his response, a demonstration of his independence and self-sufficiency, his worthiness and adequacy.

Wright felt a strong resentment of his need for sexual and human companionship from women. After the publication of *Native Son,* he engaged in an experiment with Frederic Wertham, a psychoanalyst, to discover whether there were any direct associations of Bigger's murder of Mary in Wright's background. Wertham and Wright probed for some connections between Wright's experience in white households in the South during his youth and the key scene of Bigger's smothering Mary in the presence of her blind mother. Wright began to recall working for a young couple who lived with the wife's mother when he was about fifteen years old. The woman was very friendly to Wright, "and he felt this was a second home to him." He tended the fireplace, lighting the day's heat on winter mornings. One morning he opened a door in the course of these duties to discover the young woman partly dressed; he was reprimanded and told to knock.

As a careful reading of *Black Boy* makes clear, in Wright's life the ego ideal derived from the mother and not the father. And Wertham notes that "the very symbol of the seeing eye that is blind fits the mother image." By extension, of course, all the blind, questing authorities in *Native Son,* who seek to punish Bigger for his transgressions against the two women, are derived from Wright's own mother. In the experience explored with Wertham, the patterns of response to female authority, sexuality, and affection which had been set at home, made themselves manifest in a situation that was also socially charged with threat: even at fifteen, Wright knew the danger of being accused of sexual improprieties with a white woman.

In the novel, the "outering" of these conflict patterns in the life of Bigger Thomas is more complex, I believe, than Wertham and Wright's little experiment demonstrated. For in considering the total action of *Native Son—* the psychic motive out of which the events are generated—as Bigger's effort "to discover an identity," the killing of white Mary Dalton, half-accidental and unconscious as it is, is secondary to the purposeful and free act of killing black Bessie Mears.

Mary Dalton's death is Dreiserian, determined by Bigger's social conditioning and the terrible pressure of the moment. Mary's clumsy efforts at social egalitarianism and Marxist comraderie with her father's new chauffeur make only for confusion in Bigger's mind. He recoils from their attempts at intimacy, for it sharpens his shame and hatred of his status.

> He felt he had no physical existence at all right then: he was something he hated, the badge of shame which he knew was attached to a black skin. It was a shadowy region, a No Man's Land, the ground that separated the white world from the black that he stood upon. He felt naked, transparent; he felt that this white man (Jan Erlone), having helped to put him down, having helped to deform him, held him up now to look at him and be amused. At that moment he felt toward Mary and Jan a dumb, cold, and inarticulate hate.

Bigger feels vividly his condition of being "cut dead" by his social environment; Jan's and Mary's efforts at being friendly only exacerbate and intensify Bigger's sense of shame, fear, and hatred. The unreal, dreamlike quality of the murder scene later, comes into the tone of the novel here, with Bigger's uncomfortable journey across the city in the car, squeezed between Jan and Mary, who are completely blind to his terror. After the killing, Bigger realizes the absurdity: "It all seemed foolish! He wanted to laugh. It was unreal. He had to lift a dead woman and he was afraid. He felt that he had been dreaming of something like this for a long time, and then, suddenly, it was true."

Killing Mary is thus clearly, for Bigger, a release of long pentup aggressive tendencies that are both sexual and social. The act opens Bigger to a flood of realizations that he had managed all his life to repress with a half-conscious resistance. His vision cleared by his irreversible act, Bigger comes to grasp the essential blindness of both black and familial authority and white social authority. Having already grasped blind Mrs. Dalton's similarity to his mother and responded to it in kind, Bigger now sees that his own mother moves like a blind person, "touching objects with her fingers as she passed them, using them for support."

Bigger is elated by this perception of the essential blindness of all those who would censor and punish him for the as yet undiscovered murder. "His being black and at the bottom of the world was something which he could take with a new born strength. What his knife and gun had once meant to him, his knowledge of having secretly murdered Mary now meant." But this sense of power does not satisfy him. Bigger finds that he wants to tell the world what he has done:

> He wanted the keen thrill of startling them. . . . He wished that he could be an image in their minds; that his black face and the image of his smothering Mary and cutting off her head and burning her could hover before their eyes as a terrible picture of reality which they could see and feel and yet not destroy.

Bigger's sense of his act of murder as a creative expression, as an act which confers on him a meaningful identity in his own eyes, is incomplete, even though "the knowledge that he had killed a white girl they loved and regarded as their symbol of beauty made him feel the equal of them, like a man who had been somehow cheated, but had now evened the score." Something more is required. Full psychic liberation can come to Bigger only when the image of his self reflected back at him by others coincides with his own image of his self. Although the knowledge of having murdered Mary Dalton replaces in his mind the sense of security that carrying a knife and a gun had given him,

> he was not satisfied with the way things stood now; he was a man who had come in sight of a goal, then had won it, and in winning it had seen just within his grasp another goal, higher, greater. He had learned to shout and had shouted and no ear had heard him; he had just learned to walk and was walking but could not see the ground beneath his feet; and had long been yearning for weapons to hold in his hands and suddenly found that his hands held weapons that were invisible.

Charles James has pointed out that Bigger's girl, Bessie, "is the ear he needs to sound out the meaning of Mary's death. Through her, Bigger can gain some insight into his family's judgement of his act, without actually telling them." For Bessie is an oasis of motherly comfort in Bigger's world. Wright presents her and their essentially physical relationship in pastoral terms infused with stock female symbols—the "fallow field" and "the warm night sea" and the cooling and cleansing "fountain" whose "warm waters" cleared Bigger's senses "to end the tiredness and to reforge in him a new sense of time and space." This passive, maternal, all-accepting and sensually refreshing aspect of his mistress contrasts strongly in Bigger's mind with "the other Bessie," the questioning and censoring aspect of her which arouses in Bigger a desire "to clench his fist and swing his arm and blot out, kill, sweep away" all her resistance to his will and ideas.

Bessie's failure to understand and endorse the meaning Bigger has found in killing Mary Dalton dooms her. When Bigger tells her what he has done, she is terrified that she will be implicated. Her near-hysterical outburst of weak fatalism contains an explicit rejection of Bigger's very being— "I wish to God I never seen you. I wish one of us had died before we was born"—and makes Bigger realize that she can neither accompany him on his flight, nor be left behind to betray him. Bessie has proven herself to be like his mother: weak, limited, blind. "He hated his mother for that way of hers that was like Bessie's. What his mother had was Bessie's whiskey, and Bessie's whiskey was his mother's religion." Bigger begins to conceive of killing Bessie as a free act, "as a man seeing what he must do to save himself and feeling resolved to do it."

Killing Bessie, Bigger comes closer than in killing Mary to direct expression of Richard Wright's own primary inner conflict, the desire to strike out against the women who limited, repressed, censored, and punished his rebellious initiatives. Having killed Bessie with a brick, Bigger feels at last "truly and deeply" free and alive. The killings have given him a sense of freedom, and he is now able to make a direct contact with that consciousness he had for so long held at arm's length: "he had killed twice, but in a true sense it was not the first time he had ever killed. He had killed many times before, but only during the last two days had this impulse assumed the form of actual killing." His elation now is larger than the pride and sense of power he derived from killing Mary. This time, with this murder, he is brought to the brink of a philosophical consideration of his identity. As Charles James provocatively puts it, having "symbolically 'wiped out' the progenitive elements of the two things he hates most [the white societal oppressor and the black, submissive oppressed]," Bigger is free to begin thinking as an existentially liberated person:

> But what was he after? What did he want? What did he love and what did he hate? He did not know. There was something he *knew* and something he *felt;* something the *world* gave him and something he *himself* had; something spread out in *front* of him and something spread out in *back;* and never in all his life, with this black skin of his, had the two worlds, thought and feeling, will and mind, aspiration and satisfaction, been together; never had he felt a sense of wholeness.

Killing Bessie Mears puts Bigger in the position of a questor, consciously searching for an identity—"a sense of wholeness"—that will enable him to "be at home" in his society, "to be a part of the world, to lose himself in it so he could find himself, to be allowed a chance to live like others, even though he was black." From this point forward no other action has greater meaning. After the newspaper headlines announce "AUTHORITIES HINT SEX CRIMES," Bigger feels alienation settle down around him again: "Those words excluded him utterly from the world." He knows now that the meaning of his acts will be denied by the whites in their blind fury to capture and kill him. The accusation of sexual violation denies the individuality of his action, "cuts him dead" again. He knows that white society will refuse to see and confirm his new sense of identity, his real self, which he created by murdering Mary and Bessie, the dual images of his psychosocial oppression. Murdering Bessie, Charles James argues, "is Bigger's acknowledgement of his own impending death. He knows he must be caught, so from that moment his energy is devoted to salvaging 'spiritual victory.' "

The ambiguity of Mary Dalton's death required, for Wright's satisfaction, an unambiguous and legitimate murder, for which Bigger can confess and be punished. Lest he again create a story that bankers' daughters might tearfully enjoy, he wedded the American, Dreiserian naturalist tradition and the Russian, Dostoevskian existential tradition to make Bigger's passion for murder as broadly meaningful as possible. Against the resistance of his friend Jane Newton to his plan for killing off Bessie, Wright was adamant: "But I have to get rid of her. She must die!" he insisted (Fabre). Killing Bessie was thus an act of self-liberation for Wright as well as for Bigger. At the very least,

> Bigger's murder of Bessie marked a new stage in Wright's literary evolution: everything that he had learned from his naturalist models up to this point had prevented him from allowing his characters to give in to these demonic temptations, but now Bigger claimed his right to "create" in the existentialist meaning of the word, by rejecting the accidental nature of his first murder with this further proof of his power to destroy. (Michel Fabre, The Unfinished Quest of Richard Wright)

But more than this, I think, can be ventured. Wright's conception of Bigger as existential killer, forging out of the violence in his psyche a desperate and necessary identity, served also to manifest what Daniel Aaron calls "his hidden and perhaps repressed opposition to the Party." Wright's intense concern with Bigger's psychological motives and existential plight were not the flowerings of his Marxist perspective. Wright, as Aaron suggests, was leading a sort of intellectual double life:

> One side of him—the Black Marxist, very likely a true believer in the Party's fight against its enemies at home and abroad—contributed useful articles and poems and stories to the Party press. The other and private side tried to explain and define the meaning of being Black in white America, tried to discover his own identity and in effect, to create himself.

Wright's "private" perspective fostered his insistence on the personal, psychological dimensions of the black experience, and brought him, inevitably, into conflict with the essentially pamphleteering approach of the American Communists.

In a letter to Mike Gold, written shortly after Gold's defense of *Native Son* in the *Daily Worker* of April 29, 1940, Wright attacked the simplistic agitprop and proletarian-heroes-vs.-capitalist-villains mentality of many in the Party:

> An assumption which says that a Communist writer must follow well established lines of perception and feeling, must deal with that which is readily recognizable and typical, must depict reality only in terms of how it looks from a common and collective plane of reality ... might seem sound. But I think those who put forward this reasoning forget the international framework in which we live and struggle today. ... Are we Communist writers to be confined merely to the political and economic spheres of reality and leave the dark

and hidden places of the human personality to the Hitlers and the Goebbels? I refuse to believe such. . . . Not to plunge into the complex jungle of human relationships and analyze them is to leave the field to the fascists and I won't and can't do that.

This vehement dissent from Party tradition, if not doctrine, was the beginning of Wright's dissociation from the Communists. He had found a supportive community amongst them, and through that community had found friends and a wife. But now the Party too had become a limiting and censoring authority in his life. His Communist readers were puzzled and displeased with his creation, Bigger Thomas. In the same letter to Gold, Fabre reports, "Wright complained that Bigger's humanity, so obvious to him, meant so little to them, and that Ben Davis [a prominent and powerful black Communist] thought Max should have pleaded 'not guilty.' "

Part of the fault is Wright's, for his long interpolation of Max's sociological appeal, while it puts across a necessary ideological interpretation of Bigger's situation, nevertheless serves to distract the reader's attention from Bigger's strategies for dealing with his final days. Kenneth Burke has attempted to justify Wright's handling of Max by arguing that the lawyer's long address is a "conceptual epitome" of the novel's emotional themes, "a culmination of the book in the sense that an essayist's last chapter might recapitulate in brief the argument of his whole book." In Burke's view, Wright, "after the symbolic committing of the offences through his imaginative identification with Bigger, had thus ritualistically 'transcended' the offences. . . . His role as Marxist critic transcended his role as Negro novelist." As indebted as I am to Burke in general, I must disagree with him in this particular. Book 3 of *Native Son* is not a capstone, some neatly trimmed and tailored conclusion of a case study, but rather an open-ended or suspended argument in which Wright is refusing to allow Bigger's individuality to be swallowed up or subsumed by Max's social analyses.

When Bigger's crime career ends, and he is captured and brought bumpily down to earth, dragged by his ankles into the cold, white, enshrouding snow, he is forced to set aside the sense of power that the murders had given him. The motive which has impelled his behavior throughout, however—his drive to find a viable sense of identity—is not cast aside. It is in fact now his only concern. In the face of his impending death he must come to terms with his life, find some way to accept it, if he is to be "at home" in the world before he leaves it forever. The release of his repressive tension in the acts of murder was not useless; as in a dream, Bigger's expression of his internalized, repressed aggression makes subconscious data available to his conscious mind. As Bigger considers his end, then, the complex social considerations of Max's argument do not figure in his thought. Max's elaborate analogies and metaphors are lost on Bigger. The materials of Bigger's final meditations are his own perceptions of the world around him, freed from stereotype and threat by his murderous acts. The structure of book 3 is provided by Bigger's efforts to realize out of these materials a vision of social relatedness, a sense of his being and belonging in the world. He asks:

> If he reached out his hands, and if his hands were electric wires, and if his heart were a battery giving life and fire to those hands, and if he reached out with his hands and touched other people, if he did that, would there be a reply, a shock?

And in seeking an answer Bigger rejects the alternatives his life had presented to him. As Robert Bone notes, "He rejects his family ('Go home, Ma.'); his fellow prisoners ('Are you the guy who pulled the Dalton job?'); the race leaders ('They almost like white folks when it comes to guys like me.') and religion." His spiritual victory, if he is to have one, must come from within, be composed entirely of the stuff of the self. "He was balanced on a hairline now, but there was no one to push him forward or backward, no one to make him feel that he had any value or worth—no one but himself."

Bigger comes through to a sense of identification with a human community at the very conclusion of his life and story. In his last conversation with Max, Bigger is calm and composed. Max has come "to offer compassion when Bigger seeks meaning," but "Bigger takes control of that final interview and 'comforts' Max" (Charles L. James). Max tries to give Bigger hope in a future collective human salvation, a Marxist vision of men reclaiming the world from their bosses. Bigger takes from what Max says confirmation of his new inner feeling, newly arrived at, that "at bottom all men lived as he had lived and felt as he had felt." Max tells him "the job in getting people to fight and have faith is in making them believe in what life has made them feel, making them feel that their feelings are as good as those of others." The feelings that Bigger accepts in himself are not, as so many critics have asserted, those of fear, shame, and hatred. But, Paul Siegel has recently noted, "it is hard to make men hear who will not listen. Seven times in the last page and a half of the novel Bigger cries out to Max, 'I'm all right,' the last time adding, 'For real, I am.'" Bigger is all right because, as he tries to tell Max, when he thinks about what Max has said he feels that he was right for wanting what he wanted—a sense of human integration, wholeness, identity.

> "They wouldn't let me live and I killed. Maybe it ain't fair to kill, and I reckon I really didn't want to kill. But when I think of why all the killing was, I begin to feel what I wanted, what I am. . . . I didn't want to kill! . . . But what I killed for, I *am!* It must've been pretty deep in me to make me kill! . . . What I killed for must've been good. . . . I didn't know I was really alive in this world until I felt things hard enough to kill for 'em."

Now Siegel is too busy defending Max to take note of the fact that Bigger is not defending his hate and shame but rather the motive that lay behind all the actions of his short life—the unsatisfied drive to reject the negative identity that the cultural stereotypes had forced on him and to discover an adequate, integral replacement. Max, for all his good will, has never really seen Bigger's individual humanity. As Donald Gibson notes, he "cannot accept the implications of Bigger's conclusions, nor indeed, can he fully understand the position that Bigger has finally arrived at." As he departs Max gropes for his hat, "like a blind man." At the last Bigger speaks as a free man and equal human being not to Max, who can not, finally, look him in the eye, but to Jan. Jan has paid his dues, suffered, and learned to see Bigger as a human being.

IV

At least implicitly, then, *Native Son* denies the notion of human salvation and integration through the medium of social process, even radical social process. Max, as spokesman for the political and social left, is unable either to give Bigger a satisfying ideological social vision or to measure the angle of vision from which Bigger views the world. Wright's separation from the Communist view of reality is foreshadowed here in the image of failed contact between Max and Bigger. If in Bigger's murderous rage Wright was elaborating personal as well as intellectual and social aggression, then in Bigger's rejection of Max's view of reality as inadequate Wright was repudiating the masked authority of the Party. Deep down, Wright felt a continuing and unbridgeable alienation from family and society, from religion, custom, and community. The Party had, for a time, given him the support he needed to articulate, albeit in symbolic terms, the elements of his situation. The symbolic outering of inner conflicts that reached back into personal and familial history reduced the pressure within and enabled him to marry and to carry on a career, but it also made clearer to him the essential loneliness incumbent on an person who, for whatever reason, must create a sense of values for himself.

Bigger Thomas's Quest for Voice and Audience in Richard Wright's *Native Son*

JAMES A. MILLER

Critical commentary about *Native Son* has invariably focused on the meaning of the final section of the novel, particularly Max's impassioned speech to the judge in his vain attempt to save Bigger Thomas's life and the final encounter between Max and Bigger at the end of the novel. Max's appearance in the novel has been regarded by many critics—among them Irving Howe, Robert Bone, Dan McCall, Edward Margolies, and Russell Brignano—as an ideological intrusion which disrupts the artistic unity of *Native Son*.[1] To the extent to which Max speaks for Bigger Thomas and, by implication, for Richard Wright—so the argument goes—Wright succumbs to his own ideological (i.e., political) impulses at the expense of his literary artistry. One important consequence of the centrality some readers and critics confer upon Max's role in *Native Son* is that it inevitably leads to the conclusion that Bigger Thomas himself is inarticulate, incapable of negotiating the conflict between "thought" and "feeling" which defines his emotional life for a great deal of the novel, incapable of telling his own story and, therefore, of defining himself.[2] To be sure, Bigger's story is presented from the perspective of a third-person narrator who is clearly more politically informed and verbally articulate than Bigger himself, and, within the novel itself, readers are confronted with a variety of voices—ranging from Buckley, the State's Attorney, to Max—which seek to define Bigger's reality. Nevertheless, the concluding scene of the novel clearly belongs to Bigger and his recovery of his voice at this crucial moment in *Native Son* not only undermines the argument that Max functions as a spokesman for Wright's political views but also challenges the view that Bigger himself is inarticulate.

The insistence by some critics that Max functions as authorial spokesman seems to derive from the rather mechanical equation of Max's political beliefs (and legal tactics) with those of the Communist Party and, therefore, with Wright's ideological viewpoint. But this perspective tends to overlook the artistic and ideological complexity of *Native Son* and, indeed—as Mikhail Bakhtin points out—the stylistic uniqueness of the novel as a genre:

Reprinted from *Callaloo*, 9 (Summer 1986): 501–6.

its incorporation of a range of *heterogeneous* stylistic unities into a structured artistic system. In Bakhtin's words:

> The novel can be defined as a diversity of social speech types (sometimes even diversity of languages) and a diversity of individual voice, artistically organized. . . . Authorial speech, the speeches of narrators, inserted genres, the speech of characters are merely those fundamental compositional unities with whose help heteroglossia can enter the novel; each of them permits a multiplicity of social voices and a wide variety of their links and interrelationships.[3]

Bakhtin's definition of the novel as a multiplicity of voices is particularly useful in this context, it seems to me. It cautions us against isolating any single language system (in this case, Max's speech) as a direct and unmediated expression of authorial intention; it directs our attention to the possibility that there are other voices and communities in *Native Son* which deserve close attention; and it requires us to pay careful attention to the various speech communities Bigger Thomas encounters on his quest for voice and audience.

To begin with, it should be clear that Bigger Thomas is far from the inarticulate character many critics claim him to be. Bigger is sullen, brooding, brusque, and sometimes violent in his attitude towards his family and immediate community, but he is definitely *not* inarticulate. If we define the pattern of call-and-response in the Afro-American community as a dynamic exchange between speaker and audience, one which elicits responsive speech from the audience and encourages the audience to respond with its own variation on the performer's song or story, there are numerous examples of Bigger Thomas's participation in this pattern in *Native Son*. Early in the novel, for example, after Bigger and Gus have amused themselves by the ritual of "playing white," the following exchange occurs:

> "You know where the white folks live?"
> "Yeah," Gus said, pointing eastward. "Over across the 'line'; over there on Cottage Grove Avenue."
> "Naw; they don't," Bigger said.
> "What you mean?" Gus asked, puzzled. "Then, where do they live?"
> Bigger doubled his fist and struck his solar plexus.
> "Right down here in my stomach," he said.
> Gus looked at Bigger searchingly, then away, as though ashamed.
> "Yeah; I know what you mean," he whispered.
> "Every time I think of 'em, I *feel* 'em," Bigger said.
> "Yeah; and in your chest and throat, too," Gus said.
> "It's like fire."
> "And sometimes you can't hardly breathe. . . ."
> Bigger's eyes were wide and placid, gazing into space.
> "That's when I feel like something awful's going to happen to me . . ." Bigger paused, narrowed his eyes. "Naw; it ain't like something going to happen to me. It's . . . like I was going to do something I can't help. . . ."

"Yeah!" Gus said with uneasy eagerness. His eyes were full of a look compounded of fear and admiration for Bigger. "Yeah; I know what you mean. It's like you going to fall and don't know where you going to land. . . ."[4]

The ease with which Gus anticipates what Bigger is going to say, the way their voices overlap and co-mingle in this conversation tends to undermine Wright's assertion, in "How Bigger Was Born," that Bigger ". . . through some quirk of circumstance . . . had become estranged from the religion and the folk culture of his race."[5] Bigger, in fact, belongs to a specific speech community within the larger black community, one which is governed by its own norms and values: the world of the black, urban, male *lumpenproletariat*. Not only is Bigger articulate in this world, he exercises considerable power within it. Bigger realizes, perhaps more fully than Gus, Jack, and G. H., that fear and shame are the dominant forces in the world he inhabits; and, by successfully manipulating these emotions, externalizing them—as he does when he pulls his knife on Gus in the pool-room—he gains power over this world, or at least manages to keep it at bay.

Bigger Thomas's quest for voice and audience has therefore little to do with his relationships with the black community, tension and conflict-ridden as they may be, but is inextricably connected to his perceptions of the white world. In other words, Bigger's quest for voice and audience is essentially Other-directed, defined by his need to struggle with externally determined definitions of the self. As Wright observes:

> To Bigger and his kind white people were not really people; they were a sort of great natural force, like a stormy sky looming overhead, or like a deep swirling river stretching suddenly at one's feet in the dark. As long as he and his black folks did not go beyond certain limits, there was no need to fear that white force. But whether they feared it or not, each and every day of their lives they lived with it; even when words did not sound its name, they acknowledged its reality. As long as they lived here in this prescribed corner of the city, they paid mute tribute to it.[6]

The white world represents, in Bakhtin's terms, the world of "authoritative discourse":

> The authoritative word demands that we acknowledge it, that we make it our own; it binds us, quite independently of any power it might have to persuade us internally; we encounter it with its authority already fused to it. The authoritative word is located in a distanced zone, organically connected with a past that is felt to be hierarchically higher. . . . It is a *prior* discourse. It is therefore not a question of choosing it from among other possible discourses that are equal. It is given . . . in lofty spheres, not those of familiar contact. Its language is a special . . . language. . . . It is akin to taboo. . . . It demands our unconditional allegiance. . . . It enters our verbal consciousness as a compact and indi-

visible mass; one must either totally affirm it, or totally reject it. It is indissolubly fused with its authority—with political power, an institution, a person—and it stands and falls together with that authority.[7]

It is within this world of "authoritative discourse"—symbolized by the billboard of the State's Attorney in the opening pages of the novel, the distortions of African reality at the Regal Theatre, the liberal pieties [of] the Dalton family, the inflammatory rhetoric of the press, and the blatantly racist arguments of the State's Attorney—that Bigger must struggle to discover his voice and, presumably, an audience which will give assent to his testimony.

But what is the nature of the dialogue Bigger Thomas seeks, and with whom? As readers of *Native Son,* we know the sense of elation Bigger experiences in the aftermath of Mary Dalton's accidental death, the ease with which he accepts responsibility for his action and confers meaning upon it, the way in which his secret knowledge establishes further distance between himself and his family, the sense of power he temporarily achieves over a white world trapped smugly in its own assumptions of racial superiority; yet, one of the questions which has always intrigued me as a reader is: why doesn't Wright allow Bigger Thomas to escape, say somewhere between the first and second books of *Native Son?* What would be the imaginative and ideological implications of Wright exercising such an artistic choice? The text of the novel provides us with a clear answer:

> He wanted suddenly to stand up and shout, telling them that he had killed a rich white girl, a girl whose family was known to all of them. Yes; if he did that a look of startled horror would come over their faces. But, no. He would not do that, even though the satisfaction would be keen. . . . He wanted the keen thrill of startling them, but felt that the cost was too great. He wished that he had the power to say what he had done without the fear of being arrested; he wished that he could be an idea in their minds; that his black face and the image of his smothering Mary and cutting off her head and burning her could hover before their eyes as a terrible picture of reality which they could see and feel and yet not destroy. He was not satisfied with the way things stood now; he was a man who had come in sight of a goal, then had won it, and in winning it had seen just within his grasp another goal, higher, greater. He had learned to shout and had shouted and no ear had heard him.[8]

Bigger will not be satisfied, in other words, until his actions are recognized by the world whose attention he seeks. And it is here that we see how completely Bigger's quest for voice and audience are determined by his fascination with the white world.

For Bigger, in fact, *does* achieve recognition for his actions from his girlfriend, Bessie. As we know, Bessie remains an unacknowledged character—except as evidence—by the State's Attorney, by Max, and by many critics as well, yet she is an important figure in Bigger's life. Like Gus, Jack, and G. H. she participates in Bigger's world and understands its terms. Bessie knows Bigger so well that she realizes fairly quickly that he has murdered Mary Dalton and elicits a confession from him. Enlisted by Bigger as an unwilling accomplice in his inept kidnapping scheme, Bessie articulates the pain of her life with all of the passion of a blues singer, a testimony to which Bigger nods his head and assents, but a song which he clearly does not want to hear. And when Bigger rapes and murders Bessie, he effectively severs his ties to the black community. From this point in the novel until its conclusion, Bigger functions essentially as a soloist.

It is in this context that Max emerges in *Native Son* as an intermediary between Bigger Thomas and the white world. Throughout the novel, Bigger's voice falters in the presence of white people: in his encounter with Mr. and Mrs. Dalton; with Peggy, the housekeeper; with Mary and Jan, with Britten and Buckley. Virtually all of these exchanges are conducted in the interrogatory mode, with Bigger confining himself to terse, monosyllabic responses. Max interrogates Bigger too, but the difference between Max and the other white characters Bigger encounters is that Max addresses Bigger as a human being rather than as a social type. This is clearly the kind of human encounter for which Bigger has been yearning throughout the novel, one which has been presumably missing up until this point, and Bigger instinctively and immediately places his trust in Max. Nevertheless, while Max and Bigger communicate reasonably well in their private conversations, Max's defense of Bigger in the public sphere reveals that Max, too, suffers from some of the limitations of the white world.

There is, first of all, the problem of the legal strategies Max chooses to pursue in his defense of Bigger Thomas. In his review of *Native Son* for the New York *Sunday Worker,* Benjamin Davis, a leading black official in the American Communist Party during the 1940s, correctly pointed out that Max's defense of Bigger is seriously flawed and, in fact, atypical of the kind of legal defense the Communist Party would conduct. Max does not challenge the false charge of rape against Bigger Thomas, he pleads Bigger guilty to both the rape and murder of Mary Dalton, even though it is clear that the murder is accidental. Finally—Davis concludes—"Max should have argued for Bigger's acquittal in the case, and should have helped stir the political pressure of the Negro and white masses to get that acquittal."[9]

Secondly, there is the question of whether Max fully understands Bigger Thomas. It is true that Max's probing questions awaken Bigger to a sense of his own reality which he has not experienced before, but it is also clear—as Donald Gibson has pointed out—that Max is primarily concerned with the social and symbolic implications of Bigger's situation while Bigger is concerned with his personal fate.[10] Max *appropriates* many of the statements Bigger makes and incorporates them into the structure of his appeal to the judge, but it is clear that Max's argument will fall on deaf ears. Not only is Bigger's ultimate fate at the hands of the court a foregone conclusion, it is also clear that Bigger himself does not grasp the meaning of Max's speech.

Indeed, throughout the third book of *Native Son*, Bigger Thomas remains curiously detached from the action; he functions as a witness, an auditor to the public debate which rages about him, but not as a participant in the dialogue. The public exchanges between Max and the State's Attorney, Buckley, represent two attempts to define, in opposing ideological terms, the meaning of Bigger Thomas's actions—and, by extension, his existence—in the public sphere of "authoritative discourse." In the final analysis, however, Bigger repudiates both arguments—as we see in the concluding conversation between Max and Bigger, when Bigger blurts out: "What I killed for, I *am!*" and Max backs away from him, groping for his hat like a blind man.

Max does not speak for Bigger Thomas, nor does he speak for Richard Wright. He attempts to *represent* Bigger, in both a legal and linguistic sense, and fails. Nevertheless, Max's presence in the novel does have an important bearing on the development of Bigger's consciousness. Through his relationship with Max, Bigger Thomas is able to further de-mystify the power of the white world over him, a process which has been unfolding since the accidental murder of Mary Dalton. And even though Bigger does not understand Max's language, he nevertheless appropriates it for his own purposes.

"The word in language," Bakhtin observes, "is half someone else's. It becomes one's own only when the speaker populates it with his own intentions, his own accent, when he appropriates the word, adapting it to his own expressive and semantic intention. Prior to this moment of appropriation, the word . . . exists in other people's mouths, in other people's contexts, serving other people's intentions: it is from there that one must take the word, and make it one's own,"[11] seizing it and transforming it into private property.

This is precisely what Bigger Thomas does in the concluding pages of *Native Son.* Having shaken the "authoritative discourse" of the white world to its foundations and triggered off an ideological debate which seeks to define his place in the public sphere, Bigger Thomas, partly inspired by Max's rhetoric, chooses a position that places him decisively outside of the existing social framework.

Nevertheless, Bigger Thomas's achievement of the voice he assumes at the end of the novel has not been without its price. In cultural terms, the strategies Bigger pursues to evade white society after Mary Dalton's death—particularly the gratuitous murder of Bessie—only serve to isolate him from the black community. In social and political terms, Bigger's actions not only invite the wrath of a racist society but confirm his place within popular mythology. In personal terms, Bigger seems to achieve a level of human recognition—of sorts—through his relationships with Jan and Max, accepting Jan's offer of comradeship by, for the first time in his life dropping the use of "mister" in front of a white man's name. But Max—as we have seen—recoils from Bigger's final speech, and the call which Bigger issues in his assertion "I Am" does not receive responsive testimony from Max. Rather, we are left with the final image of Bigger Thomas facing his impending death in proud and lonely isolation, a soloist listening to the sound of his own song.

Notes

1.   See Irving Howe, *A World More Attractive* (New York: Horizon, 1963) 104; Robert Bone, *Richard Wright* (Minneapolis: U of Minnesota P, 1969) 23; Dan McCall, *The Example of Richard Wright* (New York: Harcourt, 1969) 90; Edward Margolis, *The Art of Richard Wright* (Carbondale: Southern Illinois UP, 1969) 114–15; and Russell Carl Brignano, *Richard Wright: An Introduction to the Man and his Work* (Pittsburgh: U of Pittsburgh P, 1970) 81.

2.   See Robert B. Stepto, "I Thought I Knew These People: Richard Wright & the Afro-American Literary Tradition," *The Massachusetts Review* 18:3 (Autumn 1977): 525–42.

3.   M. M. Bakhtin, "Discourse in the Novel," in *The Dialogic Imagination* (Austin: The U of Texas P, 1981) 262–63.

4.   Richard Wright, *Native Son* (New York: Harper & Brothers, 1940) 18–19.

5.   Richard Wright, "How Bigger Was Born," reprinted in Richard Abcarian, ed., *Richard Wright's Native Son: A Critical Handbook* (Belmont, Ca.: Wadsworth, 1970) 19.

6.   *Native Son* 97.

7.   Bakhtin 342–43.

8.   *Native Son* 110.

9.   John M. Reilly, ed., *Richard Wright: The Critical Reception* (New York: Burt Franklin, 1978) 75. See also Paul N. Siegal, "The Conclusion of Richard Wright's *Native Son.*" in Richard Macksey and Frank E. Moorer, eds., *Richard Wright: A Collection of Critical Essays* (Englewood Cliffs, N.J., Prentice-Hall, 1984) 106–16.

10.   Donald B. Gibson, "Wright's Invisible Native Son," in *Richard Wright: A Collection of Critical Essays* 98.

11.   Bakhtin 293–94.

Tone in *Native Son*

Robert J. Butler

The novel's unique point of view helps create a tone that is consistently ironic. As we have seen, sharp ironies are often produced by the discrepancy between Bigger's explicit views and the author's implied attitudes. After Bigger has seen a film about upper-class whites, he thinks the film has given him new insights about white people that will lead to "something big" (36) because he can now discover how they make money and dominate society. But Wright's implied attitudes make it ironically clear to the reader that the film has given Bigger a number of misleading stereotypes that will blind him to the true nature of whites and cause him real trouble later on. Likewise, Bigger thinks his extortion plot will give him money and power, but Wright's narrative voice undercuts his views with blatant ironies because Bigger's plan is so crudely envisioned and executed that it is bound to blow up in his face. In the same way, when Bigger is tricked by Buckley into signing his confession he thinks such an act will make him feel better, but Wright presents the scene as a cheap betrayal of Bigger that results in his feeling even worse about himself, for after he has signed the confession and realized how he has been manipulated by Buckley, he feels "empty and beaten" (288).

Irony is also produced from Bigger's own perspective as he continually observes a wide gap between the democratic promises of American life and the harsh realities around him. This kind of irony is particularly evident in an early scene in which Bigger and Gus hang around the streets and consider their opportunities as black people in a white-dominated society. Bigger is fascinated with the movement he detects in the world around him because he instinctively associates this movement with expanded possibilities leading to human growth. As he watches the clouds drift by, the cars whirring through the streets, and people walking about, the narrator tells us, "Every movement in the street evoked a casual curiosity in him" (19). Bigger's deepest yearnings are evoked when he spots a plane overhead skywriting the word "USE." Although he would like to "use" his life productively by becoming a pilot, he knows Gus is right when he reminds Bigger that such "flying" is reserved for

Reprinted from *Native Son: The Emergence of a New Black Hero* by Robert J. Butler (Boston: Twayne, 1991): pp. 88–103, with the permission of Simon & Schuster and the author.

whites. Bigger realizes he will never get a chance to use his talents, and so he cultivates an essentially ironic view of American life.

This ironic view is dramatized powerfully when he and Gus "play white" (21) shortly after they have discussed the plane flying overhead. Parodying the roles of generals directing armies, J. P. Morgan dominating the business world, and the president of the United States organizing a cabinet meeting, they "leaned against the wall and laughed" (22). Although this game makes them fully aware of their impotence in a white-dominated society, the rich ironies they enjoy as they enact the roles of whites gives them a way of psychologically coping with their situation, for such irony not only results in laughter-producing awareness but also enables them to translate their anger into a kind of social protest. As Bigger enacts the role of president, he indirectly articulates his anger about being black in a white-dominated society:

> "Well, you see, the niggers is raising sand all over the country," Bigger said, struggling to keep back his laughter. "We've got to do something with these black folks."
> "Oh if it's about the niggers, I'll be right there, Mr. President," Gus said. (22)

The ironies of this scene closely resemble those found in the blues, a form of black folk art Wright admired for its "paradoxical" ability to make "an almost exultant affirmation of life" even while carrying a "burden of woe and melancholy."[1] Like the blues singer, Bigger is able to look at the painful facts of his situation as a black person victimized by a racist society, frankly observing, "We black and they white" (23), and "They don't let us do *nothing*" (22). But like the blues musician, he can also cope with his situation and to some extent psychologically master it through an act of ironic awareness, for blues irony produces both laughter, which transforms pain into pleasure, and awareness, which gives the underdog a psychological weapon to use against his oppressors. As Ralph Ellison observed, the blues have a "sheer toughness of spirit"[2] that enables blacks not only to survive American racism but to overcome some of its psychological burdens. When Gus and Bigger "play white," they clearly exhibit this toughness of spirit, turning a condition of physical oppression into a state of ironic awareness.

Blues ironies resonate throughout *Native Son,* from its very first words to its final image. The novel's title establishes the central character as a representative American figure who desires to achieve the American dream but who has to live an American nightmare because history has excluded him from the mainstream of American life. And the novel's final sentence describes Bigger's "faint, wry, bitter, smile" (392) as he considers the ironic fact that Max, whose political convictions commit him to a belief in universal brotherhood, cannot translate such ideas into action in the real world by simply turning around and confronting Bigger face to face as a human being.

Similarly, most of the novel's major characters are named in a way that reinforces the novel's ironic tone. As we have seen, Bigger's first and last names call to mind the stereotypes of "Uncle Tom" and "nigger," but his portrayal in the novel ironically establishes him as a human being who transcends these stereotypes, even though almost none of the people around him are aware of this transcendence. The Daltons are ironically named after a form of color blindness called Daltonism. Although they see themselves as good liberal people who are "color-blind" in the positive sense of being without racial prejudice, the novel establishes them as "color-blind" in the negative sense, for it reveals that they are tragically blind to the way a white system oppresses blacks and how they as slumlords are part of the problem. Bigger's brother is named Buddy to suggest a close personal relationship, but in fact the two are strangers to each other because ghetto life has divided members of the black family against one another, separating them with "walls" of fear and mistrust. Mary Dalton's first name might initially suggest a parallel with the mother of Christ; but the allusion is bitterly ironic because she is neither a virgin nor a person who can offer Bigger redemptive love; on the contrary, the "love" she offers Bigger leads him to his doom. Jan Erlone's name is also heavily ironic. Although he sees himself as a sort of Janus figure who will lead people to a new world of brotherhood, he is unable even to overcome his own condition—suggested by his last name—of being alone. The ideology that has promised to give him a sense of solidarity with the masses has ironically set him apart from others, making him a sort of pariah.

Given the novel's overall tone of irony, it is not surprising that many of its central scenes are powerfully ironic inversions of conventional scenes from traditional literature; that is, they use motifs from these scenes but turn their meanings inside out, producing effects exactly the opposite of those contained in the original scenes. Bigger's killing of Mary Dalton, for example, is a remarkable inversion of a love scene from a romantic novel. This scene—perhaps the most revealing one Wright ever wrote—ironically describes violence in terms of romantic lovemaking to suggest that Bigger's creative and destructive drives have been snarled, locking him in a psychological trap that suffocates his deepest human impulses. The episode begins in a simple, erotic way, with Mary attempting to arouse Bigger sexually. In the car she tells him he is "very nice," deliberately sprawls her legs "wide apart" (80), and leans her head on his shoulder. When she catches him looking at her exposed legs, she laughs and asks him to carry her out of the car, while her "dark eyes looked feverishly at him" (81). Although she is somewhat intoxicated, she is much more in control of herself than she allows Bigger to realize. Swaying against him, she asks him to take her up the "back way" (82) to her room. Although she is surely conscious enough to give him directions and reject his advances if she wishes, she does not resist "the tips of his fingers feeling the soft swell of her breasts" (82). Indeed, she clearly desires to make love to him, her world's forbidden fruit. As he carries her up the stairs, "she pulled heavily on him, her arm around his neck" (82) and her hair brushing his lips. Fully aroused now, Bigger feels "possessed" (83) by her, *his* world's forbidden fruit.

Several erotic images are then used to describe the two entering Mary's room. As his fingers spread over Mary's back "her face came toward him and her lips touched his" (84). Although he wants to leave after he has "laid" (84) her on the bed, he is overtaken by sexual desires. When he tightens his fingers on her breasts and kisses her twice, she moves toward him, clearly encouraging his actions.

Mrs. Dalton's entry into the room abruptly turns their lovemaking into death-making. But Wright artfully persists in using erotic images to describe the scene, turning them inside out for shockingly ironic effect. As Mrs. Dalton approaches them, all of Bigger's violent tendencies become "erected": "he grew tight and full, as though about to explode" (84). When Mary's fingernails tear at him, he covers her entire face with a pillow, and her suffocation is described in terms of copulation: "Mary's body surged upward and he pushed downward upon the pillow with all of his weight, determined that she must not move or make any sound that would betray him. . . . Again Mary's body heaved and he held the pillow in a grip that took all of his strength. For a long time he felt the sharp pain of her fingernails biting into his wrists" (84–85). After her "surging and heaving" (85) body finally relaxes and Mrs. Dalton leaves the room, Bigger orgasmically utters "a long gasp" (85). In the afterglow of this strange experience, he is depicted as "weak and wet with sweat" (85), listening for some time to his heavy breathing filling the darkness.

Bigger's reaction to his killing Mary can likewise be seen as an ironic reversal of the sort of "conversion" experience depicted in Christian tradition dating back to St. Augustine's *Confessions*. Although such religious conversions depict a dramatic moment of awakening in which a person turns from an "old" life that has trapped him in sin to a "new" life that cleanses him of sin and points the way to redemption, Bigger's killing of Mary is not a dramatic change in his character but instead, the culmination of violent tendencies that have been boiling in him for a long time. When Bigger thinks "he had murdered and created a new life for himself" (101), his thought is ironically undercut by the fact that such a "murder" will lead directly to his death in the electric chair rather than to a new life. Likewise, Bigger is wrong when he sees himself as undergoing a baptism through his killing of Mary. Such violence does not make him "like a man reborn" and it does not make him "like a man risen up from a long illness" (106); instead, his acts of violence come from the "old" Bigger, a person made sick by a pathological society intent on destroying him.

The novel's final scene is also a revealing inversion of the endings of conventional gangster movies and crime stories appearing in popular magazines. As Ross Pudaloff and others have pointed out, Wright was fascinated by popular films and was also an avid reader of such magazines as *Argosy All-Story Magazine* and *Flynn's Detective Weekly,* which featured sensationalistic stories about hideous crimes being solved and criminals being justly punished for such crimes.³ In writing the ending of *Native Son,* Wright consciously used many of the conventions of popular films and stories about crime but inverted them for subtly ironic effect. He rejects altogether the simple moralistic allegory that prevails in popular films and detective fiction in favor of a much more complex and ironic vision. The popular crime literature of Wright's day always presents execution as an appropriate punishment for "murderers" and suggests that society is cleansed when it destroys such people, who are a threat to the social order. But as Wright presents the ending of *Native Son,* society has wrongly condemned a man to death for two reasons: (1) Legally, it has convicted him of crimes he did not commit, since Bigger did not rape Mary and his killing of her was accidental, and (2) morally, such a punishment is not justified, because Bigger is not a pathological monster who is a threat to the social order but a person who has undergone a profound psychological change that has cleansed him of his compulsion for violence. Because society's killing of Bigger cannot be justified on either legal or moral grounds, Wright ironically links society's actions with Bigger's earlier killings of Mary and Bessie. All three deaths take place when intimate human activity is initiated but is then aborted by environmentally induced fear and hatred. Just as Bigger's and Mary's lovemaking is inverted into killing when Mrs. Dalton strikes terror into Bigger's heart, Bessie is murdered when Bigger's attempts to "love" her are overcome by his fear that she will somehow reveal his whereabouts to the police. In a comparable way, the serious conversation begun by Bigger and Max at the end of the novel is cut off by Max's terror, Bigger's incomplete understanding, and society's fear that the real human bonds might eventually develop between two such hated people. *Native Son* therefore concludes with the same brutal irony that has vibrated throughout the novel: Death comes precisely at the threshold of our most deeply human experiences. This finally becomes Wright's most terrible revelation of a social world that encourages and even necessitates fear and hatred but violently blocks love and understanding wherever it emerges. Drawing upon popular films and stories that formulaically conclude with reassuring allegorical scenes equating criminals with evil and society with goodness, Wright transforms these materials, ending his novel with provocative ironies that force us to think well beyond the clichés of popular art.

Wright not only used such ironic inversions in key scenes but also employed broader patterns of irony throughout the novel. His handling of Christian imagery and symbolism is a particularly good example. Wright, who was brought up in part by a grandmother who was deeply committed to fundamentalist religion, rebelled strongly against conventional Christianity at a very early age, but he consciously used Christian motifs, usually for ironic purposes, in all his major fiction. This is particularly true of *Native Son.* From the very beginning of the novel the conventional religion practiced by Bigger's mother is ironically juxtaposed against the harsh realities the Thomas family has to face. Rather than helping her cope with these harsh realities, the religion practiced by Mrs. Thomas encourages her to escape to a world of illusion that temporarily enables her to feel better but in the long run makes her problems worse. At the end of the novel's first scene, which portrays the Thomas family trapped by a racist environment, Mrs. Thomas sings a spiritual that envisions life as a liberating journey directed by a powerful and benevolent God. But while the song imagines human life as a "mountain railroad" controlled by an "engineer" who helps people make "the run successful from cradle to grave" (14), the actual circumstances of the Thomas family ironically contradict this uplifting view, for since the death of Bigger's father in a southern race riot, nobody has been able to direct the family in any effective way. As a result, their life has been anything but a smoothly run journey and they have alternated between utter paralysis and purposeless drifting. The song "irked" (14) Bigger because he sees its affirmative imagery as a bleak contrast to his family's actual situation. He also is annoyed a few minutes later when his mother says grace at breakfast, thanking the Lord for "the food you done placed before us for the nourishment of our bodies" (14). Ironically, the only food they can afford to eat will give them little nourishment, consisting as it does of small amounts of coffee, bacon, and bread. Bigger therefore sees his mother's otherworldly religion as a cruel joke and often identifies such religion with the whiskey Bessie consumes, because both are palliatives that allow people to withdraw from reality, all the while eroding their will to change reality.

Whenever Bigger confronts the sort of religion his mother practices he responds to it in a bitterly ironic way. After he hears his mother saying during her evening prayers, "Lord, I want to be a Christian in my heart" (37), he immediately goes to his room, takes his gun from under his mattress, and puts it inside his shirt. While conventional Christianity reminds Bigger of his family's impotence and resignation, his gun provides him with a sense of power. In book 2 he likewise rejects the otherworldly religion he observes black people practicing during a church service. As he listens to them singing "Stealaway to Jesus" (237–38) he consciously rejects such passivity and "surrender" (237). He instead defines himself in terms of violent rebellion, refusing to surrender to the police and resolving to use his gun rather than prayer as a means of coping with his difficulties. He rejects Reverend Hammond's Christianity in book 3 for the same reasons. When Reverend Hammond begs him to forget the earthly world and pray for deliverance in the next world, Bigger imagines the preacher's religion as "a vast black silent void" (263). Ironically, Bigger at this precise moment of his life feels the need for light rather than darkness, and self-actualization rather than self-abnegation.

Conventional religious imagery is repeatedly undercut by irony throughout the novel. When Mrs. Dalton enters Mary's bedroom and discovers that her daughter has been drinking, she instinctively prays over Mary so that Mary will mend her ways, little realizing that her daughter is quite dead.

When Bigger holds a hatchet over Mary's head before decapitating her, he is described as "pausing in an attitude of prayer" (91). While his outward posture might suggest sorrow over what he has done and even a desire to seek mercy, his inward thoughts, ironically, reveal only his grisly desire to cut off Mary's head so that he can fit her corpse into the furnace. Mr. Dalton is later perceived by Bigger as an omniscient "god" (164), but the ironic fact is that he is as blind and powerless as Bigger before a social system he can neither understand nor control.

Some readers have seen Bigger as a Christ figure who is "crucified" by white society and then achieves a kind of religious "salvation" by the end of the novel. But it is difficult to support this interpretation with a close reading of the novel. Unlike such books as Ken Kesey's *One Flew over the Cuckoo's Nest,* William Faulkner's *Light in August,* and Ignazio Silone's *Bread and Wine,* which tell the hero's story against a sustained pattern of allusions to Christ, *Native Son* makes but few explicit references to Christ's narrative when telling Bigger's story. And the few allusions to Christ in the novel are strongly ironic. Bigger certainly is not interested in taking Reverend Hammond's advice: "Be like Jesus. Don't Resist" (265). On the contrary, Bigger attacks his attackers and rebels against his condition in a most un-Christ-like way. When he removes the small cross from the chain around his neck and angrily throws it at the white people tormenting him, he shouts, "I can die without a cross" (313). As they torment him further by reminding him that only God can help him now and he had better put his soul in order, he cries out, "I ain't got no soul" (314).

Then too, Bigger's death at the end of the novel takes place on a much more private level than the death of Christ. While Christ was motivated by a love of humankind, Bigger goes to his death instead with a renewed sense of self-awareness. Even though Bigger does acquire a broader sympathy for those around him, these sympathies extend only to those with whom he has had personal contact. When Max asks him, "Do you love your people?" Bigger's reply is simply, "I don't know, Mr. Max" (330). And Wright certainly does not depict Bigger's death in messianic terms, as something that will regenerate the world. Unlike Christ, whose death created the possibility of salvation for humankind, Bigger dies "alone" (380) and his death leaves society and history unchanged. Bigger's story, when seen against the background of Christian narrative, therefore produces irony because its meanings jar so violently against the meanings of Christ's story.

Another broad pattern of ironic inversion in *Native Son* is the way it subverts the meanings of the Horatio Alger novels. As Michel Fabre has pointed out, Wright as a young man was "an avid reader of Horatio Alger" and believed deeply in "the myth of the self-made man, in the great American dream whereby everyone had an equal chance."[4] As an adult he came to see how the Alger myth was little more than a cruel joke for black people, since the doors of American opportunity were systematically closed to blacks because of their skin color. *Native Son* is therefore a conscious parody of the Alger novels, reducing to absurdity Alger's vision of America as an open society in which poor boys could go from "rags to riches" through good character, hard work, a little luck, and the support of a benevolent rich man. Boiled down to their simplest terms, all Alger novels repeat the same formula: A young orphan boy works his way from poverty to middle-class security by working hard at various menial jobs, educating himself at night, and performing heroic acts that eventually impress a gentleman who becomes his "sponsor." The typical Alger novel ends with the young boy proving his moral purity by altruistically performing an act that saves the life of a rich man's daughter. He is rewarded for his bravery in two ways: (1) In the short run, he is given a job in the rich man's business and is thus provided with an opportunity to work his way up the ladder of success, and (2) in the long run, he will marry the boss's daughter, securing his emotional happiness as well as his financial prosperity.

The Alger novels can be seen as secularized conversion narratives, in that they portray a dramatic transformation of a person from a penniless social outcast to a respectable citizen with unlimited possibilities. But the hero's "new life" is not generated by a mystical experience centered in Christ; rather, it is brought about by purely secular means, the hero's good character expressing itself in worldly acts of "service." The decisive force in such a process is not God's grace but a gentleman's goodwill. And the sign of conversion is not an inward sense of well-being but the accumulation of outward wealth and status.

Like Dreiser and Fitzgerald, Wright was fascinated with the Alger stories, seeing them as the expression of a fundamental American myth. *Native Son,* like *An American Tragedy* and *The Great Gatsby,* generates many of its most powerful meanings by consciously echoing and then ironically inverting the conventions of the Alger myth. To begin with, Bigger Thomas is like Alger's young hero in that he is at the bottom of American society and feels radically alone. Although he is not literally an orphan, he has lost his father in a race riot and has seen what is left of his family destroyed by the economic, social, and psychological pressures of American life. Like the Alger hero, Bigger wants to "rise" in American life, and he thinks he might be able to do this by coming to know a rich white man who will unlock the doors of American capitalism and show him the way to wealth. Coming out of the movie theater with Gus after they have watched a film about rich white people, Bigger is suddenly "filled with a sense of excitement about his new job" (35) because he feels that such a job will put him in contact with people who know the system and can teach him how to advance in it:

> Those were smart people; they knew how to get hold of money, millions of it. Maybe if he were working for them something would happen and he would get some of it. He would see just how they did it. Sure it was all a game and

white people knew how to play it. And rich white people were not so hard on Negroes; it was the poor whites who hated Negroes. . . . It was the rich white people who were smart and knew how to treat people. He remembered hearing somebody tell a story of a Negro chauffeur who had married a rich white girl and the girl's family had shipped them out of the country and had supplied them with money. (36)

Bigger's job as chauffeur therefore puts him precisely at the point where Alger's orphan boy is when he sells newspapers to rich men or shines their shoes. Although the job is menial, it locates him at the exact spot where poor and rich meet, thereby inspiring dreams of rising from a condition of poverty and magically entering the world of the rich. In its most romantic form, Bigger's dreams of success consist of marrying a "rich white girl" whose parents will transport him to a world of wealth and security. Bigger now sees rich white people as sponsors in a rags-to-riches novel, "smart," powerful people who can teach him to play the "game" of American success. Unlike poor whites, whose lowly status puts them in economic competition with blacks, rich whites are envisioned as benevolent mentors interested in helping deserving black people. Bigger's romantic vision of rich whites seems confirmed in his first meeting with the Daltons, when he discovers that they are liberal people who are well disposed toward blacks, have given large amounts of money to Negro education, and have also helped their previous chauffeur ascend the ladder of American success by sending him to evening school.

A closer look at the Daltons, however, reveals that they are quite different from the sponsors appearing in Alger novels and that Bigger ought to be very careful in his dealings with them. (As the novel turns out, he would have been better off had he obeyed his gut instincts and avoided them altogether.) Unlike Alger's gentlemen, who are moral guardians of the American system and oversee that system in an almost godly, omniscient way, the Daltons are "tragically blind" (362) and are therefore unable to help Bigger in his search for a better life.

First, they are blind to their own motives. Considering themselves to be philanthropists who unselfishly improve the lives of poverty-stricken blacks, they are unaware that they are instead driven by guilt stemming from the fact that their wealth is created by renting overpriced, substandard housing to blacks. Second, Mr. Dalton is blind to the nature of the economic and social system in which he participates. Although he consciously believes that hard work and good character enable a person to be a success in American life, he has made his fortune not by demonstrating good character but by exploiting ghetto blacks. When Max tries to make him see the connection between his wealth and the suffering of black people, he refuses to acknowledge this link, blindly declaring, "What do you want me to do? . . . Do you want me to die and atone for a suffering I never caused? I'm not responsible for the state of the world. I'm doing all one man can. I suppose you want me to take my money and fling it out to the millions who have nothing?" (274).

What Mr. Dalton fails to see is that he is *not* doing all he can to make America the open society it is portrayed to be in the Alger novels. By making his wealth from the systematic exploitation of black people and by not doing "something of a more fundamental nature" (274) to change the system, Mr. Dalton is closing, not opening, doors to people like Bigger Thomas. Mr. Dalton's "cold" question to Max implies that he lacks the human warmth truly to understand how he has caused much of the suffering he says he wants to alleviate. Rather than being a kindly sponsor to Bigger, Mr. Dalton is therefore one of Bigger's oppressors.

Similarly, Mary Dalton is an ironic inversion of the boss's daughter typically portrayed in the Alger books. Whereas Alger idealizes such figures as paragons of moral purity, Wright depicts Mary as sexually promiscuous and a heavy drinker. Whereas Alger sees the hero's marriage to the boss's daughter as a reward for the hero's own virtue, ensuring his entrance into a stable, fruitful, middle-class world, Wright makes it clear that Bigger and Mary could never marry, because a racist society forbids such unions. Despite the impressions he has received in movies and from apocryphal stories of chauffeurs marrying rich white girls, Bigger is barred from forming any kind of human relationship with Mary. As Max tells the court, American society has made people like Bigger and Mary strangers to each other. While they might occasionally engage in casual and secret sex, they could never develop a sustained and loving relationship, because society regards such relationships as the ultimate taboo. The final reward in Alger's novels is therefore forbidden to Bigger—he can never have the money, power, and status that Mary has by birth, and he can never "marry into" the comfortable world that Mary takes for granted. Ironically, his contact with Mary results not in expanded possibilities and a new life for Bigger but in his death.

That Bigger senses all this on a deeply subconscious level explains why his actual treatment of the Daltons is such a grim parody of how the typical Alger hero responds to his sponsors. Whereas Alger's orphan boy has a childlike trust in the rich gentleman who eventually becomes a father surrogate for him, Bigger is instinctively suspicious of the Daltons from the start and actually brings his gun with him on the day he reports to work. Whereas Alger's hero is eager to perform selfless acts of "service" to others in order to prove his moral worth to his sponsor, Bigger engages in criminal activity, trying to extort money from a rich man who represents an amoral system from which Bigger feels excluded. In a supremely ironic inversion of the central act of the Alger myth, Bigger does not fall in love with and marry the boss's daughter but instead kills her, decapitates her, and incinerates her in a furnace.

Wright's startling reversal of the Alger myth vividly emphasizes two main points. First, Wright clearly stresses that American capitalism does not work for blacks and other minorities. Such a system oppresses poor people on a daily basis, regardless of their good character or capacity for hard work. At best, American capitalism can make token gestures, for example, when the Daltons patronize their chauffeur by sending him to night school but then refuse to hire him in their business after he has graduated. Second, Wright emphasizes that blacks and other minorities must overturn American capitalism, pushing for radical changes that will ensure they become the "native sons" who fully share in the democratic possibilities of American life. Because the present system is rotten and corrupts people on all levels of society, from poor boys to rich sponsors, it must be replaced by a new system. As Max tells Mr. Dalton, "Something of a more fundamental nature must be done" (274) to make America the just and open society envisioned by the Founding Fathers and sentimentalized in the Alger books.

In "How Bigger Was Born" Wright observed that in writing *Native Son* he did not want to write a piece of fiction like his first book, *Uncle Tom's Children,* that could be mistaken for a sentimental story that would blur his reader's perceptions with tears: "I had written a book of short stories which was published under the title *Uncle Tom's Children.* When the reviews of that book began to appear, I realized I had made an awfully naïve mistake. I found that I had written a book which even banker's daughters could read and weep over and feel good about. I swore to myself that if I ever wrote another book, no one would weep over it; that it would be so hard and deep that they would have to face it without the consolation of tears" (xxvii).

Native Son's consistently ironic tone produces a "hard and deep" book that results in a lucid awareness of American reality rather than a sentimental outlook that gives the reader the "consolation of tears." It is essential to realize, however, that Wright's ironies are not so bitter and reductive that they make *Native Son* a bleakly nihilistic book that cancels out all human meaning to Bigger's experience. Wright manages to make important affirmations after his novel's corrosive ironies have dissolved what is false in American life. Even though conventional religious values are ironically undercut throughout the novel, Wright stresses that Bigger does have a need for "certainty and faith" (109) and that he has a powerful spiritual yearning to find "a center, a core, an axis" (238) to his life. As we have seen in previous chapters, he finally discovers a center to his life when he develops an existential "faith" in himself. Even though Wright strips this faith of standard religious meanings and surrounds it with the irony that the state will execute Bigger shortly after he has fashioned a human identity for himself, Wright does indeed celebrate the psychological "conversion" that Bigger achieves.

Even Wright's handling of the Alger myth is not ultimately pessimistic. After he has used irony to demolish the sentimental clichés of the Alger novels, he makes one more twist of irony to establish Bigger as a kind of "success story" after all. Just as Alger's hero achieves selfhood in his attempts to educate himself so that he can go from a condition of illiteracy to an ability to read and write, Bigger finally becomes a new kind of self-made man who has educated himself to the realities of American life and his own human nature. He clearly rejects the sort of formal education that Mr. Dalton proposes when he offers to send Bigger to night school, because Bigger realizes that such an education will enclose him in the impenetrable "night" that has blinded Dalton. Nevertheless, Bigger does informally educate himself by closely examining his own actions in the real world. This kind of self-education opens his eyes and enables him to undertake a decisive psychological journey. *Native Son* therefore subverts the conventions of the Alger myth in order to redefine that myth, ultimately positing a new kind of psychological and moral "success" for its hero.

Unlike fundamentally pessimistic works—such as Jean-Paul Sartre's *Nausea,* Samuel Beckett's *Happy Days,* and Louis-Ferdinand Céline's *Journey to the End of Night*—that employ massive patterns of irony to undercut all human meanings and thus envision modern experience as a colossal void, *Native Son* uses irony both to attack false values and to create new values in their place. As a result, Wright's masterwork possesses a thematic complexity missing in many modern books, especially those arising from existential and naturalistic traditions.

Notes

1. Foreword to *The Meaning of the Blues,* by Paul Oliver (New York: Collier Books, 1960), 9.
2. Ralph Ellison, *Shadow and Act* (New York: New American Library, 1966), 104.
3. Ross Pudaloff, "Celebrity as Identity: Richard Wright, *Native Son,* and Mass Culture," *Studies in American Fiction* 11 (Spring 1983): 4.
4. Michel Fabre, *The Unfinished Quest of Richard Wright,* trans. Isabel Barzun (New York: Morrow, 1973), 51.

An American Hunger

Andrew Delbanco

I first read *Native Son* in unreflective fascination when I was 16. I remember feeling queasy during the early scenes when the bubbly Chicago heiress Mary Dalton and her fast-talking radical boyfriend patronize a ghetto boy and conscript him as a tour guide for a cruise through the "black belt." Reading these scenes made me think of the time in grade school when I had invited a black child from the "projects" to my suburban home. After introducing him to my mother, I waited for him to join us for lunch, until his plate of ravioli had grown cold and I discovered that he had climbed out the window of our first-floor bathroom and run back down the hill to school. For nearly ten years I had not begun to imagine the mental storm that must have sent him out that window—until I read of Bigger's panic over whether to enter the Daltons' house through the front door or back, of his shrinking when the white house-maid approaches so close that he can "see a tiny mole at the corner of her mouth," and of his "misjudging how far back he was sitting" in an overplump chair, so that, "conscious of every square inch of skin on his black body," he has to struggle to his feet when the "amused" Mr. Dalton arrives to interview him for the job of chauffeur. These passages made me retrospectively embarrassed and confused.

When next I read *Native Son,* I was living near Boston, and it delivered a different shock of recognition. It compelled me to move in memory between the scenes in which Dalton's private detective, trying to scare the truth out of Bigger about Mary's disappearance, calls him a "*goddamn* black sonofabitch!" and a sunny afternoon at Fenway Park when, sitting for once in a really good box seat, I had found myself behind a pair of plaid-slacked fans who spent the whole game heckling the Red Sox first baseman for being a "black bastard," in a voice loud enough for him to hear.

And now that I have read *Native Son* again, this time with a mind clogged by other books, I find myself in the grip of an entirely new experience. This is partly because Arnold Rampersad and the editors of the Library of America have given us not the original published version of 1940, but the

Reprinted from *The New Republic,* 206 (30 March 1992): 28–30, 32–33, with the permission of *The New Republic,* © The New Republic, Inc.

text of the bound galleys that lay, for weeks during the fall of 1939, on the submission desk at the Book-of-the-Month Club, while the directors fretted over whether they could tolerate Bigger masturbating in a movie theater, or Mary Dalton moving her "hips . . . in a hard and veritable grind" against his black body. Richard Wright was a young writer tasting his first chance for fame, and so when the verdict came in that these scenes had to be cut if the Club was to select his novel, he agreed. At last, with the deletions now restored, we have, as Rampersad says, the words of the book as Wright "wanted them to be read."

It is always a tricky business to disqualify a text that a living author has at least tacitly approved. A few years ago a group of scholars, working on the premise that Theodore Dreiser had been bullied into making changes in the text of *Sister Carrie* just before it went to press, put forward a new text based on his typescript, and the Library of America wisely refrained from following suit. This time the Library has rejected the text in which an American classic has been known for half a century. The publication of this new edition is not just an editorial innovation, it is a major event in American literary history.

There can be no doubt that the book is better for the restorations. For one thing, the restored text solves some consistency problems, as when the State's Attorney tells Bigger that "I knew about that dirty trick you and your friend Jack pulled off in the Regal Theatre"—a statement that floats without antecedent in the 1940 text, but, in the intact version, refers to Bigger's "polishing his night stick" in the movie house. More important than such textual repairs is their total effect: we now have the first book in our literary history that represented the full, urgent sexuality of a young black man—here as he moves upon Bessie's body, with whom he lies among the garbage and rats in an abandoned tenement where they are hiding from the vigilantes and police:

> The loud demand of the tensity of his own body was a voice that drowned out hers. In the cold darkness of the room it seemed that he was on some vast turning wheel that made him want to turn faster and faster; that in turning faster he would get warmth and sleep and be rid of his tense fatigue. He was conscious of nothing now but her and what he wanted. He flung the cover back, ignoring the cold, and not knowing that he did it. . . . His desire was naked and hot in his hand and his fingers were touching her. . . . He heard her breathing heavily and heard his own breath going and coming heavily. *Bigger.* Now. All. All. Now. All. *Bigger.* . . .
> He lay still, feeling rid of that hunger and tenseness and hearing the wail of the night wind over and above his and her breathing. He turned away from her and lay on his back again, stretching his legs wide apart.

Native Son is a book about the imperatives of the body—about Bigger's panic-sweat beading on his skin; about his convulsive stomach pain when he gulps water after parched days on the run; about his struggle to will his erection to subside while a white woman and man have sex on the car seat behind him. There are brilliant descriptions of Bigger forcing a street crony to lick the blade of his knife in an act of public submission, and of his chewing frantically his first loaf of bread in days, until it bulges his cheeks like a trumpeter's and coaxes the scarce saliva from his tongue.

The book has an almost brutal immediacy, which the newly restored text not only confirms, but heightens. I have never been able to drive past the severe houses of Hyde Park, or through the tangent black neighborhoods, without seeing Bigger huddled against a steamed window in a passing streetcar, or seeing the snow fall softly, as if flake by flake, onto the Daltons' blue Buick that he has left parked in their gated driveway. One feels pushed by the wind off the lake toward the edge of the plains; one peers with Bigger through the "gauzelike curtain of snow" at the streetlights that taunt him with the promise of warmth—"street lamps covered with thick coatings of snow, gleaming like huge frosted moons above his head."

For Theodore Dreiser forty years earlier (from whose *An American Tragedy,* published in 1925, Wright may have gotten the idea of a half-conscious murder), these lamps had been "blinking lines of gas-lamps, fluttering in the wind," but they were already Chicago's visual signature—tiny fires disappearing in long perspectival lines that lead out of the city into the prairie distance. Like Dreiser, Wright was not a native-born Chicagoan; his Mississippi origins are the subject of *Black Boy* (1945), the book in which he recounted his awakening from a brutal childhood. The son of an illiterate sharecropper who deserted the family, Wright struggled against poverty and the intransigent reality of Southern racism. He was bounced from grandmother to aunt to orphanage while his mother sank into invalidism and despair. His brilliance and his discontent began to find literary expression during his schooling in Memphis, and, at 19, he moved to the great Midwestern city where he quickly became, in his guts, a Chicago writer. Wright was aware, as New England and Southern and even New York writers were less likely to be early in this century, that all class distinctions in America were of absurdly recent vintage, and vulnerable to a surge or drop in the commodity market or to the perpetual real-estate scramble. Wright was a student of both the dreamless poor and the cocksure rich, whom he found locked in vicious interdependence in Chicago.

Though he had broken with the Chicago Communist Party in 1937, he did not leave the national party until 1942, and was still trying to construct *Native Son* within the framework of a class analysis. He had been active in the '30s in the John Reed Club, a largely white literary organization sponsored by the Communists, and later became Harlem editor of *The Daily Worker.* His early novel *Lawd Today!* (published posthumously) is largely an evocation of soul-deadening labor; its central character, like Wright himself (who held jobs during these years as a ditch-digger, delivery boy, dishwasher, hospital worker), is a postal clerk whose body becomes a mechanical extension of the canceling machine, and whose mind can only accommodate "images [that] would flit [in] . . . and then aimlessly out again, like stray cats." The early stories, collected in *Uncle Tom's Children* (1938), look back to the South, and are concerned with the gathering desperation of rural blacks, whose inarticulate rage against a world owned by white men was beginning to take the form of apocalyptic expectation.

This implicit Communist criticism of capitalist society is still at work in *Native Son,* in which Wright gives Bigger an incipient proletarian consciousness, a desire to "merge himself with others and be a part of this world, to lose himself in it so he could find himself, to be allowed a chance to live like others, even though he was black." As part of the same allegory of class conflict, Wright draws the kindly Mr. Dalton as a stock figure from agitprop fiction—a giver to causes who sends his servants to night school even as he rakes in the rent from black tenants who live five to a rat-infested room (a contradiction of which "in a sullen way Bigger was conscious"). And if Dalton keeps a human screen of "house niggers" between him and the brutal reality of the plantation, he has an overseer to do his dirty work—Britten, the thick-necked security man, who studies Bigger to see if he waves his hands about and if his voice rises at the ends of sentences (clues that would clinch his theory that he has been fraternizing with Jews).

Here, under rough interrogation, Bigger begins to see the futility of his plan to blame Mary's murder on Jan, her Communist boyfriend: "Britten loosened his fingers from Bigger's collar and shrugged his shoulders. Bigger relaxed, still standing, his head resting against the wall, aching. He had not thought that anyone would dare think that he, a black Negro, would be Jan's partner." This remarkable phrase, "black Negro," is not a tautology, but a clue that the concept of "Negro" is, for Wright, not fundamentally a racial idea. "Negro" is a generic word for hopelessness and degradation. The early pages on Bigger—his portrait as a gang leader who compensates with cruelty for his sense of exile from the world of satisfactions—are almost indistinguishable in social content from James T. Farrell's portrait of the Irish thug in *Studs Lonigan* (1932–35).

But a "black Negro" is something quite different—something for which Bigger hates himself more than he hates his oppressor. A "black Negro" is worse, he knows, than the refuse of the white world, since he is a creature held by whites of every class (from tycoons to vigilantes, they all close ranks in his pursuit) to be not only low and incorrigible, but foul and poisonous. A wall stands between Bigger and the sensations he craves. He finds himself smacked back like a dog that lifts its head to the table rather than wait for the white man's scraps to fall to the floor. Not merely exploited, he is despised; and *Native Son,* almost in spite of itself, is a book about this distinction.

It is, in other words, a book about self-hatred—about a young man who loathes his own color and physiognomy and dialect and all the features of his irreparable social ugliness. Bigger is not so much an autonomous consciousness as he is the projection of the white imagination, a figure whose closest precursors in American fiction come not from previous black writers, but from racist white writers (such as Thomas Dixon, author of *The Clansman,* 1905) for whom black men were nothing more than clothed apes. Earlier black writers had certainly remarked the "peculiar sensation," as W. E. B. DuBois famously put it, of a "double-consciousness, this sense of always looking at one's self through the eyes of others, of measuring one's soul by the tape of a world that looks on in amused contempt and pity." But before Wright, black novelists had tended to approach this psychological dilemma from a connoisseur's distance and with Jamesian finesse—as in the tradition of the mulatto novel, which dramatized the mixed relief and guilt of light-skinned blacks who tried to solve the problem of double-consciousness by obliterating their black identity altogether.

In the 1920s and '30s black literary intellectuals (especially those who participated in what became known as the Harlem Renaissance) turned more openly to a celebration of their African identity—a gesture with which Wright sympathized, but which he suspected of self-delusion and accommodation to the prurient white taste for the exotic. Wright was working toward an unblinking confrontation with the problem of black identity in *Lawd Today!* and in the stories of *Uncle Tom's Children.* But it is in *Native Son,* despite Bigger's lumpish inarticulateness, that he gives full voice to the anguish of the "black Negro":

> What did he want? What did he love and what did he hate? He did not know. There was something he *knew* and something he *felt;* something the *world* gave him and something he *himself* had; something spread out in *front* of him and something spread out in *back;* and never in all his life, with this black skin of his, had the two worlds, thought and feeling, will and mind, aspiration and satisfaction, been together; never had he felt a sense of wholeness . . . only under the stress of hate was the conflict resolved.

What Bigger discovers in the moments when he kills is that his reactive life of shame and fear can become hideously creative, that he can animate the ghostly world through which he has been wandering in numb fright. A cup of hot milk, a shot of whiskey, the touch of Bessie's flesh, even the very conditions of hunger and desire, become reassurances of life itself:

> The memory of the bottle of milk Bessie had heated for him last night came back so strongly that he could almost taste it. . . . He saw himself take the top off the white bottle, with some of the warm milk spilling over his black fingers, and then lift the bottle to his mouth and tilt his head and drink. . . . He felt in his hunger a deep sense of duty, as powerful as the urge to breathe, as intimate as the beat of his heart. . . . He wanted to pull off his clothes and roll in the snow until something nourishing seeped into his body through the pores of his skin. He wanted to grip something in his hands so hard that it would turn to food.

But the terrible honesty of *Native Son* was its acknowledgment that people to whom life has been denied can only learn contempt from those who deny them. (Wright understood how effective was the fascists' appeal to unappeased resentment.) And so Bigger begins to live through a kind of aesthetics of hate:

> He was living, truly and deeply, no matter what others might think, looking at him with their blind eyes. Never had he had the chance to live out the consequences of his actions; never had his will been so free as in this night and day of fear and murder and flight.

For Bigger there is an almost erotic pleasure in seeing his picture in the papers, and his terror mixes with thrill while he watches from the rooftop as the white mobs converge upon him. He has provoked them, enraged them, even eluded and confounded them. After a lifetime of being owned, he now possesses them.

Bigger's sensory awakening is a version of Wright's own (right down to the consoling taste of warm milk), which he describes in *Black Boy:*

> The days and hours began to speak now with a clearer tongue. Each experience had a meaning of its own. . . . There was the drenching hospitality in the pervading smell of sweet magnolias. . . . There was the dry hot summer morning when I scratched my bare arms on briers while picking blackberries and came home with my fingers and lips stained black with sweet berry juice. . . . There was the drugged, sleepy feeling that came from sipping glasses of milk, drinking them slowly so that they would last a long time, and drinking enough for the first time in my life.

For Wright, the resurrection of his senses was a liberating event, benign and even gentle, evoked in almost pantheistic terms borrowed from Walt Whitman. For Bigger, it was the discovery that he had the power to damage and destroy white lives.

In 1940 Bigger's was an almost unwritable violence. Explosive, indiscriminate, he finds that he has a taste for killing: hours after burning Mary Dalton's body in the furnace he crushes Bessie's head with a brick, this black woman whom he both loves for her tenderness and hates for her despair. Wright's editors and sponsors worried that this squalid story might prove unreadable. They were wrong. *Native Son* sold 215,000 copies in three weeks—in a world poised on the verge of a conflagration in which the human capacity for systematic and spontaneous violence would be proved larger than anyone dreamed.

Wright had invented a young black man who awakens to himself by discovering his capacity for rage, by punching through the racial wall into moments of bodily contact (carnal and lethal) that confirm the aliveness of his body. In the autobiography that he wrote five years later, Wright makes it clear that he, too, had found salvation in the life of the body. He recalls the electric moments when, in his early days as a dishwasher in Chicago, a white waitress brushed casually against him without complaint—and another turned to him for intimate help:

> One summer morning a white girl came late to work and rushed into the pantry where I was busy. She went into the women's room and changed her clothes; I heard the door open and a second later I was surprised to hear her voice:
> "Richard, quick! Tie my apron!"
> She was standing with her back to me and the strings of her apron dangled loose. There was a moment of indecision on my part, then I took the two loose strings and carried them around her body and brought them again to her back and tied them in a clumsy knot.
> "Thanks a million," she said grasping my hand for a split second, and was gone.

In the South this incandescent moment would have been read by virtually any observer as a hint of miscegenation. But Wright discovered a new world in Chicago—not a place where taboos could be broken, but a place where the dividing line of race could simply be forgotten in the press of daily life. He delighted in Chicago because it occasionally offered anonymity: "It was strange to pause before a crowded newsstand and buy a newspaper without having to wait until a white man was served." And it was wonderfully strange to ride the trolley beside a white man who, instead of pulling away, "was still staring out the window, his mind fastened on some inward thought. I did not exist for him; I was as far from his mind as the stone buildings that swept past in the street."

In the mid-1940s Wright moved to Paris (a "city of refuge," he called it) and became part of the literary circle including Gertrude Stein (whose "Melanctha" had been an early influence) and André Gide, as well as leading intellectuals of the "Négritude" movement—Léopold Senghor, Aimé Césaire, and others. Wright, in turn, gave encouragement and patronage to younger black American writers like James Baldwin and Chester Himes. In the later '40s and early '50s he devoted himself to a new novel, *The Outsider* (1953)—the story of a black intellectual who begins life with a new identity after being presumed dead in a train wreck. Wright composed this novel, whose theme is the exhilarating loss of a burdensome self, under the personal influence of Sartre and de Beauvoir, and after considerable reading in Heidegger and Husserl. Like the second section of his autobiography (which he had agreed to drop, again at the behest of the Book-of-the-Month Club, and which was published after his death under the original title of the whole work, *American Hunger*), *The Outsider* contained a bitter attack on the Communist Party as a purveyor of false messianic hope.

Along with the second part of the mutilated autobiography (now reattached to *Black Boy* in the Library of America edition), *The Outsider* is a candid record of Wright's disillusionment with the Communist promise. Blaming the Party for intervening with friends at the Book Club to drop the offending section of his memoir, he again acceded to the pressure, but went on to publish some of the deleted chapters separately—including one long section, "I Tried to be a Communist," that appeared in *The Atlantic* and was widely read in Richard Crossman's notable book, *The God That Failed* (1950).

In 1954 Wright brought out *Savage Holiday,* a novel about a white psychopathic murderer that was well received in France but pretty much ignored at home. By now he was becoming a little formulaic in his demonstration of savagery—this time not beneath the servility of a black youth, but just below the civility of a middle-class white man. Spanning the decade from the end of the Second World War to the height of McCarthyism (Wright reverted to his native Mississippi for the setting of his last novel, *The Long Dream,* 1958), all of this writing has sporadic power and historical interest. But his artistic imagination had been nearly exhausted by *Native Son*—the book in which he had faced up to the blood-dread between whites and blacks, and had shown, in horror and sorrow, how impervious it was to rationalist solutions offered by both reformers and radicals.

Wright did not want to believe in the intractability of the problem. He felt himself fleetingly released from it among the waitresses in the Chicago kitchen, and even in *Native Son* he reached for themes that transcend it. His early stories, as Baldwin remarked after his death, "did not make me think . . . particularly of Negroes. They made me think of human loss and helplessness." One of the rewards of coming back after years to *Native Son* is to see how reductive it is to read it as merely a tract about race. It can be read as a transcription of an adolescent dream, as a portrait of a man for whom guilt is a half-formed emotion, as a criticism of philanthropic sentimentality.

It is also a prescient anticipation of contemporary insights into the pathologies of the ghetto family, and of the indictment of black men, lately handed down in black feminist writing, for punishing black women in recompense for their stolen dignity. It is certainly, too, a tour de force of psychological manipulation: when the bloodhound reporters, milling about in the Daltons' overheated basement, tell Bigger to clear out the ashes to quiet the furnace, we shudder with him as Mary's unconsumed bones drop down through the grate. Our allegiance is with Bigger, even as we apprehend more and more of his animal ferocity.

"Shattering" is a critical word that has been properly consigned to service as an adjective in blurbs. But there *is* a class of books for which this word, or some synonym that conveys the idea that a book can do real violence to the mind, is indispensable. Not all great books work by this kind of assault, but some do, and thereby they are fatal to whatever mental structure the reader inhabits when he sits down to read them. *Native Son* is such a book. It is all the more remarkable because it achieves its destructive power not by exposing the inadequacies of conventional thinking, but by dramatizing conventional ideas in such a way that they can never be held casually again. *Native Son* was indeed the book Wright swore to write so that "no one would weep over it," the book that "would be so hard and deep" that it would deny its readers "the consolation of tears." It was the first book that forced Americans to take their racial fears seriously, and it did so by turning their most vicious thoughts against themselves.

It is a profound irony that the arc of Wright's career moved downward after *Native Son* because of his refusal to be imprisoned by the thematics of race. His move to France, where he partook of the prestige attached to the man of color in exile from crass America, did not enlarge him as a writer. He became, perhaps, a more cosmopolitan artist. Still, as Baldwin said, speaking from within the same paradox, Paris "would not have been a city of refuge for us if we had not been armed with American passports," and "it did not seem worthwhile to me to have fled the native fantasy only to embrace a foreign one."

In his moving eulogy, Baldwin reflected that Wright was "one of the most illustrious victims" of "the war in the breast between blackness and whiteness." Writing in the heady atmosphere of postcolonial possibility, Baldwin added that "it is no longer important to be white—thank heaven—the white face is no longer invested with the power of this world; and it is devoutly to be hoped that it will soon no longer be important to be black." Such a dissolution of difference was Wright's hope, too. All his work was a plea that racial identity be submerged in the colorless fact of being human. But his enduring greatness as an artist will be owed, I think, to his unprecedented ability to convey the horror of being black in America. What he wished for was to lose his subject. After reading *Native Son,* no one can doubt his willingness to make the sacrifice.

The City Without Maps in Richard Wright's
Native Son

CHARLES SCRUGGS

Ah! but in some low and obscure nook,—some narrow closet on the ground floor, shut, locked and bolted, and the key flung away,—or beneath the marble pavement, in a stagnant water-puddle, with the richest pattern of mosaic-work above,—may lie a corpse, and still decaying, and diffusing its death-scent all through the palace! The inhabitant will not be conscious of it, for it has long been his daily breath!

—Nathaniel Hawthorne, *The House of the Seven Gables*

We have in the oppression of the Negro a shadow athwart our national life dense and heavy enough to satisfy even the gloomy broodings of a Hawthorne.

—Richard Wright, "How Bigger Was Born"

Me and the Devil was walking side by side.

—Robert Johnson, "Me and the Devil Blues"

The movement of black people from the south to the cities of the north, which had been a series of small waves since 1900, became a flood with the entrance of the United States into World War I. The war meant jobs because of a shortage of workers in northern industry, and thus there was reason and opportunity for blacks to move. The *Chicago Defender,* which for all its criticism of conditions for blacks in the south had never advocated immigration, changed its editorial policy in 1916: the new word was "Come on up."[1] "From 1916 to 1919," James Grossman states, "between fifty and seventy thousand black southerners relocated in Chicago," and thousands more would continue to arrive year by year in the decade of the 1920s, most following a route along the Mississippi River via Memphis and St. Louis which blues singers would describe in countless songs and eventually make symbolic of all the transient conditions of modern life.[2] One unexpected result of this

Reprinted from *Sweet Home: Invisible Cities in the Afro-American Novel* by Charles Scruggs (Baltimore: The Johns Hopkins University Press, 1993), pp. 68–99, 251–60, with the permission of The Johns Hopkins University Press.

migration is that now in Florence, Italy, there can be heard groups of young German (or English or Swedish) musicians painfully pronouncing a list of railroad lines, highway numbers, juke joints, women and long-abandoned plantations along that route. This is a "Florentine urbanity" in reverse, one only partially glimpsed by Alain Locke and by most of the black intellectuals of the 1920s. Not only were blacks going to be changed by the city and its new mass culture, they were going to contribute hugely to the making of that culture.

When Alain Locke's *New Negro*—the manifesto of the Harlem Renaissance—was published in 1925, Richard Wright was a young man halfway to Chicago. His migration, from Mississippi via Memphis, fit the archetypal pattern exactly, and in fact it was Wright rather than any contributor to Locke's book who would be the "New Negro." The Great Depression would be the breaking point, the obdurate historical fact set between Wright and the writers of the Harlem Renaissance. Not only did Wright differ from these writers in background and situation, but the Depression meant that he would come to live in a city where the desperate conditions for blacks could no longer be ignored. These conditions, the invisible city of economic relations made all too visible, would demand new explanations and a new sociology, and Wright's Marxism would in turn lead him to depict the urban life of blacks from the underside. *Native Son* was a novel from which there was no going back; Wright made it impossible for anyone to make an important statement on black urban life without considering the racist social setting of the city. In this sense, Irving Howe is absolutely right: "The day *Native Son* appeared, American culture was changed forever."[3]

There is another divide between Wright and the Harlem Renaissance which perhaps because of his social focus is less evident: for literary models Wright looked to a generation of writers who were only tangentially influential upon most renaissance authors. In 1937 Wright published in a magazine called *New Challenge* an essay that amounted to a small *ars poetica* for his work:

> . . . for the life of the Negro people is not simple. The presentation of their lives should be simple, yes; but all the complexity, the strangeness, the magic wonder of life that plays like a bright sheen over the most sordid existence, should be there. To borrow a phrase from the Russians, it should have a *complex simplicity*. Eliot, Stein, Joyce, Proust, Hemingway, and Anderson; Gorky, Barbusse, Nexo, and Jack London no less than the folklore of the Negro himself should form the heritage of the Negro writer.[4]

"Blueprint for Negro Writing" is an effort to theorize about the necessary political dimension of black literature, but the authors Wright invokes include Gertrude Stein, T. S. Eliot, Marcel Proust, James Joyce—the pantheon of the great modernists. In Wright's view, there is no contradiction between social themes and modernist technique for the black writer: "Every iota of gain in human thought and sensibility should be ready grist for his mill." Even political works require a "remaking": "The relationship between reality and the artistic image is not always direct and simple. The imaginative conception of a historical period will not be a carbon copy of reality."[5] Wright is usually placed in the tradition of literary naturalism or "realism," yet his "realism" is a quite different matter from that of a Walter White or even a Jessie Fauset, and his "naturalism" often expresses a "divided stream" of the facts and the fantastical.[6]

In actuality, *Native Son's* documentary realism is almost always spilling over into myth.[7] In "How Bigger Was Born," Wright describes Chicago in terms of two kinds of myth, one related to the history of the city and one that emerges from an archetype:

> Then there was the fabulous city in which Bigger lived, an indescribable city, huge, roaring, dirty, noisy, raw, stark, brutal; a city of extremes: torrid summers, and sub-zero winters, white people and black people, the English Language and strange tongues, foreign born and native born, scabby poverty and gaudy luxury, high idealism and hard cynicism! A city so young that, in thinking of its short history, one's mind, as it travels backward in time, is stopped abruptly by the barren stretches of wind-swept prairie! But a city old enough to have caught within the homes of its long straight streets the symbols and images of man's age-old destiny, of truths as old as the mountains and seas, of dramas as abiding as the soul of man itself![8]

The city is "fabulous" and "indescribable" and mythic like the heavenly city—as well as being a specific, historical city with extraordinary extremes of weather, an odd mixture of peoples, "high idealism and hard cynicism," and an indomitable will to succeed in a place where no sane person would believe a city could be founded, much less flourish. In this passage, Wright surely has in mind Carl Sandburg, Chicago's epic bard: "out of prairie-brown grass crossed with a streamer of wigwam smoked—/ out of a smoke pillar, a blue promise—out of wild ducks woven in greens and purples—/ Here I saw a city rise and say to the people round the world: Listen, I am strong, I know what I want."[9] However, one key theme in *Native Son* is that the city, despite its strong will (or perhaps because of it), does *not* know what it wants. That confusion of intention or motive that Wright describes is part of the mythic dimension of the modern city, the city as Pandemonium or as Babel; it is, as with Dunbar's immigrants, the vision of the city seen by the outsider, which of course is what Bigger is. Bigger's vision is not his alone, however; it stands as well for the social fragmentation that is the general condition of modern urban civilization.

One fact in Chicago's history directly linked the city to the mythic; not only was this "fabulous" city young even by American standards, but it had been rebuilt since the great fire of 1872. It is no wonder that Wright was fascinated by *Crime and Punishment,*[10] for Petersburg was a city like Chicago, created de novo from the egg of the intellect.[11] Just as Peter the Great's platonic conception of the city emerged from the marshes in Western dress, so too Chicago sprang into being after the great fire on the shores of Lake Michigan. Much of this city was abstracted from the heads of architects and city planners, having little to do with the living reality of people like Bigger. Living in a rootless city, Bigger, like Dostoevsky's Raskolnikov, is a rootless man attracted to whatever electrical currents pass through the city's streets. For Wright, the city was also "fabulous" in the manner in which Dreiser had depicted it in *An American Tragedy.* According to Ellen Moers, Dreiser had complained in 1921 of the "dead end at which American realism had arrived." He saw the urban landscape as the means by which the "power of the imagination" might be revived, for the modern city in American life was something out of the Arabian Nights: "If there are all the chain cigar stores, chain drug stores, haberdasheries, movie theatres, and big hotels in Manhattan, here are also Hell, Heaven and Purgatory of the soul, which Dante would have found. . . . He would have gone beyond mere realistic description and shown us the half-monstrous proportions of our city like a giant sphinx with wings."[12]

Although it is true that *Native Son* is a "proletarian novel," the only time that we see Bigger actually working is in the context of a fairytale situation: he has a twenty-five-dollar-per-week job (during the Depression), with a room of his own in a rich man's house, and his only duty (besides tending the furnace) is to chauffeur the princess of the castle around the town. Here is the "fabulous" city that seduced Clyde Griffiths, one whose magnetic poles (positive and negative) Wright also felt when he came to Chicago: "There is an open and raw beauty about that city that seems either to kill or endow one with the spirit of life. I felt those extremes of possibility, death and hope, while I lived half hungry and afraid in a city to which I had fled with the dumb yearning to write, to tell my story."[13] Bigger also feels those extremes, death and hope, and in *Native Son* Wright will connect Bigger's possible fates to the two faces of the "fabulous" city he lives in, the demonic city that belongs to State's Attorney Buckley, and the paradisal city of community that his lawyer Boris Max offers Bigger at the novel's end.

Wright's attitude toward Chicago suggests that what is "real" about this "unreal city" (as he called it in *American Hunger,* thinking no doubt of *The Waste Land*) cannot always be pinned down. Indeed, his first impression of the actual city was that its "houses . . . were sinking slowly into the dank prairie."[14] The implications of this insight are important for *Native Son.* If the material city seemed fantastic, then Max's vision of a city of democratic community at the novel's end cannot be dismissed as Marxist doctrine or utopian fantasy. It is as "real" as the City of the Big Shoulders, the city of might. For as Wright said in *American Hunger,* the idea of community was a human need, made even more acute if one were "a Negro in America": "The problem of human unity was more important than bread, more important than physical living itself; for I felt that without a common bond uniting men, without a continuous current of shared thought and feeling circulating through the social system, like blood coursing through the human body, there could be no living worthy of being human."[15] The outlines of Max's utopian city trace, though faintly, the shapes of the city of *caritas* (Paul and Augustine), the city of civilization (Cicero), and the city of light and openness (Book of Revelation). The allusions to community are a reality beneath layers of chaotic impression; but myth and metaphor, as Kenneth Burke observed in a book that Wright owned (*Permanence and Change* [1935]),[16] move us with as much force as do empirical facts, because they give life a sense of purpose.[17] To Wright, Chicago's "straight streets" are empirical facts that lead us in the direction of myth and metaphor, even as the order of an urban pattern is deceptive because it doesn't reveal the disorder of urban life. As Wright says of Bigger, "Sometimes, in his room or on the sidewalk, the world seemed to him a strange labyrinth even when the streets were straight and the walls were square."[18] What Bigger doesn't know, but Wright does, is that Chicago's grid, laid out in accordance with the Land Ordinance of 1785, is not neutral but contains within its apparent rationality a secret record of money, power, and racial prejudice. As Mario Gandelsonas has shown, an invisible wall separates "north Chicago from south Chicago, white Chicago from black Chicago. This wall [is] implied from the fact that the monumental north-south axes seem to come to an abrupt end at the point where the streets change their name from north to south, marking a significant shift in the social geography of the city."[19] Even though Bigger finds his way around some of Chicago's walls, others equally invisible will effectively exclude him.

Bigger's sense of the city as labyrinth is as much an existential perception as a spatial one: a vision of the immigrant lost in the welter of conflicting cultural messages, straight streets leading nowhere, square walls that dissolve into a collage of bright social images, billboards whose real texts remain hidden. The question becomes, urgently, how to perceive coherence or find a way through the labyrinth. Or, from another viewpoint—Wright's—is there some coherence being imposed whose form is an apparent disorder? Wright's friend the Chicago sociologist Louis Wirth, who elaborated on the theories of his teacher Robert Park, attempted to answer that latter question in 1938. Because the modern city is made up of heterogeneous, segmented worlds, each with its own spatial and moral regions, "the masses of men in the city," said Wirth, remain isolated from each other and hence "are subject to manipulation by symbols and stereotypes managed by individuals working from afar or operating *invisibly* behind the scenes through their control of the instruments of communication" (my italics).[20] Those in control of the city's "instrumentalities" are masters of illusion: through newspapers and movies, they forge a myth that the city is still a homogeneous whole, still a village of shared values. It is a myth that disguises their own power, their attempt to reduce urban complexity to a manageable "normality," yet it is a myth that is attractive because it so closely imitates an invisible archetype of community—the heavenly city in the Book of Revelation, for example—that men and women desperately want to believe in.

The manipulators of the media pretend to a sense of community and a cohesive moral order that in fact has no basis in urban experience, especially in the experience of urban blacks who, like Bigger, recognize that the myth of a moral order is a mask for social control. But although mass media become the means by which moral order is contrived, control through their agency is always problematic, for there is something intrinsically subversive about these media. In particular, the appeal newspapers and movies make to a democracy of desire challenges the illusion of moral order and exposes the segmented, class-ridden city. As H. L. Mencken observed of Hollywood morality in an *American Mercury* book review: "The astounding thing is not that there are so many young criminals; but that there are so few. The public school, with its witless goose-stepping, is a natural hatchery of them. The newspapers and movies help, not so much by teaching that crime pays, as by teaching that virtue doesn't. The rich, it appears, do not have to obey the laws."[21] Since Wright was reading "the *American Mercury* from mid-1926 on,"[22] he might have recalled this observation as he imagined Bigger's response to *The Gay Woman,* a film Bigger sees shortly before he goes to work at Mr. Dalton's house.[23] For the moral lesson that Bigger remembers from the movie, despite its moralistic ending, is that "the rich . . . do not have to obey the laws." The Hays Code of Film Production (1934) demands that the gay woman return to her deceived husband and that her immorality be displaced onto a convenient scapegoat, a Communist bomb-thrower, but the movie's most potent meaning is the meaning Bigger takes away from it: Hollywood's heavenly city is a city of capitalist consumption. The word *gay* in the movie's title refers to the desire for pleasure that the movie instills in its audience; its visual luxury is the real message: "Then came *The Gay Woman* in which, amid scenes of cocktail drinking, dancing, golfing, swimming, and spinning roulette wheels, a rich white woman kept clandestine appointments with her lover while her husband was busy in the offices of a vast paper mill" (26). Bigger receives a message intended for a white, middle-class viewer rather than for him, for although the geographical boundary lines of the city are firmly fixed, movies and newspapers cross those lines, and their messages are registered and reworked in the minds of those who represent an invisible audience and who recreate an invisible city of desire.[24]

This moral ambiguity within the city's media points to the moral ambiguity of the city itself, which from the nineteenth century on has been the scene of America's great integration, the "melting pot" where various immigrant groups were more or less Americanized. In this century the means of integration has increasingly been a mass culture that, through the instruments of the media, has produced the popularizing, leveling, and homogenizing to make people of very different cultural backgrounds alike. But Wright's *Native Son* is in one sense a story of the failure of integration (though that failure is paradoxically a kind of salvation), and it is a failure phrased in terms of city space, city maps, horizons and perspectives, and views from windows. By extension, those views could even be said to include scenes framed by the motion picture screen or the advertising billboard. In the most general terms, this means simply that the city Bigger sees and moves through is a *different* city than the one Wright's white characters perceive.

The urban geographer Kevin Lynch has coined the phrase "cognitive map" to describe an individual's unique but limited view of his or her environment, a view importantly determined by social divisions of class, gender, race, or age. The perception of a city is "an active transaction between person and place," said Lynch, noting that "self-identity" seems to be "reinforced by a strong identity" with place.[25] In *Native Son,* Bigger boasts that he knows "the South Side from A to Z," (126), but the historical and cultural intention of the city's monuments escapes him. Thus, cognitive maps cover not only districts, streets, or houses but also other, less tangible, cultural formations. In *Native Son,* perception becomes an index of one's relationship to the city, and although Chicago's monuments are part of a "featureless environment" (Lynch's phrase) as far as Bigger is concerned, he perceives the city's media in ways that would shock its ruling class.

In "How Bigger Was Born," Wright said that "Chicago's physical aspect—noisy, crowded, filled with a sense of power and fulfillment—did so much more to dazzle the mind with a taunting sense of possible achievement that the segregation it did impose brought forth from Bigger a reaction more obstreperous than in the South." Yet Bigger's mind is dazzled primarily by the media, for, Wright added, "the environment supplies the instrumentalities through which the organism expresses itself," and Bigger's urban world is circumscribed by the "instrumentalities" he is allowed to perceive: "It was when he read the newspapers or magazines, went to the movies, or walked along the streets with crowds, that he felt what he wanted: to merge himself with others and be a part of this world, to lose himself in it so he could find himself, to be allowed a chance to live like others, even though he was black."[26] His city's "instrumentalities" are not Du Bois's university, or even Wright's Memphis library. He may share a desire for community, but his desire is mediated by movies, magazines, and newspapers rather than by the library and the university.

However, because of his race Bigger is an outsider even from the ersatz village of the media; and pushed by the desires the media create, he is left to try to find his way in a jungle of illusion. Throughout, the invisible city in the form of a labyrinth confines Bigger in a world of darkness and misapprehension. In "Fear," book 1 of the novel, the antithetical "rhythms" of Bigger's personality—fluctuating, as it does, between violence and nonviolence, silence and anger, "brooding and intense desire"—emanate from a "far-away invisible force": "He was like a strange plant blooming in the day and wilting at night" (24–25). Later, outside Ernie's Kitchen Shack, Bigger backs away from Mary Dalton "as though she were contaminated with an invisible contagion" (62). In book 2, entitled "Flight," after the murder, he feels the he has "shed an invisible burden" (97), that he is no longer "enclosed in the stifling embrace of an invisible force" (127). Or as Wright's narrator says of Bigger, *after* he has killed Mary: "For the first time in his life he moved *consciously* between two sharply defined poles: he was moving away from the threatening penalty of death, from the death-like times that brought him that tightness and hotness in his chest; and he was moving toward that sense of fullness he had so often but inadequately felt in magazines and movies" (127; my italics). The irony of this passage is that although the murder frees him from the labyrinth of his powerlessness and places him in that media world he associates with power and success, he is now even more helpless, because a fugitive.

One visual image that is intended for black Chicago, and that world alone, is the movie-screen-sized face of State's Attorney Buckley on the billboard outside Bigger's apartment building. Indeed, Buckley's piercing eyes are cinematic, seeming to follow the viewer until they disappear "like a movie blackout" (11). Underneath Buckley's face is the inscription "IF YOU BREAK THE LAW, YOU CAN'T WIN!" (11), but Bigger intuitively understands this poster in light of his reading of the movies. The poster argues not for a universal code of moral behavior but for one directed at black people alone; it is, as Bigger recognizes, an instrument of power—a perception revealed in Bigger's cynical, "You let whoever pays *you* off win!" Buckley *could* be an honest official—Bigger has no way of knowing that he is corrupt—but Bigger's perception of Buckley depends on the same observation Mencken made: what Bigger has learned from the movies is that only the poor have to obey the laws. And who wants to be poor? Instead of rejecting Buckley out of hand as morally reprehensible because he belongs to a corrupt world, Bigger identifies with him. He wants what Buckley has—money, power, and pleasure, the city of material consumption that hides behind the billboard or glitters beneath the Hays-code text of *The Gay Woman.*

Against the city as labyrinth or as desire is set Max's city of a utopian future, one that has both a Marxist and an American foundation. Throughout *Native Son,* Wright flirts with the possibility that the ideals of the Republic will become incarnated within the city, that they will forge the connecting link between city and civilization. Like Ellison, Wright believed that the nation's sacred documents do not go unnoticed even by its lowliest citizen, and "that every man and woman should have the opportunity to realize himself, to seek his own individual fate and goals, his own peculiar and untranslatable destiny. I don't say that Bigger knew this in terms in which I'm speaking of it; I don't say that any such thought entered his head. His emotional and intellectual life was never that articulate. But he knew it emotionally, intuitively".[27]

Yet it is precisely here that Wright differs from Ellison, who would complain that Wright never gave Bigger the imagination that he, Wright, possessed.[28] That is, in fact, Wright's point: Bigger, unlike Ellison's invisible man, cannot tell his own tale, because the city is never made real to him in the full extent of its mythic possibilities. Unlike Ellison's protagonist, Bigger cannot articulate his conception of American ideals in any other terms *but* those of the movies, magazines, and newspapers. Ironically, in the novel's conclusion Wright will enclose Bigger's story within the frame of Hollywood's cinema, but will rewrite that story's ending to fit a life that is more authentic—more truly "pious," to use Kenneth Burke's term—than those lived on the silver screen.

George Steiner has observed that the setting of the Gothic novel in the nineteenth century changed from the country mansion house to the "encroaching vastness of the city."[29] At the end of "How Bigger Was Born," Richard Wright links *Native Son* to the Gothic tradition in American literature because of the ongoing "oppression of the Negro": "If Poe were alive, he would not have to invent horror; horror would invent him."[30] What Wright does in *Native Son,* as Poe did in "The Man of the Crowd," is use the city as the setting for a contemporary horror story in which both the city and the city's creation, Bigger, are labyrinths that do not permit themselves to be read.[31] And in this sense, Wright is writing not only a Gothic novel, but also a detective story in which the ultimate crime remains unsolved.

At first, Bigger can read his own surroundings only in terms of somebody else's moral map: "Thou shalt not." This restriction is lifted when he kills. When, before the murder, he walks the ten blocks to the Dalton house, he is lost in a strange new world, trapped in a displaced country mansion whose separate rooms replicate a social power-structure he cannot comprehend. By the act of murder, imposing the negative upon others, he begins his long journey toward self-definition, a journey partly measured by his reordering of social space.

Wright employs a technique from "The Man of the Crowd"—the description of views from a window—to represent various attempts by characters in the novel to see the city as a whole. Yet seeing the world through a frame always yields an unreliable image, one that makes a direct appeal to experience, to *seeing,* but discounts the way in which the frame itself restricts the view. Ultimately all attempts to see a single pattern to the city fail, but not all fail in the same way or to the same degree. Indeed, Wright forces us to judge his characters in terms of what pattern they see in the city's mosaic. Thus Kevin Lynch's "cognitive map" is connected to what Kenneth Burke calls the different levels of power in the novel and their "interrelationships,"[32] for power reflects class and race, and class and race determine what one sees in (and of) the city. For Wright, there is no purely "aesthetic" view; each "cognitive map" is a reflection of a political stance and social placement in the urban world.

In an early scene in "Fear," Jan and Mary are in a car with Bigger on the Outer Drive, and the two white lovers, full of themselves and the beauty of the evening, look at the city's skyline through the car's windows:

> "Isn't it glorious tonight?" she asked.
>
> "God, yes!" Jan said.
>
> Bigger listened to the tone of their voices, to their strange accents, to the exuberant phrases that flowed so freely from their lips.
>
> "That sky!"
>
> "And that water!"
>
> "It's so beautiful it makes you ache just to look at it," said Mary.
>
> "This is a beautiful world, Bigger," Jan said, turning to him. "Look at that skyline!"
>
> Bigger looked without turning his head; he just rolled his eyes. Stretching to one side of him was a vast sweep of tall buildings flecked with tiny squares of yellow light.
>
> "We'll own all that some day, Bigger," Jan said with a wave of his hand. "After the revolution it'll be ours. But we'll have to fight for it. What a world to win, Bigger! And when that day comes, things'll be different. There'll be no white and no black; there'll be no rich and no poor."
>
> Bigger said nothing. (59)

Bigger says nothing because he doesn't see what they see; he can find his way to the Outer Drive, to Adams Street, then to Lake Street in the Loop, but he has no "cognitive map" of that world. If, as Lewis Mumford has said, architecture is "legible script,"[33] then Bigger is confronted with a sign system that he cannot read, for he has been excluded from the "symbols and images" of Jan and Mary's civilization (353), as Wright continually reminds us. To Bigger, the skyline is simply made up of "tall buildings," but to Jan and Mary the buildings are symbols within an urban text, symbols that are immediately recognized. Not only are these "buildings" particularized but only some of them are "tall" or even buildings. Jan and Mary would see the Wrigley Building and the Tribune Tower and possibly the Buckingham Fountain, the aquarium, the planetarium, and Soldier's Field. And hidden from view would be the Chicago Art Institute, the Chicago Public Library, and the home of the Chicago Symphony Orchestra. For Jan and Mary, these are all monuments to high culture—even the sports venue of Soldier's Field, with its classical architecture—and they would all be part of Chicago's skyline.[34]

The lovers see the city's skyline as beautiful because they have inherited an urban aesthetic tradition that has taught them to see the city as static and pictorial.[35] And buried in the image of Chicago's skyline is the legendary history of Chicago itself: the Columbian Exposition of 1893 and its famous White City, and Daniel Burnham's 1897 plans to remake Chicago into "Paris by the Lake."[36] Architecture was to have an important place in Chicago's cultural ambitions at the turn of the century, and one building built in the 1920s deserves particular mention: the Tribune Tower. In 1922, the *Chicago Tribune* ran a competition among architects for the design of the Tribune Tower, and even solicited suggestions from its readers; yet the competition was more or less determined beforehand, because what the *Chicago Tribune* preferred as a model was the medieval cathedral—even though one artist's rendering of the tower depicted it as a huge Doric column. Whether the motif was to be Gothic or classical, the calculated effect was to be the same: the Tribune Tower (1925) would express the values of Western civilization and guarantee their "guardianship" by the media.[37] In Wright's novel, the *Chicago Tribune* will give its demonizing account of Bigger's capture and trial, and that, too, may be a reflection of some of those values.

This, of course, points to the underlying irony of Jan and Mary's enthusiastic raptures over Chicago's skyline. Jan may be a Communist, and Mary a Communist sympathizer, but they are still full members of Western civilization. Products of an elite middle-class culture, Jan and Mary perceive the skyline in terms of the "picturesque," perhaps the most bourgeois of all visual perspectives because it implies an immense satisfaction with the status quo. What this aesthetic perspective ignores, of course, is that the skyscrapers represent the power of Dalton's economic system, and their obverse is the slum where Bigger lives. Replacing the skyscrapers' owners with new owners is a neat rhetorical slight of hand, a revolutionary trompe-l'oeil, as it were, but it does not touch the reality of Bigger's poverty or his myopia. In this context, Bigger is like John Locke's imaginary child who cannot see the skyline because he grows up in a house with no doors and no windows; but Jan and Mary are blind as well—outside the frame of the panoramic view of Chicago's skyline is the enclosed space of Bigger and his family's "kitchenette."

The limits to Mary's map of the city become apparent when Jan turns off the Outer Drive and into Bigger's neighborhood. Looking through the car window at "tall, dark apartment buildings looming to either side" of the car, Mary innocently comments to Bigger, "I've long wanted to go into those houses . . . and just *see* how your people live" (60). Although plainly meant to be sympathetic, her remark triggers an internal rage in him, making him wish he could "stand in naked space above the speeding car and with one final blow blot it out" (60). What Bigger responds to is the same pictorial perspective that allowed Mary to see the skyline in a certain way, although, in this context, the pictorialist becomes a voyeur. Because Bigger knows the misery of his own world so intimately, he perceives the obscene element in Mary's wish. Bigger's inarticulate rage represents a felt knowledge of existence that Mary is not privy to, hence his rejection of the kind of sympathy Mary has to offer: she only wants to *see*.

So extreme is Bigger's reaction that he remembers Mary's precise words on four separate occasions in the novel, and Wright seems to link his killing of her to those words. His anger represents a long history of enforced separateness which Mary's "innocent" remarks cannot begin to broach. On this history, Sam Warner, Jr., notes that in the nineteenth century the word *slum* began to be used to express the growing spatial divisions within the modern city. As poor people became more and more segregated, and hence isolated from what was seen to be the only authentic way of life (that is, middle-class life), the word *slum* took on a metaphoric and exotic character. A "slum" was like a foreign country that could be visited, as by tourists; it was also a place set apart, having no connection to "normal" life: "No one went slumming when the poor lived on the alley behind her or his house." Moreover, the word *slum* tended to hide the possibility that there might be an economic cause for such a place: "Slums were just there, facts of life, found objects." As such, slums "assumed a special role in contemporary ideological structure . . . [and] performed what Roland Barthes called the task of 'denomination.' The new symbol, by separating the slums from the conditions of urban employment, told us that the slums were a part of English and American cities, like smoke, or bricks, or saloons. By denomination, an historical event, something of a specific time and place, was transformed into a general fact of life."[38]

Wright anticipates Warner's remarks when he refers to Bigger's world as "this *prescribed* corner of the city" (97; my italics). The word *prescribed* suggests a fact of life so permanent that it was ordained *before* it was written down, thus justifying that "corner's" inclusion within the official, written map of the city. It is no wonder, then, that Bigger looks at the white people who prescribe him to *his* "corner of the city" not as human but as "a sort of great natural force" (97). The word *prescribed* also suggests that "space has absolute properties. . . . that structures, people and land parcels exist in a manner that is mutually exclusive each of the other in a three-dimensional, physical (Euclidean) space."[39] What enrages Bigger is the contrast he perceives between his fixed place in three-dimensional, physical space, and the fluid space of the cinema (or of an airplane), in which he can imaginatively move at will. And what he will end up doing is rearranging the space of the Daltons' house, making their space his own. Not only does he usurp the space of Mary's room by killing her, but after her death he transforms the basement—his space in the social spectrum—into the symbolic center of the house.

When Bigger first comes to the Daltons' neighborhood, its space is like that of a foreign land, "a cold and distant world; a world of white secrets carefully guarded" (37). He is bewildered, hesitating at the front door, wondering if he should use the rear entrance, which he cannot find. When he is ushered into the living room by Peggy, the Daltons' cook, he is again made anxious by the cold elegance of the house, which has nothing of the opulence he has come to expect of the rich of the movies: "He had not thought that this world would be so utterly different from his own that it would intimidate him" (39).

His experience of this alien space continues to disorient him until he ends up accidentally trapped in the house's most forbidden enclosure, the daughter's room, and he kills her. After Mary's death, the spatial focus within the house completely changes. Before, movement and activity are concentrated in the living room and kitchen: ordinary domestic space. After the death, the house begins to revolve around the furnace, the sun of Bigger's new system. Peggy, Britten (a detective), the Daltons, and the reporters are all drawn like satellites to a new planet, and the social hierarchy of the house's space is reversed; now the invisible basement where the black servant works becomes its center. Bigger has drawn himself a new map of the house, and it is at last a map he can read.

The slum is only an image in Mary's mind, one that provokes a sympathetic tear or an anthropological interest (both motivations are behind Mary's desire to "just *see* how your people live"). Yet ironically, in wishing to close the gap between the segmented worlds that make the city difficult to comprehend as a whole, Mary also feels both Bigger's frustrated response to living in "a strange labyrinth" and his desire to "understand it" (204). In this desire to find a map to the whole city, rich and poor almost meet. Wright, however, never lets us forget that Mary's activism is that of a dilettante. Although she is different from her father, who shuts his eyes to the real nature of the economic arrangements of the city, she has none of the understanding of Max, who recognizes that Bigger's alienation from society cannot be overcome by gestures of goodwill alone.

Wright also emphasizes that Bigger's struggle to make sense of the city is linked to an existential question—"Who am I?"—while Mary's curiosity is that of the tourist who will never have to concern herself with a final destination, never have to give an answer to an overwhelming question. From Bigger's perspective, she is a careless meddler: what she wants to *see* is an obscenity that should remain hidden; what she wants to expose is a raw wound that she has no way of healing. For Bigger, blotting out the car means returning the world to blank space, to a primal emptiness, where all "prescribed" conditions disappear.

Like his daughter, Mr. Dalton also treats the slums he creates as a "general fact of life." He hides his relationship to Bigger's neighborhood by devoting himself to philanthropy and owning a car that is not a Rolls Royce or a Cadillac but only a dark-blue Buick sedan. Dalton's reluctance to consume conspicuously is not a moral choice, however, but a moral obfuscation: he pretends, even to himself, that his millions are neutral millions. The house is a symbol of power used to hide power, and in this sense it belongs to the world of the movies Bigger watches, the "democratic" medium that celebrates wealth and power at the same time that it claims to censure them.

Mr. Dalton also hides behind a legal fiction. Even as holder of "the controlling stock" of a corporation called the South Side Real Estate Company, he can tell himself that he does not exploit people, for his corporation operates in an amoral realm that doesn't touch individuals but only abstractions: supply and demand, his competitors, and so forth (277). A corporation is a kind of parody of the Beloved Community, for as Alan Trachtenberg has noted, a corporation is an "association . . . understood as strictly contractual, not necessarily comprised of people acquainted with each other or joined by any common motive other than profit seeking."[40] Moreover, it is a single "body" (from the Latin *corpora*) in which the whole is greater than the sum of its parts. "The advantage that the corporation has over the individual entrepreneur," said Louis Wirth in a moment of rare humor, ". . . derives not only from the possibility it affords of centralizing the resources of thousands of individuals or from the legal privilege of limited liability and perpetual succession, but from the fact that the corporation has no soul."[41] One can be sure that Wright, in his depiction of Mr. Dalton, didn't let this paradox slip by. Mr. Dalton washes his hands of any responsibility for Bigger's fate because the standards for Bigger's housing are set by the soulless corporation, a legal "body." Thus the reversal of the Christian paradox: in giving his soul to the corporation, he has lost it—he has become an abstract "body." Later in the novel, Max will pun upon "corporation" and "corpse" in the trial scene, trying to draw a connection between Mr. Dalton's attempt to distance himself from Bigger's life through a legalistic form, and Dalton's responsibility, because of this act, for his own daughter's death.

Bigger's compulsive gesture, blotting out the mapped universe, is an unconscious response to the invisible forces that govern his life. After he has killed both Mary and Bessie, he stands at the window of an empty apartment building gazing upon the city under snow, seeking for the pattern that continually eludes him:

> The snow had stopped falling and the city, white, still, was a vast stretch of rooftops and sky. He had been thinking about it for hours here in the dark and now there it was, all white, still. But what he had thought about it had made it real with a reality it did not have now in the daylight. When lying in the dark thinking about it, it seemed to have something which left it when it was looked at. Why should not this cold white world rise up as a beautiful dream in which he could walk and be at home, in which it would be easy to do and not to do? If only someone had gone before and lived and suffered or died—made it so that it could be understood! It was too stark, not redeemed, not made real with the reality that was the warm blood of life. He felt that there was something missing, some road which, if he had once found it, would have led him to a sure and quiet knowledge. (204)

The snow outside the window destroys the last aura of Bigger's dream, a dream that had hinted that a pattern of the city's labyrinth could be found. For the white snow, which obliterates all shape, all pattern, is the city that Bigger lives in, a world that denies him a map. That Bigger lives outside the "symbols and images" of civilization means that he lives in a blank space, and the resurrected Christ cannot substitute for the dream: Christ's warm blood will not thaw the city's snow, or reveal the invisible City of God beneath the formless surface of the city. Indeed, the burning cross set to intimidate Bigger when he is forced to return to the scene of the crime is Wright's reminder that Christ's compassion is exclusive. The real Chicago is governed by myths that the Buckleys and the Daltons have imposed—these substitutes for God have created a mockery of community whose substance is the cold, white snow. Only Mary's death momentarily convinces Bigger that he is free to read the invisible traces and, like Prometheus, to challenge the gods of the city, to answer power with power.

The last section of the novel (book 3, "Fate") brings Bigger into the toils of Chicago's judicial system, a heart of darkness where the city's contradictions become flesh in the characters of the agents of the state. Calculating that he can be reelected if Bigger is executed for murder, Buckley visits Bigger in his cell, hoping to obtain a confession. He "led Bigger to a window through which he [Bigger] looked and saw the streets below crowded with masses of people in all directions. 'See that, boy? Those people would like to lynch you. That's why I'm asking you to trust me and talk to me. The quicker we get this over with, the better for you' " (258). Of all the window views of the city in *Native Son,* Buckley's is the most essentialist, reducing society to the expression of brute force. And Bigger yields momentarily to the voice claiming to explain the city, for it explains a city of power he himself has recognized and embraced. By the window Buckley manipulates Bigger's fear by exposing him to the people's monolithic wrath; at the trial, Buckley will arouse the people's fear by depicting Bigger as a beast, demonizing what is different. The intention of both rhetorical occasions is to freeze by means of terror the city's protean potential for change.

That Buckley is Bigger's sinister "double" is made clear early in the novel, when Buckley's face on the billboard glares at Bigger, and Bigger glares back. Buckley is both antagonist and doppelgänger—that is why Bigger reads the image on the billboard with such accuracy. He identifies with Buckley because he understands that the empirical reality operating in the city precludes the possibility of virtue being rewarded. In book 2 of the novel, the sense of freedom and release which Mary's murder gave to Bigger is quickly diffused among the city's conflicting, ephemeral narratives. Because of Bessie's chance mention of the sensational Leopold-Loeb case, Bigger associates his own situation with that half-known story, seeing a means to defend himself and to exploit his single act of identity. But here, as elsewhere, Bessie defines the nature of his estrangement more absolutely than any other character in the novel: his brutal murder of her illustrates that the only new identity he can conceive of assuming is the godlike persona on a movie screen or billboard.[42] In a city where the only maps trace circuits of power, Buckley is all that Bigger can imagine becoming.

At the trial, Buckley's relationship to the world of power is subsumed in his role of defender of the laws of the city, the written code that gives the city its formal rationale. Wright reminds us of the falsity of this legal assumption not only by alluding to Paul ("The letter killeth. . . .") but also by connecting Buckley's histrionics to the moralistic endings of Hollywood movies. The laws that Buckley stresses in his courtroom speech all illustrate what he calls God's "thunderous 'NO'!" (344). His civilization is defined in terms of negatives, and his strategy is to make Bigger nonhuman, "a rapacious beast," a "maddened ape," and so forth—he will ensure the safety of the city by destroying the beast that threatens it.

But the beast that Bigger stands in for, of course, is the scapegoat. In *Permanence and Change,* Kenneth Burke says that society's choice of a scapegoat often reflects a metaphor gone wrong. For, like a window frame, a metaphor is a way of seeing, an orientation; and "a way of seeing is also a way of not-seeing." Laying the city's sins upon a scapegoat should allow the city's residents to see that there but for the grace of God go they—the sins that Christ takes upon himself are humanity's sins. But making Bigger the scapegoat blinds the citizens of Chicago to the true nature of their society and its problems, an effect that Burke refers to as "trained incapacity."[43] Buckley's metaphor of the beast frames a Manichean view of the urban landscape, one that distracts the hearer's attention from the economic and political facts, just as the sublime aesthetics of the skyline sublimate questions of practical power.

Both Buckley and Dalton symbolize invisible forces that freeze the city's potential for change. The empty, skeletal buildings on Chicago's South Side are objective correlatives of Dalton's wintry world, illustrations of an architecture that, in Lewis Mumford's words, no longer reflects the "living functions" of an organic society.[44] The dead buildings in Mr. Dalton's slums are the reverse side of the gleaming classical architecture in the White City of the Columbian Exposition of 1893; they call into question the values ostensibly expressed by the city's Gothic cathedrals. They are what high culture divorced from the *demos* has created, a Gothic nightmare, where the freeze-frame of Buckley's face on the billboard (only the eyes move) overlooks a necropolis.

This connection between power, stasis, and death is emphasized at the inquest by the character of the coroner (literally, the agent of the *corona,* the crown) who presides over corpses. He obscures the story of power by constructing an alternative myth out of scattered icons. At the inquest, Bigger looks up to see on a table

the pile of white bones . . . beside them lay the kidnap letter, held in place by a bottle of ink. In the center of the table were white sheets of paper fastened by a metal clasp; it was his signed confession. And there was Mr. Dalton, white-faced, white haired; and beside him was Mrs. Dalton, still and straight. . . . Then he saw the trunk into which he had stuffed Mary's body, the trunk which he had lugged down the stairs and had carried to the station. And, yes, there was the blackened hatchet blade and a tiny round piece of metal. (265)

The last is Mary's earring, which the coroner focuses upon to build, step by step, a symbolic history. Encouraged by the coroner, Mrs. Dalton describes the ancestry of this pair of earrings (only one of which was found in the furnace), observing how they were passed down from generation to generation within her family.

The coroner's rhetorical strategy is obvious, but it involves much more than a sentimental picture of the Dalton family. He uses the earring to construct the moral history of what he conceives to be civilization, his method that of the archaeologist, a search for an *archē* (beginning). Where does civilization begin, he is asking, in what place and with what intimate gestures? For him, the scattered objects on the table illustrate the desecration of the sacred. In this sense, they are like objects in a museum in that they attempt "to give by the ordered display of selected artifacts a total representation of human reality and history." The museum implies a static world, a "Newtonian model [that] moves from point of presence to point of presence and does not have, intrinsically, a temporality that describes systems as changing."[45] It is a nineteenth-century metaphor for order, for things being in their place; it will be replaced by the twentieth-century furnace, a metaphor for things once solid melting "into air." In the furnace, objects go "from a differentiated state to an undifferentiated state."[46] Such change, which removes all difference, all distinctions between things, is an apt metaphor for the urban experience of "leveling," the transformation of culture caused by a predominantly commercial motivation. Hence there is a basic contradiction between the coroner's myth of stasis, stability, and the ordered march of civilization, and the corporate powers behind Mr. Dalton which create and manipulate the city's mass culture. The furnace in *Native Son* obliterates the Dalton family narrative. Mr. Dalton's daughter has literally melted into air in his own basement, and this is what Wright perceives the true meaning of the earring to be. It is a deeply ironic, and frightening, conception of the "melting pot."

In his summation speech at the trial, Max, too, wants to remove all illusion of difference, to look at a new "map." Those "colonists" you romanticize, he tells the jury, "were faced with a difficult choice: they had either to subdue this wild land or be subdued by it. We need but turn our eyes upon the imposing sweep of streets and factories and buildings to see how completely they have conquered. But in conquering they *used* others" (328–29). Wright, perhaps following Lewis Mumford, links the first city-builders in America and the white settlers' westward movement with naked aggression.[47] Theirs, continues Max, was "the imperial dream of a feudal age," the ultimate irony of a civilization that claimed to be based on the natural rights of man. The pilgrims and pioneers had fled the "cities of the old world where the means to sustain life were hard to get or own," but they became like the people who had oppressed them, for in creating their "streets and factories and buildings" they had them-selves oppressed others. Late in the novel, Max will try to get Bigger to see how his present discontent contains a future promise, how dead stone might be reanimated by living spirit; but in his summation speech he confronts the city's citizens with the horror of a civilization that claims to be a uniquely just human society but has in fact simply repeated the sins of the past.

The point he makes to the city's citizens is that there *is* a beast in the city, but it is the creation of their civilization's failure. And that beast is a corpse that will not stay dead: "It still lives! It has made itself a home in the wild forest of our great cities, amid the rank and choking vegetation of slums! It has forgotten our language! In order to live it has sharpened its claws! . . . By night it creeps from its lair and steals towards the settlements of civiliza-tion!" (331). Wright takes Eliot's "Dog . . . that's friend to men" in *The Waste Land* and reworks it for use in another "Unreal City." Eliot's dog digs up the corpse of corruption beneath the placid philistine surface of the city, and in so doing is transformed into an agent of doom, James Thomson's "hound of heaven."[48] The city of Chicago is still close to the forest, the word *settlements* reminding us how recent, tenuous, and fragile its walls are. Dalton rejects any connection to this "forest," but the connection is made by the corpse of his daughter, who suffers the indignity of imitating how Bigger lives. Bigger can-not squeeze her into the trunk, having to bend her legs to make her fit, and later must cut off her head to make her fit into the furnace. The literalization of the Procrustes myth comments on Mr. Dalton's blindness; in death, Mary's body mirrors the physical and spiritual bends that he inflicts upon the black people who live in his buildings. Those "settlements" are built upon corpses, and the civilization they project is as illusory as a picture on a movie screen.

It is at the invisible boundary line separating civilization from wilderness that Wright wants the city to confront itself. The city, he insists, is lost within an illusion of its monuments, of its institutions, of its dreams of becoming a Paris on the Lake. It pretends that its white city is an accurate measure of its status as a culture, that the facade of its classical and Gothic architecture reflects a city of *civitas*. But throughout his novel, Wright has underscored a connection between power and high culture, greed and elegance. Those like Mr. Dalton who represent high culture are self-deceived, because they refuse to acknowledge their connection to power, and those like Buckley who repre-sent power hide their greed behind a myth of civilization, the city's skyscraper skyline.

When Jan and Mary attempt to speak to Bigger, despite their leftist rhetoric they unconsciously employ the symbolic image of the skyline. But Bigger can't see that city, because he has been excluded from it. When Max finally succeeds in communicating with him, it is because Bigger's fear has been transformed, first to an illusion of power, then by a collapse into despair. For Wright tells us at the beginning of the novel's third book that the identity Bigger created for himself by the negative act of murder has failed him, and that he exists in a kind of moral limbo, his only desire to sink into the "dark face of ancient waters" (234). At this point Max approaches him by indirection, as part of a professional interrogation that by degrees leads to uneasy friendship. The questions Max asks about Bigger's background and motivation have the unintended effect of causing Bigger to try "to see himself in relation to other men, a thing he had always feared to try to do, so deeply stained was his mind with the hate of others for him" (306). Indeed, so successful has Max been in stimulating Bigger to think of himself in terms of others that Bigger has a vision of community that bears some resemblance to Max's final appeal. He sees himself "standing in the midst of a vast crowd of men, white men and black men and all men, and the sun's rays melted away the differences, the colors, the clothes, and drew what was common and good upward toward the sun. . . . Had he been blind all along? . . . Was there some battle everybody was fighting, and he had missed it?" (307). Wright's image overcomes the terror of the furnace that melts down difference: the sun discovers a common humanity beneath that difference. But if Max's vision already lies dormant in Bigger, why then doesn't Bigger respond to it in the novel's final scene?

In fact, the novel's third book begins in a way that anticipates a Christian ending, or at least one whose themes are reconciliation, acceptance, and humility. Bigger's despair seems to demand an upward ascent, the one expected by the Christian-oriented literature of Western civilization. And indeed Max seems to play the part of Dante's Beatrice, who will lead Bigger out of his despair to a higher moral awareness, because his questions cause Bigger to probe the meaning of his own life and to connect it to something more lofty than mere ego. The scene is apparently set for a kind of Marxist and/or Christian redemption at the novel's conclusion. But there is a paradox here.

Even Max must use the "symbols and images" of a civilization that had betrayed the values that they stand for. If Mumford is right that the architecture of a civilization is a "sure index of what the people are subjectively,"[49] then is it possible to free the Wrigley Building from the chewing gum, or the Tribune Tower from yellow journalism? Max implicitly rejects Jan and Mary's picturesque view of these buildings—they will only be beautiful, he tells Bigger, when their stone is reanimated, not merely repossessed; his point is that humanistic values can be recovered when the "symbols and images" that express them are reconnected to an Ur–impulse: the passion to create an egalitarian society. Max wants Bigger to see the *figura* of the future buried within American civilization's frozen architecture;[50] but as Max implies at the trial, the prime mover behind these buildings, even if some of them look like cathedrals, was not God but the Faustian thrust of greed and power. This conflict between what is and what ought to be points to the tragic dilemma of the novel's final scene.

After the governor has refused Max's plea for clemency, the lawyer goes to Bigger's cell for a last meeting. Anxious for more than consolation, Bigger says to Max, "How can I die!" but he is asking in essence, "What did my life mean?" (354). Max tries to make Bigger see that he must join the human community in spirit if he is to understand that meaning. He takes Bigger to the window of his cell in the Cook County Jail, and Bigger sees "in the distance the tips of the sun-drenched buildings in the Loop" (356).[51] He tells Bigger that "those buildings sprang up out of the hearts of men. . . . Men like you." Human desire for fulfillment, Max continues, "keeps those buildings in their place. . . . What you felt, what you wanted, is what keeps those buildings standing there. When millions of men are desiring and longing, those buildings grow and unfold" (356). But a few men, he continues, have gotten control of the buildings and blocked the entrances; and the buildings "can't unfold." The meaning of Bigger's life, Max posits, is seeing himself in relationship to those "men like you [who] get angry and fight to re-enter those buildings, to live again" (357). Max wants Bigger to see his life in terms of living architecture, in terms of the vital polls, in terms of the *archē* of a true civilization. And he wants Bigger to join, if only in his imagination, with others in humanity's struggle to fulfill itself, a theme also implicit in the epilogue to *Invisible Man.*

Max's visionary portrait of the redeemed city is a classic statement of humanistic ideals, Christian and pagan. The vision from the window is like the vision Ezekiel sees of the New Jerusalem from high atop a mountain, and it also echoes the Book of Revelation, the ending of Milton's *Paradise Lost,* and book 6 of the *Aeneid.*[52] In this final scene from *Native Son,* we are reminded, as Maynard Mack has said in another context, of "man's recurring dream of the civilized community only one of whose names is Rome."[53] If Max gives his redeemed city a Marxist bias, Wright makes sure that readers see it in a more universal light through its archetypal setting.

Why then does Bigger reject Max's visionary city, especially since it reflects an image of community which he desperately seeks? Wright's answer is that one can imagine a holy city only if one perceives that the real city bears some resemblance, no matter how slight, to the archetype. Yet as Wright says of Bigger, in lines that precede Max's imaginary rendering of Chicago as an image of community and civilization: "He had lived outside of the lives of men. Their modes of communication, their symbols and images, had been denied him" (353). Just as he could not *see* Chicago's skyline as an image and symbol of civilization (having been excluded from that civilization), so too he cannot perceive the figura in Max's buildings. In order to make the cognitive leap to Max's buildings, Bigger would have to have some unifying principle in his mind to pull together the disparate images that exist there, and this would only be possible if the ideals of America's sacred documents had been made real to him *as ideals.* In other words, Max exists as Dante's Virgil for Bigger, showing him the various levels of Hell, but he cannot become Bigger's Beatrice. The only city Bigger knows is Chicago, and that city is either a maze or a prison; the only ideal city he can imagine is the one given to him by the mass media.

To look at the ending in another way, Wright makes it clear that Bigger is a political animal in an Aristotelean sense: he feels the need to belong to a polis. Indeed, that need is so powerful, Wright said in "How Bigger was Born," that it might have taken the form of either fascism or communism. The problem is, America presents Bigger with no viable form of the polis that he can believe in, so that when Max's heavenly city is presented to him at the novel's conclusion, it appears to him not as something abstracted from his own experience but simply as an abstraction. Paradoxically, Dalton's and Buckley's urban abstractions—corporations and laws—are more real to him, because they cloak motivations that he knows all too well. As Wright reminds us in an oft-quoted passage from *Black Boy,* the human values we take for granted must be learned:

> How hollow our memories, how lacking we were in those intangible senti-
> ments that bind man to man. . . . Whenever I thought of the essential bleak-
> ness of black life in America, I knew that Negroes had never been allowed to
> catch the full spirit of Western civilization, that they lived somehow in it but
> not of it. And when I brooded upon the cultural barrenness of black life, I
> wondered if clean, positive tenderness, love, honor, loyalty, and the capacity to
> remember were native with man. I asked myself if these human qualities were
> not fostered, won, struggled and suffered for, preserved in ritual from one gen-
> eration to another.[54]

This passage has been criticized as too narrow an interpretation of black life, specifically black folk culture, yet we might consider it a just interpretation of Chicago in *Native Son.*[55] Within Chicago, Bigger sees the invisible cities of economic power and the mythologies of mass culture, but he doesn't see "ten-derness, love, honor, loyalty and the capacity to remember . . . preserved in ritual from one generation to another," because *that* heavenly city does not exist in Chicago. And there is perhaps a deeper ironic level than this: in *Native Son,* Bigger lacks those "intangible sentiments that bind man to man" because he mirrors a city that in turn is a mirror of a nation that never caught "the full spirit of Western civilization." In this sense, he is the native son of *both* Chicago and America. That Wright was a student of Van Wyck Brooks, Waldo Frank, and Lewis Mumford, as well as H. L. Mencken, is significant here; these critics had also pointed to an undeveloped American culture, and in *Lawd Today!* Wright had used epigraphs from both Brooks and Frank which reflected on the absence of the Beloved Community in black urban cul-ture, in Chicago, and in America at large.[56]

Hence Bigger opts for what he knows, his own experience, which in itself is difficult to pin down. (Wright is determined to leave no easy answers.)

As Emerson saw, self-reliance is a vague concept: "Speak rather of that which relies, because it works and is."[57] Behind Emerson's transcendental philosophy is a tough-minded pragmatism, and this too is what Bigger accepts when he tells Max, "what I killed for, I *am!*" Bigger's sense of self "relies" upon "what I killed for," that is, upon desire made manifest through action. As a person excluded from American culture, Bigger is only able to define himself in opposition, by the act of murder, and that definition becomes so important to him that he will not give it up. Paradoxically, like any good American, Bigger "wanted to be happy in this world, not out of it" (302), yet his concept of happiness was shaped by the "instrumentalities" that his urban environment provided. Bigger authenticates himself by murder, and the only city he can imagine at the novel's end is one that created his life as a criminal, shaped it, and gave it meaning. And in choosing individual identity over community—a decision, we might say, that paradoxically marks him as an American—Bigger also fulfilled Kenneth Burke's definition of the truly "pious" life.

"What I killed for, I *am*": in Burke's terms, the "what" defines the man; it is the substantive pronoun, the "sub-stance," that "stands under" the human. Bigger killed to live—that is, in essence, the "what" that he killed for. In *Permanence and Change* (1935), Burke insists that true piety is "*the sense of what properly goes with what*";[58] and Bigger's decision to remain true to his "sense of what . . . goes with what" explains why he rejects Max's vision. That vision does not express Bigger's sense of personal propriety: "When I think about what you say I kind of feel what I wanted. It makes me feel I was kind of *right*" (358). That is, "right" in terms of "what properly goes with what": right to kill, right even to die in the electric chair. To accept Max's vision as his own—to see himself as belonging to a community of human beings all striving to achieve utopia—would deny the rightness of actions that make up the pattern of life he can understand. It is right that he die in the electric chair, because this sense of an ending makes him read his life as a whole text for the first time. The electric chair is a fitting conclusion to a life that was one long act of rebellion against what society officially considers pious.

Native Son's Gothic ending is indebted to Poe, Hawthorne, and Conrad—all favorite authors of Wright's—but it was also shaped by Hollywood movies. (As Michel Fabre tells us, Wright was an inveterate moviegoer; "he sometimes went to as many as three movies a day").[59] The debt is an indirect one, yet there is a suggestive coincidence of chronology, character, theme, and narrative maneuver between Wright's novel and the gangster movies of the 1930s. After 1934 the Hays code legislated that Hollywood would not depict gangsters in a favorable light; they had to die as a lesson to the supposedly impressionable audience, sometimes with just the hint of Christian redemption.[60] A film that fulfilled all the nominal requirements was *Angels with Dirty Faces,* released in 1938, while Wright was working on *Native Son.* The general structural similarity of plot (the poor boy turns to crime, has a brief success, and comes to a bad end), as well as Wright's use of the name "Buckley" (a crooked police captain in the movie) and other details make it possible that Wright had *Angels* in mind while writing *Native Son*.[61] But whether he had or not, the distinctive parallels between the ending of the novel and that of the movie help illuminate the last scene of *Native Son*.

Angels is a gangster movie set during the Depression; its locale is the city during hard times, and it focuses on those hit hardest by hard times, the poor. Thus it makes a claim on our conscience as we watch one bad boy, Rocky Sullivan (James Cagney), grow up in a tough neighborhood to become a gangster. Parallel to Rocky's glamorous rise from reform school kid to mobster is the humble vocation of the local parish priest, Jerry Connolly (Pat O'Brien), who was Rocky's boyhood chum. Although he and Rocky had engaged in petty crimes together as juveniles, he is determined now to save the teenagers in his parish from Rocky's influence and his fate. The movie ends with Father Connolly asking Rocky to die a coward in the electric chair so that the impressionable kids of their old neighborhood will despise his memory. Connolly's argument is that although Rocky's life is over, Rocky can perform one Christian act before he passes from the scene: to save the kids by not giving them a defiant and rebellious image to admire. Although Rocky at first resists so outrageous a request, he whimpers and whines in the death room, and the camera zooms in to a close-up of Connolly's face as we hear Rocky's weeping in the background. In the Rembrandt lighting that Hollywood in the 1930s reserved for Christians and virgins, Father Connolly is shown thanking God for the mysterious ways in which his wonders are performed, and the movie ends on this saccharine note. What began as a criticism of the city as social system ends as a celebration of Christian piety and of the triumph of good over evil.

The movie's ending would have appeared to Richard Wright as an example of Hollywood immorality, and when he came to write the ending of his own novel, he allowed Bigger to complete the cycle of piety, to frame his life in his own terms, in a way Hollywood's gangsters were never allowed to do. However, what makes *Angels* particularly interesting in reference to Wright's novel is that the movie's ending could be understood as very similar to the conclusion of *Native Son*. The penultimate shot of the film suggests that Connolly's motivation has been not a love of Christ but a love of power, and that it is as a figure of power that he has replaced Rocky in the boys' hearts. This shot is low-angle, looking upward at Father Connolly, who is wearing a fedora at a rakish angle and standing at the top of the basement stairs with bars of light behind him, as he ostensibly confirms Rocky's "yellow" behavior in the death chamber.[62] What this shot actually confirms is that beneath the Hollywood story line there has been a dark, *film noir* side to Father Connolly's behavior through the entire movie. He sees himself competing with Rocky for the boys' admiration, and he resents the infatuation of Lori Martin (Ann

Sheridan) with his rival: it is at that point that he suddenly "converts" to active opposition. He quickly becomes a media figure and a power broker, using radio and newspapers as effectively as any propagandist and, incidentally, making once again the point of mass culture's moral ambiguity—Rocky has been (like Bigger) partially a creation of "the news." But Connolly is driven to his evangelical fury by a barely visible web of unpriestly motivations—jealousy, envy, lust, and the desire for power. Michael Curtiz, the film's director, seems to know exactly what he is doing; he tells one story for the Hays-code censors and tells another story, through innuendo and visual imagery, for whoever in his audience cares to see.[63] It is easy to imagine that if Bigger Thomas were in the audience watching *Angels,* he would have understood Connolly's will to power just as he understood Buckley's.

It is Rocky, not Father Connolly, who is truly pious in Kenneth Burke's sense. Rocky's contempt for the law, his will to succeed, his refusal to be anyone's dupe, and his arrogant mannerisms—these give him a consistency of character that only his bravery in facing the electric chair could complete. Rocky, like Bigger, is held up as a grotesque by the newspapers, but both men draw an invisible sustenance from their caricatures, becoming more and more like poisonous flowers, deadly nightshades, that gain their strength from being planted in dung.

The newspaper campaigns against Rocky only revitalize him, making him all the more determined to go out with guns blazing. What destroys his own sense of piety is an appeal made to him on the basis of another kind of piety. He allows Connolly to manipulate him, to use their boyhood friendship for his own ends; hence Rocky violates the sacred space of his own making, which is based upon rebellion, and resistance to a hypocritical city.

In *Native Son*'s original version, Wright has Bigger die in the electric chair like Rocky, though without Rocky's feigned cowardice. The published ending is more effective. Indeed, the slamming of the "far door" in the prison is one of the most terribly final conclusions in American literature. We recognize that the door is closing not only on Bigger's life but also on a myriad of hopes and illusions of American civilization, and it is ironically appropriate that we can measure the extent of our loss by comparing Bigger's end to Rocky's. In *Native Son,* Wright gave Bigger a much greater threat to his integrity than a hypocrite like Father Connolly; he made him square off against an honest man, one who represents a vision of the city that Bigger already wants to believe in, the idea of a Beloved Community in which a true democracy prevails. The heavenly city that Connolly presents to Rocky and the neighborhood kids is Dalton's corporation, a hierarchy with Connolly at the top (as shown by the *film noir* final shot). The tragedy of *Native Son* is that Bigger ultimately can only resolve the dilemma by choosing self-definition over a community with others. But it is, of course, no solution, because as Bessie's death clearly illustrates, by accepting "why all the killing was" (358), Bigger places himself beyond the pale of *caritas* and of the Beloved Community. The novel's tragic center is the fact that Bigger's definition of self include not one but two corpses, one murder "accidental," the other done in cold blood.[64] And it is that last murder that places him outside any refuge within the black community. Yet it is that definition of self based on murder which is the only thing in his life that makes sense: "What I killed for must've been *good!* . . . I didn't know I was alive in this world until I felt things hard enough to kill for 'em" (358; my italics). If there is a tragedy in *Native Son,* as one critic has argued, then both the reborn Bigger and the idealized city must be seen as *good* at the novel's end. For if the novel is a tragedy, then we need a tragic dilemma. And a tragic dilemma is one in which there are no satisfactory solutions.[65]

Through Bigger, Wright accepts the Lockean (even Hobbesian) implications of America's past. Bigger is a native son because, like other Americans, he lacks the cohesive glue of tradition, the *substance* that might close the large gap between the ideals contained in the nation's sacred documents and the quotidian world that he experiences. As Lewis Mumford had argued in the *American Mercury* in 1926, the American was a "stript European." The pioneers and puritans who emigrated to these shores were no longer "buoyed up by memorials of the past." They were modern men who shed the rich and varied intellectual heritage of the medieval-Renaissance world view and had only their Enlightenment grids to replace it. Coming to America, they wandered in the wilderness without a spiritual guide "to lead them . . . and here they have remained in exile," Mumford adds with a touch of understatement, "a little more than the Biblical forty years."[66] The diaspora for blacks was even longer and even more culturally traumatic. The problem of Max's vision of the city on the hill, and perhaps of John Winthrop's as well, is that it belonged to the piety of another time, another place.

At the end of *Native Son,* Max tries to counter the naked id with a vision of the Beloved Community, and we might say that through both Max's vision and Bigger's rejection Wright is speaking for us. It is precisely here that he anticipates, but with a different emphasis, Ellison's famous last sentence of *Invisible Man:* "Who knows but that, on the lower frequencies, I speak for you?" Ellison would have us identify not only with the invisible man's alienation but also with his desire to reconnect himself to the American polis. In the epilogue the invisible man hints that he is going to leave his cell, "since there's a possibility that even an invisible man has a socially responsible role to play." Because the city, whose true founder is Proteus, has taught him to be protean, he hopes to make the "sacred papers" live in and through him. Bigger, too, intends to be more than a disembodied voice at the novel's end: "What I killed for, I *am*" means that in accepting himself as a murderer, he has refused society's definition of him as an invisible man. But this means that, again paraphrasing Poe's "Man of the Crowd," he is a text that not only can't be read but also remains somewhat opaque even to himself: "When I think of *why* all the killing was, I begin to feel *what* I wanted, *what* I am"

(358; my italics). Even Bigger cannot reconcile the paradoxical relationship between murder and creation; all he knows at the end is that the vision of the ideal place is unsubstantial compared to the places in the heart where he has in fact lived.

In *Native Son,* Wright accepts the Romantic paradox of Cain, who is both a homeless pariah and the first city-builder. The American Cain defined himself by rejecting somebody else's definition of him, but he in turn used others to build his city—aggression became its foundation.[67] Max fails at the novel's end not because his vision of the redeemed city is a pretty picture but because it is a picture that has no Cain in it. Bigger only knows the city at the bottom, and thus Cain's city is the only city he knows: "Bigger was gazing in the direction of the buildings; but he *did not see* them. He was trying to react to the picture Max was drawing, trying to compare that picture with what he had felt all his life" (357; my italics).[68] Max, too, is speaking for us through this "picture," but he leaves Bigger's cell with his eyes "full of terror," because he is brought face to face with the fact that the Founding Fathers' dream of "a more perfect union" may be an illusion. For Max, like them, is a rationalist who believes in humanity's capacity to recognize evil and remove it. This ultimately is the basis of his appeal in the courtroom: the corpse we have created can be put to rest if we ourselves can be brought to see its true nature. In the novel's final scene, Max is like Joseph Conrad's Kurtz, who has looked into the abyss and confronts a truth at the heart not only of this civilization but, perhaps, of all civilizations: there are no civilized cities. Each is based on a primal crime that cannot be eradicated. The true implications of his courtroom speech come home to him as he leaves Bigger's cell, for in describing Bigger's history he has also described the history of civilization and of its cities.

Notes

1. James R. Grossman, *Land of Hope: Chicago, Black Southerners, and the Great Migration* (Chicago: University of Chicago Press, 1989), 81. The *Defender* was the largest black newspaper of the time, and during World War I it increased its circulation in the south from 50,000 (1916) to 125,000 (1918): "It was said that in Laurel, Mississippi, old men who did not know how to read would buy it because it was regarded as precious" (Emmett J. Scott, *Negro Migration during the War* [1920; reprint, New York: Arno, 1969], 30). It was "precious" because it was tangible proof of a black city existing somewhere in an unseen world. Moreover, it created an imagined community of readers held together by the printed word; see Benedict Anderson, *Imagined Communities: Reflections on the Origin and Spread of Nationalism,* rev. ed. (London: Verso, 1991), 25. For a concise and often amusing account of the black newspaper, see Eugene Gordon, "The Negro Press," *American Mercury* 8 (June 1926): 207–15. Gordon notes the existence of 220 black newspapers in 1926. Also see David Gordon Nielson, *Black Ethos: Northern Urban Negro Life and Thought, 1890–1930* (Westport, Conn.: Greenwood, 1977), 9–12, 18–20. The first full study of the black newspaper is Frederick D. Detweiler, *The Negro Press in the United States* (Chicago: University of Chicago Press, 1922). The migration to the city at the turn of the

century roughly coincides with the founding dates of seven major black newspapers with close ties to metropolitan areas: the *New York Age* (1880) and the *Amsterdam News* (1909); the *Pittsburgh Courier* (1910); the *Philadelphia Tribune* (1885); the *Boston Guardian* (1902); the *Baltimore Afro-American* (1892); and the *Chicago Defender* (1905). The *Defender* is an interesting illustration of how a social movement like the Great Migration both created a newspaper and was in turn spurred on by it. For an illustration of the latter theme, see Langston Hughes, *Not without Laughter* (1930; reprint, New York: Macmillan, 1969), 191, 255–56. Set for the most part in rural Kansas, Hughes's novel shows the *Defender* to be an important link in a chain of circumstances that leads the major characters to Chicago.

2. Grossman, *Land of Hope*, 4.

3. Irving Howe, "Black Boys and Native Sons," in *Critical Essays on Richard Wright,* ed. Yoshinobu Hakutani (Boston: Hall, 1982), 41; first published in *Dissent*, 10 (Autumn 1963): 353–68.

4. Richard Wright, "Blueprint for Negro Writing" in *Richard Wright Reader,* ed. Ellen Wright and Michel Fabre (New York: Harper & Row, 1978), 44–45; first published in *New Challenge* 2 (Fall 1937): 53–65. The connection of the Harlem Renaissance to literary modernism is still an open question. Houston A. Baker, Jr., has argued that black writers from the turn of the century up through the 1920s worked out their own brand of modernism within the parameters of Afro-American culture; see his *Modernism and the Harlem Renaissance* (Chicago: University of Chicago Press, 1987). Arnold Rampersad has linked Langston Hughes with "populist" modernism, noting that reading Carl Sandburg freed the young poet "from the tyranny of traditional forms." Moreover, Hughes corresponded with Pound and was published in Harriet Monroe's *Poetry* magazine (Arnold Rampersad, *The Life of Langston Hughes* [New York: Oxford University Press, 1986], 1:29, 129, 237). During the writing of *Cane* (1923), Jean Toomer was part of a home-grown modernist group consisting of Waldo Frank, Sherwood Anderson, Hart Crane, Gorham Munson, and Kenneth Burke, although Toomer's "Kabnis" could be considered a rewriting of James Joyce's "The Dead" (or of *A Portrait of the Artist as a Young Man*). Similarly, Sterling Brown employed Eliot's "mythical method" in his poetry, as did Zora Neale Hurston in her most famous novel. (See Cyrena N. Pondrom, "The Role of Myth in Hurston's *Their Eyes Were Watching God,*" *American Literature* 58 [1986]: 181–202). Yet no one in the Harlem Renaissance of the 1920s, with the possible exception of Toomer, immersed himself in modernism with quite the thoroughness that Wright did. For instance, Wright's *Lawd Today!* (New York: Walker, 1963), written in 1936 and published posthumously, was clearly a seminal black novel; its broken narrative and the text's weave of allusion to and quotation of both high and low culture, especially black street culture, was useful to Ralph Ellison, as was Wright's modernist allegory "The Man Who Lived Underground," in *Eight Men* (Cleveland: World, 1961). For an intelligent discussion of Wright as a modernist, see Craig Werner, "Bigger's Blues: *Native Son* and the Articulation of Afro-American Modernism," in *New Essays on "Native Son,"* ed. Keneth Kinnamon (Cambridge: Cambridge University Press, 1990), 117–52.

5. Wright, "Blueprint for Negro Writing," 48.

6. The phrase "divided stream," of course, comes from Charles Child Walcutt's classic study *American Literary Naturalism: A Divided Stream* (Minneapolis: University of Minnesota Press, 1956). Also see Eric J. Sundquist, ed., *American Realism: New Essays* (Baltimore: Johns Hopkins University Press, 1982), 3–24. Sundquist makes perceptive connections between realism and romance, "the gothic and naturalism" (13).

7. Bernard W. Bell, *The Afro-American Novel and Its Tradition* (Amherst: University of Massachusetts Press, 1987), 161. Influenced by Robert Scholes (see p. 284), Bell states that in *Native Son* "Wright's image of black character is consciously more mythic than mimetic" (161). It would be more accurate to say that the two modes—mimesis and myth—form a kind of dialectic interplay in the novel.

8. Richard Wright, "How 'Bigger' was Born," in *Twentieth Century Interpretations of "Native Son,"* ed. Houston A. Baker, Jr. (Englewood Cliffs, N.J.: Prentice-Hall, 1972), 39. The open space of the "wind-swept prairie" foreshadows LeRoi Jones's "horizon" in "Each Morning."

9. Carl Sandburg, *The Complete Poems of Carl Sandburg* (New York: Harcourt, Brace, 1970), 81.

10. Michel Fabre, *The World of Richard Wright* (Jackson: University of Mississippi Press, 1985), 21.

11. See Burton Pike, *The Image of the City in Modern Literature* (Princeton: Princeton University Press, 1981), 90–96.

12. Quoted from Ellen Moers, *The Two Dreisers* (New York: Viking, 1969), 277.

13. Richard Wright, Introduction to *Black Metropolis,* by St. Clair Drake and Horace R. Cayton, 3d ed. (New York: Harcourt, Brace, 1970), xvii.

14. Richard Wright, *American Hunger* (New York: Harper & Row, 1977), 1.

15. Ibid., 63.

16. Michel Fabre, *The World of Richard Wright* (Jackson: University of Mississippi Press, 1985), 23. For an insightful treatment of Kenneth Burke's influence on Richard Wright's writings, see Eugene E. Miller, *Voice of A Native Son: The Poetics of Richard Wright* (Jackson: University of Mississippi Press, 1990), 174–211.

17. Kenneth Burke, *Permanence and Change: An Anatomy of Purpose* (1935; reprint, Los Altos, Calif: Hermes, 1954), 182–83.

18. Richard Wright, *Native Son* (New York: Harper, 1940), 204; in this chapter, unless otherwise noted, page numbers for subsequent citations of this work are given in parentheses and refer to this edition.

19. Mario Gandelsonas, *The Urban Text,* with essays by Joan Copjec, Catherine Ingraham, and John Whiteman (Cambridge: MIT Press, 1991), 23. Also see Joan Copjec, "The Grid and the Logic of Democracy," in Gandelsonas, *Urban Text,* 13. Thomas Jefferson's original proposal "called for the . . . extension of the chess-board divisions and subdivisions of Eastern cities over the Western territories." Also see John R. Stilgoe, *Common Landscape of America, 1580 to 1845* (New Haven: Yale University Press, 1982), 99–107. Congress severely qualified Jefferson's "model example of Enlightenment abstraction," but even their "compromise" recognized the value of the grid, as townships were mapped out in terms of "six statute miles square divided into thirty-six lots of 640 acres each" (103). According to Stilgoe, "by 1820 the grid concept was permanently established in the national imagination" (104).

20. Louis Wirth, "Urbanism as a Way of Life," in *Louis Wirth: On Cities and Social Life. Selected Papers,* ed. Albert J. Reiss, Jr. (Chicago: University of Chicago Press, 1964), 82. Wright specifically calls attention to Wirth's essay in his Introduction to Drake and Cayton, *Black Metropolis,* xx. Wright need not have gone to Wirth for this insight about metropolitan "communications"; in 1938 Wright could have found a similar observation about radios and newspapers in Lewis Mumford's *Culture of Cites* (New York: Harcourt, Brace, 1938), 256: "The swish and the crackle of paper is the underlying sound of the metropolis. . . . What is visible and real in this world is only what has been transferred to paper. The essential gossip of the metropolis is no longer that of people meeting face to face on the crossroads, at the dinner table, in the marketplace: a few dozen people writing in newspapers, a dozen more broadcasting over the radio, provide the daily interpretation of movements and happenings. . . . It is a short step from a yellow journal proprietor, skillfully manipulating the day's news, to a propaganda ministry in a war government or a fascist dictatorship."

21. H. L. Mencken, "The Ways of the Wicked," *American Mercury* 13 (March 1928): 381.

22. Fabre, *World of Richard Wright,* 14. In *American Hunger* Wright notes, "One afternoon [in Chicago, 1927], the boss lady entered the kitchen and found me sitting on a box reading a copy of the *American Mercury*" (15). And of course everyone by now knows of Wright's famous encounter with the writings of H. L. Mencken, which Wright described in *Black Boy* (New York: Harper, 1945).

23. As Keneth Kinnamon and Arnold Rampersad have recently shown, Wright was forced to write this scene as a replacement for one objected to by Edward Aswell, Harper's

editor. See Keneth Kinnamon, Introduction to Kinnamon, ed., *New Essays on "Native Son,"* 12–14; *Richard Wright: Early Works,* ed. Arnold Rampersad (New York: Library of America, 1991), 912, 924. In the latter compilation, which includes the Library of America's new edition of *Native Son,* Rampersad includes the original scene (472–75). Although some of the revisions forced on Wright "diluted" (Kinnamon's word) the impact of *Native Son,* the scene at the Regal Theater he rewrote is actually better than the original. In the original scene, Bigger and Jack masturbate in the movie house, and then watch a newsreel in which Mary Dalton appears in a pseudo-documentary context that highlights the rich and famous: Mary, in her swimsuit, sports with Jan Erlone on Florida's beaches, while the newsreel's commentator alludes to her companion's politics and her father's chagrin. Wright was meticulously accurate when it came to the texture of realism—he wanted a detailed map of Chicago's "South Side" (see Kinnamon, ed., *New Essays on "Native Son,"* 28), and he corrected street names in "later printings" of *Native Son* (*Richard Wright: Early Works,* 913). What was to be gained by the unlikely coincidence of Bigger's seeing Mary in a newsreel that morning and meeting her in the Dalton home that afternoon? True, Wright obviously wanted to show the contrast between the newsreel's titillating portrait of the rich playgirl and the actual Mary, an irony nicely refined by the fact that Mary herself is acting out the script of Jan's left-wing ideology. Yet the same irony is secured, and even intensified, by substituting for the newsreel the generic film *The Gay Woman.* This substitution, as I shall show, gives Wright the opportunity to examine, through the movie's plot, the ways in which mass culture manipulates its audience, never taking into account how someone like Bigger "reads" its fictions. Wright, of course, invented *The Gay Woman*—there is no such movie—but its composite plot points to several film genres of the 1920s and 30s. The early melodramas of Cecil B. De Mille could have provided a model. See Lary May, *Screening Out the Past: The Birth of Mass Culture and the Motion Picture Industry* (New York: Oxford University Press, 1980), 209. Wright perhaps borrowed the name from the Fred Astaire-Ginger Rogers musical *The Gay Divorcee* (1934), the general ambience of luxury from a number of screwball comedies dealing with divorce and remarriage (e.g., *The Awful Truth* [1937]), and the right-wing motif from a gangster movie such as *G-Men* (1935).

    24.   There was, of course, an attempt to regulate how Hollywood promoted this desire. The Hays code, which came into force in 1934, was very specific about what forms sexuality might take in the movies, and its norms were carefully monitored by Joseph Breen and his spies (see Gerald Gardner, *The Censorship Papers: Movie Censorship Letters from the Hays Office, 1934 to 1968* [New York: Dodd, Mead, 1987], xv–xxiv, 207–14). Before 1934 a previous Hollywood code (1927) had been in effect, but although it, too, insisted on sexual "good taste," its cursory list of "don'ts" and "be carefuls" was often ignored. After Breen began managing the Hays Office, however, self-censorship (as well as subtle evasions of the code) became a way of life for Hollywood film makers. The 1927 code condemned the cinematic depiction of miscegenation, but racial mixing went unmentioned in the 1934 code (in keeping with the Hays Office's "progressive" attitudes toward ethnic groups and minorities). Nevertheless miscegenation, as we know, remained an invisible taboo in Hollywood. One form of desire the code wouldn't restrain, of course, was the desire for consumption; in fact, it modestly claimed to promote it. As Hays said, "More and more is the motion picture being recognized as a stimulant to trade" (May, *Screening Out the Past,* 236).

    25.   Kevin Lynch, "Reconsidering the Image of the City," in *Cities of the Mind: Images and Themes of the City in the Social Sciences,* ed. Lloyd Rodwin and Robert M. Hollister (New York: Plenum, 1984), 152, 155. Lynch's famous book on this theme is *The Image of the City* (Cambridge: MIT Press, 1960).

    26.   Wright, "How 'Bigger' Was Born," 29; idem, *Native Son,* 204. As he was writing *Native Son* in 1938, Wright used *Chicago Tribune* accounts of a murder trial involving two black youths, Robert Nixon and Earl Hicks, to show how the media shaped the circumstances sur-

rounding Bigger's trial. See Keneth Kinnamon, *The Emergence of Richard Wright: A Study in Literature and Society* (Urbana: University of Illinois Press, 1972), 121–25. Also see Margaret Walker, *Richard Wright: Daemonic Genius* (New York: Warner, 1988), 122–25.

27.   Wright, "How 'Bigger' Was Born," 37–38.

28.   Ralph Ellison, *Shadow and Act* (New York: New American Library, 1966), 121–22: "Wright could imagine Bigger, but Bigger could not possibly imagine Richard Wright."

29.   George Steiner, *Tolstoy or Dostoevsky: An Essay in the Old Criticism* (New York: Random House, 1961), 195–96.

30.   Wright, "How 'Bigger' Was Born," 47.

31.   In Poe's story, the ambiguous pronoun *er* ("er lasst sich nicht lesen"—it [or he] does not permit itself [or himself] to be read") applies to both city and to the old roué whom the narrator follows in an attempt to discover who and what he is. See Edgar Allan Poe, "The Man of the Crowd," in *The Norton Anthology of American Literature*, ed. Nina Baym et al., 3d ed. (New York: Norton, 1989), 1412; hereafter this volume is cited as *Norton*.

32.   Kenneth Burke, *The Philosophy of Literary Form: Studies in Symbolic Action*, 2d ed. (Baton Rouge: Louisiana State University Press, 1967), xxi–xxii.

33.   Mumford, *Culture of Cities*, 403.

34.   See in particular Levine's account of the history of the Chicago Symphony Orchestra and the Chicago Public Library; what began as democratic expressions of culture soon hardened into exclusive institutions controlled by wealthy patrons and/or patrician attitudes. (Lawrence Levine, *Highbrow/Lowbrow. The Emergence of Cultural Hierarchy in America* [Cambridge: Harvard University Press, 1988], 115–99, 128, 130, 159, 160).

35.   See Burton Pike, *The Image of the City in Modern Literature* (Princeton: Princeton University Press, 1980), 28–30.

36.   Joan E. Draper, "Paris by the Lake: Sources of Burnham's Plans of Chicago," in *Chicago Architecture, 1872–1922: Birth of a Metropolis*, ed. John Zukowsky (Munich: Prestel-Verlag, 1987), 107–19.

37.   John W. Stamper, *Chicago's North Michigan Avenue: Planning and Development, 1900–1930* (Chicago: University of Chicago Press, 1991), 74, 69. For the design of the tower as a Doric column, see Zukowsky, ed., *Chicago Architecture,* 302. The design chosen was one submitted by John Mead Howells and Raymond Hood, "based on a thorough study of the formal features of a Gothic Tower." Howells gave the project added luster, because he was the son of William Dean Howells, novelist and "former editor of the *Atlantic Monthly*" (Stamper, *North Michigan Avenue,* 70, 74). Thus an aura of sanctimoniousness surrounded the tower's planning and construction, which was perhaps a reason for Lewis Mumford's 1931 complaint that the tower illustrated the "fake religion of business" (Lewis Mumford, *Brown Decades: A Study of the Arts in America, 1865–1895* [New York: Harcourt, Brace, 1931], 140).

In 1919 William Wrigley, Jr., the chewing-gum magnate, hired the firm of Graham, Anderson, Probst, and White to design a plan for the Wrigley Building (completed in 1922), which they modeled after the Giralda Tower of Seville, a cathedral erected at the height of the Spanish Renaissance (Stamper, *North Michigan Avenue,* 32, 40). These twin monuments on North Michigan Avenue were to inspire the citizenry to keep the barbarians outside the gates of the essential city.

In 1934 the *Tribune* built a Gothic-style annex north of the Tribune Tower to house WGN, its radio station, making its "guardianship" complete in terms of media control of the city. The *Tribune*'s ownership of WGN did not escape Wright's notice in *Lawd Today!* Wright opens his novel with this radio station's slick, patriotic celebration of Lincoln's birthday. It is worth noting that the only radio station Wright allows Jake to hear in *Lawd Today!* is WGN, just as the only newspaper that exists in *Native Son* is the *Tribune*. Wright's insights about media "guardianship" are similar to the Frankfurt School's and look forward to Fredric Jameson, who has discussed in our own day the omnipresent pervasiveness of mass media as one manifestation of "late capitalism." For a good discussion of this last theme, see David S. Gross,

"Marxism and Resistance: Fredric Jameson and the Moment of Postmodernism," *Canadian Journal of Political and Social Theory* 12, no. 3 (1988): 71–85.

38. Sam Warner, Jr., "Slums and Skyscrapers: Urban Images, Symbols, and Ideology," in Rodwin and Hollister, ed., *Cities of the Mind,* 187–89.

39. David Harvey, *Social Justice and the City* (Baltimore: Johns Hopkins University Press, 1973), 168.

40. Alan Trachtenberg, *The Incorporation of America: Culture and Society in the Gilded Age* (New York: Hill & Wang, 1982), 83.

41. *Louis Wirth,* 72. Following the Apostle Paul, Josiah Royce argues that the Beloved Community grounds itself in the paradoxical notion of a spiritual "body": "This new being is a corporate entity,—the body of Christ, or the body of which the divinely exalted Christ is the head. Of this body the exalted Christ is also, for Paul, the spirit and also, in some new sense, the lover. This corporate entity is the Christian community itself" (Josiah Royce, *The Problem of Christianity,* [New York: Macmillan, 1913] 1:92).

42. The figure of Bessie and her fate in the novel have led some critics to accuse Wright of being indifferent or actively hostile to his female characters. See Trudier Harris, "Native Sons and Foreign Daughters," in Kinnamon, ed., *New Essays on "Native Son,"* 63–84; Houston A. Baker, Jr., "Richard Wright and the Dynamics of Place in Afro-American Literature," in ibid., 108–13. To accuse Wright of misogyny—as Harris does—because of his representation of Bessie is to simplistically conflate author and character. Bigger's murder of Bessie is Wright's comment on the impotence of his character's illusion of power. It is an act of an existentially "free" man; and that is the act's ultimate horror (as Wright would have known, if only from reading *Crime and Punishment*). To wish that Bessie were depicted as an empowered black woman, or as a woman connected to a vital black community, is to ignore Wright's judgment about the effects of a racist social structure on relations between Afro-American women and men. Baker contends that Wright's Marxist frame of reference forces him to devalue Bessie (and black women in folk culture), yet Baker admits that Bessie "possesses the most lucid vision in *Native Son*" (110), is Bigger's most perceptive critic, and embodies the blues tradition in the novel. One could quarrel with Baker's interpretation of Marx, or indeed with his interpretation of the "Marxist" author of *Native Son,* yet the real issue here is Bessie. The question Baker never answers is, why such profound sympathy for and understanding of Bessie if Wright cannot find any "intellectual space" for her? One explanation is that it is Bigger, not Wright, who is incapable of sympathy and understanding. Three times in *Native Son* Wright mentions the "narrow orbit" of Bessie's life—her exhaustion, fear, loneliness, and desire to escape via intense pleasure—and these always occur in the context of Bigger's response to her. Bigger *knows* her life, but that knowledge does not lead to pity; rather, in their first long meeting after Mary's murder, he sees Bessie's vulnerability as something he can use to control her. Later, forced to flee with Bigger from her apartment, Bessie repeats again the details of her painful life and his dishonesty, but Bigger's only response is to see "what he must do to save himself" (195): he decides to murder her. Finally, at the inquest, when they bring out her mutilated body to prove him a monster, Bigger does have a different comprehension of her life—he sees that even in death she is still owned by her white employers. Yet this is as far as Bigger's compassion and understanding go; it is Wright, not Bigger, who makes us *see* that Bigger has abused Bessie in the same way that white society has abused Bigger. This is Wright's true Marxist perspective, the knowledge that oppression creates endless circles of cruelty among the oppressed. And although Bessie is indeed the bearer of a blues tradition (was she named after Bessie Smith, who had died in 1937, mutilated in a traffic accident and reportedly denied access to a white hospital?), in Wright's view that tradition by itself is helpless to change the conditions of black life. An expanded version of Baker's essay on Wright appears in Houston A. Baker, Jr., *Workings of the Spirit: The Poetics of Afro-American Women's Writing* (Chicago: University of Chicago Press, 1991), 102–33.

43. Burke, *Permanence and Change,* 49, 14–16.

44. Mumford, *Culture of Cities,* 406.

45. Eugenio Donato, "The Museum's Furnace: Notes toward a Contextual Reading of *Bouvard and Pécuchet,*" in *Textual Strategies: Perspectives in Post-Structural Criticism,* ed. Josué V. Harari (Ithaca, N.Y.: Cornell University Press, 1979), 221, 234; see Donato's discussion of "archēs" on 220.

46. Ibid., 234–35. Also see Marshall Berman, *All That Is Solid Melts into Air: The Experience of Modernity* (1982; reprint, New York: Penguin, 1988), 15–36.

47. Lewis Mumford, "Origins of the American Mind," *American Mercury* 8 (July 1926): 354. This article later appeared in a revised form as the first chapter of Mumford's *Golden Day* (1926). Wright here also deromanticizes Frederick Jackson Turner's frontier thesis, and Locke's application of that thesis to the city in *The New Negro.* See Paul Kellogg, "The Negro Pioneers," in *The New Negro,* ed. Alain Locke (1925; reprint, New York: Atheneum, 1969), 271–77. The Mumford-Wright view of the westward expansion has now become the accepted historical paradigm.

48. T. S. Eliot, *The Waste Land,* lines 60–75, in *The Complete Poems and Plays, 1909–1950* (New York: Harcourt, Brace & World, 1952), 39.

49. These are Louis Sullivan's words, which Mumford quotes with approval (Mumford, *Brown Decades,* 157, 158).

50. See Eric Auerbach, *Scenes from the Drama of European Literature* (New York: Meridian, 1959), 45: "The notion of the *figura* under which something other, future, true, lies concealed."

51. Wright carefully worked out his geography in this scene. A 1933 map of Chicago locates the Cook County Criminal Court Building and Jail between Twenty-sixth and Thirty-first streets (north/south), and between California and Sacramento boulevards (east/west), that is, within easy visual distance, on a clear day, of the tops of buildings such as the Tribune Tower and the Wrigley Building.

52. See Ezek. 40–48; Rev. 20–21; John Milton, *Paradise Lost,* 12, lines 549–51; *Aeneid,* 6, lines 752–95.

53. Maynard Mack, *The Garden and the City: Retirement and Politics in the Later Poetry of Pope* (Toronto: University of Toronto Press, 1969), 3.

54. Wright, *Black Boy,* 33.

55. See, for instance, Robert B. Stepto, "I Thought I Knew These People: Richard Wright and the Afro-American Literary Tradition," in *Chant of Saints: A Gathering of Afro-American Literature, Art, and Scholarship,* ed. Michael S. Harper and Robert B. Stepto (Urbana: University of Illinois Press, 1979), 195–211.

56. The Van Wyck Brooks epigraph for the first part of *Lawd Today!*—"Commonplace"—illustrates a theme explored by Brooks in *America's Coming-of-Age:* the assertion that in America there is no "common life," only "a vast Sargasso Sea—a prodigious welter of unconscious life, swept by ground-swells of half-conscious emotion" (Claire Sprague, ed., *Van Wyck Brooks: The Early Years* [New York: Harper & Row, 1968], 149. Brooks's next sentence, which Wright does not quote, is even more appropriate to the sterile urban landscape of *Lawd Today!:* "All manner of living things are drifting in it, phosphorescent, gayly colored, gathered into knots and clotted masses, gelatinous, unformed, flimsy, tangled, rising and falling, floating and merging, here an immense distended belly, there a tiny rudimentary brain (the gross devouring the fine)—everywhere an unchecked, uncharted, unorganized vitality like that of the first chaos. It is a welter of life which has not been worked into an organism" (149–50). The quotation from Frank that Wright uses for the novel's second section—"Squirrel Cage"—contains an idea common to Brooks, Bourne, Frank, and Mumford: without the Beloved Community there is no personal growth, no organic wholeness.

57. Ralph Waldo Emerson, "Self-Reliance," in *Norton,* 965.

58. Burke, *Permanence and Change,* 74.

59.　Michel Fabre, *The Unfinished Quest of Richard Wright,* trans., Isabel Barzun (New York: Morrow, 1973), 200. Also see Walker, *Richard Wright,* 220–21; Walker notes that "Edward G. Robinson . . . and Jimmy Cagney films" were among his favorites. Two Edward G. Robinson films—*Double Indemnity* (1944) and *The Woman in the Window* (1944)—influenced the writing of Wright's *Savage Holiday* (New York: Avon, 1954).

60.　See Gardner, *Censorship Papers,* 207–14. For a penetrating analysis of the implications of the Hays code, see Richard Maltby, *Harmless Entertainment: Hollywood and the Ideology of Consensus* (Metuchen, N.J.: Scarecrow, 1983), chap. 4.

61.　Jerry Connolly, the Irish priest in the movie, uses basketball, as Mr. Dalton does ping-pong, to keep potential troublemakers in the city off the streets. And in both *Native Son* and *Angels,* the ubiquitous newspaper paradoxically indicts and validates the existence of the protagonists. Finally, in the movie there is a chase scene across the rooftops of the city which mirrors the conclusion of the second book of *Native Son.* However, the real parallel between movie and novel lies elsewhere. In the endings of movie and novel, Rocky Sullivan and Bigger Thomas are faced with the electric chair, and each is provided with a guardian angel who offers him an alternative to damnation.

62.　He also lies. He tells the boys they should all pray for "a boy who could not run as fast as I could." In truth, it was Rocky who was the faster runner: in an early scene, with the police on their trail, Rocky returns to help a slower Connolly, and this act of friendship lands him in reform school.

63.　There is possibly an additional irony here. Gerald Gardner points out that a "Jesuit priest" had actually written the Hays code, and that Joseph Breen, the head of the Hays Office, was a "catholic journalist." Moreover, the Legion of Decency, created by a group of Catholic bishops, was a major factor in forcing Hollywood to regulate itself (Gardner, *Censorship Papers,* xvi, xviii, xix). If Curtiz did indeed satirize Connolly, he may have had a larger target in mind than one power-mad priest.

64.　Bigger's emotions when he kills Mary are complicated, even contradictory—fear, sexual desire, and rage—and thus, to a degree, we are capable of feeling sympathy for him; but his gratuitous murder of Bessie removes that sympathy and makes us look upon him with fascination and horror, much as Max does at the end of the novel. One could argue that his relationship to Mary reflects both his fear of and his attraction to white culture, but he doesn't fear Bessie, and he is attracted to her only as a sexual object. Wright's point is that racism creates self-contempt, which is then transferred to others as powerless as oneself.

65.　Joyce Ann Joyce, in her *Richard Wright's Art of Tragedy* (Iowa City: Iowa University Press, 1986), places Bigger within a context of Aristotelian tragedy, and yet by denying Max a significant part of the tragic action, she actually reduces Bigger's significance as a tragic hero. For Joyce, Max is shallow, "self-serving," and in the long run not much better than State's Attorney Buckley (103–4, 113–16). Yet to be a tragic hero, Bigger needs a real antagonist; and Max, as the voice of the invisible city, plays that role.

66.　Mumford's "Origins of the American Mind," 354.

67.　Compare James Baldwin's observation in *The Fire Next Time* (New York: Dial, 1963), 54–55: "In the same way that we, for white people, were the descendants of Ham, and were cursed forever, white people were, for us, the descendants of Cain."

68.　Compare Martin Heidegger's observation in *Poetry, Language, Thought,* trans. A. Hofstadter (New York: Harper & Row, 1975), 147, that the German word *bauen* (to build) "originally means to dwell," and that this word has the same root as the German *ich bin* (I am). Heidegger not only sees a connection between *being, building,* and *dwelling,* but also between *bauen* and civilization: "this word *bauen* however *also* means to cultivate the vine." Denied a place within Western culture, Bigger's felt existence lies outside buildings that define someone else's "being."

ORIGINAL ESSAYS

◆

Native Son, Pudd'nhead Wilson, and Racial Discourse

Yoshinobu Hakutani

When *Native Son,* Richard Wright's first novel, appeared in 1940, critics as well as readers hailed it the most influential racial discourse American literature had produced.[1] Some readers, however, have not considered *Native Son* a successful novel. James Baldwin, for example, considered Bigger Thomas a monster that does not reflect the complex truths of the black experience in America. To Baldwin, Wright fails to understand the true meaning of humanity and the genuine struggle of African American life; Wright merely records "that fantasy Americans hold in their minds when they speak of the Negro."[2] The serious limitation Baldwin saw in Bigger's character is not Wright's use of Bigger as a representation, but the absence of the social and human relations underlying that representation. Baldwin also disagreed with Wright in portraying the ordeal of black people, since *Native Son,* to Baldwin, is rooted in the tradition of naturalistic protest fiction. The protest novel, Baldwin argued, is written out of sympathy for the oppressed but fails to transcend their trauma or the rage such a novel expresses.

Although it is often true that literature and sociology, as Baldwin cautioned, are not synonymous, it is also true that protest fiction can be successful discourse, a work of art that transcends the limitations of didactic writing. One of Wright's techniques to transform this sociological book into a well-made novel is the creation of a Marxist lawyer, Boris Max, to defend Bigger.[3] Bigger, of course, is the major character but he is not Wright's deepest concern until the very end of the novel. Through Max, Wright speaks for and to the nation, thereby creating a narrative voice, a point of view that is indeed sympathetic to Bigger but entirely impersonal in shaping racial discourse.

Half a century earlier Mark Twain used a similar technique in writing *Pudd'nhead Wilson,* another important racial discourse in American literature. Just as *Native Son* proves to be an authentic literary document, Twain's book is dramatic, unsentimental, and uncompromisingly realistic.[4] While Wright and Twain both provide their works with sensational, violent actions, they

This essay was written specifically for this volume and is published here by permission of the author.

succeed in presenting objective and judicious observations about the most agonizing racial issue in America.

As racial discourse, *Native Son* thrives on Max's long speech before the jury in Book III, entitled "Fate." Since this scene takes place in the final section of the novel, it makes a great impact not only on Bigger, the oppressed protagonist, but also on the nation, the oppressive antagonist. At the climactic moment in presenting his argument, Max declares: "Multiply Bigger Thomas twelve-million times. . . . Taken collectively, they are not simply twelve million people; in reality they constitute a separate nation, stunted, stripped, and held captive *within* this nation, devoid of political, social, economic, and property rights."[5] Max then poses a rhetorical question to the court about whether capital punishment would deter black people from committing murder. "No!" Max says. "Such a foolish policy has never worked and never will. The more you kill, the more you deny and separate, the more will they seek another form and way of life, however blindly and unconsciously" (p. 365).

How strongly Max's speech contributes to the argument of the novel is ironically shown by the weakness of Max's statement as a plea for Bigger's individual life. Not only does Max's plea fail to save Bigger, but it is doubtful that the plea convinces many readers in view of Bigger's brutal treatment and murder of his girlfriend Bessie. It does, however, convince the reader of the general plight of African Americans. Other scenes that have taken place long before Max's speech also contribute to its success. At the beginning of the novel Bigger complains to his friend Gus: "Goddammit, look! We live here and they live there. We black and they white. They got things and we ain't. They do things and we can't. It's just like living in jail. Half the time I feel like I'm on the outside of the world peeping in through a knot-hole in the fence . . ." (p. 23). Bigger is aware of a fence of discrimination that exists around the aviation school he dreams of attending. The poverty-stricken atmosphere in which his family is forced to live makes relationships strident and inhuman. In order to recreate for the audience in the court the condition of a family like Bigger's, Max says: "This vast stream of life, dammed and muddied, is trying to sweep toward the fulfillment which all of us seek so fondly," the pursuit of happiness guaranteed in the Constitution (p. 365).

Wright presents Max's speech as a sociological analysis depicting racial conditions in the thirties in terms of a modern version of slavery. Similarly, Twain creates in his novel a young lawyer from upstate New York named David Wilson to provide a scientific analysis of the racial issue in the nineteenth century and of slavery in particular. The difference between the two works is obvious: *Pudd'nhead Wilson* was written not only by a white man but by an individual, unlike Wright, who was not personally involved in the racial problems the work addresses. But Wilson's role resembles Max's, for both lawyers on behalf of the authors establish a distance from life and create an impersonal vision, a requirement for fiction as social discourse. For Twain as well as for Wright, the structure of the story is therefore endowed with the author's logic and objectivity.

In *Adventures of Huckleberry Finn,* a somewhat romantic novel of race, slavery is obscured in the happy ending for Jim, and other subtle and disturbing aspects of the race question are not raised. By contrast, *Pudd'nhead Wilson* ends tragically for all the major characters, white and black alike, and this connects it strongly to *Native Son.* In both works, the system of slavery, whether it is actual slavery in *Pudd'nhead Wilson* or racial discrimination and oppression in *Native Son,* is realistically portrayed. Although the story in each case is fiction, its development rests on American history. Tom Driscoll's tragedy took place in Dawson's Landing on the Missouri side of the Mississippi in 1830, and Bigger Thomas's occurred in the South Side of Chicago a century later. In each novel, several generations of American experience, a nation, a society, a local community, and an era all coalesce into a unified vision.

Another similarity is the concept of determinism Wright and Twain both use in analyzing the issues of race. From the moment *Native Son* begins, Bigger is placed in an oppressive environment; his killing of a large rat is representative of suppressed violence and tension. Whether he lives in a sordid, one-room apartment with his mother, brother, and sister or roams about a pool parlor with his friends, he is a frustrated young man prone to violence and transgression. Even though he is lucky enough to land a job as chauffeur for the family of a wealthy businessman, he cannot help noticing a glaring contrast between the money and power of the white ruling class and the poverty and misery of black people. This contradiction would stimulate his ambition to become "somebody," but if he were to be denied such an opportunity, he would instinctively defend himself at all costs.

In *Pudd'nhead Wilson,* as in *Native Son,* Twain intends to demonstrate that men and women, both black and white, are victims of society at large. In such a deterministic world there are no heroes, no villains; only white society, the system of slavery in particular, becomes the culprit. No character, whether it is Roxy or Wilson, acts as an individual. The reader scarcely knows what a character thinks. Man or woman is merely a victim of circumstance and history. Just as Wright's major concern is with racism rather than with Bigger's character, Twain's aim is to assail slavery rather than the individuals involved. This is the reason some critics do not consider *Pudd'nhead Wilson* a great novel. Richard Chase, for instance, compares it unfavorably with *Huckleberry Finn,* a great novel strengthened by Twain's characterization of the hero. Chase argues that in *Pudd'nhead Wilson* "there are no characters who are capable, either by themselves or in relation to each other, of giving the book a sustained organic life."[6] Although Chase is right in maintaining that even Roxy, who is as courageous and human as anyone in Twain's stories, is not a credible character, Chase is wrong in assuming that *Pudd'nhead Wilson* is intended as a novel of character.

The most significant affinity between the two novels is that Twain and Wright both narrate in the full conviction that the crimes they dramatize are inevitable products of American society. They both convince the readers that the protagonists are morally free of guilt. It is much easier, therefore, to understand the author's intention if the work is regarded as what Emile Zola called an "experimental novel."[7] Zola called the experimental novelist an "experimental moralist" (p. 178), for the mission of such a novelist is to determine the causes of social ills so that "we wish to reach better social conditions. . . . To be master of good and evil, to regulate life, to regulate society, in the long run to resolve all the problems of [society], above all to bring a solid foundation to justice by experimentally resolving questions of criminality, is that not to do the most useful and moral human work?" (p. 177).

Because Wright's mission in Native Son as racial discourse is to determine the cause of Bigger's murders, Wright places his emphasis on the third section of the book. As several critics have pointed out, Book III is the best part of the novel and as a result Wright is able to shift the burden of Bigger's guilt to society.[8] As Wright's development of the story clearly indicates, Native Son is built on the inevitable results of Bigger's unpremeditated murder of a white girl. However gruesome and unbelievable his actions may appear, Bigger finds no other way to defend himself but to burn her body and make false accusations. And he cannot help killing Bessie, lest she implicate him. It is inevitable as well that Bigger gets captured by white police and is brought to a trial by an all-white jury. Given a racist climate, all the scenes take place one after another without a hitch. The denouement of the story is convincing not only because Wright adheres to Zola's deterministic philosophy but because the plot is partly based on the actual murder of a white woman by a black man as reported in the Chicago Tribune in 1938.[9]

Book III, and Max's speech in the court in particular, are solidly built upon what has transpired before the trial in the novel. As the lawyer Wilson discovers scientific evidence to prove Tom Driscoll's murder in Pudd'nhead Wilson, Max's speech seizes upon sociological evidence for the causes of Bigger's murders. Max argues with logic and eloquence that Bigger's murders have resulted from white racism rampant in Chicago. To Max, as the first two sections of the novel have proven, Bigger merely falls victim to the racist forces so familiar to the American public. As an idealist who believes in the American dream, Wright takes pains to provide a picture of what young Americans try to be—independent, economically self-reliant, and happy. Young and full of energy as Bigger is, he urges himself to pursue his dreams. If it is racism that prevents him from realizing these ideals, the result of his frustration is to save himself at the risk of killing his enemy.

Just as the concept of determinism is more important than the characterization of Bigger in Native Son, Twain's interest in Pudd'nhead Wilson lies more strongly in the effects of environment on individuals than in the individuals themselves. Wilson thus conducts an experiment on behalf of the author Twain. Whether or not Wilson is a fully developed character is moot, because he is an outside observer like Max. "Isn't that pleasant—& unexpected!" Twain wrote in a letter. "For I have never thought of Pudd'nhead as a *character*, but only as a piece of machinery—a button or a crank or a lever, with a useful function to perform in a machine, but with no dignity above that."[10]

The approach Twain and Wright take to determinism, however, differs from Zola's. Zola attributes Gervaise's tragedy in *L'Assommoir,* for example, not only to her environment but to her heredity as well. Throughout *Native Son*, Bigger's behavior has nothing to do with his mother's, and there are no discernible similarities among Bigger, his sister, and his brother. In *Pudd'nhead Wilson,* Tom, the assumed white child, grows up and develops a distinctive pattern of behavior clearly traceable to his white environment but not to his black heredity. When Roxy, Tom's biological mother, reveals to her son that he was in fact born a slave, she argues that his despicable behavior derives from his black gene. "Pah! it make me sick!" she cries out. "It's de nigger in you, dat's what it is. Thirty-one parts o' you is white, en on'y one part nigger, en dat po' little one part is yo' *soul*."[11] But Roxy is wrong in her observation because she herself had been indoctrinated with the prejudice that black people are genetically inferior to white people. In the course of the story, Tom exhibits the worst traits ascribed to the corrupt white society: he is spoiled as a child, goes to Yale but comes home with offensive mannerisms, gambles away his allowance, steals, and finally murders Judge Driscoll, his benefactor.

Tom's most heinous act is the betrayal of his own mother Roxy, since he willingly sells her down the river after she has helped him pay his debts. But his atrocities are not shown to derive from his being black; they are caused by the training the institution of slavery has forced upon black and white people alike. Having been trained over the generations to treat black people as properties and commodities, white and black people both regard black people as "animals," not as human beings. Whatever is base and inferior in Tom has stemmed not from the black blood but from the white training. The black heredity, in fact, is shown superior: the white woman, the mother of the real Tom Driscoll, died shortly after she bore her son while Roxy, when she gave birth to Chamber, Twain says, "was up and around the same day, with her hands full, for she was tending both babies" (p. 5). Genetically Roxy was far more capable than her white counterpart. Moreover, Roxy "was of majestic form and stature, her attitudes were imposing and statuesque, and her gestures and movements distinguished by a noble and stately grace" (p. 8).

Twain expresses his concept of determinism with poignancy in the climactic scene where Tom has no choice but to kill Judge Driscoll. Just as Bigger's killing of Mary Dalton is accidental, Tom's killing of the Judge is not premeditated since his mission late that night is to steal money from his uncle's safe. He has had no intention of murdering him as Twain writes:

"When he was half way down he was disturbed to perceive that the landing below was touched by a faint glow of light. What could that mean? Was his uncle still up? No, that was not likely; he must have left his night-taper there when he went to bed." Since Tom feels no malice toward his uncle, he is pleased "beyond measure" when he sees his uncle soundly asleep on the sofa. But when his uncle stirs in his sleep, Tom is seized with panic and draws "the knife from its sheath, with his heart thumping and his eyes fastened upon his benefactor's face." No sooner has Tom felt "the old man's strong grip upon him, and a wild cry of 'Help! help!' [rung] in his ear," than his own fear and confusion overwhelm him and any vestiges of free will are negated at once. "Without hesitation," Twain says, "he drove the knife home—and was free" (p. 94). Tom's actions, therefore, are remarkably similar to those of Bigger when Mrs. Dalton's entrance into Mary's bedroom causes him to panic: "He turned and a hysterical terror seized him, as though he were falling from a great height in a dream. A white blur was standing by the door, silent, ghost-like. It filled his eyes and gripped his body" (p. 84). In each case, the protagonist falls victim to the forces of social environment working against his free will and causing him to act as though he were a trapped animal.[12]

From the vantage point of slaveholders, Tom's killing of Judge Driscoll is deemed not only criminal but immoral simply because Tom murders his benefactor. Similarly in *Native Son,* racist society refuses to recognize Bigger's killing of Mary Dalton as accidental and calls it rape and murder. In each novel, the ultimate irony is created by the narrative voice, a point of view in opposition, which informs the reader of the fact that the protagonist's killing of a white person has resulted not from his hatred of that person but from white racism, the racist conditioning of black people imposed on them by white society.

In contrast to *Native Son,* the success of *Pudd'nhead Wilson* as racial discourse largely comes from Twain's use of irony in the style and structure of the book. The opening scene is deceptive: everything seems orderly. But as the story unfolds, things are not in order as they appear. Society is corrupt: the effect of slavery on the lifestyle of Dawson's Landing is gradually revealed. The irony rests in the fact that there is a clear line of demarcation between black and white people, slaves and slave owners. As the story progresses, a deeper irony emerges: the racial distinction has become obscure through generations of miscegenation. Roxy looks white, but her blood is one-sixteenth black. The color line becomes even more obscure since Tom is one thirty-second black. Moreover, he is switched with a pure white baby in the cradle. Despite his black heritage, he becomes a white man and the heir to Judge Driscoll. The dramatic irony is further intensified because nobody knows Tom's background except for Roxy and the reader. The doctrine of determinism underlies Twain's theme and technique, as it does Wright's, but what enhances the effect of the story is this ironic incongruity between appearance and reality.

What is more, Twain's irony does not spare white men their lack of moral conscience. For Twain, miscegenation as condoned in the South is unquestionably immoral; he accuses slave owners of hypocrisy. His disclosure of the tradition of miscegenation is ironic, for they regard black people as animals and yet they themselves behave like animals. They take advantage of black women for sex but fail to take paternal responsibility for their offspring. In contrast to a black woman like Roxy, these men are judged clearly immoral. What she did in switching the babies is deemed moral because her action came out of her heart, a mother's genuine love for her child.

The most subtle irony is reserved for the ending of the novel. Immediately after Wilson's fingerprint collection proves Tom's identity, the real Tom is rescued from the throes of slavery. Twain then comments on a final scene: "The real heir suddenly found himself rich and free, but in a most embarrassing situation. He could neither read nor write, and his speech was the basest dialect of the negro quarter. . . . The poor fellow could not endure the terrors of the white man's parlor, and felt at home and at peace nowhere but in the kitchen" (p. 114). Twain's satire is now complete: the seeming slave is free, but is doomed to live like a slave for the rest of his life.

Twain's disparagement of white society is also tempered with humorous commentary on American life. Pudd'nhead Wilson's famous calendar records Twain's witty but serious charges against American society at large. Although many of such remarks have little bearing on the major themes of the novel, some of them are eloquent expressions about human folly. Twain highlights one of Wilson's calendar notes in the middle of the story. Chapter 21, for instance, opens with this note:

> *April 1. This is the day upon which we are reminded of what we are on the other three hundred and sixty-four.*
> —PUDD'NHEAD WILSON'S CALENDAR. (p. 105)

The most satiric remark is recorded in the concluding chapter:

> *October 12, the Discovery. It was wonderful to find America, but it would have been more wonderful to miss it.*
> —PUDD'NHEAD WILSON'S CALENDAR. (p. 113)

This remark on Columbus Day is followed by Twain's concluding argument. Twain asserts at the end of the story that if "Tom" had been white and free, he should rightfully have been punished. But if he had been a slave, as he should have been since he was born black, Twain suggests, he would not have committed the murder in the first place. "As soon as the Governor understood the case," Twain writes, "he pardoned Tom at once, and the creditors sold him down the river" (p. 115). From a deterministic point of view, slavery was indeed the murderer and Tom was an innocent victim. Throughout the text, then, a master novelist's skill is on display, for Twain is able to create indisputable racial discourse with a pointed sense of humor and irony.

To present a sociological observation based on determinism, Wright uses in *Native Son* a variety of devices quite different from those in *Pudd'nhead Wilson*. There is a clear distinction, first of all, between the motives of the two novelists. Twain, a liberal thinker, wrote out of deep sympathy for the oppressed, and the fault he had to avoid was sentimentality. Wilson, neither the oppressor nor the oppressed, can take a neutral stand. Not only does Twain's point of view sound scientific and impersonal, but it is conveyed with humor and seldom turns into an expression of pity. Wright, on the other hand, was motivated by wrongs he had personally suffered and his vision had no room for humor or levity. Unlike *Pudd'nhead Wilson*, *Native Son* from the first page keeps the reader vividly aware of the protagonist as the inevitable product of his environment. As the story unfolds, this portrait is gradually intensified with the events that follow his capture. The lurid trial and his defense by a radical attorney enable *Native Son* to express the whole tragedy of black people rather than one individual's pathology.

Wright's most effective technique in *Native Son* is the conversion of Max's speech into a narrative voice, which in turn coordinates the findings of a sociological analysis with Bigger's personal grievances. Such a voice triumphantly counteracts the travesty that is the state's case. Unable to support his claim with factual evidence or rudimentary logic, the prosecutor piles up in his speech the statements of racial prejudice and hatred reminiscent of those of Ku Klux Klansmen. Those who regard Max's speech as didactic and uninspiring are surprised at Bigger's intellectual growth at the end of the trial. The views Bigger expresses toward the end of his life become abstract, because he has earlier been compelled to act by his social environment but through Max's speech he begins to establish his own identity. As a result, he is able to conceptualize the meaning of his act and is proud of his manhood and independence. What he achieves at the end of his life, despite the death sentence, thus contributes to Wright's thematic design.

Max's role in pleading for Bigger, then, differs from Wilson's in identifying the murderer. Max, being Jewish, has a deeper understanding of the conflict of races in America than does Wilson. Wilson, characterized as absentminded, keeps himself out of the racial strife in the local community. One can only speculate why Wright deleted in the 1940 Harper edition of *Native Son* a reference to Max's being a Jew, but because Wright's intention was to indict American society, he made Max's speech reflect a racially impersonal point of view.[13] Max's observations on Bigger's condition in America strike the literary public, not the courtroom audience, as eminently true and brilliant. The objectivity in Max's vision therefore contrasts sharply but finely with the bigotry in the prosecutor's probing.

Despite the obvious difference in the roles Max and Wilson assume, the visions their speeches create are both ironic. As Wilson tells the court that Tom is an innocent victim instead of a murderer, Max testifies that society instead of Bigger is a murderer. Even the well-meaning Daltons—like Judge Driscoll, "respected, esteemed, and beloved by all the community," who considers himself a "free-thinker" (*Pudd'nhead Wilson*, p. 4)—are depicted as prejudiced and condescending. Though they appear philanthropic since they donate money for black boys to buy ping-pong tables, they are in fact exploiters of the poor and disadvantaged. At the coroner's inquest Max questions Mr. Dalton with sarcasm: "So, the profits you take from the Thomas family in rents, you give back to them to ease the pain of their gouged lives and to salve the ache of your own conscience?" (p. 304). As Ben Davis Jr. pointed out in his review of *Native Son*, Dalton's philanthropy as Max satirizes it resembles that of "the class of hypocritical Carnegies, Fords and Rockefellers, who are the very causes of the unemployment, poverty and misery among the Negro people, which their million-dollar gifts are falsely alleged to cure."[14] Max's final speech in the court also abounds in irony. While Max is aware of the racist tone of the press against Bigger, he deplores "the silence of the church" (p. 356). "What is the cause of all this high feeling and excitement?" he asks. "Is it the crime of Bigger Thomas? Were Negroes liked yesterday and hated today because of what he has done?" (p. 356). Indicting the judicial system, Max says: "Gangsters have killed and have gone free to kill again. But none of that brought forth an indignation to equal this" (p. 356). Personally as well, Max satirizes the landlord Dalton who refuses to rent apartments to black people anywhere but in the black belt. According to Max, then, it turns out that confining Bigger "in that forest" as a stranger had in fact made him an acquaintance of Mary, whom he murdered (p. 362). And to Mrs. Dalton, Max ironically utters: "Your philanthropy was as tragically blind as your sightless eyes!" (p. 362).[15]

In creating literary discourse, Wright uses other stylistic and structural devices to transcend the limitations of sociological prose. The first scene, where Bigger and his brother Buddy corner a big rat, and Bigger smashes it with a skillet, suggests the plight of black people in white society. Such violent scenes take place throughout the first two sections of the novel to imply the conditions and frustrations of African Americans in general, but their dramatic impact is not fully appreciated until Book III, where Max delivers the eloquent speeches at the inquest and at the trial.

The scenes of confinement and estrangement are also reflected in the languages of the people involved. When Mrs. Dalton is introduced to Bigger by her husband at their residence, she speaks: "Don't you think it would be a wise procedure to inject him into his new environment at once, so he could get the feel of things? . . . Using the analysis contained in the case record the relief sent us, I think we should evoke an immediate feeling of confidence . . ." (p. 48). Bigger tries to listen to their conversation, "blinking and bewildered." Her expressions such as "using the analysis contained in the case record" and "evoke an immediate feeling of confidence" make "no sense to him; it was another language. . . . He felt strangely blind" (p. 48). Not only does her language indicate how strange the white world appears to Bigger, but Wright also improvises such a dialogue to satirize the condescension and esotericism of social workers.

Bigger's estrangement from the white world, on the other hand, is reflected in the languages of his friends and enemies. When Bigger and his friend Jack go to see a bourgeois movie called *The Gay Woman,* they are both puzzled by certain words used in the dialogue:[16]

> "Say, Jack?"
> "Hunh?"
> "What's a Communist?"
> "A Communist is a red, ain't he?"
> "Yeah; but what's a red?"
> "Damn if I know. It's a race of folks who live in Russia, ain't it?" (pp. 34–35)

Later Bigger meets Mary and her Communist friend Jan, and their talk about Communists, demonstrations, class struggle, and black liberation bewilders him. However sympathetic their demeanor may appear, Bigger finds it difficult to understand their language. Feeling alienated from his black friends and resentful toward Mary and Jan, he even resists going in Ernie's Kitchen Shack, where he would dread his black friends' asking one another: *"Who're them white folks Bigger's hanging around with?"* (p. 71). Jan tells Bigger that Communists like Jan and Mary have been fighting to *"stop"* the kind of killing in a riot in which Bigger's father was also a fatality, but Bigger fails to see the connection between the Communist and Civil Rights movements. To make Bigger as uninformed and innocent a youth as possible, Wright seems to have omitted in the Harper edition a dialogue in which Peggie, the maid at the Daltons, intimates to Bigger that Mary's "wild ways" vex her conservative parents.[17]

Another significant omission in the Harper edition is a page-long passage of Max's speech that characterizes Mary as a compassionate woman. In this passage, Max reminds the court that despite the racial segregation rampant in the country, including the very court where Bigger is standing accused of murder, she genuinely had tried to have sympathy and understanding for Bigger. "It has been said," Max emphasizes, "that the proof of the corrupt and vile heart of this boy is that he slew a woman who was trying to be kind to him. In the face of that assertion, I ask the question: Is there any greater proof that his heart is not corrupt and vile than that he slew a woman who was trying to be kind?" (*Early Works,* p. 818). Deleting such a passage, Wright made *Native Son* less didactic and avoided a cumbersome recapitulation of the earlier scene. Leaving this passage, on the other hand, would undermine Wright's attempt to portray a black youth like Bigger as estranged from Mary, a representation of white society. The passage would also contradict Wright's assertion that the estrangement between Bigger and Mary rather than the emotional affinity between them is what caused Mary's death. Wright attempted to prove that racism, not their infatuation with each other, resulted in the whole tragedy.

Not only do Max's speeches in the way they are delivered in the published version awaken in Bigger a consciousness of freedom and autonomy of which he has not been aware before, but they also form a singular contrast to the talk of Mr. and Mrs. Dalton, which is larded with sociological jargon. "Bigger," as Wright intimates, "was not at that moment really bothered about whether Max's speech had saved his life or not. . . . It was not the meaning of the speech that gave him pride, but the mere act of it" (p. 371). That is, Max's final speech is not a description of something, but, as Aristotle had said of tragedy, an action. Wright approaches Aristotelianism in the way he structures Max's dialogue with Bigger in Book III, for Bigger's response to Max is not simply a description of Bigger's sensations at the end of his life but the dynamic development in Bigger's character. This development alludes to Max's earlier observation that the actions leading to the death of Mary and Bessie were "as instinctive and inevitable as breathing or blinking one's eyes. It was an act of *creation!*" (p. 366).

In contrast to *Pudd'nhead Wilson,* then, the success of *Native Son* as racial discourse also stems from a thematic design that enables Bigger to achieve a sense of freedom and independence despite his death sentence. Wright takes pains to show that Bigger has undergone an enormous development from an innocent, alienated youth to a mature, reflective person. In *Pudd'nhead Wilson,* on the other hand, Twain's chief interest is not in character development. Courageous and daring though Roxy is, she is not portrayed as an individualist such as Bigger becomes at the end of his ordeal. In the beginning she has some of Bigger's rebelliousness, but by the end of the story she has been reduced to the religious passivity of Bigger's mother.

These stylistic, structural, and thematic elements that buttress *Native Son* were not, of course, excised in the 1940 edition. As Twain's use of anecdote, humor, and satire in *Pudd'nhead Wilson* made the novel a unique accomplishment, Wright's devices in *Native Son* transformed what James Baldwin called "everybody's protest novel" into a successful one.[18] To Baldwin and to Wright's detractors, Bigger Thomas is not much of a character but merely a racial representation, and the novel suffers from Wright's excessive reliance on symbolism and didacticism. But *Native Son* displays, as does *Pudd'nhead Wilson,* a complex interplay of personal, racial, and social experiences seldom seen in American literature. For both novelists, the result was a remarkably skillful fusion of the naturalistic and psychological traditions in American fiction.

Notes

1.   See the reviews of *Native Son* collected in John M. Reilly, ed., *Richard Wright: The Critical Reception* (New York: Franklin, 1978), pp. 39–99. Subsequent references to these reviews are cited as Reilly.

2.   James Baldwin, "Many Thousands Gone," *Partisan Review,* 18 (Nov.–Dec. 1951): 672.

3.   Malcolm Cowley, generally very positive about *Native Son,* deplored Max's courtroom plea for Bigger's life as thematically weakening. He argued that Max's speech, on behalf of the whole black population, would be quite meaningful but that Bigger must die to stand as an individual, not a symbol. See Reilly, pp. 67–68.

4.   For a well-annotated analysis of *Native Son* as protest fiction, see Keneth Kinnamon, "*Native Son:* The Personal, Social, and Political Background," *Phylon,* 30 (Spring 1969): 66–72. The most incisive analysis with respect to the history of the composition of *Pudd'nhead Wilson* is given in Hershel Parker's "The Lowdown on *Pudd'nhead Wilson:* Jack-leg Novelist, Unreadable Text, Sense-Making Critics, and Basic Issues in Aesthetics," *Resources for American Literary Study,* 11 (Autumn 1981): 215–40.

5.   Richard Wright, *Native Son,* 1940 (New York: Harper, 1966), p. 364. Later page references in parentheses are to this edition.

6.   Richard Chase, *The American Novel and Its Tradition* (New York: Doubleday, 1957), p. 156.

7.   Emile Zola, "The Experimental Novel," *Documents of Modern Literary Realism,* ed. George J. Becker (Princeton: Princeton UP, 1963), pp. 162–96.

8.   Edward Kearns, in "The 'Fate' Section of *Native Son,*" *Contemporary Literature,* 12 (Spring 1971): 146–55, argues that despite the abstractness of Bigger's speech, the third section of the novel enables Bigger to achieve his identity, a thematic strategy which serves Wright's aim. Paul N. Siegel, in "The Conclusion of Richard Wright's *Native Son,*" *PMLA,* 89 (May 1974): 517–23, regards Max's long speech in the courtroom as original and suggests that it does not have a Marxist party-line defense. As for Wright's shifting of Bigger's guilt to society, see Phyllis R. Klotman, "Moral Distancing as a Rhetorical Technique in *Native Son:* A Note on 'Fate,' " *CLA Journal,* 18 (Dec. 1974): 284–91.

9.   See Keneth Kinnamon, "*Native Son:* The Personal, Social, and Political Background." While writing the first draft of *Native Son,* Wright read in a long series of *Tribune* articles that the case of murder "involved Robert Nixon and Earl Hicks, two young Negroes with backgrounds similar to that of Bigger." One of the articles, 27 May 1938, reported that one Florence Johnson "was beaten to death with a brick by a colored sex criminal . . . in her apartment." The two black men, Kinnamon writes, "were arrested soon after and charged with the crime. Though no evidence of rape was adduced, the *Tribune* from the beginning called the murder a sex crime and exploited fully this apparently quite false accusation" (68).

10.   Mark Twain, *The Love Letters of Mark Twain,* ed. Dixon Wecter (New York: Harper, 1949), p. 291.

11.   Mark Twain, *Pudd'nhead Wilson* and *Those Extraordinary Twins,* ed. Sidney E. Berger (New York: Norton, 1980), p. 70. Subsequent textual references to this edition are indicated in parentheses.

12.   Robert Butler calls Bigger's killing of the rat, his near killing of Gus, and his killing of Mary Dalton "scenes of entrapment in which various forces inside and outside the central character restrict his consciousness and limit his free will." See Robert Butler, *Native Son: The Emergence of a New Black Hero* (Boston: Twayne, 1991), p. 41.

13.   In the manuscript version of *Native Son,* Max states: "And, because I, a Jew, dared defend this Negro boy, for days my mail has been flooded with threats against my life. The

manner in which Bigger Thomas was captured, the hundreds of innocent Negro homes invaded, the scores of Negroes assaulted upon the streets, the dozens who were thrown out of their jobs, the barrage of lies poured out from every source against a defenseless people—all of this was something unheard of in democratic lands." This passage is deleted in the Harper edition. See Richard Wright, *Early Works,* ed. Arnold Rampersad (New York: Library of America, 1991), p. 806. Subsequent textual references to this edition of *Native Son* are indicated as *Early Works.*

14.   Ben Davis Jr., (New York) *Sunday Worker,* 14 April 1940, sec. 2, pp. 4, 6; Reilly, p. 70.

15.   As several critics have noted, the most significant element of artistry in *Native Son* is the imagery of blindness. Through his killing of a white girl, Bigger is able to see himself as an individual. See, for instance, James Nagel, "Images of 'Vision' in *Native Son,*" *University Review,* 36 (Dec. 1969): 109–15.

16.   This dialogue, part of which is quoted here, is a replacement for the original passage in the manuscript. The manuscript version of the dialogue indicates that both Bigger and Jack are well acquainted with Communism and that Bigger identifies the man kissing Mary Dalton in the movie as a Communist. Wright's portrayal of Bigger and Jack in the original manuscript, therefore, makes them more knowledgeable about world affairs than they are in the published version (see *Early Works,* pp. 472–75).

17.   In the Harper edition, Wright omitted Peggie's speech and part of Wright's comment that follows it. The omitted passage reads:

> "She's a sweet thing," she said. "I've known her since she was two years old. But she's kind of wild, she is. Always in hot water. Keeps her folks worried. The Lord only knows where she got her wild ways. But she's got 'em. If you stay around here long, you'll get to know her."
> Bigger wanted to ask about the girl. . . . (*Early Works,* p. 498)

18.   James Baldwin, "Everybody's Protest Novel," *Partisan Review,* 16 (June 1949): 578–85.

The Politics of Spatial Phobias in *Native Son*

CAREN IRR

Why kill Bessie Mears? This question has been at the root of much of the controversy surrounding *Native Son* in the last 20 years. Why, critics have asked, did Wright double the number of murders in an already violent, calamity-filled novel? And, once he had killed off the only character of any significance who was both black and female, why did he not exert authorial energy to make this death significant? Why do the trial scenes in the last third of the novel so conspicuously return Bessie's corpse to view without explaining her horrible fate?

The usual answers to these questions reveal the critics' motivations for asking them. By and large, the consensus has been that Bessie's murder results from Wright's politics. Following James Baldwin's lead, most critics agree that Wright is "a spokesman for the militant men and women of the thirties" and that the Communism of that period is inherently misogynist.[1] Furthermore, it is commonly claimed that misogyny has no place in multiculturalism (usually associated with feminist politics) and the latest revival of interest in African American culture. Thus, to the extent that Wright is influenced by Communism, the argument goes, he sets himself outside and against African American culture, and the mutilated corpse of Bessie Mears bears witness to his alienation. Her corpse is a blot on Wright's novel as well as on the African American community so far as critics such as Houston Baker and Henry Louis Gates are concerned.[2] In light of the adulation heaped on writers hostile to Wright, such as Zora Neale Hurston, one wonders whether one motivation for recent attention to *Native Son* has been a desire to discredit Wright as a parent of African American literature. Perhaps some cultural historians would prefer to replace Wright with a more politically comfortable figure—someone not encumbered by an embarrassing interest in Communism.

This post-Baldwin consensus mistakes the bandage for the wound by interpreting Bessie Mears' body as evidence of Wright's supposedly simplistic Communism rather than as a sign of his critique of Communism. Instead,

This essay was written specifically for this volume and is published here by permission of the author.

Wright makes Bessie's corpse a blot on his text quite explicitly. Far from wit-lessly reproducing a putative Communist misogyny, Wright leaves Bessie's body mangled and unexplained so that he can foreground his critique of con-temporaneous Communist literary practices. In *Native Son,* Wright is an internal critic of Communism—a position that necessitated neither misogyny nor rejection of his cultural heritage.

An increasingly large body of revisionist scholarship on the cultural life surrounding the American Communist Party supports this last point. While earlier scholarship tended to focus on the theoretical statements of party functionaries, the new work concentrates on cultural and political practices and illustrates the relative flexibility and variety of Communist cultural politics during the 1930s. Paul Buhle's study *Marxism in the United States* fol-lows the deep roots of Marxist thought and activity in various non-English-speaking immigrant communities. Robin D. G. Kelley's work on Alabama sharecroppers demonstrates that the Communist Party attracted thousands of African American members in the South, in part because of what rank-and-file members saw as a basic compatibility between Communist and Christian world views.[3] Similarly, Paula Rabinowitz and Barbara Foley have both accounted for the complex appeal that the literary forms sponsored by the Communists had for women writers of the 1930s. Rabinowitz argues that women writers confronted the sexism evident in critical calls for a macho pro-letarian fiction and created their own genre of women's revolutionary fiction.[4] Foley describes an even closer fit between feminism and Communism; in her view, the Communist Party offered one of the most forward-looking sets of policies and literary practices on gender available during the 1930s. There-fore, it had a natural appeal for feminist-minded writers of that period. The Communists should be applauded, Foley argues, for promoting so-called women's issues, employing female spokespersons, and supporting women's organizations long before it was customary to do so.[5] Altogether, this new work demonstrates that there was not a necessary link between Communism, misogyny, and white supremacism. Also, the work of Kelley et al. suggests that it will be necessary to rethink figures like Wright in light of a more nuanced, practice-oriented view of ideology. If we are to understand the poli-tics of Wright's work, we will need to supplement our knowledge of his out-right statements with analyses of the particular tensions evident in his fiction. We will need to understand not only the ways that Wright was a spokesper-son for the militants of the thirties, but also the ways that, in the act of speak-ing for others, he altered the significance of their statements. We will discover how he encodes his critique in the manner that he chose to articulate his political vision.

In *Native Son,* Wright's primary target for revisionist critique is the pro-letarian novel—the focus of his revision being this genre's representation of space. The proletarian novel was a genre of political fiction promoted by Communist intellectuals and executed more and less skillfully by a variety of writers during the Depression. It was a controversial form, and even one-time supporters such as *New Republic* editor Malcolm Cowley came to describe the genre as formulaic and dogmatic:

> . . . most of the [proletarian novels] have essentially the same plot. A young man comes down from the hills to work in a cotton mill (or a veneer factory or a Harlan County mine). Like all his fellow workers except one, he is innocent of ideas about labor unionism or the class struggle. The exception is always an older man, tough but humorous, who keeps quoting passages from *The Communist Manifesto.* Always the workers are heartlessly oppressed, always they go out on strike, always they form a union with the older man as leader, and always the strike is broken by force of arms.[6]

While this description does not fairly represent the actual variety of setting, characterization, and style in the radical fiction of the 1930s, Cowley does draw attention to an important feature of the genre: a proletarian novel is almost always set in a white community, often an isolated "folk" community of the type found in the Appalachians during this period. The implicit thesis was that these communities did not share the values of the modern industrial world; radicals expected to appeal to an inherent sense of justice based in local traditions. They considered these communities "cultural islands" which, when bridged together, would serve as a base for the revolutionary upheaval of the whole of American society.[7]

Not surprisingly, this monochromatic tendency in the proletarian novel did not go unnoticed by Wright. In fact, in *American Hunger,* the volume of his autobiography that describes the 1930s, he describes the following incident: after his first visit to the Chicago John Reed Club, an important Communist arts organization, inspired by a newfound sense of community and audience, Wright pounds out "a wild, crude poem in free verse," or he does so until his mother enters the room:

> She hobbled to the bed on her crippled legs and picked up a copy of the *Masses* that carried a lurid May Day cartoon. She adjusted her glasses and peered at it for a long time.
>
> "My God in heaven," she breathed in horror.
>
> "What's the matter, mama?"
>
> "What is this?" she asked, extending the magazine to me, pointing to the cover. "What's wrong with that man?"
>
> With my mother standing by my side, lending me her eyes, I stared at a cartoon drawn by a Communist artist; it was the figure of a worker clad in ragged overalls and holding aloft a red banner. The man's eyes bulged; his mouth gaped as wide as his face; his teeth showed; the muscles of his neck were like ropes. Following the man was a horde of nondescript men, women, and children, waving clubs, stones, and pitchforks.
>
> "What are those people going to do?" my mother asked. (p. 64)

His mother's horrified questions ("What's wrong with that man?" and "What are those people going to do?") allow Wright to borrow "her eyes" for a moment. From her perspective, the "worker" associated with the proletarian novel appears grotesque and menacing. The exaggerated muscularity of the Communist figures promises violence and mob action very much at odds with his mother's "ideal" of "Christ upon the cross" (p. 65). On the strength of this contrast between symbolic vocabularies, Wright decides that his task will be to "tell Communists how common people felt and . . . tell common people of the self-sacrifice of Communists who strove for unity among them."[8] As several commentators have already noted, foremost among the translations he will make is the adaptation of the proletarian novel to African American culture.[9] In *Native Son,* Wright portrays his hero's search for a language that will link Communist culture to the ghetto, but, unlike the proletarian novelists, he stresses the difficulty of this project. In Wright's view, cultural isolation wreaks psychological damage, and much of his novel can be read as a warning to those who would romanticize "folk" communities. Enclosure on the folk "island," Wright demonstrates, does not usually produce the kind of resistance the Communists desired. In fact, the space of "folk" culture can even breed resistance to the Communists' overtures. For this reason, in his role as mediator, Wright finds it necessary to alter the radicals' map; he writes in and against the conventions of the proletarian novel in order to complicate its conclusions. He supplements Communist cultural geography with his own sense of African American social psychology.

NATIVE SON AND SPATIAL PHOBIAS

The major psychological pattern that Wright traces is claustrophobic anxiety. By way of revising the map of culture proposed in the proletarian novel, *Native Son* manifests symptoms of a fear of enclosure; then, it briefly becomes agoraphobic, until it finally relapses into an enhanced, even utopian, form of spatial anxiety. These phobic effects are produced cumulatively, as well as in particular symbolic details, but recreating the flow of Wright's narrative should clarify some of the unique features of his political and literary practice.

Native Son begins with depictions of enclosed spaces and the psychology of living in them. Readers of *12 Million Black Voices,* Wright's "folk history" of African American life, immediately recognize that the spaces portrayed in the first pages of the novel are those that Wright considered typical of the limited circuit of African American urban life: the kitchenette, the pool room, and the movie theater.[10] In these initial settings, Wright establishes the kernel of his novel; he sketches the phobias that organize the novel and exhibit its implicit critique of the proletarian novel.

The "narrow space" of the kitchenette is one of the novel's most significant locations.[11] In the first scene, Wright uses the closeness of this space to establish a clear parallel between the two Thomas boys and a rat they trap in a corner of the apartment. His mother tells Bigger to " 'Put that box in front of the hole so [the rat] can't get out!" (p. 9). This command is then transferred to Bigger, when she repeatedly threatens him: " 'if you don't like it, you can get out' " (p. 13). Of course, both comments function ironically, since neither Bigger nor the rat can "get out." Bigger cannot escape from his family or from a sense of responsibility for his family. Like the rat, Bigger wants "a wider choice of action" but does not have it (p. 16). Both of them are cornered in the kitchenette.

To cope with his feeling of entrapment, Bigger places himself "behind a wall, a curtain" (p. 14). This self-imposed isolation is a personal version of the ritual his family has developed to preserve their collective modesty while dressing; Bigger figuratively turns his head aside to create the kind of privacy he desires. This seemingly passive withdrawal is not, however, the only element of Bigger's ritual; when he begins to fear his own entrapment, he also violently displaces that fear. In the kitchenette scene, this displacement has two stages. First, Bigger kills the rat with an excessive amount of force; he distances himself from his fear by hysterically overacting a version of it. Then he uses the evidence of his compensatory violence to frighten his "scary" sister (p. 10). The word "scary" is clearly important in this passage, since it is repeated several times and is one of the first colloquialisms used in the novel.[12] These two items suggest that Vera is not only easily frightened but also that she is "scary" to Bigger and that part of his purpose in killing the rat was to slaughter and displace his fear of her. Being trapped in the kitchenette involves, for Bigger, being forced into an oppressive and repressed awareness of the proximity of the black female body, and he responds to that body (as represented by his sister) with anger and fear. This at least is one of the novel's initial answers to Vera's question "How come Bigger acts that way?" (p. 12).

The psychological pattern established in the kitchenette scene recurs in the following scenes in the pool room, and only a few elements are altered. Although all the pool players are male and Bigger's victim in this scene is his buddy Gus, not Vera, Bigger again violently displaces his fear of enclosure. Again, his anger takes an object (Gus or the rat) that seems a substitute for something else. In the pool room scenes, this something else receives a name: race. Bigger explicitly attributes his feeling of suffocation and constriction to the "white folks" who live "right down here in [his] stomach" (p. 24). So, once again, we find Bigger being made physically uncomfortable by his proximity to an other. This suggests that Bigger might be eliding his anxieties about women and "white folks"; the two others fill the same position in his pattern of violent response.

However, be this as it may, it is certainly clear that, as in the previous scene, Bigger's anxious response follows on the heels of a thwarted desire for freedom of movement (desire to fly an airplane) and a ritual behavior that is designed to lessen the pain of the thwarted desire (Bigger and his friends playing " 'white' "). Also, as in the kitchenette scene, Bigger's displacement of his fear is so excessive, overblown, and neurotic that it prompts others to voice his own desires. After he attacks Gus in the pool room, he is so concentrated on substituting rage and hate for fear that he deliberately slices the felt of the pool tables. This gratuitous (and therefore psychologically significant) action leads the owner of the pool room to repeat his mother's threat: "Get out, before I call a cop! . . . Get out of here! . . . Get out before I shoot you!' " (p. 42). Having once again provoked another to command him to fulfill his desires, Bigger leaves the site of his claustrophobic panic—with some sense of relief.

Once we understand that Bigger habitually externalizes both his fears and his desires, then we are well placed to interpret the third of the three scenes that open the novel. When Bigger and his friends go to the movies, what they find there is an external representation of their fantasies of escape. In the giddy, fast-paced whirlwind life of the socialite on the screen, they see another version of the "SPEED" promised by the airplane Bigger would like to fly (p. 20). When supplemented by folk stories that suggest that this world of wealthy whites might open up to include them, the movie becomes the embodiment of their desires. Bigger, in particular, finds that the movie allows him to hope: "Maybe if he were working for [white people] something would happen and he would get some of [their money]" (p. 36).

Of course, Wright ensures that we notice the improbability of Bigger's hope by spotlighting its dependence on chance ("something will happen"); however, he is not proposing that the movie offers a false consciousness or a simply wrong view of the world.[13] Rather, Wright has carefully laid the psychological groundwork so that we understand how the movie fits into Bigger's interpretation of the world. Bigger's willingness to accept the movie's fantasy of escape, we see, is part and parcel of the desperation with which he seeks escape. The movie is one of several ways that Bigger represents his desires to himself, and the improbable hopes that it inspires actually induce him to take steps towards escape. It is, in part, the fantasy codified in the movie that encourages Bigger to leave his "one corner of the city" and strike out for the Daltons' home on the other side of "the 'line' " (pp. 23–24). Mass culture offers him a way out of his panic-inducing environment.

Unfortunately, when he arrives in the "spacious white neighborhood," Bigger does not realize his fantasies; if anything, he feels more "constricted and ill at ease" (p. 45). True, he is delighted to have a room of his own, but even this room is covered with "pictures of Jack Johnson, Joe Louis, Jack Dempsey, and Henry Armstrong . . . Ginger Rogers, Jean Harlow, and Janet Gaynor" (p. 60). Hemmed in by this symbolic crowd, whose combination of black men and white women prefigures his own future difficulties, he feels uncomfortable in white space, and he does not know which rituals to use to negotiate it. Should he enter at the front or the back of the house? How should he sit in his chair? Where should he put his eyes? These are the dilemmas that reveal the continuation of Bigger's spatial anxiety in the Daltons' home.

Then the entrance of Mary Dalton exacerbates his fear even further. Her questions about unions threaten to cut Bigger off from even the pretense of escape through his job, and Jan's insistence on sitting too close to him in the car makes him feel that he has entered "a shadowy region, a No Man's Land" (p. 67). Their familiarity heightens his awareness of his body. He feels that he cannot move and that he is caught "between two vast white looming walls" (p. 68). When they compound his fear further by insisting on transgressing color lines and eating at one table in a black restaurant, he again feels "ensnared" in a physical and logical trap. As in previous instances, the manifestation of this fear is the sense "that the very organic functions of his body had altered" (p. 73). He cannot chew; he is not hungry; he only wants to leave his body behind him and float "along smoothly through the darkness" (pp. 77–78). Only an alcoholic haze allows him to escape the shame and tension he feels at being brought too close to these peculiar characters.

Ultimately, though, it is alcohol that provokes the greatest crisis of claustrophobic panic in the novel. When Bigger realizes that Mary is too drunk to walk, he takes her up to her room, and, in the process, he begins to hate her again. She is forcing him to cross the invisible lines that divide up the house; her drunkenness sends him on an agonizing trek through the hall, up the stairs, and onto the landing. There his unfamiliarity with the white area of the house creates tremendous anxiety. " 'Where's your room?" he asks several times. "Was this really her room?" he wonders, "Was she too drunk to know? Suppose he opened the door to Mr. and Mrs. Dalton's room?" (p. 83). His base-level response to this unusual situation is fear—fear of entering the wrong space.

When Bigger does find Mary's room, his anxiety does not abate. On the contrary, his worst nightmare is realized when Mrs. Dalton enters the room. Total "hysterical terror" and an accompanying sensation of losing contact with his body seize him. He feels there are too many people in the room. He is "afraid to move" and, in another hysterical gesture of displacement, asphyxiates Mary so that she will not betray his presence (pp. 84–85). His fear of the "white folks" who live in his stomach and prevent him from breathing is externalized violently and excessively until Mary cannot breathe, until the girl who provoked his desire can no longer reveal that fact to the mother.

Only when Mrs. Dalton leaves the room and his spatial transgression is no longer subject to detection does Bigger's panic subside. He becomes "aware of the room" again and begins to figure out how he can "get out of the room" (p. 86). This relief lasts only a moment though—until he realizes that he has killed Mary and begins to imagine "the vast city of white people" closing in on him (p. 86). Prompted by this renewed bout of panic, he again enacts his entrapment on Mary's body—locking her "*in* the trunk" and burning her "*in* the furnace" (pp. 87, 89; Wright's emphases). Again, he "wanted to run. . . . But he could not" (p. 91). Finally, the only form of escape he can manage is a return to the narrow space of the kitchenette, and he returns there with a severely heightened and generalized sense of the limitations of that space.

It is in Book Two of *Native Son*—the book titled "Flight"—that Bigger's claustrophobia transforms into agoraphobia. The shift from fear of enclosure to fear of exposure, however, is not a simple reversal; it is, instead, a transformation whose neurotic logic Wright carefully documents. It is this logic that ultimately leads to the murder of Bessie Mears, and so to understand how and why Wright included this second murder, we will need to trace this transformation in Bigger's phobic spatial relations.

In the first scenes of "Flight," Bigger is freshly aware of the confining aspects of the "narrow space" of the kitchenette. Now that he has experienced the relatively more spacious world of the Dalton home—a place where "each person lived in one room and had a little world of his own"—he views the kitchenette from a new perspective (p. 100). He considers himself "outside of his family now" and he feels, temporarily, safe in that "outside" world (p. 101). It is the very narrowness of the kitchenette world that ensures his safety, since the people who live on the inside are "blind." Their ideological entrapment will not allow them to perceive his crime and, so long as he remains "outside," he has "a safer way of being safe" (p. 102).

While still in the throes of this exultation over his escape from the claustrophobic nightmare, Bigger visits Bessie. In one of the most frankly utopian scenes in the novel, they banter and fall into bed. There Bigger experiences their lovemaking as an erasure of fear and hate, and he discovers "a new sense of time and space." He feels that he does "not need to long for a home now" (p. 128). He has drawn Bessie to his outside world, and he is safe.

However, we quickly learn that this sensation of safety is illusory and one-sided. After sex, Bessie begins to question Bigger about his job—thus revealing her distance from him. This in turn leads Bigger to withdraw from her and imagine how he can "use her" (p. 131). He once again pictures the "narrow orbit of her life," and "the look on her face . . . separated him from her body by a great suggestion of space" (p. 133). The rift is completed once she becomes suspicious about his role in Mary Dalton's disappearance. When she returns his gaze and demonstrates her own independent outside-ness by asking " 'Bigger, you ain't done nothing to that girl, is you?' " his fear returns (p. 137). At this point, Wright anticipates her murder; Bigger feels "suddenly that he wanted something in his hand, something solid and heavy: his gun, a knife, a brick" (p. 137). In other words, at this point Bigger begins to feel that his being "outside" the "narrow orbit of [Bessie's] life" leaves him exposed; he develops a fear of her gaze—a fear that, in his usual pattern, becomes rage at the object that inspired the fear. Because he fears being seen, he turns against the woman who would see him. "The feeling of being always enclosed in the stifling embrace of an invisible force had gone from him," Wright writes, only to be supplanted by new and equally dangerous fears (p. 142).

Thereafter, Bigger begins to act out his fear of being exposed. He begins to hide, to seek ways *into* enclosed spaces. He panics when Mr. Britten, the detective, arrives to question him; he dreams of "an urgent need to run and hide"; he even plans the kidnapping scheme around a return to an abandoned kitchenette (pp. 156–57). In this last context, his fear of Bessie increases. During their visit to an empty apartment, she cries out when another trapped rat runs past; this typically claustrophobic response elicits another angry, fearful response from Bigger: " 'What you trying to do? . . . Tell the whole world we in here?' " (p. 172). Her claustrophobia provokes his agoraphobia.

Later, this fear of exposure extends from Bessie to the furnace and especially to the journalists. Fear of public space is generalized, we might say, into fear of publicity. Bigger does not want to be photographed or interviewed (he panics when the cat jumps on his shoulders for a dramatic picture), but he does want "ever so badly to read" the newspaper accounts of the crime (p. 194). He wants to be the observer, looking from the outside, but he cannot bear to be seen. Only as long as he can look, without being looked at, can he manipulate the situation.

This utilitarian, agoraphobic logic reaches its pinnacle when Mary's body is finally discovered in the furnace. Then Bigger finally runs away from the house, recognizing that "here it was. He had always felt outside of this white world and now it was true" (p. 207). He runs, of course, to Bessie—half hoping that she will be "with him," protecting him by recreating their utopian bond beyond the law (p. 211). When she panics and despairs of hiding, though, when she resists the forces of his neurosis, he turns it on her even more fully. Thinking "coldly" of her, he plans her murder: "he thought of it calmly, as if the decision were being handed down to him by some logic not his own, over which he had no control, but which he had to obey" (p. 215). Such a logic—one that he imagines originating in a space outside or above his own—ensures Bigger's distance from Bessie, and it is in this hyperrational, detached frame of mind that he rapes and murders her.

In a grim, horrible rewriting of the love scene, Wright insists in the rape scene on Bigger's being outside himself, and we learn that watching himself from afar is central to Bigger's neurotic logic. During the rape, Bessie's voice came from "a deep, far-away silence." Bigger hears her moaning "from far away," and then an imaginary wind "lifted him high into the dark air" (p. 219). Refusing guilt, Bigger once again projects responsibility for his crimes onto the victim: "it was her own fault," he concludes (p. 220). So, the obsessive phrase that he uses to justify her murder takes over his consciousness.

Repeating the Manichean logic prompted by his fear of exposure, he mentally chants "he could not take her with him and he could not leave her behind" (pp. 220–21). Then, applying a distant discipline akin to that "used" on Bessie, he marshals his "will," experiences a temporal and spatial distortion, and smashes Bessie's skull with a brick. Through the horror of this scene, the reader discerns that Bigger is repeating (with a twist) his attacks on the rat, Gus, and Mary. In each case a spatial phobia overtakes Bigger and he purges himself of it only by violently displacing his fear onto the object that inspired it.

The twist in the murder of Bessie, though, is that her death does not rid Bigger of his agoraphobia; it worsens it. "Fear was in him again" only seconds after her death (p. 223). Killing her, in fact, makes him more vulnerable to the exposure he fears since "somebody might find her" when he throws her body outside (p. 223). Afterward, he can not rest; he finds no relief. Tossing and turning in the abandoned kitchenette, he feels that "a chance for [sure and quiet knowledge] was gone forever" (p. 226). There is now no "home" to which he can return. He is stranded in the public world that his murders have constructed around him. In an agoraphobic's nightmare, there is no safe place for him to hide, and no one to accompany him out into the public eye.

After this crisis, the agoraphobic logic can no longer function on its own, since it is premised on the possibility that one could return home or be safe in some way. So, for the remainder of the "Flight" section, Bigger experiences a perverse admixture of claustrophobia and agoraphobia. Fleeing desperately, he runs along the borders of the spaces he fears, and he experiences both inside and outside as traps.

For instance, claustrophobia returns with a vengeance when Bigger examines the map of the city printed in the newspapers. The "white portion" representing the parts of the city yet to be searched by the police is shrinking, and Bigger feels himself to be "trapped" in the white square representing the black South Side (p. 230). With a twinge of paranoia, he imagines that "all of the black men and women were talking about him" and "hating him for having brought this attack upon them" (p. 231). Consequently, he is not at home in or outside this area of the city. He roams the ghetto, reflecting in a defamiliarized fashion on the cramped conditions, examining buildings for rent, and listening through the walls. This last posture typifies his situation. Crouching silently on one side of the wall, he has space and a certain amount of dangerous freedom, but he cannot stray too far from his fellows. He wants to hear what they say about him; he wants to be (and is) both in and outside the life of the kitchenette.

This precarious perch causes peculiar distortions of Bigger's perceptual apparatus. As in the moment of killing Bessie, he experiences hallucinations and splits in his persona. "There were two Biggers," we learn: one that slept and one filled with terror, one observing social life and one crippled with hunger (pp. 236–37). His doubled phobias begin to split his personality in two.

Finally, the long-awaited chase begins, and Bigger unifies himself by escaping to the ambiguous space of the roof. As an emblem of his psychological condition, the roof is ideal, since it is both an open, exposed area and a limited, confining one. On the roof (whose entrance, the "trapdoor," also represents this spatial paradox), he is simultaneously free and not-free. Running to avoid the spotlight and the official gaze that will entrap him, he excels in applying his utilitarian logic, until, at last, the water hoses catch him at an unexpected angle and he once again goes "outside of himself" and looks "down at himself freezing" (pp. 250–53). When he can not sustain the conflict between his detached utilitarianism and his panic, he performs the ultimate flight and loses consciousness.

Upon awakening in the final "Fate" section, Bigger finds that his fear has transformed once again. In this section, he directly confronts the "fear of death" which has perhaps been his underlying fear all along (p. 256). The novel makes it clear that there is little chance Bigger could escape the death sentence; it is his "fate" to be at the mercy of the court. But, at the same time, Wright does not seem to be justifying Bigger's fear. This is not a neurotic novel that glories in the psychological extremes to which its central character is pushed. Instead, Bigger's final fear pushes us toward recognition of a utopian side of his anxieties. While facing his fear of death, Bigger realizes how strong his desire for "a new mode of life" is, and he begins to try to communicate that desire (p. 256). "Life," here, represents a kind of positive fulfillment—something similar to, but more active than, the "home" sought earlier in the novel.

Although this conclusion veers toward the existentialist, it does not abandon the more sociological depiction of space so important in the first two sections of the novel. However, in "Fate," space is no longer the source of anxiety or a screen for the source; here, space becomes the scene of the psychological drama. Space has a resonant, symbolic aspect that can be consciously considered. When Bigger begins to formulate his thoughts and visions of space, he becomes what Wright called, in another context, one of the "men in the making."[14] Bigger sorts through his spatial phobias and ultimately realizes a conscious, utopian desire for "life."

The transformation of space into the scene of "life" begins in the first episode in the "Fate" section. Here Wright carefully distorts the plausible space of the prison cell. As he noted in "How 'Bigger' Was Born," he brings a preacher, Jan, Max, the prosecutor, the Daltons, Bigger's family and friends all into the cell because he wants "to elicit a certain important emotional response from Bigger."[15] This response, though, is not the claustrophobic panic explored earlier in the novel; in fact, the effect of this mass visit is just the opposite. At its conclusion, Bigger falls to the floor, exhausted and afraid because he is "alone, profoundly, inescapably"; his inability to satisfy the "impulsion to try to tell" why he had killed leaves him drained and isolated (p. 288). In this case, the space of the cell is not what entraps him; the cell becomes merely the physical correlative for his existential solitude. The flexible walls of the cell balloon outwards to contain all these people so that Wright can dramatize Bigger's isolation in a world without communication.

From this traumatic transformation of claustrophobic space into scene, the novel moves into the public arena of the courtroom. Significantly, the room itself is not described in these scenes. Only the physical evidence of the crime attracts the narrator's eye—the kidnap note, the pile of bones, the Daltons, the trunk, the hatchet (p. 290). This space is clearly designed to be invisible except where it offers a reenactment of the crime. The courtroom is a theater, and the conventions of theater demand that one ignore all of the room except that designated for the drama. Like the rooftop, the court is ambiguous—it is a public space for dramatizing private conflicts.

Bigger's responses to this space follow the conventions of the theater. For most of the inquest scene, we assume that his attention is directed to the drama of the court, since the narrative ignores him—until one key moment. When Bessie's mutilated corpse is brought forward as evidence, the theatrical routine of the courtroom is disrupted. Identifying briefly (and too late) with Bessie, Bigger is "crushed, helpless"; he reflects anxiously on the staging of the courtroom (p. 306). He concludes that her body is being "used" by the white authorities to make a scene, much as he had "used" Bessie to plan the faux kidnapping (p. 307). At this point, Bessie's body is revealed and Bigger flinches. He lifted "his hands to his eyes and at the same instant he saw blinding flashes of the silver bulbs" (p. 307). He tries to withdraw from the scene and cut off his senses, but his withdrawal is made public by the relentless eye of the press. Thus, although aware of the scenic properties of the courtroom, Bigger still relapses simultaneously into both of his previous phobias. He experiences a frozen panic at being too close to the body and a cynical fear of his image entering the public realm. So long as he is without language or the power to represent himself, this dual phobia is his only response to crisis.

However, a major awakening takes place immediately after the inquest when the authorities drag Bigger back to the Daltons' home to reenact the crime in its original space (pp. 308–15). Understanding that the police simply desire another gratuitous spectacle, Bigger refuses to play his role. But the important revelation for Bigger arrives when he sees a burning cross on a building outside. At first, he thinks it is there to remind him to love Jesus; then "it gripped him: that was not the cross of Christ, but the cross of the Ku Klux Klan" (p. 313). In a flash, he understands that symbols are appropriated for entirely different purposes by different groups of people, and he tears off his own cross and throws it away. This act initiates a string of antiphobic, even curative, behaviors. Instead of shielding his eyes as he did with Bessie's corpse, from this point on Bigger works to represent himself. He refuses to reenact the drama in the bedroom for the white observers because he is beginning to stage his own scene.

Thereafter, the novel concerns various attempts to interpret the scene of the crime. Bigger begins to articulate to Max the way that " 'they choke you off the face of the earth. . . . They make us stay in one little spot,' " and this speech helps him find "a cool breath of peace" (pp. 327, 332). Talking suddenly seems to him "a recognition of his life, of his feelings, of his person" (p. 333). As a direct result of this eye-opening experience, he reimagines the space around him. He has a revelatory vision, "a dark vast fluid image" of the world "as a black sprawling prison full of tiny black cells in which people lived" (p. 334). In contrast to his earlier phobias, this image of enclosure does not panic Bigger. Instead, it arises from and sponsors a desire for "a set of words which he had in common with others, words which would evoke in others a sense of the same fire that smoldered in him" (p. 337). Bigger is no longer responding phobically to his situation as a publicly confined person; he is attempting to find another way out through interpretation. The symbolic dimension is taking precedent over the spatial.

Of course, the speeches in the courtroom—Max's and the prosecutor's—are also attempts to direct interpretation of the scene of the crime. They are long and abstract, and they do not read well because they work over ground that is too familiar to the reader by this point in the novel. We already know that "the relationship between the Thomas family and the Dalton family was that of renter to landlord" (p. 302) and that the authorities "mean to keep Bigger Thomas and his kind within rigid limits . . . within the ghetto-area of the city" (p. 363). However, criticism of Max's speech in particular has been misplaced.[16] This speech is not positioned as the moral of *Native Son*. It is, rather, one of several attempts to reflect on Bigger's phobias and come to a conscious understanding of their utopian aspect. Wright knows that the speech is not a sufficient effort in that direction, and his narrator remarks that "It was not the meaning of the speech that gave [Bigger] pride, but the mere act of it" (p. 371). For Bigger and the social world of which he is a part, fears and hatred do not disappear simply because they are named and placed in a historical narrative. Only when the whole social space is conceptualized anew is "life" confirmed.

The final scene of the novel, then, is Wright's last attempt to demonstrate how such a reconceptualization might take place. Under the shadow of death, Max and Bigger talk together, although they find it difficult to understand one another. Bigger feels that "Max was upon another planet, far off in space," and he wants "to break the wall of isolation" (p. 386). Bigger has trouble expressing himself; he tends to shout. But finally "the desire to talk, to tell" takes hold of him, and he blurts out another condensed version of the source of his fears and anger: " 'They were crowding me too close; they wouldn't give me no room. . . . So I fought 'em' " (p. 388). Then he wants to know if other people feel as he does—if they, too, have "life." Across "a gulf of silence," Max responds by leading Bigger to the window and drawing his attention to the city outside. He draws his own map of the city for Bigger:

"Those buildings sprang up out of the hearts of men, Bigger . . . When millions of men are desiring and longing, those buildings grow and unfold" (pp. 389–90). Max offers Bigger this consciously humanist interpretation of the space surrounding them as a way of communicating his faith in life and social transformation. Although the vision has a strongly sentimental side to it, Bigger recognizes and respects the impulse behind it.

However, once again, Wright insists that Bigger does not swallow Max's vision whole. "Bigger was gazing in the direction of the buildings," he writes, "but he did not see them. He was trying to react to the picture Max was drawing, trying to compare that picture with what he had felt all his life" (p. 390). Wright does not tell us what Bigger concludes about the fit between the two pictures. Instead, he leaves us with Bigger exulting in some sort of new, unnamed knowledge and frightening Max—his final words suggesting that he has found a way out of fear that cannot quite be expressed. When the "far door clanged shut" on Bigger, he is still confined and marked for death, but he smiles "a faint, wry, bitter smile" that intimates he is aware of the irony of his impending death (p. 392). He faces his own certain demise with the knowledge that he can place himself in the sweltering, throbbing human life of the city. He seems to have reimagined social space in such a way that he is no longer afraid. He is, instead, focused on his powerful discovery of a new sort of symbolic space within himself and in language.

POLITICS AND THE INTERSPACE

The narrative of phobias and the promise of a cure traced in the previous section is made manifest in *Native Son;* the narrator presents Bigger's anxieties in habitual phrases and metaphors throughout the novel. However, we might also notice that this free indirect discourse foregrounds the narrative frame by drawing our attention to the fact that these feelings are indirectly narrated.[17] With comments such as "the feeling of being always enclosed . . . had gone," Wright brings both Bigger's dilemma and his own position as the author of this dilemma into focus. He creates an optical illusion in which one's attention alternates between the active and descriptive layers of the text.

Now, to describe the novel's geography, one need not concentrate on the narrative level of the text; one could also turn to some of Wright's commentary on *Native Son*. In "How 'Bigger' Was Born," for example, Wright makes it quite clear that he told his story "in close-up, slow-motion" because "this was the best way to 'enclose' the reader's mind" (p. xxxii). He says he "restricted the novel" so it would become the reader's "private theater"; he used a "short space of time" and "limited" himself so the novel would allow no escape from "the forces and elements against which Bigger was striving" (p. xxxii). In this essay, Wright is also clear about the fact that he imagined Bigger as one link in a chain of comparable oppressions—Bigger's experience stands metonymically for the "Bigger in Nazi Germany and Bigger in old Russia" (p. xix). One could use such passages to argue that this chain of equivalents was as important to Wright's imagination as the specificities of the African American situation. Both led him to grasp the *"drama"* of Bigger's situation; that is, both the enclosure and open-endedness of Bigger's character were crucial to this literary formulation of Wright's political principles (p. xx).

This sort of evidence is readily available. However, I chose to limit myself to what Slavoj Zizek, a follower of Jacques Lacan, calls "the inter-space."[18] If we think of the novel as resembling a dream, the manifest level represents the imagery of the dream, while its political content (its critique of Communism) parallels the anxiety represented in the dream. The fit between these two—the logic that leads one to represent a certain anxiety in a partic-ular dream language—is the "interspace" in which the unconscious is at play. To describe the interspace of *Native Son,* it was useful to draw attention both to the organization of the text and to its statement—to both the manifest and latent contents. Now that both of these have been outlined, we can cre-ate a sort of overlay by placing *Native Son*'s map of culture over that of the proletarian novel. Doing this should allow us to learn how Wright's politics emerge from his literary practice.

From the manifest narrative of *Native Son,* it is clear that Wright's map of culture has similar contours to that proposed in the proletarian novel. In both cases, the significant contrasts are between small, local spots and the large, general exterior. In both cases, the texts strive to establish bridges between the small localities. Proportions are the key; the communication of two localities across a much vaster distance is the constant factor.

However, while the proletarian novelists imagined that linking white Appalachian communities to the industrial mainstream would propel culture as a whole into a newly organized future, for Wright space had a more backward-looking resonance. For Wright, space comes to represent history. The spatial phobias and critique of Communism fit together for him because together they embody the specific history of the urban African American community. As we know from *12 Million Black Voices,* Wright considered the migration of Southern black farmers from one-room shacks to the kitchenettes of Northern cities such as Chicago one of the definitive features of his era. For Wright, this movement represented the historical transformation of feudalism into capitalism, and the fact that, for African Americans, it was "all enacted within a *short* space of his-torical time" made his community central to twentieth-century American cul-ture.[19] He knew from personal experience that the speed of his generation's shift from peasant to worker had wreaked especially significant, historically spe-cific forms of psychological damage on that generation, and it is this fast-paced historical drama that he portrays in his "close-up, slow-motion" novel.

In the end, confined space and psychological panic about space represent for Wright not a potential resistance to capitalism but the crisis provoked by entering modern capitalist, urban life. Wright found it necessary to dramatize this phase of historical development because he felt that some of his peers on the Left had ignored it in favor of more sanguine hopes that feudalism could leap suddenly forward into socialism, and the psychology of space became the vehicle of his critique of sanguinity because, in space, seemingly incompatible historical modes may coexist. As *Native Son* demonstrates, a rural mindset can occupy an urban space; neofeudal ghettos can hide within the spacious neighborhoods of wealthy industrialists; and seeds of something more lifelike and egalitarian can inhabit the same cell as the fears generated by the alienating and contemporary environment of inner-city slums. The spatial dimension offered Wright a cross-section of history, and portraying the psychology of space allowed him to put that history in motion in the mind of a violent, damaged, but ultimately hopeful native son.

Notes

1. James Baldwin, "Many Thousands Gone," in *Notes of a Native Son* (Boston: Beacon, 1955), 33. For discussions of Wright's misogyny, see Jane Davis, "More Force than Human: Richard Wright's Female Characters," *Obsidian II*, 1 (1986): 68–83; Trudier Harris, "Native Sons and Foreign Daughters," in *New Essays on Native Son,* ed. Keneth Kinnamon (New York: Cambridge, 1990), 63–84; Alan W. France, "Misogyny and Appropriation in *Native Son,*" *Modern Fiction Studies,* 34 (1988): 413–24; and Houston Baker Jr., "Richard Wright and the Dynamics of Place in Afro-American Literature," in Kinnamon 1990, 85–116.

2. Studies of African American intellectual life regularly qualify their praise of Wright with the mention of his "overreliance on the Communist ideology with which he encumbered his powerful indictment of society" (Margaret Just Butcher, *The Negro in American Culture* [New York: Knopf, 1956], 178); see also Harold Cruse, *The Crisis of the Negro Intellectual* (New York: Morrow, 1967), 182; S. P. Fullinwider, *The Mind and Mood of Black America: Twentieth-Century Thought* (Homewood, Illinois: Dorsey, 1969), 191. A more contemporary anti-Communist argument is Houston Baker's assertion that "a Marxian problematic forces the writer to devalue women" (Baker, 108).

3. Paul Buhle, *Marxism in the United States* (New York: Verso, 1987); Robin D. G. Kelley, " 'Comrades, Praise Gawd for Lenin and Them!': Ideology and Culture Among Black Communists in Alabama, 1930–1935," *Science and Society,* 52 (1988): 59–82; Kelley, *Hammer and Hoe: Alabama Communists During the Great Depression* (Chapel Hill: University of North Carolina Press, 1990).

4. Paula Rabinowitz, *Labor and Desire: Women's Revolutionary Fiction in Depression America* (Chapel Hill: University of North Carolina Press, 1992).

5. Barbara Foley, *Radical Representations: Politics and Form in U.S. Proletarian Fiction, 1929–1941* (Durham: Duke University Press, 1994), 213–48.

6. Malcolm Cowley, *The Dream of the Golden Mountains* (New York: Penguin, 1964), 250–51. Cowley's judgment is consistent with the mainstream critical opinion on the proletarian novel such as Walter Rideout's *The Radical Novel in the United States* (Cambridge: Harvard University Press, 1954).

7. The phrase "cultural islands" comes from the Workers Cultural Federation manifesto "ART IS A WEAPON!" *New Masses,* (August 1931): 11–13. R. Serge Denisoff argues that leftists saw folk music as containing a latent "cry for justice"; see *Great Day Coming: Folk Music and the American Left* (Urbana: University of Illinois Press, 1971). On the construction of supposedly premodern aspects of Appalachian life, see David Whisnant, *All That Is Native and Fine: The Politics of Culture in an American Region* (Chapel Hill: University of North Carolina Press, 1983), chapter 1.

8. Richard Wright, *American Hunger* (New York: Harper & Row, 1977), 64–66.

9. Keneth Kinnamon remarks that "Wright's effort in [*Native Son*] is to reconcile his sense of black life with the intellectual clarity and the possibility of social action provided by Communism, to interpret each group to the other" in his introduction to *New Essays on Native Son,* 3; in the same volume, John M. Reilly argues that Wright rewrote the "social novel as a black text" ("Giving Bigger a Voice: The Politics of Narrative in *Native Son,*" 41). Barbara Foley also sees *Native Son* as a performative dialogue in "The Politics of Poetics: Ideology and Narrative Form in *An American Tragedy* and *Native Son,*" in *Narrative Poetics: Innovations, Limits, Challenges,* ed. James Phelan (Columbus: Ohio State University, 1987), 55–67; and Martin Kilson argues Wright adopted the strategy of the "Marginal Man" in "Politics and Identity among Black Intellectuals," *Dissent,* 28 (1981): 339–49. My argument differs from these in more specifically focusing on how Wright used this dialogue to reformulate the proletarian novel.

10. Richard Wright, *12 Million Black Voices: A Folk History* (1941; rpt. New York: Arno and *New York Times,* 1969).

11. Richard Wright, *Native Son* (1940; New York: Harper & Row, 1968), 7. All further references will appear in the text.

12. For an interesting discussion of Wright's use of dialect, see Lynda Hungerford, "Dialect Representation in *Native Son,*" *Language and Style,* 20 (1987): 3–15.

13. Ross Pudaloff convincingly argues that Wright sees mass culture as a challenger to folk traditions in "Celebrity as Identity: Richard Wright, *Native Son* and Mass Culture," *Studies in American Fiction,* 11 (1983): 3–18.

14. Wright, *12 Million Black Voices,* 141–48.

15. Richard Wright, "How 'Bigger' Was Born," repr. in *Native Son,* xxxi. Orig. pub. (New York: Harper, 1940).

16. For a discussion of Wright's didacticism, see Edward Margolies "*Native Son* and Three Kinds of Revolution," in *Bigger Thomas,* ed. Harold Bloom (New York: Chelsea, 1990), 43–53.

17. This understanding of free indirect discourse is adopted from Gilles Deleuze's discussion of Passolini in *Cinema 1: The Movement-Image,* trans. Hugh Tomlinson and Barbara Hammerjam (Minneapolis: University of Minnesota Press, 1986), 72–76. Deleuze, in turn, is borrowing from Bakhtin's *Marxism and the Philosophy of Language.*

18. This phrase appears in an interesting discussion of the congruence of Marx and Freud's strategies for interpretation: "the unconscious desire . . . intercalates itself in the interspace between the latent thought and the manifest text." Slavoj Zizek, *The Sublime Object of Ideology* (New York: Verso, 1989), 13.

19. Wright, *12 Million Black Voices,* 142.

On the Lower Frequencies:
Sound and Meaning in *Native Son*

ALESSANDRO PORTELLI

I. FEAR: EVERYBODY'S TEXTUAL NOVEL

Certainly he does not write by ear unless he is tone deaf.[1]
...a bad authorial ear...[2]

In a landmark essay, Robert Hemenway pointed out years ago that in the criticism of African American literature "the direction of commentary is always outward, away from the text," toward "social allegory."[3] This has been especially true concerning Richard Wright's *Native Son*, which has been consistently read (praised and, at least in certain phases of its critical history, condemned) as a political, philosophical, autobiographical statement, and only rarely analyzed (and frequently dismissed) as a verbal artifact. Zora Neale Hurston's early attack on Wright's use of language established the grounds of this dismissive approach; Bloom's verdict is only one among the many mechanical repetitions of Hurston's by-now canonical judgment.

"Everybody's protest novel" must, by definition, be all signified and no signifier (and therefore, ultimately, have very little meaning at all). Though recent work in African American literary criticism has somewhat modified the state of things denounced by Hemenway, much remains to be done. Even those critics who have treated *Native Son* as a work of art have considered mostly its imagery.[4] The present essay reconsiders *Native Son* primarily in terms of language, on the basis of a computer-aided reading and concordance of the text.[5] Doing so, we shall find that the problem concerns less the lacking authorial ear than the prejudiced and insensitive ears of the critics.

This essay was written specifically for this volume and is published here for the first time by permission of the author.

II. FLIGHT: AN EXPERIMENT IN CRITICAL LISTENING

1. Sound and Meaning: Critical Clusters

The coroner rapped for order, then rose and stepped to the table and with one sweep of his arm *flung* the sheet *back from Bessie's body.* The sight, *bloody and black,* made Bigger *flinch* involuntarily and lift his hands to his eyes and at the same instant he saw *blinding flashes* of silver *bulbs flicking* through the air. His eyes looked with painful effort to the back of the room, for he *felt* that if he saw Bessie again he would rise from his chair and sweep his arm in an attempt to *blot out* this room, and the people in it. (p. 755)

This is one of the most intentionally theatrical scenes in *Native Son.* Bigger Thomas has murdered, more or less accidentally, Mary Dalton, his white employers' daughter, and burned her body; later, he murdered in cold blood his girlfriend, Bessie Mears. Now, in the courtroom, the prosecutor makes up for the absence of Mary's corpse by exhibiting Bessie's battered body. The intensity of the passage is underlined by the dramatic clustering of words and alliterations featuring certain sounds: *b, bl; f, fl.*

Because these sounds play a very important role in the text, they may be the key to some of its less visible meanings. They reverberate through all of the crucial scenes, including the killing of Mary and the disposal of her body:

Would there *be blood?* . . . He touched the sharp *blade* to the throat, just touched it, as if expecting the knife to cut the white *flesh* of itself, as if he did not have to put pressure behind it. Wist*fully,* he gazed at the edge of the *blade* resting on the white skin; the gleaming metal re*flected* the tremulous *fury* of the coals. Yes; he *had* to. Gently, he sawed the *blade* into the *flesh* and struck a *bone.* He gritted his teeth and cut harder. As yet there was no *blood* anywhere but on the knife. *But* the *bone* made it difficult. Sweat crawled down his *back.* Then *blood* crept outward. . . . (p. 531)

The Blur and the Blaze

From the moment Bigger first lays eyes on the furnace to the shutting of the lid on Mary's body, the initial cluster *bl* occurs no fewer than 13 times in two pages (6 *blood,* 3 *blade, blur, blaze, blast, black*). In the four preceding pages, in which Mary is killed, the formulaic syntagm *white blur* (referring to Mary's blind mother, whose presence frightens Bigger into choking her) is used eight times.[6] *Blind* enters the text the moment Bigger enters the Dalton home (p. 488) and appears six times before the murder scene begins; in the course of the novel it will be attributed to all of the characters (see p. 543, where it occurs 9 times).

Blind is part of a paradigm of visual terms which includes, among others, *blink* (also in the variant *unblinkingly,* a typical Richard Wright word) and the *blue* light in Mary's room. Among other *bl* words, we may take *black* for granted, but Wright takes care to alliterate it frequently in order to foreground its sound shape. In the most crucial moments, Bigger is always tempted to *block out* something or someone, possibly with one single *blow*. And the white man Bigger and his pals prepare to rob is named *Blum*. There are 694 occurrences of words beginning with *bl* in *Native Son*. Besides *black* (302 occurrences), the most important are *blood* (50) and *blind* (46).

Around these "key entries" we can observe an area of "halo entries" in which *b* and *l* are not directly in contact (*b**): *bulb* (16 occurrences), *bulge, balk,* and the formulaic syntagm *white {looming} bulk* (repeated 4 times). A further circle includes "marginal entries" in which the nexus occurs in positions other than initial (**bl**), such as *oblong* ("the *oblong Black Belt*"), *mumble* (54 occurrences, also applied to each character), and *table* (84). At a further remove, many important objects and actions are designated by words in *b:* the *bed* on which *Bigger* kills Mary and the *basement* in which he *burns her body* and saws her *bone;* and the *brick* with which *Bessie* is murdered on a *blanket*. The number of character names in *b* has often been noted (beside *Bigger, Bessie,* and *Blum,* also *Buddy, Britten,* and *Buckley*). Even the Dalton automobile is a *blue Buick*. "Halo" and "marginal" entries are in evidence, together with *b* initials, in several crucial passages. For instance:

> He *blinked* his eyes and stared at Mary's face; it was darker than when he had first *b*ent over her. Her mouth was open and her eyes *bulged* glassily. Her *b*osom, her *b*osom, her—her *b*osom was not moving! He could not hear her *b*reath coming and going now as he had when he had first *b*rought her into the room! He *b*ent and moved her head with his hand and found that she was relaxed and limp. He snatched his hand away. Thought and feeling were *balked* in him. . . . (p. 527)

Floating and Flying

Much the same considerations apply to the other critical cluster identified in the courtroom scene, *fl* (381 occurrences). Book One ends with alliteration suggesting a sigh of relief; when Bigger steps outside after putting Mary's body in the furnace, "a *few fine flakes* of snow were *floating* down" (p. 532). Around such words as *floor* (121 occurrences), *flash* and *flashlight* (58), *flat* (32), *flood, fly, flight,* and others can be found the halo of indirect *f*l* clusters. Forms of *fall* (106 occurrences) and, most of all, *feel* (no less than 744 occurrences, of which 336 are accounted for by *felt*) create a thick halo around the key entries. Also, a number of important entries, *fire, furnace, freeze,* and *fear,* begin with *f.* Symmetrically, they occur in a significant passage at the end of Book Two: "He *felt* cold, *freezing;* his *blood* turned to ice . . . Then he was *falling.* He landed on the roof, on his *face* . . ." (pp. 697, 698). Of course, the three sections of the novel alliterate in *F: Fear, Flight, Fate.* The Daltons' cook is Peggy O'*Flagherty.*

"Helden"

The key entries (and their surrounding halo and margin) tend to agglomerate in the vicinity of the most emotionally important scenes. These sound clusters are qualitative as well as quantitative terms. Their function is not unlike that of "Helden" in alliterative old German poetry: a continuous bass note, a constant burden, reverberating in the lower frequencies of the text to emerge in its most dramatic moments.[7]

2. Foreshadowings and Echoes

This use of sounds is anticipated or reiterated frequently in Wright's other works. One typical moment, which anticipates the equivalent passages in *Native Son,* is the orgasm scene in "Long Black Song": ". . . a high red wave of hotness drowned her in a deluge of silver and *blue that boiled her blood and blistered* her *flesh bangbangbang.* . . ." A few lines above, an agglomeration of *fl* and *f* words (*flicking, fingers, face, folds, flood*) surrounds another occurrence of *blood.*[8] When the heroine in "Bright and Morning Star" comes to from her faint, "a vast *white blur* was suspended directly above her. For a moment she could not tell if her *fear was from the blur or if the blur was from her fear.* Gradually the *blur* resolved itself into a huge white *face* that slowly *filled* her vision" (p. 424). A *white blur* haunts *Native Son;* in *Black Boy* (a phonetically significant second choice for *American Hunger*), the origin of it all is revealed in the "huge *wobbly white bags*" of a fearful childhood memory.[9]

These clusters are connected to images of fire and water: ". . . the *flood* rustled, gurgled, droned, glistening *blackly,* like an ocean of *bubbling* oil" ("Down by the Riverside," p. 287). In "The Man Who Lived Underground," we find water "*bl*ossoming" around a dead baby's body. The opening scene of *Black Boy,* in which Richard sets fire to the curtains, includes 12 occurrences of words in *b* in nine lines, including *black* and *blaze.* Wright's controversial descriptions of black life in the South are sustained by alliterations: the "*bleakness of black life,*" "a *bare, bleak* pool of *black* life," and "our *flight,* our *fears,* our *frenzy* under pressure."[10]

In "Big Boy Leaves Home" (and in "Bright and Morning Star") most characters have names in *b: Bobo, Buck,* and *Big Boy.* In this story, *blinking* and *blade of light* are used throughout. According to Michel Fabre's biography, Wright's first appreciation of fiction and storytelling was aroused by the story of *Bluebeard.*[11]

The butcher shop scene in "The Man Who Lived Underground" is dominated by the same sounds as that of Mary's murder: it opens with a "*frigid blast*" as the narrator is "*blinded* by light" and the meat is cut with "a *bloody* meat cleaver" and placed on a "*bloody* wooden *block*" until the butcher "wiped *blood* off the wooden *block.*" Later, the narrator "placed the *bulb* on the dirt *floor* and the light cast a *blatant* glare on the *bleak* clay walls": 9 out of 11 words contain the sound *l,* including *gl* and *cl* clusters that, as we will see later on, play a role again in *Native Son.*[12]

Wright resorted to these devices also in his later work. In *The Outsider* and *Savage Holiday,* he alliterates in *D* and *A* the titles of book sections. While entries and alliterations in *d* dominate *The Outsider,*[13] *Savage Holiday* takes up the *fl* and *bl* paradigm with a vengeance: in the three pages describing Fow*l*er's murder of Ma*bel,* there is a total of 20 occurrences of such key entries, nearly always alliterated halo and marginal ones (for a total of 39 occurrences, including 8 occurrences of *table*): "He heard the sound of *blood* dripping into pools that had *b*egun to *f*orm on the *floor.* He started away from the ta*b*le, then turned back and tossed the *bloody* *b*utcher knife carelessly on top of the slashed and *bleeding* stomach."[14]

This, however, could be merely a personal mannerism as James T. Farrell suggested in his review of *Uncle Tom's Children,* criticizing the emphatic overuse of certain figures of sound and flow: "He has bare feet whisper too much in the dark, and there is too much ebb and surge in the blood of his characters."[15] In *Native Son* alone among Wright's works, however, these devices are patterned in a complex, if tentative, grammar of sounds, foregrounded in the demarcative structures of the text, the three alliterating book titles, and the symmetry of the opening and closing scenes.

The very first lines immediately call our attention to sound, with a clamorous onomatopoeia and a sequence of sound icons, critical clusters, and alliterations:

Brrrrrriiiiiiiiiiiiiiiiiiinng!
An alarm *clock clanged* in the dark and silent room. A bed spring *creaked.* A woman's *voice sang out* impatiently:
"Bigger, shut that thing off!"
A *surly grunt* sounded above the *tinny ring* of metal. Naked feet *swished* dryly across the planks in the wooden *floor* and the *clang* ceased abruptly.
"Turn on the light, Bigger."
"Awright," came a sleepy *mumble.*
Light *flooded* the room and revealed a *black boy standing in a narrow space* *b*etween two iron *b*eds, ru*bb*ing his eyes with the *b*acks of his hands. (p. 447)

The first verb and first sound of the novel—"clanged"—are also the last: "He heard the ring of steel against steel as a far door clanged shut" (p. 850).

3. Arbitrary Language, Motivated Sounds

"Son et Sense"

Becoming aware of a possible pattern of sounds in *Native Son,* we need to understand its meaning and its structure. Since Saussure, a basic law of linguistics (with a number of exceptions, even in ordinary usage) is that of the essentially "arbitrary" nature of language; on the other hand, a basic law of literary theory is that nothing can be assumed to be arbitrary in a literary text. A literary text is a place where two basic laws of language conflict and negotiate a perennial tension between arbitrariness and motivation. Paul Valery's punning definition of poetry as a hesitation between "sense" and "sound" (homophonous in French) is a good description of how poetical language works upon the ordinary matter of language, and is especially applicable to the African American tradition, with its historical grounding in the sounds of speech and music.

Most discussions of this aspect of language, however, refer to poetry rather than fiction. In poetry, sound is inherent in rhythm, rhyme, and alliteration; the brevity and subjectivity of most modern poetic genres allow sound to sustain sense with little interference from the referential functions of ordinary speech. In a novel, however, sheer length and the requirements of plot and characterization accentuate the resistance of the referential function to the shaping force of literary language. The originary asystematic quality of arbitrary referent-sign relationships curbs the teleological systematicity of literary language: the "prose of the world" interferes with the world of prose. Therefore, in a novel, any grammar of sounds will be much more tentative, unfinished, and contradictory than in a sonnet. In *Native Son,* this incompleteness of the system mirrors, at the level of the signifier, Wright's motif of the *resistance of language.* "Wrestling with words gave me my moments of deepest meaning," he wrote in *American Hunger;* in *Native Son,* the tension of referent, signified, and signifier underscores Bigger's almost physical struggle with words.

The concept of a tension between different levels of signification within the sign also clarifies the difference between the theoretical status of Wright's use of sound and the romantic and transcendentalist tradition of a direct, natural link between "words" and "natural fact." Interestingly, linguists and writers had based this theory precisely on sounds and graphemes that are central to the meaning of *Native Son: l, b, f, st.* In 1842, for instance, the linguist Benjamin F. Taylor wrote that "The liquid L, flows like the object to which it is applied. The guttural C, is hollow like the cave that it imitates. The sound *st,* is *st*rong, *st*able, and *st*ubborn, as the object to which it is applied." A few years later Thoreau developed this graphemic and phonemic iconism in his famous passage on the globe and the leaf.[16]

It is important to bear in mind that any meaning of sounds in Richard Wright's works is not spontaneously inherent in them, but projected, evoked, often forcibly wrested, in the process of artistic creation. In fact, even in everyday speech, the relationship of sound and meaning is usually latent (otherwise any ordinary conversation would be impossible), and is "awakened," as it were, by consistent and patterned textual foregrounding.

For instance, the *b*l*l* cluster in such a commonplace word as *table* does not attract our attention until we find it in the phonetically charged context of the courtroom scene (twice alliterated with the ominous *oblong*). We then remember that we had encountered it in the violent context of the poolroom scene ("Gus . . . gra*bb*ed a *billiard ball* from the ta*b*le," [p. 482]). In this light, the irony of Mr. Dalton's gift of ping-pong tables becomes utterly painful.[17]

In another example, the semantically elementary opposition of "black" and "white" is charged in *Native Son* by the usually dormant phonetic opposition between the explosive *bl* and the blurred *wh,* underscoring the ghostlike quality of whites (especially if, as Melville suggested, we voice the *h*) and the hard-vs.-soft paradigm to be discussed later.[18]

In order to create this effect, Wright uses a set of increasingly complex textual devices. The most important are *onomatopoeia, articulation, lexicon, rhetoric,* and *syntax.*

Onomatopoeia

The use of this figure in the opening scene of *Native Son* (as, earlier, at the beginning of "Long Black Song") is self-explanatory. We may, however, note that this scene displays two levels of onomatopoeia: imitation of nonlinguistic sounds (*brrrrrrriiiiiiiiiiiiiiiiiiiiinng!*) or lexicalization of sound icons (*grunt, swish, screak, clang*). One thing about such words is that, like images, they literally require no translation. Even such lexicalized onomatopoeias as "clang" or "mumble" are regularly untranslated, for instance, in Italian translations of American comics (and adopted in Italian comics imitating American models).

Onomatopoeia is situated in the no-man's-land between language and not-language, between "natural" sounds and "conventional" speech. We will see later that the concept of no-man's-land, or borderline and liminal stages of consciousness, is crucial to the symbolism of *Native Son.* A function of onomatopoeia in this text seems indeed to be the underscoring of the uncertain zone between sleep and wakefulness, reverie and daydream. The sound of the alarm clock shakes Bigger from sleep to wakefulness; later, half asleep on his bed, he half dreams of "the heavy trunk going *bump-bump-bump* down the stairs" (p. 562) and then of hurling Mary's "bloody head squarely into their faces *dongdongdong*" (p. 599). In both cases, a sudden sound (a knock, a ring) startles him awake.[19]

It makes sense, then, that onomatopoeia and sound icons should mark the beginnings of texts, the threshold and border between writing and absence. Besides *Native Son* and "Long Black Song," it is also the case with the muffled sounds that open *The Outsider:* "*F*rom an invisi*b*le February *s*ky *s*himmering curtain of *s*now*fl*akes *fl*uttered down upon Chicago."[20]

Articulation

Synesthetic and symbolic overtones often accrue to articulation, both in terms of mode and place. In *Moby Dick,* Melville proclaims that *h* is the most important part of *whale:* its origin in the depths of the body, its unobstructed progress toward the outside, charge it with spiritual meaning. A similar logic applies to Wright's use of sounds.

"B": Tension and Explosion

Place of Articulation. The labial articulation of *b* suggests a zero degree, a prelinguistic, prearticulate ("baby-talk"?) stage of the language, especially when accompanied by the "liquid" *l*. This is the implication of Whitman's "*blab* of the pave" (repeated in "I too . . . *blubb'd, blushed* . . ."), the "*babble*" of Hawthorne's "*brook*", Huck Finn's "*blubbering*", even Emily Dickinson's busy "*bumblebee*." In Melville, such names as *Babo, Billy Budd,* and *Bartleby* designate characters whose language is forcibly impeded or willfully restrained. The Italian word for Billy Budd's stutter would be *balbettio,* suggesting again the translinguistic implications of prelinguistic evocations of sounds. Both Italian and English share *blah-blah* to designate utterance without meaning, and the mythical place where all languages were one and became meaningless to each other is aptly called *Babel.*

Bigger takes his move from this stage of the language. He is "inarticulate and incommunicative throughout most of the novel,"[21] and is first heard in a "surly grunt" and a "sleepy mumble": on the threshold between sound and silence, sound and language, as represented by the labial articulation of his own name. On the other hand, everybody in *Native Son* "mumbles"; inarticulateness is not just Bigger's problem, but an effect of the inability of language to convey what Wright, in the closing sentence of *American Hunger,* describes as "the inexpressibly human,"[22] a condition shared, like blindness, by all the players in the drama.

Mode of Articulation. The phoneme *b* is a voiced stop. Stops are also described as "plosive" (or "explosive") sounds, in which the flow of air is blocked and then suddenly released; "voiced" consonants are uttered with tense vocal chords and the application of a great deal of energy.[23] Energy, tension, obstacle, explosion: almost a capsule summary of at least the first section of the novel, in which Bigger's long-repressed "tensity"[24] explodes, as does Billy Budd's, to supplement a symbolically impaired language. A symbolic speech impediment resolves into (accidentally?) murderous violence. "My stroke is heavier than my groan," says Wright's biblical epigraph. Part of what it means is that what the "mumble" and the "grunt" cannot voice is articulated by the "blow."

"F": Laxity and Repose

Place of Articulation. The implications of *b* (all but latent in ordinary use of the language, and evoked here by their correspondence with other levels of the text) are underscored by the binary opposition with *f.* In terms of place, *f* is a labio-dental consonant and shares with *b* the preverbal symbolism of the labial articulation; in terms of mode, however, it creates a significant pattern of opposition.

Mode of Articulation. *F* is an *unvoiced continuant.* Unvoiced sounds are formed with relaxed vocal chords; the connotations of laxity in *f* are thus opposed to the tension and energy in voiced *b.* As a continuous sound, characterized by length and by the lack of a very sharply defined beginning and end, *f* evokes static duration vs. the punctual, discrete action in stopped *b.*[25] The pattern of relaxation, tension, explosion is relevant to other levels of the text. For instance, the opposition of lax continuant *f* and tense explosive *b* coincides with the alternation in Bigger's life of "indifference and violence; periods of abstract brooding and periods of intense desire; moments of silence and moments of anger" (p. 471).[26]

Lexicon

The existence of "constellations of words having similar meanings tied to similar sounds" was recognized by Roman Jakobson, among others.[27] While this phenomenon is often only the evolution of an etymological species, some semantic fields are bound together by shared sound clusters in an implicit synesthesia. Among the many possible examples is a semantic field that ties tension and vision in a paradigm of words in *gl: glance, glare, gleam, glimpse, glitter,* and *glow.* Another similar field, closely related to the area of physical "tensity," includes such words as *clamp, clench, cling,* and *clutch.* It is the nature of language, of course, that not all words designating the same semantic field begin with the same sound and that not all words including a given sound belong to the same semantic field. By combining a constant foregrounding of sound with careful structuring of contexts, however, *Native Son* manages to draw toward a semantic field associated with a given sound also words that do not share the same immediate semantic implications. Thus, *glass, glaze,* or *clock, clang,* often with the help of context, acquire connotations of physical tension from the *gl* and *cl* paradigms. This lexical linking of sounds and meaning is, of course, central to the uses of *bl* and *fl* words, as will be discussed under the heading of syntax, where the lexical level becomes activated.

One should mention also the activation of morphological sounds. One possible ground for Wright's predilection for modal adverbs formed from gerunds is that the juxtaposition of the -ing and -ly suffixes generates a new *gl* nexus, as in his favorite "unbl#*kin*gly." Adjectives formed by the -ful suffix also generate adverbs with an *f*l* nexus. Especially in Book Three, Wright also uses a number of -ble suffixes ("inevita*bl*e," "incomprehensi*bl*e," "unescapa*bl*y").

Rhetoric

Alliteration and Emphasis. As I already noted, the rhetorical motivation of sound may be either inherent to generic requirements (rhyme, alliteration, rhythmic poetry) or freely used in order to draw attention to specific textual passages. Alliteration is, in a sense, the zero degree of rhetoric, the most facile of figures. If the careful interplay of selected sounds can be compared to a musical modulation of language, an indiscriminate accentuation of alliteration per se is like turning up the volume to attract attention. Wright is often prone to the temptation of emphatic alliteration. As Bigger and Bessie make love, the modulation of critical clusters to suggest a pattern of repose and underlying tension is almost lost in a general increase in the rate of alliteration:

> He *felt* two soft palms holding his face tenderly and the thought and image of the *whole blind world which* had made him *ashamed and afraid fell away as* he *felt her as a fallow field* beneath him stretching out under a *c*loudy sky *w*aiting for rain, and he slept in her body, ri*s*ing and sinking with the ebb and *flow of her blood, being wi*lling*ly* dragged into a *w*arm night sea to *rise renewed* to the sur*face to face* a *w*orld he *h*ated and *w*anted to *blot out* of existence, *c*linging *close* to a *f*ountain whose *warm waters washed* and *c*leaned his *s*enses, *c*ooled them, made them *s*trong and *k*een again to *see and smell* and *touch and taste* and hear, *c*leared them to end the *t*iredness and to reforge in him a new *s*en*s*e of *t*ime and *s*pace. . . . (p. 570)

Formulaic Genres.   A further and emblematic use of formulaic alliteration occurs in the sociological and legal language of Book Three: "commit a crime," "suffocation and strangulation," "make a motion," "opportunity to offer," "present a paper," "rules and regulations," "reserve the right," and "crowded conditions." These alliterations suggest the formulaic quality of legal discourse. Though ideologically opposed, Max and Buckley draw from the same linguistic materials. Though their positions and their demands are not the same, they both use "placed in a position" and "demand the death penalty." In fact, the unfairness of the trial may consist precisely in Max's having no other language to address the judge and jury than his opponent's.

Though the use of legalistic and sociological formulas is not without justification, the two courtroom speeches share so much linguistic matter and take up so much textual space (especially in the "restored" text of the Library of America edition) that the quality of their language leaves its mark throughout the last section. This type of formulaic alliteration, in fact, also spills over into the narrator's idiom: in more than one case, alliterative sequence crosses the quotation marks, linking diegesis and mimesis, and vice versa. The patterned use of critical clusters is less organized in Book Three, weakening the deeper structures of sound that shape language in the rest of the novel.

4. Syntax

The most important level of semantization of sounds is syntax. As we already noted, and as Roman Jakobson explains, latent phonetic symbolism comes alive only when it finds some kind of "correspondence" in a given text or performance; only then is the reader or listener made aware of sound as an autonomous vehicle of meaning.[28] The syntactic semantization of sounds takes place on two levels: the relationship between sounds (the system of *oppositions*) and the position of sounds in discourse, that is, the relationship of sounds and plot (i.e., distribution).

Distribution

Key, halo, and margin entries, and related figures of sound, are distributed in the three books of *Native Son* as shown in Table 1 (numbers are based on the coefficients explained in note 5). Although the numeric coefficient is highest in Book Two, the actual impact of the critical sounds is higher in Book One, if only because the most important ones occur there for the first time. In fact, a number of occurrences in Book Two are found in Bigger's recollection of the scene of Mary's death, in which the same sounds are repeated. Book Two, however, combines these repetitions with the first occurrence of highly frequent entries, such as *flat* (noun), *floor* (of a building), and *flashlight* (35 out of 37 occurrences are in Book Two). In other words, "Fear" combines both the sounds of violence and murder and those of the tension of escape.

Book Three is the least tightly organized, not only because relevant entries are less frequent, but also because they tend to be accounted for by entries with lower emotional impact. *Blame* (20 occurrences out of 24) and *bless* are among the words that appear only in this section. As already pointed out, the less tightly organized grammar of sound is a sign of the impoverishment of language in this section.

Lows. If we divide the text (arbitrarily) into five-page units, we immediately see that the lowest coefficients of sound patterning occur in dialogue sections (see Table 2). The same holds for the next-ranking five units. The first law of the text's syntax of sounds, then, is that all the lows are concentrated in passages in which dialogue is predominant; the critical clusters belong to the narrative voice (diegesis) rather than to the speech of the characters (mimesis). Their function, therefore, is not realistic (a reproduction of actual speech) but symbolic.[29] Again, inarticulateness is not Bigger's personal problem, but a fundamental inadequacy of language in grasping Bigger's world.[30] All characters "mumble" and, figuratively, so does the narrator.

Table 1 Distribution of Key, Halo, and Margin Entries

Book	bl	fl	Total	Average per page
"Fear"	3736	3359	7095	81.55 (42.94, 39.6)
"Flight"	8551	8126	16677	100.46 (51.31, 48.95)
"Fate"	5700	5316	11016	72.95 (86.10)

Table 2 Coefficients of Sound Patterning by Five-Page Units

Pages	Coefficient	Scene
588–92	28	Bigger's interrogation by Britten
745–49	48	Inquest
740–45	83	Inquest
513–17	107	Conversation with Jan and Mary
493–97	128	Bigger's interview with Mr. Dalton

Interestingly, the only character who seems to contradict this rule and uses a number of critical entries is the preacher who talks to Bigger in jail. On the one hand, the rule of separation is maintained by the fact that the entries found in his speech are idiosyncratic (*bless, bloom, flowers,*) and hardly occur in the narrator's language. On the other hand, the continuity of sounds between the narrator and this character might suggest that the gulf between the narrative voice and vernacular speech is not as wide as critics have described. Perhaps, on the lower frequencies, the narrative voice derives from the sounds of folk speech—stylized and abstracted to be sure, its sensitivity to certain sounds, and to sound in general.

Highs. I have already noted that the peak occurrences coincide with the tensest and most dramatic passages in the text. The intensification of crucial formal characteristics of texts in the vicinity of crucial plot passages has been noted by Federico Orlando and developed by Franco Moretti. The latter speaks of an "accelerating rate of figuration" at crucial moments[31]; we may speak here of an "accelerating rate of sound figuration" in *Native Son.* Thus, the five-page sequence that displays the highest concentration of critical sounds is pages 528–33, describing the killing of Mary and the disposal of her body; next are pages 664–68, including the rape and murder of Bessie.

The single pages that display the highest occurrence of critical clusters are listed in Table 3.

Table 3 Highest Occurrences of Critical Clusters per Single Page

Page	Coefficient	Scene
662	345	Bigger, Bessie reach the empty building
755	341	Bessie's body in the courtroom
677	341	Bigger's flight
543	319	List of "blind" characters
622	318	Bessie's rape and murder
532	284	Mary's murder

Distribution and Meaning: Bessie and "habeas corpus." Three of the five top scenes listed in Table 3 center around Bessie; among the immediate runners-up is page 570 (coefficient of 229), which includes the first scene of lovemaking between Bigger and Bessie. This is intriguing, since "Bessie remains an unacknowledged character—except as evidence—by the State's attorney, by Max, and by many critics as well."[32] The plot could hold very well without her death, which in fact remains somewhat contrived.[33] Even the first readers of the novel's draft objected to her death. According to biographer Michel Fabre, Wright shouted down their objections, screaming, "I have to kill her! she must die!"[34] Just as he felt he had to raise his voice in order to justify her death to his friends, Wright uses emphatic alliteration and the thickening of critical clusters to indicate that, though imperfectly justified in terms of plot, Bessie is a centrally significant element in the text.

It is Bessie's death that makes *Native Son,* as Wright put it, a novel over which "bankers' daughters" could not weep, and it is quite disturbing to modern students. As he progresses from the "accidental" killing of Mary to the cold-blooded murder of Bessie, Bigger turns from victim (of society, of chance) to protagonist by retroactively creating the meaning of his first murder. Bessie's meaning, then, is in the first place the meaning she retroactively projects on Mary: she is a signifier to Mary's signified. This is dramatically reinforced in the courtroom scene, where again Bessie "means" Mary: "they were using his having killed Bessie to kill him for his having killed Mary" (p. 754), thinks Bigger, underlining the thought with a chiastic form crossing over "him."

Bessie's body is dragged into the courtroom in an obscene travesty of "habeas corpus," a concept which, in its literal sense of "having the body," is a key to the deeper meaning of Bessie's presence in the text. In the courtroom scene, not Bessie but Bessie's *body* stands for Mary, whose body cannot be exhibited because Bigger has destroyed it. Bessie's body is the real subject of the other scenes in which she appears. In the bedroom as in the courtroom, she replaces Mary. Bigger has almost had Mary, the inaccessible white woman, and takes Bessie instead (in manuscript Wright changed "Bessie" to "Mary" twice, as a revealing lapse in Bigger's free indirect discourse).[35]

Later, Bigger injects in the murder of Bessie the intentional violence which he now attributes to his killing of Mary (in both cases he goes for the face).[36] Bessie's body, however, resists him: he destroys Mary's body in fire but fails to destroy Bessie's in ice. To underline the relationship, however, both are killed in or by air: Mary choked, Bessie thrown in the "air-shaft."[37] Later, he forgets Bessie, whose indestructible body reappears to damn him in the courtroom ("He had completely forgotten Bessie during the inquest of Mary" [p. 754]), and allows Mary's dissolved body to haunt his visions and memory. Both in the bedroom and in the courtroom, then, Bessie is represented as inevitable presence and body, Mary as haunting absence and image.

This is foreshadowed from Bigger's first contact with Mary, when he notices that her body is much softer than Bessie's.

Thus Bessie is revealed as one of the symbolic centers of the novel.[38] The symmetry of Bessie and Mary is much more complex than a one-way relationship of secondary signifier to primary signified. For one thing, here the signifier has an indestructible material substance, while the signified is elusive. The relationship is again reversed at another level, as the body (Bessie) becomes the signifier of the image (Mary). And the symmetry of Mary and Bessie appears again in the symbolism related to sexual and racial politics in this very complex novel.

Syntax of Sounds and Semantic Fields

The symmetry of Bessie and Mary is the contact point of distributional and relational syntax in the book's grammar of sounds. The mirror image of their respective deaths, in which the opposition of death in water and death in fire crosses the coincidence of death by air, is related to the list of *bl* and *fl* words, for water, fire, and air constitute the semantic field that holds together the major portions of these paradigms.

Vision and Violence: The Paradigm of "bl" Words. There are 22 *bl* entries[39] in *Native Son*, for a total 695 occurrences (of which 302 are accounted for by *black* and its forms). They may be grouped into two fields: violence, fire, blood (field A), and vision, light (field B). Tables 4 and 5 list their occurrences in the three books. There are 142 occurrences (27, 72, 43, respectively by sec-

Table 4 Occurrences of Field A (Violence, Fire, Blood) Words

Word	Total occurrences	"Fear"	"Flight"	"Fate"
blade	15	8	4	3
blast	10	1	7	2
blaze	15	4[40]	8	3
blood	75	10	37	28
blow	24	3	16	5
blurt	3	1	–	2

Table 5 Occurrences of Field B (Vision, Light) Words

Word	Total occurrences	"Fear"	"Flight"	"Fate"
blank	7	3	1	3
blind	58	6	30	22
blink	26	4	18	4
blur	23	10	7	6

tion) of six words belonging to field A, and 114 occurrences (23, 56, 35, respectively by section) of four words belonging to field B.

Two words bridge these two fields and bring them together: *blot out* (14),[41] a violent gesture of removing something from sight, and the connotations of darkness and violence in the forms of *black* (302 occurrences). Other entries are attracted to these fields by contexts that foreground certain connotations: the formulaic "hazy blue light" draws *blue* (21) to the semantic area of vision and light, and *blanket* (7 occurrences, 5 in the scene of Bessie's death) and even *Blum* (thanks to the formulaic syntagm "rob[bing] Blum," which occurs in 11 of the 28 occurrences of this name) are also peripheral to the area of violence. Altogether, fields A and B account for 627 occurrences, 90.2% of all *bl* occurrences. Other words—*block, bloom, blizzard* (28, 5, 4)—are assimilated to paradigms of space and air, which are dominated by *fl*. Only five entries, for a total of 31 occurrences, cannot be accounted for by any paradigm. These occurrences are overwhelmingly located in Book Three (the distribution is 1, 8, 22), the most important being *blame* (24: 0, 8, 16).[42]

Fluidity, Tension, and Space. The semantic organization of the *fl* paradigm is looser. The total number of occurrences is smaller (403: 92, 194, 117), while the number of entries is higher (43). This in itself makes for more semantic diffuseness and a higher number of occasional words. Also, almost one-third of the occurrences (121) are concentrated in one entry (*floor*), while many entries (15, as opposed to 3 in *bl*) occur only once. Over half of these one-time occurrences, or *hapax legomena,* occur in Book Three. On the other hand, such all-important marginal entries as *feel* (734: 154, 242, 338) and *fall* (73: 6, 46, 21) contribute to the overall relevance of this phonetic zone but also blur the distinctness of the key entries vs. halo and margin entries.

We may tentatively identify two fields: water, liquids (field C), and air, flying, falling (field D). Tables 6 and 7 list their occurrences in the three books. There are 49 occurrences (15, 18, 16, respectively by section) of seven words belonging to field C, and 33 occurrences (13, 8, 12, respectively by section) of nine words belonging to field D.

Table 6 Occurrences of Field C (Water, Liquids) Words

Word	Total occurrences	"Fear"	"Flight"	"Fate"
flake	4	1	3	—
flask	1	—	1	—
float	16	8	6	2
flood	7	1	2	4
flow	15	4	4	7
flush	5	1	2	2
fluid	1	—	—	1

Table 7   Occurrences of Field D (Air, Flying, Falling) Words

Word	Total occurrences	"Fear"	"Flight"	"Fate"
flap	2	1	1	—
flee	3	—	—	3
fleeting	4	—	—	4
flight	5	—	2	3
flip	1	—	1	—
flop	2	1	1	—
fluffy	1	1	—	—
fly	13	10	3	—
flutter	2	—	—	2

Field D has a very intense halo, created by the high occurrence of *fall*, about twice the rest of the relative key entries. Though some of the words included in the list may seem occasional and fanciful, we should not discount them a priori. For instance, Michel Fabre has revealed the intense connotations of apparently innocuous words such as *fluffy*, as in the "fluffy white curtains" Richard sets on fire in *Black Boy*—an interesting crossover of the fields of air and fire. *Fluffy* is frequently associated with the perception of white people. The one occurrence in *Native Son* is "white plumage, like coils of fluffy paste being squeezed from a tube."[43]

Table 8 includes occurrences of words describing blinding or uncertain light (field E). There are 66 occurrences (7, 49, 10, respectively by section) of six words. Table 9 includes occurrences of words describing physical tension or relaxation (field F). There are 67 occurrences (17, 27, 23, respectively by section) of nine words.

Although they occur only once, and might therefore appear occasional, the meaning of *flaccid, florid*, and the adjectival form *fleshy* is underlined by the fact that they are always alliterated with *face* (*flayed*, in turn, is in co-occurrence with *fear*). *Flank* is included in this paradigm because of its military implications: in Book One, Bigger speaks of the "enemy's flank," and in Book Three he is twice flanked by policemen.

While criticism of Wright's work has correctly identified the much more predictable vertical imagery of walls,[44] it has all but ignored the pervasive horizonal imagery of *floor, flat*, and the like. These images of urban space can be collected into field G, with 136 occurrences (33, 69, 34, respectively by section) of three words (see Table 10).

Field G has a high contextual connotation of tension and violence. "*Blood on the floor*" occurs 3 times, both in connection with Mary's body and with the killing of the rat.[45] The rat hunt and the anarchist bomb-throwing (in the movie in the 1940 edition) both take place on the *floor*, as does Bessie's murder. The expression "in the middle of the floor" recurs formulaically 11

Table 8 Occurrences of Field E (Blinding or Uncertain Light) Words

Word	Total occurrences	"Fear"	"Flight"	"Fate"
flash	21	6	11	4
flashlight	37	–	35	2
flare	2	–	–	2
flick, flicker	5	1	2	2
flit	1	–	1	–

Table 9 Occurrences of Field F (Physical Tension, Relaxation) Words

Word	Total occurrences	"Fear"	"Flight"	"Fate"
flaccid	1	–	–	1
flank	6	3	–	3
flat (adj.)	17	5	10	2
flayed	1	–	1	–
flesh	14	3	6	5
flex	10	4	4	2
fling	12	1	3	8
flinch	5	–	3	2
florid	1	1	–	–

Table 10 Occurrences of Field G (Urban Space) Words

Word	Total occurrences	"Fear"	"Flight"	"Fate"
flat (noun)	15	–	15	–
floor (of apartm.)	106	33	42	31
floor (of building)	15	–	12	3

times (7 in association with "standing"). *Floor* is also associated frequently with *s*taring (3 times; once with *g*laring) and with *s*tonily: "he looked stonily at the floor." The clause "Mrs. Dalton in *flowing* white clothes was standing stone-still in the middle of the kitchen *floor*" (p. 501) brilliantly contrasts the rigidity associated with the floor to the liquid motion of the ghost.[46]

All these co-occurrences reinforce the connotation of tension associated with flat space, bridging the gap with the G field also through the isomorphy of *flat* as adjective and noun and such syntagms as "sank on the floor." We can then unify the F and G fields under the label of "tension/relaxation," associated respectively with the body and with urban space. Taken together these two unified fields account for 203 occurrences.

On the other hand, the tension associated with flat spaces crosses the boundary between the *fl/bl* paradigms. A typically flat and tense space associated with violence is, as we have seen, *table* (84 occurrences).[47] On the other hand, a *bl* entry such as *block* (17 occurrences) indicates both frozen motion and a unit of urban space (composed of *buildings* [82] divided into *floors* and *flats*); this paradigm is overwhelmingly present in Book Two.

We can therefore extend this paradigm to indicate a general association of tension with urban space, which helps account for the fact that the longest sustained high-occurrence sequence is the one in which Bigger goes from the Daltons' home to the South Side and then, first with Bessie and then alone, deeper and deeper into the surrounded zone. At which point, perhaps, it may occur to us that even "wa*ll*" shares at least one key phoneme with *floor*.

The semantic fields C, D, E, and F/G account for 344 occurrences, a percentage of 89.8%, almost the same as the more tightly organized *bl* paradigm.

Combined Fields: Correspondences and Contradictions

The next step, already suggested by the unification of fields F and G, is to cross the sound paradigms, creating semantic fields based on patterns of opposition and analogy rather than on univocal connotations. These fields "of the second degree" are structured by oppositions which are, in turn, blurred by deep currents of communication and overlapping meanings.

The first of these combined "second degree" semantic fields is fluidity (field I). This field (190 occurrences, 13 entries) originates in the relationship of A (violence, fire, blood) and C (water, liquids). A syntagm like "*flow of her blood*" alerts us to the fact that *blood* is a liquid and thus related to C (on the other hand, a C entry like *flush* refers more often to blood than to water). Fire can be a metaphorical liquid ("a furious blaze of liquid life-energy" [p. 820]) and a literal liquid ("coals blazed and quivered with molten fury," [p. 530]); water can be "warm" and blood can turn to ice, as in the capture scene. The furnace, as Emanuel notices, also sucks in air, a function which alerts us to the fluid quality implied in field D (air: "the fire whispered in the furnace" [p. 641]), and reconciles to this field the "fire" words in *f* like *furnace, fire,* and *flame*. The concept of fluidity designates the recurrent theme of the melting of solid objects, the loss of outlines, identities, and borders in a world of fluid, ungraspable, shifting shapes.

The second combined second degree field is hindered vision (field II). This field (189 occurrences, 8 entries) is generated by the inevitable encounter of B (vision, light, darkness) and E (blinding or uncertain light). Both the "hazy *blue* light" and the "*blinding flashes*" impair vision, either by absence or by excess of light. This concept is revealed by the oxymoronic and formulaic "*blinding flashlights*" of the newsmen's cameras (and, by contrast, by the uselessness of Bigger's lone flashlight in the dark flats and floors of the abandoned buildings). The key word, a visual parallel to physical fluidity, is *blur,* indicating a perception of unfocused objects, not sharply distinguished from the background, and the state of consciousness in which such objects are perceived.

Often this field includes connotations of E (violence), usually evidenced by the critical clusters: "a *gleaming blade flashed*" joins light and violence. Weapons issue light, and light can be a weapon: "*blade* of light" is formulaic in "Big Boy Leaves Home," and light can be a leaden shaft in *Native Son.* Bigger's eyes are bloodshot; the field of imperfect vision, when crossed with the field of violence, creates what could be best defined as *blinding violence/blind violence.* The key word, of course, is *blot out.*[48]

The third combined second degree field is tension/explosion/relaxation (field III). This is the sequence with which we have become acquainted in our analysis of the semantization of articulation in *b* and *f.* We find it again at the semantic level when we connect the connotations of relaxation of field C (water) and D (air) with the tension/relaxation paradigm of body and space created by F and G and the explosion of violence implied in A. Rather than a static opposition, this field describes a linear sequence, based on the splitting of *fl* paradigms in the opposites of tension and letting go surrounding the explosive paradigm of *bl.*

In phonetic terms, in fact, *fl* words can be ranked according to whether the initial cluster is followed by long and full vowels (as in *float, flood, flow, flight*), or by short and reduced ones (as in *fling, flinch, flick, flare, flap, flat, flit*). As Bolinger points out,[49] length is perhaps the most evident case of sound symbolism; the opposition between long and short vowels suggests the opposition between repose and tension/action, supplementing the opposition between long continuants and punctual stops. Although this is far from being an absolute rule (*floor* being the most obvious exception), it helps us identify a sound correlative for the tension and relaxation grouped under the *fl* cluster.

5. Sound Patterns as Indications of Plot

The linear sequence of tension, explosion, relaxation (field III), ideally defined by the pattern of *fl + short vowel/bl/fl + long vowel,* is a phonetic correlative to the cycles of the plot and the alternation of "desire," "violence," and "indifference" in Bigger's life. This is a logical, "ideal" relationship rather than a literal one. It is a fact, however, that in both murder scenes, in a framework of a higher density of critical clusters, we find that *bl*s dominate the scene of the actual killing while *fl*s all but disappear, to surface again when the deed is over (and *bl*s disappear in turn). The pattern is clear in both murder scenes. In Book One, after a general prevalence of *bl* (especially in the poolroom scene), from the moment Bigger lifts Mary into her room to the apparition of Mrs.

Dalton's floating blur (pp. 522–26), the *fl* paradigm takes over (415 vs. 322) until Bigger realizes that Mary is dead. At that point, the pattern is reversed until the body is disposed of (496 *bl* vs. 276). This done, Book One ends with a whispering sigh of relief as Bigger steps outside: "a few fine *flakes* of snow were *floating* down" (p. 533).

The pattern is repeated in the second murder. When Bigger and Bessie leave her apartment to hide in an abandoned building and he takes her by force (pp. 661–66), there is an overwhelming and unique prevalence of *fl* entries (929 vs. 221 *bl*). The ratio is reversed in the murder scene (pp. 667–69: 335 *bl* vs. 211 *fl*). After the murder, as if again drawing a breath of relief, Bigger "lifted the *flashlight*" to look at Bessie's body; and the 30 pages that follow, to the end of Book Two, are the only prolonged section in the book in which *fl* (key, halo, and margin) systematically prevails over *bl* (3329 vs. 2151).

Of Love and Death

A sequence of tension, explosion, relaxation (or "desire," "violence," "indifference") looks more like the description of an orgasm than of a murder. In fact, the book contains both, and one of its hidden but discernible themes is the formal analogy and psychological connection between the act of murder and the sexual act. The act which merges sex and violence is rape. When questioned by Max about Mary, Bigger—against whom this charge was automatically levelled by the media and the prosecutor—admits that, yes, he was a little "inclined that way."

"Inclined": he might have but he didn't. Both Mary and Bessie were, indeed, *almost* raped. Mary might also have been "inclined," as her hip-grinding seems to suggest, but the intercourse is not consummated (death takes its place) and she was so drunk that it might have been stretching the point to describe her as willing. Bessie is clearly unwilling, but Bigger forces sex on her before he kills her.[50] The fact that she was "his girl," that they have had sex before, intentionally veils—for some readers at least—the lack of consent which makes his act a rape.

In both cases, then, rape is evoked but either ultimately avoided or "technically" veiled. Both the presence and "absence" of rape are important here (again, mirroring the presence and absence of Bessie's and Mary's bodies). As "presence," rape is revealed as one of the necessary and yet unmentionable emotional cores of the novel, blurring distinctions of love and hatred, life and death. As "absence," the fact that both are intended to appear, for different reasons, as "not quite" rapes calls into question the idea of distinct consciousness, rationality, intentionality, consent; the twilight zone, the threshold between consciousness and unconsciousness in which both murders and orgasms are consummated becomes the crucial psychological region of the novel.

6. Sound Patterns as Indications of Symbolism

While field III (tension/explosion/relaxation) indicates the cycles of plot sequence, fields I and II (fluidity, hindered vision) point toward the patterns of symbolism and imagery. In order to read them more accurately, however, we need to touch on a broader syntactic pattern of sounds.

It will be clear by now that the opposition of *fl* and *bl* words has been isolated for methodological purposes and for clarity of discussion, as well as because it is the most important pattern. But this opposition is far from the only significant feature of the grammar of sounds in *Native Son*. Here we can explore briefly another area of sounds structured around the continuant/stop and vowel/consonant patterns, because it bears to the racial politics of the book the same relationship that the *bl/fl* pattern bears to its sexual politics.

The Hard and the Soft

As Bigger and his friends stand talking in the streets of the ghetto, "The *sharp* precision of the world of *steel and stone* dissolved into *blurred* waves. He *blinked* and the world grew hard again, mechanical, distinct. A weaving motion in the *sky* made him turn his eyes upward; he saw a *slender streak* of *billowing* white *blooming* against the deep *blue*" (p. 459). The sense of blurred vision and fluidity evoked by the *bl* entries (this is the only context in which they are consistently and explicitly associated with air) plays against the metallic sharpness of *steel and stone*. The initial occurrence of *s* is, of course, too common to allow for semantic focalization. We can, however, identify a tendential pattern in which the continuant and unvoiced qualities of *s* (not unlike those of *f*) play against the punctual sharpness of the stop in *st* and *sk* clusters. In this passage, the initial alliteration of *dis*solved and *dis*tinct draws our attention to their semantic contrast, underscored by the phonic contrast of the internal *ss/st* clusters.

Thus, a paradigm including *silent, soft, swell, sink, soft and shapeless, silk and satin,* and *suffusing him with . . . sensitive sorrow* plays very much the same role as other continuant sounds in evoking a state of repose, relaxation, and passivity, whereas *standing, straight and stonestill, stare, stiff, steel, sting, stop, strike, stagger, stretch, startle,* and *stick* connote tension and rigidity.

There is no need to reiterate that this is a very general rule. In the passage quoted above, for instance, *sky* and *streak* denote air, not metal or concrete. Yet this basic opposition reinforces the basic patterns of space symbolism. The *st* cluster rules Bigger's ghetto environment; in the first draft, Bigger is *staring abstractedly* out of the window at *streetcars* "rattling" and "clanging" in the *streets* of *steel and stone*. Though the scene is removed, these words are prominent in the finished draft. The closing sentence, "*steel* again*st steel,*" assimilates the sound of the jail to those of the ghetto.

As Bigger enters into the world of the Daltons, he also moves from the domination of *st* to *s* sounds: from noise and sharpness to quiet and softness (from hard Bessie to soft Mary). The opposition between the steel of the streetcars and the "*swift* rubber tires" of automobiles divides two universes of sounds and two types of space (the crowded streetcars and the privacy of the automobile). In the "guarded secrecy" of the white world, even streetcars no longer rattle and clang: "he heard a street car rumbling faintly behind him" (Harper 1940, p. 68).

Bigger's first contact with the Dalton home is a sound shock. He rings the bell and is "*startled* to hear a *soft* gong *sound* within" (p. 486). Wright had originally written "a loud gong"; the change shows that he intentionally shaped the opposition between the two worlds in terms of loud and hard vs. soft and resilient. Thus, he creates a paradoxical contrast in that Bigger is startled out of balance by softness rather than loudness. In his environment, Bigger has become inured to the tangible resistance of loud noises, and he implicitly braces himself against such a resistance as he rings the bell. When he encounters softness instead, it is as if the house itself had given way beneath the pressure of his finger. This is a metaphor of all of his future experience at the Daltons'. Bigger braces himself to face white hostility and hatred, and he panics when he encounters paternalism and misplaced good intentions. Like Mary's body, so much softer than Bessie's (Mary is killed with a soft pillow, while Bessie survives, if temporarily, a battering with a hard brick), the world he now tensely steps into is carpeted, yielding, "dim," "hazy," "faint": "dim lights glowing from a hidden *source*" while "a *faint sound* of piano music *floated* to him" (p. 487). From his world in distinct black and white, he walks into a "shadowy" one of dissolved, shaded, and blurred colors.

Throughout the episode, like the classic blues character, Bigger stumbles, but has no place to fall. He attempts to sit in a shapeless soft armchair, only to be thrown off balance by its yielding: "He rose *slightly* to *sit farther* back; but when he *sat* down he sank down *so suddenly*. . . ." What follows is one of Wright's most brilliant phonosymbolic inventions: as the chair gives in beneath him Bigger is first startled, then "he *sank distrustfully down* again" (p. 487). The sounds of *distrustfully* are a synopsis of the entire sequence and a synthetic representation of a state of mind: Bigger's tension (the twice repeated *st* cluster, the sound-stopped alliteration in *d*) and his uneasy surrender (the *f*l* cluster, with its connotations of relaxation). Bigger will be rudely awakened from this world of soft and floating sounds when the sound of the furnace lid on Mary's body brings it all back home and foreshadows his fate in a loud *rattling* of coal again*st t*in (p. 532).

Ghosts

Bigger has scarcely recovered from his encounters with softness when Mrs. Dalton walks in "like a ghost." In a brilliant passage, unfortunately omitted from the "restored text" of the Library of America edition, the very sounds of Mrs. Dalton's speech define her in terms of a terrifying lack of hard materiality: "Don't you think it would be a wise procedure to inject him into his new environment at once? . . . I think it's *important emotionally* that he feels free to trust his *environment.* . . . *Using the analysis* contained in the case record the relief sent us, I think we should *evoke an immediate* feeling of confidence . . ." (Harper 1940, p. 40). Within a few lines, Mrs. Dalton uses 8 occurrences of six polysyllabic entries beginning with a vowel. This passage accounts for one-third of the total occurrences of these entries in the novel, marking Mrs. Dalton's brief speech as a very specific idiolect. The shortest, *evoke,* occurs a total of 7 times; but this is the only occurrence of *analysis.* There is one other instance of *inject,* and *emotionally, environment,* and even the commonplace *important* appear only three more times.[51] Over half of these occurrences are in Book Three, where they are used only by one other character, the lawyer Max (together with such words are "emotional attitude," "excitement," "exultation," "elation"). Mrs. Dalton's sociological lexicon is, therefore, in anticipation of the language of Book Three (as confirmed by the formulaic alliteration "contained in the case record") and, more significantly, of a "benevolent" white attitude that frightens Bigger to death.

More importantly, however, the sound quality of this passage is constructed as a unicum in the novel. As she speaks, "Bigger listened, *blinking and bewildered*" to the "long strange words." The form of the words—their length—bewilders him as much as their ungraspable meaning. Polysyllables contain a higher number of unstressed vowels, resulting in "shwa" (i.e., blurred) sounds and in short and reduced vowels. The high incidence of vowels in the initial position draws attention to this pattern by blurring the outline of words, the border between sound and silence.

The sound shape of a word like *environment* reproduces the indistinct and threatening environment Bigger finds himself in, soft like the gong, shapeless like the armchair. The four words containing the continuous *f* (the alliterated *feels free,* relief, con*f*idence, *feeling*) reinforce the pattern of indistinct and continuous sounds, with no clear-cut beginning and end, no sharp distinction between sound and silence. Mrs. Dalton sounds like a "white blur" before she appears as one. The vocalic immateriality of her disembodied language announces her for what she really is: "Her face and hair were completely white; she seemed to him like a ghost" (p. 488).

The loss of this passage in the "restored" text is most unfortunate in that by inserting it Wright created a phonological correlative to Bigger's perception of white people. "To Bigger and his people," the narrator explains, "white people were not really people. They were a sort of great natural force, like a stormy sky looming overhead, or like a deep swirling river stretching suddenly at one's feet in the dark." According to the sociolinguist Ken Johnson, "Black people equate the lack of pigmentation with lifelessness"[52]; he lists, however, a Black vernacular designation of whites as "grays," indicating not so much lack of color as a shifting, uncertain, in-between one.

The "vagueness" of Bigger's perception of white people is, therefore, as Keneth Kinnamon has argued, far from a case of inadequate characterization.[53] It places Wright, instead, in the very mainstream of African American folk and literary imagery. Olaudah Equiano's first image of white people is one of ghosts and spirits: white skin is transparent, suggesting the absence of a solid body. Or it is no skin at all, and white people are seen as "men without skin," forms with no shape or outline, in Toni Morrison's *Beloved*. Ralph Ellison is certainly referring to Bigger's plight in the car with Jan and Mary when his Invisible Man is pushed against "a mass of whiteness . . . looming two inches from my eyes," like "a formless white death."[54]

The disembodied, expanding formlessness of white people is the source of Bigger's fear. Having no substance (again, Bessie's body vs. Mary's absence), they cannot be grasped and held still; having no skin, they recognize no limit, no distinction, and no border between them and their inarrestable expansion in the world.[55] There is no way of telling where they begin and where they will stop. They are *some sort* of natural force; there is even no telling *which* one, but certainly a fluid one of stormy skies and swirling rivers in the dark.

Loomings

The formulaic "white blur" at the end of Book One is reiterated by a formulaic "looming white *bulk*" at the end of Book Two. "Looming" is a word that is very dear to Wright, almost always associated with whiteness; but it has other, revealing literary associations. "Loomings," it will be remembered, is the title of the first chapter of *Moby–Dick,* in which the white whale "rolled its island *bulk*." The white whale is another "shrouded phantom," and its terror emanates from its "indefiniteness," from the lack of a distinct color and shape. The "whiteness of the whale" is not a color but "the visible absence" of color (like the visible absence of ghosts, in the whiteness of white people in African American tradition), and at the same time "the concrete of all colors."[56] The white whale, then, is another "looming bulk" and another "floating blur," existing in a liquid realm, "ungraspable," unfocused, and contourless until it can no longer be distinguished from the universe it stands for. And just as the essence of "whale" is the *h,* so perhaps the same immaterial, disembodied sound is the essence of "w*h*ite."

Borders

Although much is made, with reason, of the "wall" imagery in *Native Son,* Bigger's fear comes as much from impalpable and invisible as from impassable barriers, as much from the blurring as from the sharpness of the distinction between his world and the white universe. He finds himself not on the opposite side of a border, but in "a *shadowy* region, a No Man's Land" (p. 508), neither here nor there. He sinks in the Daltons' armchair, as if in water, and panics because Mary has "waded right in" (p. 500) as if she came from the other side of a river rather than of a wall.

Walls and buildings are always dissolving and melting away during Bigger's brief experience with the Daltons. As he drives Jan and Mary around the park, "his sense of the city and park fell away" (pp. 518–19); later, when he realizes he has killed Mary, "The reality of the room fell from him; the vast city of white people that sprawled outside took its place" (p. 527). As the walls fall away, he finds himself naked and vulnerable, in the middle of a wide open and formless (white) space. This is one of the sources of the unsustainable tension evoked by the formulaic "standing in the middle of the floor"; away from the walls, he is defenseless, like the rat who is killed (and "exposed" [p. 450]) when it can no longer hide in its hole in the wall.

The image of characters lying flat or standing "stone-still in the middle of the floor," then, captures the vision of a frozen movement in a tension equivalent to the building of a wall around one's body and mind to replace physical walls that are distant, absent, collapsed. The opposition of horizontal floors to vertical walls parallels the vertical movement from enclosed, warm basement to open, icy, "flat" rooftop—from the space of secret power to that of public capture.

Walls, then, are both exclusion and inclusion. While there is oppression, violence, frustration in being shut in the ghetto, an enclosed and self-defined space also offers a sense of certainty, shape, even of protection and refuge. But Bigger soon finds out that, in the existing social relationships, walls exclude him but do not enclose him; they keep him in, but do not keep dangers out. The ghetto is a closed space from which he is not allowed to stay out, but is an open territory in which the whites can penetrate and expand at will: ". . . they make us live in one corner of the city . . . they don't let us fly planes and run ships" and yet they live "right down here in my stomach" (pp. 463, 464).

Whatever protection ghetto walls allow is ultimately dissolved when the Daltons' paternalistic liberalism blurs distinctions without abolishing hierarchies and difference—only making it impossible for Bigger to grasp and control them. He has no power to prevent Mary and Jan's invasion of his social space, just as Mr. Dalton owns his family's physical space to begin with. He knows that their friendly openings are one-directional. They can ask him to sit next to them or shake their hands, but he cannot make the same gesture toward a white person. Or should he? Do gestures of inclusion abolish walls of exclusion, or do they just abolish whatever painful certainty and security the walls grant?

One of the consequences of injustice, then, is the blurring of Lotman's spatial model of culture which associates "inside" with protection and familiarity, and "outside" with alienation and hostility.[57] When this horizontal paradigm encounters the vertical paradigm of power, the inside space of home and community is an alienated desert, and relatives and friends become shapeless and vulnerable.[58]

The contrived and awkward scene in which all the book's characters gather in Bigger's jail cell has at least this symbolic justification. Even the jail walls are a one-way enclosure; they keep Bigger in, but cannot keep anyone out. While dramatically weak, the scene symbolically "signifies" on consolatory clichés about freedom. "Stone walls do not a prison make," sang Richard Lovelace, "Nor iron bars a cage." In Bigger's case, this is literally true, not because "in my soul I am free" but because stone walls do not grant him even the freedom of seclusion that allows Lovelace to "take/ That [prison] for an hermitage."[59] Ellison's hero's invisibility in his illuminated cellar is also a trickster's protection and "power"; in jail, Bigger is *both* invisible and nakedly exposed. His cell is the ultimate panopticon.

7. *Liminality*

On the Threshold

Wright's "looming white bulk" and Melville's "rolled its island bulk" also bear a phonic resemblance in the broad central *i* at the center and, most of all, in the alliterating *l*s. Ultimately, it is fitting that "looming" should begin with *l,* the sound that pervades all the critical clusters and semantic fields, the true "Helde" of this text, the shared ground that structures oppositions.

The sound of *l* is often impressionistically described as "liquid." The French linguist of the Enlightenment, de Brosses, wrote that the "caractère liquide" of the *fl* cluster "est affecté au fluide, soit igné, soit aquatique, soit aerien."[60] While the description would be difficult to substantiate in hard phonological terms, the imagery has its value, and in fact de Brosses' description coincides with our identification of *fluidity*—water, fire and air—as one of the major semantic fields of *Native Son*. And, of course, we have already noted the liquid imagery in the earlier quotations from Benjamin F. Taylor ("The liquid L, flows like the objects to which it is applied") and Thoreau.

Roman Jakobson attributes to "liquid" sound a "liminal," "fluid" position: "an intermediate place" between vowels and consonants, and (in length) between silence and sound.[61] "Liminal" is apt, because the concept of threshold is crucial to this novel, from Bigger's "staring abstractedly" at the glass pane of his window to Mrs. Dalton's apparition on the threshold of Mary's room. More importantly, *l* illuminates the connection of liminality and liquidity; most thresholds here are fluid, as indicated by the reiterated melting away of walls by Mary's "wading in" and by Bigger's sense of a "shadowy . . . No Man's land."

The concept of a liquid threshold underscores Bigger's "liminal" consciousness at the crucial moments of his experience. Liquids flow in the text to define sexuality as blurred and numbed consciousness. Bessie drinks whisky to numb herself, and Bigger gives her liquor for the same purpose. Rum is passed around as Bigger drives Mary and Jan through the park, "*simply sit-ting and floating*" and getting "numb" (p. 518). On the porch (another threshold), Mary is drunk enough to be on the threshold of consent. Blood and water also flow in sexual abandon and in murderous explosion, in the subliminal mechanics of the first murder and in the intentional numbing of consciousness in the second. Bessie is a "fountain" as Bigger makes love to her and "a sodden mass . . . a wet wad of cotton, some damp substance" when he kills her. "Blood [is] running slowly" out of Bessie's body, and "oozing out" of the newspapers on the basement floor, under the gaze of the cat's "burning pools" of eyes, after Mary is thrown, as if to drown in fire, into the "molten fury" of the furnace.

The Chill, the Stupor, Then the Letting Go: The Waters of Identity

The liminal and liquid state once more associates sex and violence, orgasm and murder. These are both the fusional moments of loss of self and abandon-ment of control, and the highest moments of presence and fulfillment. Big-ger, says Wright in "How 'Bigger' Was Born," "is in a nascent state,"[62] another liminal image. His search for selfhood and humanity floats between the possibilities of humanity as "fusing," "union, identity . . . supporting one-ness," "merg[ing]" with mankind (pp. 784, 671), and humanity as an outline of separate, distinct personal identity. Both forms have promise and danger. To merge and "be a part of this world" is "to lose himself in it" (671); to gain and retain an individual selfhood may "freeze" him into the numbness of iso-lation and silence. In the liminal zone of sexuality and violence, Bigger grasps at the possibility of reconciling fusion and selfhood. This is, perhaps, why his murder became "an act of creation."

One consequence of the concept of a liquid threshold is that it replaces a static border of binary oppositions with a fluid region of mobility. It says that one is not either conscious or unconscious, but may grope in the shadowy and blurred region in between. Even more importantly, I think, it shows that there is no linear progress from unconsciousness to consciousness, from inar-ticulateness to mastery of language, from victimization to control. Bigger ebbs forward and back, never in the same place twice, but never firmly in one place either.

The dilemma of fusion and separation, couched in the liquid imagery of freezing, floating, and melting, and the patterns of the *fl* soundscape, domi-nates the end of Book Two and the beginning of Book Three: Bigger's desper-ate defense of his freedom and his desperate letting go into numbness. Again, the memory of Bessie's body sets the pattern. While making love to her, Big-ger floated in a "warm night sea" and "warm waters," and yet as his "cling-ing" and his desire to "blot out" everything remind us, he had not been able to let go completely. He had "clung" to Bessie as "a fountain"; on the rooftop, in significant contrast, he "clung to a chimney"[63] and then he desperately holds on to the edge of the water tank, literally clinging to his separate freedom, "freezing" until his fingers become "stiff," and then he lets go, falling in the snow, "dazed," like Emily Dickinson's dying person's recollection of the snow: "first chill, then stupor, then the letting go."[64]

"He relaxed," and the sounds of the crowd reach him "like the roar of water" (pp. 698, 699). Having sensed the attempt to create a "possible order and meaning in his relations with the people about him" which would have balanced autonomy and communication, and having seen his effort frozen into isolation, Bigger now seeks safety in merging as loss of self. He goes limp, numb, and liquid: "his eyes like two still pools of black ink in his *flaccid face*" (p. 700). *Flaccid* here is an extremely eloquent *hapax legomenon,* revealing how completely Bigger's rebellious "tensity" has gone out his very body as he attempts to "sink back" into the "ancient waters . . . from which he had been first made . . . if there could be no merging with the men and women about him, there should be a merging with some other part of the natural world in which he lived" (p. 701). Throughout "Fate," Bigger floats between Max's vision of oneness with others and the recovery of his own separate self. His final cry of autonomy ("I am") and his hesitant message of solidarity ("Tell Jan hello") express these two attitudes, still not fully reconciled as death violently interrupts Bigger's nascent quest.

8. A Flow Chart

We can now go back to the first two semantic fields of fluidity (I) and blurred vision (II) that we derived from the lexical paradigms associated with the critical clusters. We have already seen how field III (tension/explosion/relaxation) suggests the temporal and emotional dynamics of the *plot.* Fields I and II, in turn, supported by the unifying presence of *l,* support the patterns of *imagery,* the liquid liminal state that forms the continuous undercurrent of meaning.

The fields of fluidity and vision consist of binary oppositions, as described in Figure 1. The four elements (merging and freezing, blindness

I. fluidity $\left\{\begin{array}{l}\text{merging}\\\text{freezing}\end{array}\right.$

II. blurring $\left\{\begin{array}{l}\text{blindness}\\\text{(excessive) light}\end{array}\right.$

Figure 1

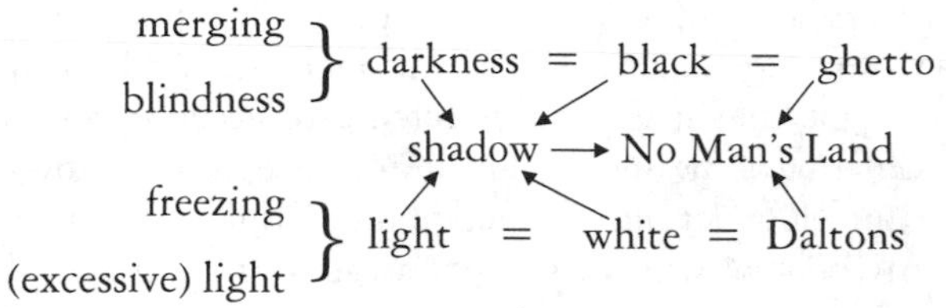

merging ⎫
blindness ⎭ darkness = black = ghetto

shadow ⟶ No Man's Land

freezing ⎫
(excessive) light ⎭ light = white = Daltons

Figure 2

and [excessive] light) can be reshuffled in ways that reinforce underlying patterns of meaning. The image of the "dark waters," for instance, relates merging to darkness and through it to blindness; on the other hand, the glaring ice associates freezing with excessive light. The new pattern is provided in Figure 2. Another combination would give us the pattern shown in Figure 3.

The visual figure of the shadow,[65] the spatial figure of the no-man's-land, and the psychological figure of numbed consciousness are all liquid liminal zones with the original fields of blurring and fluidity. On the lower frequencies, then, this is what *Native Son* is about: the hazy, blurred, liquid, shadowy threshold between death and love, unconsciousness and consciousness, nonbeing and being (the ghosts), blindness and vision, silence and sound, sound and language, and one person's doomed effort to cross this no-man's-land and come out alive on the other side.

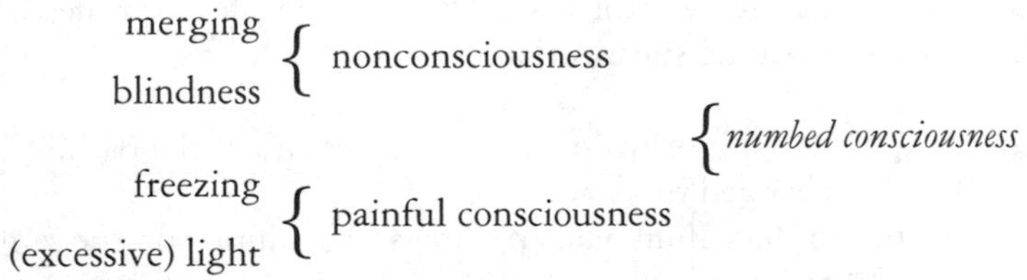

merging ⎰
blindness ⎱ nonconsciousness

⎰ *numbed consciousness*

freezing ⎰
(excessive) light ⎱ painful consciousness

Figure 3

9. An Act of Creation

Now, the question anyone is bound to ask after such exposition of the grammar of sounds and its meaning in *Native Son* is: Is it intentional? Did Wright consciously plan this pattern of *f*s and *b*s and *l*s? The intentional fallacy has so long mired critical work on Richard Wright in discussions of biography and ideology that one is tempted to refuse to deal with intention at all. But then the same question—Was it intentional?—is also the question asked, in the text and in criticism, about the murder of Mary Dalton. There is enough, in this coincidence, to motivate a closer look.

The answers are no, yes, and no again. The first "no" is based on Wright's own warnings against the intentional fallacy. "I am not so pretentious as to imagine that it is possible for me to account completely for my own book, *Native Son,*" he says in his alliterating essay, "How 'Bigger' Was Born." With an eloquent liquid metaphor, Wright continues: "There are meanings in my book of which I was not aware until they literally spilled out upon the paper."[66] In fact, when he became aware of the sound patterns, he tried to curb their pervasiveness; writing the stage version of *Native Son* and realizing (as he explained in a letter) that too many characters' names began with *b,* he changed Bessie's name to Clara.[67]

The "yes," however, is made inevitable when we go through the copy of the first draft of the manuscript in the Schomburg Collection of the New York Public Library and, on page 10, make a startling discovery: with a stroke of the pen, the character "Selchenger" becomes *Blum.*[68] One of the most problematic and unnecessary *bl* words has been intentionally created and inserted in the text in the course of revision. Since there is no referential reason for this change, the only motive can be the way it sounds. At the other end of the semantic polarities, we find the most intensely referential word, *black.* As we look at its occurrences, we discover that these also were mainly inserted in the text in the course of revision. *Black* dominates two crucial scenes that were added at a later stage of composition: the killing of the rat and Bigger's street-corner conversation. Often, these newly inserted occurrences are alliterated (e.g., *black, body,* [p. 488]).

In a number of passages the text was revised to introduce critical clusters; the opposite is hardly ever the case. The following list provides only a fraction of the most revealing substitutions in Book One:

> P. 467, "the cop is way down at the other end of the park."
> "Park" is changed to *block.*
> P. 476, "do that Blum haul" becomes "ro*b* Blum"; on the same page, "that Blum job" becomes "ro*bb*ing Blum." After replacing Selchenger with *Blum,* Wright surrounds it with the alliterating formulaic verb "ro*b,*" thus stressing the sound pattern.
> P. 480, "a gleaming knife flashed" becomes the syntagm we have already noted, "a gleaming *blade* flashed."
> P. 481, "knife" is twice replaced with *blade.* There was already another occurrence; the result is three rhythmic repetitions of a critical cluster and term, *blade,* within very few lines. This procedure is repeated at other points of the manuscript.
> P. 487, in "a *faint* sound of piano music *floated,*" both *f* words were inserted at different stages in composition; first Wright penned in the adjective in manuscript, later he created the alliteration that appears in the definitive text.

P. 487, "sunk slowly back" becomes "sank *distrustfully* down."

P. 504, *blinked* is inserted

P. 510, "with one final stroke *blot it* out" gains an alliteration as it becomes "with one final *blow blot it* out."

P. 515, "he saw a *blinding flash*" is eliminated: this would have been the only occurrences in which this syntagm did not refer to the media or the police. The elimination reinforces the pattern of meaning.

Pp. 525, 526, "*white blur floating*" and "*hazy blue light*" are inserted.

P. 529, "hard ache" is supplemented by the insertion of "*blazing* terror."

Pp. 530, 531, both *blazed* and *ablaze* are added. It looks, from the manuscript, as if at some time in composition Wright became aware of the potentialities of this word and began to use it consistently.

Pp. 531, 532, occurrences of *blood, blade, floor* are added (some were inserted just before printing, and therefore are missing in the new "restored" text). Throughout the sequence, the motif of vision is attenuated and that of violence is heightened, thus sharpening the contrast with the visual images in the pages before.

P. 532, "*a few fine flakes of snow were floating down*" is added.

Wright seems to have continued revising along these lines all the way through the final editing of the manuscript for the 1940 edition. Several new occurrences were inserted at this stage: a number of occurrences of *flashing, floor, fling, flash* in the cinema sequence (Harper 1940, pp. 26–28); the apparition of Mrs. Dalton on the threshold of Mary's room "*standing in flowing* white and *staring with stony blind* eyes" (1940, p. 71); the exhaust fan passage at the end of Book One with another occurrence of *blades* in a rich alliterative context.

It seems, then, that many of the syntagms and passages studied in this analysis were later insertions, at one stage or another. Because they were inserted during the final revision, many are missing in the "restored" text. Yet the fact that they reinforce a pattern that can be recognized in the text and in the process of its formation would suggest that they correspond to actual authorial intention rather than editorial interference, and ought therefore to have been preserved.

Wright seems to have revised "Fear" before he went on to compose "Flight" and "Fate." Thus in the second and third books the draft already incorporates the intentionality revealed by the corrections in "Fear," and the pattern of revision is less evident. However, once again most of the syntagms and clauses that have attracted our attention turn out to be later insertions. Such is the case with Mrs. Dalton's idiosyncratic language (again, intentionally inserted for the 1940 publication), *"felt her as a fallow field"* and *"flow of her blood"* in the love scene, *"flung the sheet back from Bessie's body,"* and the occurrence of *blot out* in the courtroom scene. It is safe to say that any scene written after the first draft in Books One and Two is likely to have a significant incidence of critical clusters. For instance, the passage about the airplane's billowing streak and the buildings of steel and stone are part of a conversation that was not in the original draft. Often, when a passage including a critical cluster is eliminated, Wright restores the cluster to the text at the earliest opportunity.[69]

Thus the comparison of the Schomburg draft with the restored text and with the 1940 edition reveals that great care was devoted until the last moment to the development of sound patterns and the accurate use of critical clusters. At this level, then, the answer would have to be "yes."

But on page 185 of the typed draft we make another discovery: a typing error transforms *bulb* into *blub*. Throughout the manuscript, the same typo occurs at least 9 times out of about 15 occurrences. Sometimes Wright notices and corrects in ink; often, he does not notice or does not care. Although I have not submitted the draft to computer analysis, I have not noticed any other equally pervasive typo.[70] It is as though the critical clusters were literally "spilling" almost unawares onto the page from Wright's fingers on the keyboard, in that liminal zone in which both "acts of creation"—the murder and the novel—take place, the blurred borderline between sounds and silence in which both Bigger and Wright pursue their "unfinished quest" for the uncreated features of their face.

Notes

1.   Zora Neale Hurston, review of Richard Wright's *Uncle Tom's Children* (*Saturday Review of Literature*, April 2, 1938) in Henry Louis Gates Jr. and K. A. Appiah, eds., *Richard Wright: Critical Perspectives Past and Present* (New York: Amistad, 1993), p. 4.

2.   Harold Bloom, introduction to *Richard Wright's Native Son* (New York: Chelsea House, 1988), p. 2.

3.   Robert Hemenway, "Are You a Flying Lark or a Setting Dove?" in Dexter Fisher and Robert Stepto, eds., *Afro-American Literature: The Reconstruction of Instruction* (New York: Modern Language Association, 1979), p. 122.

4.   James Emanuel, "Fever and Feeling: Notes on the Imagery of *Native Son,*" in Richard Abcarian, ed., *Richard Wright's Native Son: A Critical Handbook* (Belmont, Calif.: Wadsworth, 1970); Joyce Ann Joyce, *Richard Wright's Art of Tragedy* (Iowa City: University of Iowa Press, 1986), chapter 4.

5.   For textual analysis I used a "Glossa" program developed by the Centro di Calcolo of the University of Rome "La Sapienza" and made available by the Centro di Studi per il

Lessico Intellettuale Europeo of the University of Rome and the National Research Council. Dr. Gianni Adamo and the staff of the Centro per il Lessico Intellettuale Europeo kindly assisted me in processing the text. The Library of America edition of *Native Son,* in *Early Works,* edited by Arnold Rampersad (New York: Library of America, 1991), was scanned and coded for processing by Manuela Bagnetti, a graduate student in the English department of the University of Rome. All subsequent references to the text, unless otherwise noted, are from this edition and are indicated by page numbers in parentheses in the text. This essay is a revised version of a paper I presented in 1989 at the W. E. B. Du Bois Institute at Harvard University; at the time, I had used the only available text, that of the 1940 edition (New York: Harper & Row, 1966).

Using numbers does not eliminate the critic's responsibility to judge and evaluate. Beyond word count, all the figures cited in this paper reflect my considered critical opinion of the relevance of critical clusters and sound figures. These decisions concern what is included and what is excluded in the count, and the quantitative coefficients assigned to each occurrence.

a. *Inclusions*

"Key entries": *bl* or *fl* in initial position.

"Halo entries": *b* or *f* and *l* in the first syllable. Due to their frequency and relative semantic neutrality, I have counted quantified occurrences of *black* and *Blum* as halo entries.

"Marginal entries": *bl* or *fl* not in initial position but in the same syllable (*table, muffled*). Forms of *feel* and *fall* are counted as marginal entries because of their extremely high frequency and even distribution.

b. *Exclusions*

Entries of three syllables or more, unless derived from included entries (not *assembled,* yes *unblinkingly*).

Entries in which *b* or *f* and *l,* though contiguous, belong to different syllables (*problem, public; oblong* is an exception) or are separated by two phonemes (*bail, foul*).

Clusters created by suffixes (*-ful, -ly, -ble*)

Cases of unsounded *l* (*folk*).

c. *Figures*

"Alliteration": key, halo, marginal entries in direct (*bloody and black*) or rhetorical (*blond* hair, *blue* eyes) contact with one another or with forms beginning with respective initial (*blue Buick*).

"Co-occurrence": key, halo, marginal, or initial entries within a context of 80 characters, with no syntactic or rhetorical link.

Cross-alliteration, cross-occurrence: a contact of the type described above between *bl* area entries and *fl* area entries (*blood on the floor*).

d. *Coefficients*

Key entries	25 points
Halo entries	10 points
Marginal entries	3 points
Bisyllables	−2 points
Alliterations	
key + key	16 points
key + halo	10 points
key + margin or initial	8 points
halo + halo	8 points
halo + margin or initial	4 points
margin + initial	2 points
Co-occurrences and cross alliterations	half points
Cross-co-occurrences	quarter points

6. Keneth Kinnamon points out Wright's images of blurring and blotting out in *The Emergence of Richard Wright: A Study in Literature and Society* (Urbana: University of Illinois Press, 1972), p. 128.

7. Paolo Valesio, *Strutture dell'allitterazione: Grammatica, retorica e folklore verbale* (Bologna: Zanichelli, 1967), p. 36.

8. Richard Wright, "Long Black Song," in *Uncle Tom's Children*, in *Early Works*, p. 339. Subsequent references to *Uncle Tom's Children* are from this edition and are designated with page numbers in parentheses.

9. Richard Wright, *Black Boy (American Hunger)*, in *Later Works* (New York: The Library of America, 1991), p. 9.

10. Richard Wright, *Black Boy (American Hunger)* (New York: Library of America, 1991), pp. 6, 33, 128. The syntagm "turned black and blazed" is repeated, with a small variation, in *Native Son* (p. 585). "Bleak," on the other hand, seems to be a later discovery; it does not occur in the earlier novel.

11. Michel Fabre, *The Unfinished Quest of Richard Wright*, trans. Isabel Barzun (New York: William Morrow, 1973).

12. Richard Wright, "The Man Who Lived Underground," in *Eight Men* (New York: Thunder's Mouth, 1987), pp. 46, 60.

13. *Bl* clusters do intensify at crucial moments, such as the subway wreck: ". . . his *b*ody smashing against steel; then he was aware of being lifted and *b*ruta*ll*y catapulted through *black* space and, while he was tossed, screams of men and women rent the *black* air. Afterwards Cross remembered that when the lights had gone out he had involuntarily *blinked* his eyes. . . ." *The Outsider*, in *Later Works* (New York: The Library of America, 1991), pp. 442–43.

14. Richard Wright, *Savage Holiday* (Jackson: University Press of Mississippi, 1994), p. 216. On the next page: "Finally he washed the *blood* from his hands and dried them. He paused in the *b*athroom door, staring into the kitchen with a kind of sullen, stolid pride at the nude *bloody body* stretched on the ta*b*le. Huge, gleaming pools of red *blood* had now formed on the tiled *floor.*"

15. James T. Farrell, review of *Uncle Tom's Children* (*Partisan Review*, May 1938), in Gates and Appiah, eds., *Richard Wright: Critical Perspectives*, p. 5. There are at least five closely alliterating co-occurrences of *feet* and *floor* in *Native Son*. See the quotation from the opening passage below. See the opening page of *Native Son:* "Naked feet swished dryly across the planks in the wooden floor" (p. 447), or "the scurrying of quick, dry feet over the wooden floor" (p. 661); "the ebb and flow of her blood" (p. 570).

16. Benjamin F. Taylor, *Attractions of Language, or a Popular View of Natural Language* (1842), quoted in David Simpson, *The Politics of American English* (New York: Oxford University Press, 1986), p. 239. On Thoreau, see John T. Irwin, *American Hieroglyphics* (Baltimore: Johns Hopkins University Press, 1983), pp. 14–17.

17. As we have noted earlier, the murder in *Savage Holiday* takes place on a table.

18. There are at least 29 co-occurrences of *black* and *white* in *Native Son*.

19. In "Long Black Song," Wright links onomatopoeia to another border zone of consciousness: orgasm. According to Keneth Kinnamon (*The Emergence of Richard Wright*, p. 98), this proves that "the resources of Wright's prose go beyond a simple naturalism." In *Native Son*, as we shall see, orgasm is also linked to the paradigm of liminality.

20. R. Wright, *The Outsider*, p. 369.

21. Joyce A. Joyce, *Richard Wright's Art of Tragedy*, p. 65.

22. R. Wright, *Black Boy (American Hunger)*, p. 365.

23. William H. Chapman, *Introduzione alla fonetica pratica (Introduction to Practical Phonetics)*, trans. G. R. Cardona (Roma: Officina, 1972), pp. 17, 26.

24. Wright used this word abundantly in the first draft of the novel; it appears in the first page in the manuscript. In the finished text, as we will see, its impact is absorbed by a number of *fl* words.

25. Luciano Canepari, *Introduzione alla fonetica* (Turin: Einaudi, 1979), pp. 246–47.

26. The image of an interrupted flow of air is curiously evoked early in the novel when Bigger "felt as if he wanted to sneeze and could not" (468). This is the scene in which he vents on Gus his frustration over the Blum job.

27. Roman Jakobson, "Quest for the Essence of Language," *Diogenes*, 51 (1966): 21–37.

28. Roman Jakobson, *La linguistica e le scienze dell'uomo,* transl. Lidia Lonzi (Milan: Il Saggiatore, 1978), p. 123.

29. The rule is confirmed by the fact that the key and halo entries that occur most frequently in dialogue are also the most semantically neutral ones: *black, Blum,* and, most of all, *feel.*

30. Craig Werner, "Bigger's Blues: *Native Son* and the Articulation of Afro-American Modernism," in Keneth Kinnamon, ed., *New Essays on Native Son* (Cambridge: Cambridge University Press, 1990), pp. 117–51.

31. Franco Moretti, "La teoria dell'evoluzione come modello per la storia della letteratura," paper presented at the seminar on "Materialism and Literary Criticism," Verona, Italy, March 1986, drawing on Federico Orlando, *Lettura freudiana della Fedra* (Turin: Einaudi, 1978).

32. James A. Miller, "Bigger Thomas's Quest for Voice and Audience in Richard Wright's *Native Son,*" *Callaloo,* 9 (Summer, 1986): 501–6.

33. Bigger explains that he must kill her because she knows so much about his habits that she would lead the police to him. This is a very weak explanation, because the same might be true for his family and his poolroom pals. The Hollywood version of the novel in the 1980s cuts Bessie's death altogether.

34. Michel Fabre, *The Unfinished Quest of Richard Wright,* p. 171.

35. Bigger does think of Mary as he makes love to Bessie: "He placed his hands on her breasts just as he had placed them on Mary's last night and he was thinking of that while he kissed her" (p. 569).

36. In *Savage Holiday,* Fowler also goes for the face of the doll he destroys (with a "brick bat") in his childhood memory-fantasy (p. 216).

37. The killing of Mary by air is underlined in a passage inserted in the 1940 edition, in which Bigger, in order to eliminate the smell of the burning body, turns on an electric exhaust fan that "would suck the air out of the basement."

38. The importance of Bessie is underscored by the fact that Mabel's murder in *Savage Holiday* is patterned after motives reminiscent of those surrounding Bessie. After the murder, Fowler recalls a childhood memory in which "he had taken a dirty brick bat and beaten [a] doll's head in," like Bigger with Bessie (p. 216); later, Fowler tells the police that "the body's on the kitchen table," like Bessie's in the courtroom (p. 218).

39. I count as one word variants and derived forms such as *blacken, blackness, blackly,* and also *blackout* (included in *black*), or *blameless* (included in *blame*), and *bleed* included in *blood.*

40. I include one occurrence of *ablaze,* in the basement furnace sequence (p. 531), considering it a form of *blaze.*

41. Actually, 13 occurrences of *blot out* and one of "*blot . . .* from sight."

42. The others are: *blend,* 1 occurrence; *bless,* 4; *blond,* 1; *blunder,* 1.

43. On the use of "fluffy," see Michel Fabre, "Fantasies and Style in Wright's Fiction," in *The World of Richard Wright* (Jackson: University Press of Mississippi, 1985), p. 130.

44. J. A. Joyce, *Richard Wright's Art of Tragedy,* chapter 4.

45. *Blood* and *floor* appear in the same sentence three times in the murder scene in *Savage Holiday;* they also occur together at the end of Part Two (p. 166) and the beginning of Part Three (p. 169).

46. At this point, it is also hard to avoid the connotations of rigidity implicit in "wooden" floor (7 occurrences).

47.   Aside from the narrative context, the tension associated with tables is evoked by the fact that they have "edges": "He rested his black fingers on the edge of the white table" (618); the kidnap letter is laid "on the edge of the table" (p. 619); in court and in jail, Bigger holds to the edge of the table or gropes for it (pp. 739, 837). Bigger is certainly on edge while sitting at the table in the restaurant with Jan and Mary.

48.   A subsection of this field concerns the relationship of violence, blindness, and the media. The blinding flashes always come from newsmen's cameras; the first occurrence of *blood on the floor* occurs when Bigger mops up the rat's blood with newspapers. Mary's blood also oozes out on newspapers.

49.   Dwight Bolinger, *Intonation and Its Parts: Melody in Spoken English* (Stanford, Calif.: Stanford University Press, 1986).

50.   In the 1940 edition, Wright inserted a revealing sentence that is not included in the Library of America critical edition: "Imperiously driven, he rode roughshod over her whimpering protests, feeling acutely sorry for her as he galloped a frenzied horse down a steep hill in the face of a resisting wind" (New York: Harper, 1940, p. 198). This is much better than the text in the new critical edition; apparently, not all restorations are improvements. Subsequent references to passages inserted in the 1940 edition and missing in the "restored" text are indicated in the text by 1940 and page number in parentheses.

51.   This count is based on the Harper 1940 edition.

52.   Ken Johnson, "The Vocabulary of Race," in Thomas Kochman, ed., *Rappin' and Stylin' Out* (Urbana: University of Illinois Press, 1972), p. 144.

53.   K. Kinnamon, *The Emergence of Richard Wright,* p. 131.

54.   Olaudah Equiano, *The Life of Olaudah Equiano, or Gustavus Vassa, the African, Written by Himself* in Arna Bontemps, ed., *Great Slave Narratives* (Boston: Beacon Press, 1969), p. 27; Toni Morrison, *Beloved* (London: Chatto & Windus, 1987), p. 215; Mary F. Sisney, "The Power and Horror of Whiteness: Wright and Ellison Respond to Poe," *College Language Association Journal,* 29, 1 (1985): 82–90.

55.   On Toni Morrison's use of this imagery of white ghostlike expansion in *Beloved,* see my *The Text and the Voice: Writing and Speaking and Democracy in American Literature* (New York: Columbia University Press, 1994), pp. 238–39.

56.   Herman Melville, *Moby-Dick* (Harmondsworth, Middlesex: Penguin, 1972), pp. 98, 296. Michel Fabre discusses Wright's use of "looming" (and lists Melville among the authors whose books Wright bought in 1932) in *The World of Richard Wright;* see also Kinnamon, *The Emergence of Richard Wright,* p. 131. The connotation of "looming" as impending fate is also evoked in *Native Son* by Bigger's sense that "something awful's going to happen to me" (p. 463).

57.   Jurij M. Lotman and Boris A. Uspenskij, "Il metalinguaggio delle descrizioni tipologiche della cultura," in *Tipologia della cultura,* R. Faccani and M. Marzanduri, eds.(Milan: Bompiani, 1975), pp. 145–82.

58.   Buddy has "no sharp or hard edges," his mother is "soft and shapeless," Vera is shrinking.

59.   "To Althea, from Prison" (1642), quoted in H. Bruce Franklin, *The Victim as Criminal and Artist,* p. 244.

60.   Quoted in Geérard, Genette, "Avatars du cratylisme," *Poétique,* 12.

61.   Roman Jakobson, *La linguistica e le scienze dell'uomo,* pp. 101, 22–23.

62.   Richard Wright, "How 'Bigger' Was Born," in *Early Works,* p. 866.

63.   The opposition of the fountain and the chimney restates that of water and fire; the chimney, of course, also implies the element of air.

64.   Emily Dickinson, "After great pain a formal feeling comes," in *The Complete Poems,* ed. Thomas H. Johnson (London: Faber and Faber, 1987), n. 341, p. 162.

65.   There is also a pattern of uncertain colors, from yellow to hazy blue and, of course, the ghostlike white.

66.   R. Wright, "How 'Bigger' Was Born," pp. 853, 854.

67.   Paul Green and Richard Wright, *Native Son. A Drama in Three Acts,* in Burns Mantle, ed., *The Best Plays of 1940–41* (New York: Dodd, Mead & Co., 1941), pp. 29–63. Ironically, though he dropped one *b,* Wright retained the all-important, liminal *l,* and gave Clara a name that begins with the important *cl* nexus. He explained that too many names with a similar sound might confuse the audience, which confirms that his use of sounds is not naturalistic but symbolic. In a voiced medium like theater, sound has a different, less imaginative dimension. Also, the theater version eliminates the narrator and leaves the dialogue, which, as we have seen, is the part of the text where critical clusters are less likely to occur. All the sound pattern, therefore, is defunctionalized in the play. This may be the place to point out that most names in the novel are patterned at the level of the signifier. G. H. begins with the same grapheme as *Gus* and the same phoneme as *Jack.* Pictures of *Jack Johnson, Joe Louis, Jack Dempsey* are on the walls of *Green's* room together with *Ginger Rogers, Jean Harlow,* and *Janet Gaynor* (the only total stranger seems to be Henry Armstrong). The puns on the name of the *Dalton* family and of *Jan Erlone* (approximating a vernacular pronunciation of "alone") are also self-evident. In *The Outsider,* a text dominated by the letter *d,* the narrator's name is *Damon* and his girlfriend is *Dot.*

68.   Actually, I have consulted the manuscript in microfiche at the John F. Kennedy Institut of the Freie Universität in Berlin.

69.   A passage in the billiard room scene is removed, but the clause "the *billiard balls clacked*" is reintroduced in the text at a later point. Two occurrences of *white blur* were taken out with a passage excised in what became page 73 of the 1940 edition, and two identical occurrences were inserted on page 74.

70.   A nice typo, however, has *blow of her blood* instead of *flow of her blood* in the sex scene with Bessie.

Index

♦